Lonely Planet Publications

Melbourne | Oakland | London | Paris

D0455909

Bradley Mayhew

Shanghai

The Top Five

1 The Bund
Walk Shanghai's most impressive mile, where old meets new (p86)

2 Jinmao Tower
Admire the spectacular view from the PRC's highest building (p73)

3 The French Concession
Discover 1930s architecture in Shanghai's backstreets (p92)

4 Antiques in Dongtai Lu
Browse antique stalls and search out Mao memorabilia (p148)

5 Shanghai Museum
Experience 4000 years of culture at the PRC's best museum (p64)

Contents

Published by Lonely Planet Publications Pty Ltd
ABN 36 005 607 983

Australia Head Office, Locked Bag 1, Footscray,
Victoria 3011, ☎ 03 8379 8000, fax 03 8379 8111,
talk2us@lonelyplanet.com.au

USA 150 Linden St, Oakland, CA 94607,
☎ 510 893 8555, toll free 800 275 8555,
fax 510 893 8572, info@lonelyplanet.com

UK 72–82 Rosebery Ave, Clerkenwell, London,
EC1R 4RW, ☎ 020 7841 9000, fax 020 7841 9001,
go@lonelyplanet.co.uk

France 1 rue du Dahomey, 75011 Paris,
☎ 01 55 25 33 00, fax 01 55 25 33 01,
bip@lonelyplanet.fr, www.lonelyplanet.fr

© Lonely Planet 2004
Photographs © Phil Weymouth and as listed (p229), 2004
All rights reserved. No part of this publication may
be copied, stored in a retrieval system, or transmitted
in any form by any means, electronic, mechanical,
recording or otherwise, except brief extracts for the
purpose of review, and no part of this publication may
be sold or hired, without the written permission of the
publisher.

Printed through The Bookmaker International Ltd
Printed in China

Lonely Planet and the Lonely Planet logo are trade-
marks of Lonely Planet and are registered in the US
Patent and Trademark Office and in other countries.

Lonely Planet does not allow its name or logo to be
appropriated by commercial establishments, such as
retailers, restaurants or hotels. Please let us know of
any misuses: www.lonelyplanet.com/ip.

Although the authors and Lonely Planet have taken
all reasonable care in preparing this book, we make
no warranty about the accuracy or completeness of
its content and, to the maximum extent permitted,
disclaim all liability arising from its use.

The Authors

BRADLEY MAYHEW

Bradley started his travels in Southwest China, Tibet and northern Pakistan while still studying Chinese at Oxford University. After he graduated, Bradley fled to Central America to forget his Chinese and now regularly travels to China's borderlands in a futile attempt to get it back.

Author or coauthor of several Lonely Planet guidebooks, Bradley celebrated the millennium in Shanghai selflessly researching entertainment options for the first edition of *Shanghai*. By contrast, this edition was researched with a surgical mask covering his face, trying not to breathe during two months of SARS epidemic in the city.

When not on the road, Bradley lives in Montana where he continually tries to find a decent flight connection to Asia.

CONTRIBUTORS

JAMES FARRER

James Farrer researches sexuality, nightlife and the growing international communities in Shanghai and Tokyo. Based on three years of observations and interviews in Shanghai, James' book *Opening Up: Youth Sex Culture and Market Reform in Shanghai* describes the dramatic changes in dating culture, sexual morality and commercial leisure among young people during the period of market reform in Shanghai. In this edition of *Shanghai*, he contributed the Identity section and the 'Opening Up' and 'At Home with the Wu Family' boxed texts in the City Life chapter, as well as some of the book reviews in the Arts & Architecture chapter.

James lives in Tokyo, where he teaches sociology at Sophia University, and visits Shanghai regularly.

DR VICTORIA BUNTINE

Dr Buntine wrote the Health section for this guide. She worked as a general practitioner in Shanghai for 10 years, dealing almost exclusively with expatriate workers and their families, as well as Western tourists visiting the region. She has been a regular contributor to the Australian Association of Hong Kong's magazine since 1997, and in 1999 created her own website (www.healthinasia.com) to store these articles.

PHOTOGRAPHER

PHIL WEYMOUTH

Phil's family moved from Australia to Iran in the late 1960s and called Tehran home until the revolution in 1979. Phil studied photography in Melbourne and returned to the Middle East to work as a photographer in Bahrain for several years. He then spent a decade working with an Australian rural media company. Currently he runs a freelance photojournalism business based in Melbourne, working for a variety of Australian and international media and publishing companies.

Past commissions for Lonely Planet include the Condensed guides to Hong Kong, Beijing and Shanghai. He continues to travel extensively, supplying images to Lonely Planet Images, writing stories and avoiding his office.

Lonely Planet books provide independent advice. Lonely Planet does not accept advertising in guidebooks, nor do we accept payment in exchange for listing or endorsing any place or business. Lonely Planet writers do not accept discounts or payments in exchange for positive coverage of any sort.

Introducing Shanghai

Whore of the Orient and Paris of the East; city of quick riches, ill-gotten gains and fortunes lost; the domain of socialites and swindlers, adventurers and drug runners, missionaries, gangsters and pimps, all owing more to Marlene Dietrich than Mao Zedong – Shanghai has a history so impregnated with myth that it's hard to decide whether it was once a paradise or an all-encompassing evil.

The foreign powers crashed the party in 1842 and in less than 100 years, Shanghai had swelled beyond its sensibilities and was cut short just as quickly by the communist revolution. It is this short century of Shanghai's history that makes the city so appealing and appalling, and that has left monuments like bones to ponder over.

For Shanghai put away its dancing shoes in 1949 and the masses began shuffling to a different tune – the dour strains of Marxist-Leninism and the wail of the factory siren. All through these years of oblivion, the architects of this social experiment firmly wedged one foot against the door on Shanghai's past, until the effort started to tell. Regarded with suspicion by the communists as a hotbed of Western imperialist influence, the city has for decades played second fiddle to Beijing.

Today the giant city of Shanghai has reawakened and the government is catching up at a breathtaking pace, pouring millions into the Pudong economic zone and creating a glass-and-steel skyline that rivals the Bund in a face-off between past and future. Shanghai is the world's largest construction site, evolving at a pace so unmatched by any other Chinese city that even the morning ritual of flinging open one's hotel curtains reveals new facets to the skyline. Catch the city's historical charms while you still can – slabs of old Shanghai are vanishing almost overnight.

As the past is levelled, the future, it seems, is already here. The world's tallest building is on the cards, Shanghai's stylish hotels offer aromatherapy and fusion cuisine, the latest fashion trends hang in minimalist malls way beyond the reach of most mortals, and entrepreneurs check share prices on the Internet through their mobile phones. This is China for the 21st century, a century that will be dominated by China, with Shanghai at its driving edge. There's no better place to get a taste of what the world, and indeed the rest of China, can expect from the resurgent People's Republic.

For the visitor, Shanghai is China at its most recognisable and convenient. All the luxuries of China and all the comforts of home can be bought with a credit card. Hotel rooms, guides and train tickets can be booked in advance, and restaurants serve up everything from Indian curry to Tex-Mex.

Lowdown

Population 13.4 million
Time zone GMT + 8 hours
Coffee Y20-30
Metro ticket Y2-4
Dumplings Y4

Shanghai is foremost a business city but there is still much of interest to capture the traveller's imagination: the old-world architecture; the excellent shopping; and the excitement and energy of China's most economically, ideologically and socially open city. Moreover, Shanghai is beginning to rival Beijing as China's cultural capital. The Shanghai Museum, Art Museum and Grand Theatre rank among the best in Asia. If the synthetic delights of Shanghai start to pale, the classical Chinese cities of Suzhou and Hangzhou are just two of the many accessible places within an hour or two of the city.

As the pulse of this metropolis quickens, its steps are firmer, and at this point we make an apology. A lot of what you read here will have changed by the time you have this book in your hands. But that's the fascination with Shanghai – it is constantly evolving and continually surprising. Each visit yields a unique snapshot of the city; every time you go back the landscape will have changed.

Whatever your politics, it's hard not to be impressed by Shanghai. The city has been given a unique opportunity, and the savvy with which locals have grabbed it has many nodding their heads knowingly. Shanghai is back – with a vengeance.

BRADLEY'S TOP SHANGHAI DAY

Woken by jet lag, I'd head for the Bund just after dawn for the best light and ballroom dancing action (let's face it, I'd never make it without the jet lag). Mornings are the ideal time to hit the antique markets so I'd head to the Dongtai Lu Antique Market (or Fuyou Antique Market on a weekend) for a quick rummage through the Mao memorabilia, 1930s nostalgia and dusty lacquerware pots. From Dongtai Lu it's an easy walk to Xintiandi for lunch, and if there's time, a wander through the French Concession streets, my favourite part of Shanghai. Realistically speaking, I'd probably pass on the big lunch and head for some backstreet snack bar for my daily dumpling fix (I'm an unrepentant dumpling addict).

In the afternoon, I'd down a double espresso and head for the Shanghai Museum, easily the best sight in Shanghai. For dinner, I'd opt for Shanghainese cuisine at 1221 (for something intimate) or Baoluo Juilou (with a crowd), topped off with a romantic evening stroll along the Bund again and then a late-night cocktail at the Glamour Bar or Park 97. Very nice...

City Life

City Life

SHANGHAI TODAY

Shanghai is a metropolis bubbling in what Mao would call a state of permanent revolution. As China's showcase city, it pulses with energy, continually morphing and mutating in a socialist–capitalist test tube, with projects and ideas exploding like oil in a hot wok. Epic public transportation systems seem to spring up overnight and green spaces appear out of the blue, testament to the can-do mentality of the Shanghainese. Long-term visitors will see the city visibly improving monthly before their very eyes.

If Shanghai believes in anything, it's modernity. The city is now peppered with super-chic fusion restaurants and minimalist bars, Asia's biggest malls, the world's first levitating train and soon the world's tallest building. The city's moneyed classes play golf, sip martinis, go skiing in the southern suburbs, bungee jump off the Shanghai Stadium and shop with a zeal that would make its past communist rulers turn in their graves.

Disposable income has created an endless wave of urban fads, from owning pets to downing shots of espresso. Drive around Shanghai and you can't miss the dozens of home improvement stores such as IKEA and B&Q, which cater to the growing numbers of people buying their own flats for the first time in three generations. The latest middle-class dream is to own a private car, an ambition that has Ford and Volkswagen drooling in their spreadsheets. Meanwhile, the accompanying mood of sexual openness has fuelled soaring divorce rates and an increasingly relaxed attitude to the city's gay community. These phenomena simply didn't exist five years ago. Being in Shanghai is akin to viewing a sociological time-lapse camera on fast play.

Yet for all its good looks, Shanghai lacks a certain substance; its government has created a skeleton but not yet a soul. In recent years the foreigners, the jazz, the architecture, the style and the buzz of 1930s Shanghai have all returned (along with the drugs, prostitution and corruption) but the era's creativeness, ingenuity and freedom of expression have yet to follow.

Ten consecutive years of double-digit annual economic growth have enriched many Shanghainese. The city's clubs are frequented by the *dakuans*, or new millionaires, joined by joint-venture office workers letting rip, bar girls in hot pants touting for

Symbols of Asia's fastest growing city

business and Chinese clubbers experimenting with the 'head-shaking drug' (ecstasy). Prosperity has created a youth obsessed with self-fulfilment, be it through entertainment, shopping, drugs or relationships, giving them little in common with the politically troubled past of their parents. Partying, it seems, has become more important than politics.

Most worrying to the Chinese government is the expanding gulf between the haves and have-nots, a crisis in what is after all supposed to be an egalitarian society. In the 1990s Shanghai laid off over one million state workers. Joining these are over three million migrants from other provinces who work in the city on the fringes of Shanghai society, without insurance, medical cover, pensions, or unemployment or housing benefits. Migrants often find work on the city's 21,000 construction sites, sleeping in ultrabasic dormitory accommodation, or in seedy areas of town like the train station, which are lined with barber-shop brothels. Still, the situation in economically booming Shanghai isn't anywhere near as serious as it is elsewhere in the country.

Ever since Shanghai's elite moved en masse to Hong Kong in 1949, rivalry has existed between the cities. Despite the hype and the breathtaking pace of development, Shanghai still has a long way to go to catch up with Hong Kong. However, thousands of overseas Chinese are returning to Shanghai every year to take advantage of the city's business opportunities, confirming the city as China's golden land of opportunity.

For Shanghai is imbued with a feeling of excitement and optimism. Buoyed up by the recent decision to host the 2010 World Expo in Shanghai, Shanghainese have increasing pride in their city, and with just cause. As the biggest city in the world's most populous country and with its fastest-growing economy, the city has once again managed to capture the world's imagination.

Hot Conversation Topics

- The latest, chicest, most 'chichi' bar/restaurant/club that no-one else knows about.
- The dearth of places to get a cheap beer.
- The city's latest amazing 100-storey building or breathtakingly ambitious government project.
- Shanghai's growing traffic problem.
- Arthur Jones' latest rant in the most recent copy of *That's Shanghai*.
- The pitiful state of Shanghai's live music scene.
- Five reasons why Shanghai is better than Beijing.
- The latest cheese to arrive in Carrefour.
- Expat escape plans, to Thailand, Malaysia, the Philippines...

Things You Don't Ever Hear in Shanghai

- Did you see that great programme on CCTV last night?
- This friendly guy on the metro offered my pregnant wife his seat the other day!
- Do you want to check out some 16th-century Kunju opera with me tonight?
- Pudong is just such a fun place to live!
- OK, we're finished now! (Shanghai urban planning construction teams).

CITY CALENDAR

China, like most of the rest of Asia, follows two calendars: the Gregorian (Western) calendar and the lunar calendar. Traditional holidays and festivals follow the lunar calendar and modern and imported holidays and events follow the Gregorian calendar. For a list of public holidays, see pp208–9.

JANUARY & FEBRUARY
NEW YEAR
Longhua Temple (p82) has large New Year celebrations, with dragon and lion dances. At New Year the abbot strikes the bell 108 times while the monks beat on gongs and offer prayers for the forthcoming year.

SPRING FESTIVAL
Chūn Jié
Otherwise known as Chinese New Year, the Spring Festival starts on the first day of the first moon of the traditional lunar calendar. In Shanghai there is an explosion of fireworks at midnight to welcome the New Year and ward

off bad spirits, and there are special services at Longhua Temple and **Jing'an Temple** (p76). Top Chinese restaurants are booked out well in advance for *niányèfàn* (New Year's Eve dinner). Families paste red couplets on their doors and hand out *hóngbāo*, red envelopes stuffed with money. Another explosion of firecrackers on the fifth day of the New Year heralds the arrival of the God of Wealth.

This is a bad time for a visit – planes are booked out by overseas Chinese and foreigners fleeing the madness, trains are packed with migrant workers returning home, and hotels are booked solid. If you are in China at this time, book your room in advance, don't expect to get much business done and sit tight until the chaos is over!

LANTERN FESTIVAL
Yuánxiāo Jié
5 Feb 2004; 23 Feb 2005; 12 Feb 2006
Not a public holiday, but this is a colourful time to visit Shanghai, especially the Yuyuan Gardens. People take the time to walk the streets at night carrying coloured paper lanterns and make *yuánxiao* or *tāngyuán* (sweet dumplings of glutinous rice with sweet fillings). The festival falls on the 15th day of the first lunar month.

MARCH & APRIL
BIRTHDAY OF GUANYIN
Guānshìyīn Shēngrì
9 Mar 2004; 28 Mar 2005; 18 Mar 2006
Guanyin is the Goddess of Mercy and this is a good time to visit Taoist temples or nearby Putuoshan. Guanyin's birthday is the 19th day of the second moon.

TOMB SWEEPING DAY
Qīng Míng Jié
5 Apr (4 Apr in leap years)
This is a day for worshipping ancestors. People visit the graves of their dearly departed relatives and clean their grave sites. They often place flowers (particularly magnolias, the city's flower) on the tomb and burn 'ghost money' (for use in the afterworld) for the departed.

LONGHUA TEMPLE FAIR
This fair during the first 10 days of April is eastern China's largest and oldest folk gathering, with all kinds of snacks, stalls, jugglers and stilt walkers. The fair coincides with the blossoming of the local peach trees.

MAY & JUNE
DRAGON BOAT FESTIVAL
Duānwǔ Jié
22 Jun 2004; 11 Jun 2005; 31 May 2006
Commemorates the death of Qu Yuan, a 3rd-century-BC poet-statesman who drowned himself to protest against the corrupt government. It is celebrated on the fifth day of the fifth lunar month with boat races on Dianshan Lake, and sometimes even on the Huangpu River.

SEPTEMBER & OCTOBER
SHANGHAI TOURISM FESTIVAL
Kicks off in mid-September with a parade down Huaihai Zhonglu or Nanjing Donglu and then offers a wide variety of cultural programmes.

SHANGHAI OPEN
Mid-September
In mid-September, the world's tennis stars jet into town for the Shanghai Open. See the website www.atptennis.com for tournament details.

MID-AUTUMN FESTIVAL
Zhōngqiū Jié
28 Sep 2004; 18 Sep 2005; 6 Oct 2006
Also known as the Moon Festival, this is the time to give and receive tasty moon cakes stuffed with bean paste, egg yolk, coconut, walnuts and the like. The **Xinghua Lou** (p101), **Xinya** (p100) and **Gongdelin** (p111) restaurants are Shanghai's most famous cake makers and you'll need to order from here weeks in advance. Gazing at the moon, eating duck and lighting fireworks are popular activities; it's also a traditional holiday for lovers. The festival takes place on the 15th day of the eighth moon.

NOVEMBER & DECEMBER
SHANGHAI INTERNATIONAL ARTS FESTIVAL
A month-long programme of cultural events in late November and early December that is the highlight of the arts year. Events include the **Shanghai Art Fair** (see p26), a varied programme of international music, dance, opera and acrobatics, and exhibitions of the **Shanghai Bienniale** (see p26) in 2004 and 2006.

SHANGHAI INTERNATIONAL MARATHON

This annual November event through the streets of Shanghai attracts around 12,000 runners. It starts at the Bund and ends at Shanghai Stadium. For more details send an email to info@shanghai-marathon.com.

Lesser events include the Shanghai International Tea Culture Festival at the end of April. If you fancy something stronger, the Shanghai Beer Festival staggers into town around the end of July. Of less interest to foreign visitors are the Nanhui Peach Blossom Festival in mid-April, the Osmanthus Festival (near Guilin Park) in September or October, and the Tangerine Festival in early November.

Special prayers are held at Buddhist and Taoist temples on days when the moon is either full or just a sliver. According to the Chinese lunar calendar, the full moon falls on the 15th and 16th days of the lunar month and on the last (30th) day of the month just ending and the first day of the new month.

CULTURE
CULTURAL CONCEPTS

Despite its modern image, many traditional Chinese practices and beliefs still persist in Shanghai, never far from the surface. It is important to be aware of them, particularly if you're a business traveller.

Connections

Those who have 'connections' (*guānxì*) – normally with party cadres – rule the roost in China. Businesspeople donate endless hours to cultivating and massaging their *guānxì*, normally through business dinners and banquets. Proposals that were 'impossible' a few hours earlier can suddenly become highly possible when discussed over a plate of Beijing duck and a bottle of Johnny Walker.

Hot & Noisy

Whether it be an evening meal out or a day at the park, hot and noisy (*rènào*) is how the Chinese like it. Enormous banquets featuring eardrum-blowing drinking games and top-volume karaoke sessions are about as hot and noisy as you can get. Linked to this is a cultural preference for the group over the individual, a preference that may be part communism, part Confucianism.

Opening Up *by James Farrer*
Xu Daming, 39, private businessman

'Little Xu' grew up in a rough working-class neighbourhood in eastern Shanghai in the 1970s. He wasn't interested in school, and there wasn't much to learn anyway in the chaos of the Cultural Revolution. He joined the neighbourhood boys battling gangs of youth from other streets and chatted up passing girls on the sidewalk in front of his family house. He still has the same friends today.

In the late 1970s there was little public entertainment. Boys and girls gathered in a neighbour's living room, clicked on a transistor radio, and danced cheek to cheek with the lights turned out. These private 'lights out' parties were still illegal in 1980, but in a few years Xu was a regular at the dance halls springing up all over Shanghai.

By the mid-1980s Xu was able to turn his family home facing a busy street into a clothing shop he ran with his brother. He quit his factory job and became a private entrepreneur. He had several mistresses, but he and his wife divorced after he found out she too was having an affair, with a man she met dancing.

Xu's shop did not prosper in the more competitive 1990s. He rented out the space, and he and his brother tried their hands at trading. Again bigger, better-connected competitors won out. Living off the income from the shop, Xu plays mah jong every day with his friends in cheap hotel rooms they rent for this purpose. He doesn't know what his next career move will be. There are no chances for 'little guys' anymore, he complains.

Losing Face

Face can be loosely described as 'status', 'ego' or 'self-respect', and is by no means alien to foreigners. Losing face (diūliǎn) is about making someone look stupid or being forced to back down in front of others and you should take care to avoid it. In the West it's important; in China, it's critical. Circumvent a problem with smiling persistence rather than tackle it straight on and always give your adversary a way out. Avoid direct criticisms of people. Venting your rage in public and trying to make someone lose face will cause the Chinese to dig in their heels and only worsen your situation. Business travellers should take note here – a lot of Westerners really blow it on this point.

Politeness

Linked to face are displays of respect and politeness (kèqi). Always offer gifts, cigarettes and food several times, and expect them to be refused several times before finally being accepted. It's good to refer to elders with the appellation lǎo, which means 'old'; for example, lǎo Wang means Old Mr Wang. (Remember that Chinese put their surnames first, thus Wang Zenghao is Mr Wang). You may find the old chestnut 'my English is no good' – 'no, it is very good' – 'no, my English is no good' repeated ad nauseam. One good way of conveying respect is to hand things (such as business cards) with both hands. Another way of showing respect to a prospective partner is to show them to the door of your office and even the entry of your building when they leave.

Dos & Don'ts

Don't write in red ink as it conveys unfriendliness. If you're teaching, it's OK to use red to correct papers, but if you write extensive comments on the back, use some other colour.

Don't set anything on the ground or floor. This has nothing to do with culture, but it will save you from landing your bag on a big wad of phlegm. Even restaurateurs know this and will pull up an extra chair upon which to heap your belongings.

In China there is no shame in public bodily functions, even highly vocal displays of burping, spitting, farting, chomping or yawning.

ANNOYANCES

In many ways Shanghai is unlike the rest of China and it's certainly an easier place to visit as a tourist. Public transport is largely nonsmoking and levels of service are far higher than in other parts of China. Many people speak English and are used to foreigners. However, Chinese who have had little contact with foreigners become embarrassed by the language barrier and in defence they will giggle and shake their heads. Your own emotions in these situations may run the gamut from humiliation to frustration to outright anger. The only way for you to save face is to laugh along with them.

Beggars

Yes, beggars do exist in Shanghai's 'socialism with Chinese characteristics' and they are becoming increasingly prevalent. Some beggars squat on the pavement beside posters that detail their sad story. Almost all perk up when they see a foreigner heading their way.

Crime

Crime and other hazards to life and property are not a big feature of Shanghai living. (See Safety on p215.)

Noise

The Chinese are generally much more tolerant of noise than most foreigners. People watch TV at ear-shattering volumes to drown out the karaoke from a nearby restaurant, drivers habitually lean on the horn, telephone conversations are conducted in high-decibel rapid-fire screams and most of Shanghai seems to wake uncomplainingly to the sound of jackhammers and earth-moving vehicles. If it's peace and quiet you want, bring a good set of earplugs.

Personal Space

Years of communism, communalism and Confucianism (plus living in the same house as your grandmother...) have resulted in the fact that personal space is generally not as highly valued a commodity in China as it is in other countries. No-one is ever going to get a lot of personal space in a country of 1.2 billion people but the reasons for this are as much cultural as they are physical.

Chinese rarely have that unspoken and sacrosanct 30cm halo of private space around them that foreigners expect. For example, don't expect someone to walk out of your path if you are headed on a collision course. And don't be surprised if when you are standing 30cm from a museum exhibit or notice board someone squeezes into the space between you and the plate glass, blocking out your view.

I Queue

For all Shanghai's modernity, the lining-up system hasn't exactly caught on here. If there are only two or three people in the queue then you might be able to hold your own but beyond this the line quickly degenerates into a surging mass and it's every frail old man for himself. This is Darwinian theory at its most ruthless.

The metro currently offers the most breathtaking acts of rudeness. One tip is to stand in the centre of the yellow arrows; this is exactly where the door will open. But even with your toes hanging off the platform, someone will manage to slide in front of you. Be polite if your patience persists, but don't expect reciprocation. Fortunately, no-one will think it rude when you finally give up and join the scrum.

Spitting

China's national sport, spitting, is not as widespread in Shanghai as the rest of China. Government campaigns to stamp out the practice have been reasonably successful (particularly during the 2003 SARS epidemic) but there will still be times, especially in the early morning, when you hear an ear-shattering, lung-scraping 'HOIK!'.

Most Chinese spit for health reasons, though this theory suffered a blow during the recent SARS epidemic when locals were ordered to go light on the mucous. Some Taiwanese like to joke that the mainlanders spit because they've had a bad taste in their mouths ever since the communists took power.

There's a theoretical fine of Y200 (raised from Y50 during the SARS epidemic of 2003) for spitting in a public place; if the government ever collected on this it could boost city revenues by millions of dollars a year.

IDENTITY by James Farrer

Ever since the roaring 1920s, 'Shanghai misses' have shocked other Chinese with their bold dress and liberal sexual mores, and their independence and guile in dealing with men. Even during the Cultural Revolution when everyone in China wore unisex blue 'Mao suits', Shanghai women found ways of distinguishing themselves with feminine hairstyles and more form-fitting tailoring.

Stylish young women take time out for coffee

At Home with the Wu Family *by James Farrer*

The Wus are retirees living in a three-room apartment in a low-rise, rain-stained housing project once owned by the government 'work unit' where they were both employed. They bought the apartment five years ago at a steep employee discount. Though small in comparison with the newest apartments in Shanghai, in the late 1980s when the Wus moved in, it was considered spacious. Many families, including the Wus themselves until then, shared a single room. The Wus receive a pension of about Y1200, or US$150, a month, which is enough to cover their basic expenses. There is not much money for entertainment, so like most Shanghainese they spend each evening watching TV, usually tuned to the 24-hour sports channel. Ten years before, their imported Sony TV was an impressive luxury. Now it is simply commonplace. Old Wu's favourites include the national Chinese soccer league, US basketball and professional women's volleyball.

Though their daughters moved out after marriage, the Wus do not really live alone. Every day their daughter Mei and their son-in-law Han arrive to eat the complex meals Grandma Wu prepares. Old Wu washes dishes. The real star of the family is the eight-year-old grandson Bin, an only child like almost all Shanghai children. Dinner conversations centre on Bin's progress in school, real estate prices, or the latest restaurants and shops. Occasionally, Grandma repeats the gossip she picked up among the older residents of the building, but such matters don't interest the younger couple very much. Relations among neighbours are far less important now than when everyone in a building worked for the same socialist work unit. Every afternoon Grandpa gathers at the school gate with a crowd of other retired grandparents to meet Bin. (Most of the mothers and fathers are still at work.) Grandma supervises Bin's arduous homework assignments of Chinese characters, maths problems and English vocabulary. Unlike his grandparents, Bin enjoys a rich cultural life. He has already travelled with his parents to Nepal and several Chinese provinces, including Inner Mongolia, and like most of his second-grade classmates, he enjoys birthday parties at McDonald's, Nike sports shoes and school trips.

Mei and Han are both white-collar professionals with university degrees. Although their salaries (together about Y10,000 or US$1200) are much lower than people with similar occupations in the West, they can enjoy a modern consumer lifestyle. They often sample the regional Chinese and international cuisines available in Shanghai. They have both travelled twice to Southeast Asia, once an unimaginable luxury, but now not much more difficult or expensive than travel within China. They have even purchased a small economy car and a new three-bedroom apartment across the main road from the Wu's complex.

The older Wus had a much harder life. They married in the early 1960s in a small town near Shanghai, but for the next 16 years they saw each other only once a month when Wu had leave from his Shanghai work unit. Only after their two daughters were in their teens were they able to live together in a one-room flat in Shanghai. Grandma Wu once said that if a couple were separated that much now, they probably would end up divorced. Divorce was virtually unheard of when the Wus were young; now nearly a quarter of Shanghai marriages end that way. Mei and Han try to keep some romance in their marriage. Leaving Bin with Mei's parents, they go out alone at least once a month to sample the latest fashionable restaurant.

To Westerners the Wus may seem extraordinarily generous to their children and their grandchild. In fact, Ms Wu considers herself lucky that both her daughters are financially independent. Her sister and her husband used up most of their savings to buy their son a flat in Shanghai. One wonders if the current generation of individualistic consumers growing up in Shanghai will be so generous to their own children.

Shanghai men also are known in China as well-dressed dandies and ladies' men, but even more as 'Shanghai-style husbands' willing to do *ma da sao*, Shanghai dialect for 'shopping, washing and cooking'. Macho Northerners may ridicule their masculinity, but Shanghai husbands are rather proud of their domestic devotion.

Shanghainese are said to be so eager to enjoy the status of 'going abroad' that they will go to any country for which they can get a visa. Non-Shanghainese Chinese describe Shanghainese as 'worshipping the West and infatuated with the foreign'. Shanghai women, they say, are overly fond of foreign men.

Shanghai's reputation as a melting pot of East and West arose during the century of Western domination of the city from 1841 to 1949. Shanghai was considered a 'foreign adventurer's playground'. Shanghainese nowadays are proud of their cosmopolitan history and culture, but other Chinese sometimes interpret this pride as snobbery and this love of Western culture as a loss of authentic Chinese values. Indeed, Shanghai people like to see themselves as the top of the social hierarchy in China. Marrying a foreigner may be a move up, but marrying a Chinese from the interior is generally a move down. Other Chinese are *wàidìrén* – 'outlanders'. Proud Shanghai loyalists will even snicker at rich visitors from Taiwan as parvenu *táibàzi*, or 'Taiwanese hicks'. On the other hand, Shanghai people of all ages generally welcome foreigners, especially Westerners, to the city, and the city government has set a goal of 5% foreign residents in order to become an 'international city'.

Chinese from other parts of China also describe Shanghai people as pragmatic and stingy. Looking at the same traits, Shanghainese describe themselves as modern and individualistic. Whether evaluated positively or negatively, Shanghai is one of the few cities in China where people would rather split the bill at a restaurant than fight for the honour of paying for the entire party. Shanghainese are less bound to traditions of gift-giving and elaborate ceremonies, and Shanghai weddings are often quite bereft of traditional Chinese practices. According to Shanghainese, the reason for this pragmatic individualism is that for over 100 years Shanghai has been a magnet for refugees and fortune seekers, all forced to look out for themselves in a competitive, tough environment.

Shanghai society also has its own internal divisions and stereotypes. The leafy west end of Shanghai, once home to rich foreigners and Chinese tycoons, is still known as Shanghai's 'high corner'. The industrial northeast, outside the boundaries of the old foreign concessions, is still the 'low corner'. Even today elite Party cadres and Western expatriates congregate in 'upper-corner' areas like Hengshan Lu, while 'lower-corner' areas such as Yangpu are still considered working class. Low-corner Shanghai also became home to most of Shanghai's *sūbĕirén*, poor migrants from Northern Jiangsu Province who filled many of the dirty and dangerous trades in prerevolutionary Shanghai. Even today, their descendants maintain a distinctive dialect and cultural identity. Newer divisions in Shanghai are overtaking these old ones, however. 'White-collar' professionals with foreign MBAs are the new elite, sipping cocktails at chic retro bars in Xintiandi, while working-class Shanghainese can only afford to stroll past and watch.

FASHION

The Shanghainese have the reputation of being the most fashionable people in China. 'There's nothing the Cantonese won't eat', so one version of a popular saying goes, 'and nothing the Shanghainese won't wear'. Shanghai still exudes a faded glamour that Beijing can't touch.

The city government has declared its goal to make Shanghai an Asian fashion centre to rank alongside Tokyo, London, New York and Paris but in reality the city still has a long way to go just to catch up with its own 1930s fashion scene, when images of Chinese women clad in figure-hugging *qipaos* (cheongsams) gave rise to its epithet as the 'Paris of the East'. The city-sponsored International Fashion Festival week in March/April showcases local collections and international designers such as Givenchy and Vivienne Westwood.

On the street, Chinese-language lifestyle magazines like *Shanghai Tattler, Elle, Harper's Bazaar* and *Marie Claire* crowd every corner newsstand, the latest brand of mobile phone has taken on an almost religious importance and Christian Dior, Gucci and Louis Vuitton shops glut Shanghai's top-end

Young white-collar professionals are Shanghaii's new elite

Opening Up by James Farrer
Stacey, 22, college student

'Stacey' changes her English name regularly, always when she is turning over a new leaf in what she cheerfully describes as her 'colourful life'. She is a student at Shanghai University, studying communication technology. Her entrance-exam grades only allowed her this choice although she had wanted to study English. She studies hard at exam periods, but otherwise her 'colourful life' consists of dating, partying and shopping.

Stacey's first boyfriend was a high school classmate. They hadn't even kissed when the homeroom teacher discovered them talking to one another. Without Stacey's knowledge, the teacher took the boy aside and told him to keep his mind on his studies. Dating is not permitted in Chinese high schools. If students are 'caught,' their parents are called in for a conference. If the students are found having sex, they may be expelled, a rule that applies even to university students, though selectively enforced.

Stacey's first sexual experiences were in college. She was terrified of her strict parents finding out. They cannot understand a sexual morality that allows for sexual intimacy with each new boyfriend. Stacey dated an American youth in the summer of 2002 and sported a big American flag on her sweater. A few months later, she was dating a French guy she met at a nightclub, but this relationship also soon ended.

With the growing numbers of new college graduates in Shanghai, job hunting was tough in the spring of 2003, but Stacey found a secretarial position with a small foreign company, and changed her English name again.

malls. The attending pressure to look good has apparently led to an increase in local demand for plastic surgery, once unheard of in China. By far the most popular procedure is double-eyelid surgery, which creates a fold in the eyelid to make Asian eyes appear bigger and more 'Western'.

LANGUAGE

Shanghai dialect is largely unintelligible to Mandarin speakers, but don't fear – almost all Shanghainese also speak Mandarin. Shanghainese say *nong ho* instead of *nǐ hǎo*, say goodbye with *ze wei* instead of *zài jiàn*, and say thank you with *sha ya nong* instead of *xièxie*.

ECONOMY & COSTS

COMMERCE WAS THE BEGINNING, THE MIDDLE AND THE END OF OUR LIFE IN CHINA – THAT IS TO SAY THAT IF THERE WAS NO TRADE, NOT A SINGLE MAN, EXCEPT MISSIONARIES, WOULD HAVE COME HERE AT ALL.

British trader Charles Dyce, talking about life in pre-communist Shanghai

Shanghai is the economic and trading heart of the world's fastest-growing economy and its burgeoning wealth, leadership and intrinsic self-confidence have put it miles ahead of other cities in China. Neither Beijing nor Guangzhou can match the superficial, gilt-edged feel of modernity that covers the city. Making money is in the blood of most Shanghainese.

Shanghai was left out of China's first round of economic reforms in the 1980s. Its economic renaissance dates from 1990, when it became an autonomous municipality and Pudong was established as a special economic zone. In 1992 Deng Xiaoping gave the seal of approval to Shanghai's redevelopment during his 'southern tour'. Until then 80% of Shanghai's revenue went

Pidgin

In the 1920s and '30s few foreigners ever thought of trying to learn Chinese; if the natives did not speak English they considered that to be their tragedy. Most communicated with their head servant (the 'number one boy') using pidgin, a mix of English words twisted up with Chinese grammar. Interestingly, many of the words eventually entered common English usage, like 'can do', 'savvy', 'chop chop', 'look-see' and 'chow'. Many of the phrases are a riot: a live fish is a 'walkee walkee fish'; a brain is a 'savvy box'.

straight into Beijing's pockets. Economic reforms and restructuring have since boosted Shanghai's GDP, and there has been an increase in foreign investments – the city is now a madhouse of free-market activity. In the mid-1990s an average of five new businesses were set up every hour in Shanghai. From 1992 to 1997 Shanghai experienced an annual growth rate of 13%.

Shanghai owes its economy to its position as a clearing house for the Yangzi River. Chinese like to compare the river to a dragon, with its head at Shanghai and its body coiling through half of China, draining a potential market of 400 million people (10% of the world's population).

The city also enjoys a unique position at the meeting point of both interior and coastal economic development areas. As China's economic spotlight turns increasingly westward, Shanghai is seen as the key to unlocking the nation's stumbling hinterland. Economic boosters imagine waves of economic energy shooting up the Huangpu into the Yangzi River delta economic zone and from there to the huge cities of Wuhan and Chongqing.

Shanghai's Economic Stats

Shanghai's GDP US$65.4 billion (2002).

Per capita GDP Y41,000 (US$5000), the highest in China, with a target of US$7500 set for 2007.

GDP growth Around 10.9% (2002) in Shanghai and more like 15% in Pudong.

Foreign investment US$5.03 billion in 2002, headed by Hong Kong and the USA, up 14.5% on 2001.

Annual exports US$32.1 billion (2002).

Average annual salary Around Y21,000 (US$2700), the highest in China, recently passing Guangzhou and Shenzhen.

Annual inflation 3%.

It comes as no surprise, then, that Shanghai is now said to be the world's second-busiest port and that its Jiangnan shipyard is the largest in China. The focus has shifted from the Huangpu to the Yangzi, specifically Waigaoqiao, which is being upgraded into a major container port. Yet this site is vulnerable to the silting of the Yangzi and a new deep-water container port is planned in the Yangshan Islands, to be linked to the mainland at Luchaogang by the 30km-long Luyang Bridge, destined to become the longest bridge in the world.

Shanghai is to host the World Expo in 2010 (the world's third-largest event, after the Olympics and World Cup), the first time it has been awarded to a developing country. The city is expected to spend US$3 billion on the event, which could attract up to 65 million visitors to Shanghai.

Tourism, especially domestic, is surprisingly important to Shanghai. More than 1.6 million overseas tourists (compared with Beijing's 2.4 million) and 79 million domestic tourists net the city around US$1.15 billion annually. The travel sector is still tightly state-owned. The massive Jinjiang group owns dozens of Shanghai's top hotels, plus several taxi companies and travel agencies.

INDUSTRY & FOREIGN INVESTMENT

SHANGHAI IS LIKE THE EMPEROR'S UGLY DAUGHTER; SHE NEVER HAS TO WORRY ABOUT SUITORS.

Traditional saying

The 1999 Fortune 500 summit, 2001 Asia-Pacific Economic Cooperation (APEC) summit and the upcoming 2010 World Expo have put Shanghai squarely on the global industrial map. By 2000, 254 Fortune 500 companies had set up offices in Shanghai and there were 17,600 foreign enterprises in operation. Foreign investment peaked at US$10 billion per year between 1994 to 1996 but levels have since fallen back considerably. Foreign-funded businesses now make up 60% of total imports and exports and the government, keen to keep the cash flowing in, is offering all kinds of incentives. So far the city has collected US$40 billion, the largest amount of direct foreign investment of any city in the world. Shanghai is consistently voted the best place to invest in China.

Volkswagen is the largest joint-venture operation in Shanghai (indeed the whole of China). Its plant in Pudong produces more than 50% of all the cars sold in China, including Shanghai's ubiquitous Santana taxis. General Motors has a US$1.6 billion joint-venture Buick plant in Shanghai. Both are eyeing Shanghai's burgeoning middle class, 70% of whom state that they would like to buy a car in the next decade. Other huge investors are BASF, General Electric, Phillips, Kodak and Coca-Cola.

'Made in Shanghai' has long been a symbol of quality inside China, ranging from Forever bicycles, Hero pens and Seagull cameras to White Rabbit sweets and even Long March space rockets. Recent restructuring has seen the demise of several venerable brands as Shanghai's smaller, loss-making, State-owned industries are sold off or merged to improve efficiency. Shanghai's two largest companies are the giant Baoshan iron- and steelworks and the Shanghai Automobile Corporation. Perhaps Shanghai's greatest resource is its highly skilled, well-educated and innovative workforce.

An important change looming on the city's economic horizon is China's recent entry into the World Trade Organization (WTO). Entry signifies the end of trade restrictions, which will open up China's telecommunications, banking and insurance industries to foreign competition (making Shanghai once more the insurance capital of Asia). It also means a rush of foreign goods, such as cars, into China (current import tariffs of more than 80% will be slashed) and a flood of Chinese products abroad. China's WTO status will also undermine the kind of economic incentives offered by the government in areas like Pudong. The agreement will sound the death knell for many of China's state companies, which in turn could lead to a surge in China's unemployment rate, already as high as 15% in Shanghai.

PUDONG

Shanghai's long economic malaise came to an abrupt end in 1990, with the announcement of plans to develop Pudong on the eastern side of the Huangpu River. Designed by architect Richard Rodgers, Pudong is a 522 sq km economic zone eight times larger than London's Canary Wharf, stretching from the Bund to the East China Sea. It has been variously described as a window, a bridge and a launch pad for companies wishing to get a foot into the near-mythical Chinese market. And it worked. By the end of 1999, US$30 billion had been contractually invested in Pudong and the zone was accounting for 20% of the city's GDP (expected to increase to 40% by 2010); not bad for a marshland that had nothing but fields and pig farms a decade ago.

The most visible part of Pudong is the skyscraper-filled Liujiazui financial district, home to China's stock market and the headquarters of most foreign banks. Shanghai's goal is to regain its position as a major financial centre and it plans Liujiazui to be a future Asian Wall Street. Other major investment areas in Pudong include Waigaoqiao, a tax-free foreign trade zone for

The Pudong skyline at sunset

distribution and processing in the northeast corner; the Zhangjiang hi-tech zone, the centre of China's fledgling biomedicine industry; and the Jinqiao export and processing zone, which houses General Motors, Kodak and Coca-Cola among others. Shanghai's other major hi-tech park is in Caohejing, across the river in southern Puxi. Other important trade zones are in Minhang, south of the city and Songjiang, to the north.

ECONOMIC PROBLEMS

SEEN FROM THE RIVER, TOWERING ABOVE THEIR COUCHANT GUARDIAN WARSHIPS, THE SEMI-SKYSCRAPERS OF THE BUND PRESENT, IMPRESSIVELY, THE FAÇADE OF A GREAT CITY. BUT IT IS ONLY A FAÇADE.

Christopher Isherwood, 1937

For all the hype about its 'potential market of 1.2 billion', China's economy faces several problems, foremost of which is a growing inequality in what is supposed to be an egalitarian country. Shanghai is now reckoned to be ten times wealthier than the province of Guizhou. Its average annual income of around US$1500 per year is double the national average.

Corruption is a chronic problem; the government itself admits that US$15 billion was embezzled from state coffers in 1999. Moreover, China's banks are loaded with massive bad debts and are technically insolvent. Even China's impressive economic statistics are often exaggerated by up to 30%. For all its capitalist trappings, the state retains a tight control of the economy.

Fuelled by the gushing enthusiasm of both foreign and local propaganda, Shanghai is at times gripped in a hyped-up vision that is in danger of crumpling against the sheer reality of managing a city of this size and complexity. The visionaries seem to forget that there is more to a great city than gleaming buildings and metro systems. The immature legal system offers business few safeguards. Public discourse and critique of the economy and its relationship to culture and politics are as lacking in Shanghai today as private telephones were two decades ago.

China's Party chiefs realise that Shanghai's economy is central to China's economy, and that a thriving economy is essential to their continued control of the country. When the people question the Party's economic model, it can only be a matter of time before they perhaps also question its political model.

COSTS

Wandering Shanghai's department stores it's easy to forget that factory workers and government employees earn less per month than most. Shanghai is one of China's most expensive cities and if you frequent foreign restaurants, hotels and supermarkets you'll end up paying much the same as in the West, if not more.

Other major budget-busters are cafés, which charge up to Y40 (US$5) for a coffee, and bars, where the smallest of beers costs Y30. You can get a decent meal for the

How Much?

- Meal in a local Chinese restaurant Y20.
- Meal in a top-end international restaurant around Y200, plus drinks.
- Three-kilometre taxi fare Y10.
- Entrance ticket to Shanghai Museum adult/student Y20/5.
- Three-star room US$60.

same price elsewhere. Local Chinese restaurants offer excellent value if you can navigate the Chinese menu. You can also save money by taking advantage of the city's excellent set-lunch specials or taking the kids to a department store food court.

If you are on a budget, it's worth knowing that some of Shanghai's most famous restaurants often have a less fancy downstairs option serving snacks and cheaper main dishes. Watch for extra charges like tea and napkins and send these back if you don't want them. Always check the bill carefully.

Opening Up *by James Farrer*
Wang Ying, 26, quality control inspector

Wang Ying grew up in a small town in central Henan Province in a family with four siblings. Her father had a regular government job, so she was able to attend a technical college where she completed a degree in international trade.

When she left home, she first headed to Zhengzhou, the capital of Henan Province, where she worked as a secretary. There she met a businessman, with whom she lived a few months. The relationship ended when she found out he was married and his wife confronted her publicly. She then moved on to Shanghai, becoming one of over 3 million nonlocal Chinese residents.

Unlike a few years before, it is now relatively easy for non-Shanghainese with a college degree to get a permit to live and work in Shanghai. But it is still very difficult to find a good job. Wang Ying's English was poor compared to Shanghai graduates. She ended up working as a quality control inspector in a Taiwan-owned factory, where she earned only Y1500 a month. Rent on her shabby apartment was Y1000. She rented one room to two male students at a nearby university, but they were late paying up, and she was worried she would not be able to make ends meet. Unable to afford the expensive nightlife in Shanghai or even a meal at the new local Pizza Hut, she was thinking about returning to Henan. 'Wages will be lower, but so will the cost of living, and people there won't treat me like a back-country girl.'

Discounts are common at Shanghai's hotels so always try to knock down the price – hardly any of Shanghai's hotels actually charge their rack rates.

Stay in a hostel and eat in local restaurants and you can keep costs down to US$20 a day. Upgrade to a decent hotel, eat in mid-range places, see a few sights, take a few taxis and maybe go to see the acrobats perform, then figure on anything from US$50 up. And that's without shopping, for which you should budget more than you think.

GOVERNMENT & POLITICS

Shanghai has always courted extremism in politics and has been a barometer for the mood of the nation. The Chinese Communist Party (CCP) was formed here back in 1921. Mao Zedong cast the first stone of the Cultural Revolution in Shanghai by publishing in the city's newspapers a piece of political rhetoric he had been unable to get published in Beijing. The Gang of Four had its power base in Shanghai.

The city's influence now ripples through the whole of the Party apparatus to the upper echelons of what has become known as the 'Shanghai Clique': Former president Jiang Zemin is Shanghai's ex-Party chief and former premier Zhu Rongji was the mayor of Shanghai during the Tiananmen Square Massacre. Zeng Qinghong was the deputy Party chief of Shanghai under Jiang Zemin and remains his right-hand man. Furthermore, Hong Kong's chief executive, Tung Chee-hwa, is a Shanghai man. Shanghai's current mayor is Han Zheng.

Top Five Books on Business in Shanghai

- *Insiders Guide: Doing Business in Shanghai* (China Knowledge Press, 2003) Annual guide, also publishes business guides to Jiangsu and other provinces.
- *China Business Handbook* (China Economic Review, 2003) An annual and therefore up-to-date business guide to all of China, with an economic sketch of each of China's provinces and major cities.
- *Chinese Business Etiquette: A Guide to Protocol, Manners, and Culture in the People's Republic of China* (Scott D. Seligman; Warner Books, 1999)
- *Doing Business in China* (Tim Ambler & Morgen Witzel; Routledge, 2000)
- *Shanghai and the Yangtze Delta: A City Reborn* (edited by Brian Hook; Oxford University Press, 1998) An academic look at the economic history of the region.

In the 1990s, a little-noticed reform permitted small villages with a population under 10,000 to elect their own leaders. In 1999 two million people in 2900 of Shanghai's surrounding townships cast their votes to elect their village committees in a step which some have hailed as a fledgling movement towards democracy.

Shanghai is one of China's four municipalities (the others being Beijing, Tianjin and Chongqing). The city government has a mildly useful website at www.shanghai.gov.cn.

ENVIRONMENT

Shanghai has one of the worst air qualities in China, after Chongqing, Xining, Xi'an and Chengdu. Coal briquettes, used by most homes and noodle stalls over the winter, are a major pollutant. Shanghai consumes the largest amount of energy per square kilometre in China. Drains carry more than five million tons of industrial waste and untreated sewage into the mouth of the Yangzi each day. Shanghai's restaurants throw away 673 million polystyrene boxes and 1300 million bamboo chopsticks a year. Until the 1920s Shanghai got its tap water direct from the Suzhou Creek. Now it is a fetid cesspool.

The government has started to address some problems. A US$6 billion, 15-year environmental plan was unveiled in 1999. It will include a US$1 billion cleanup of Suzhou Creek, to be completed by 2005. Green cover is increasing rapidly in the city towards a target of 35%. Five new lakes are being dug to increase water cover and 1000 buses were recently converted to natural gas.

URBAN PLANNING & DEVELOPMENT

For over a decade Shanghai has been tearing down its past and rebuilding its future at an astonishing rate. It's estimated that over 20 million sq m of old buildings have been levelled since 1988 alone. (Shanghai creates 30,000 tons of construction waste each day and finding a place to put it all is an increasing problem.) Anyone remotely interested in urban planning should check out the **Urban Planning Exhibition Hall** (p66) and its absorbing scale model of the city. Epic urban planning projects are the city government's strong point.

Future Shanghai

Shanghai is Asia's, if not the world's, fastest-changing city, which makes it a singularly difficult place about which to write a guidebook. With this in mind, here's our look into Shanghai's crystal ball, taking a wild guess at some of the things that might happen during the lifetime of this book.

There is no end in sight to Shanghai's building frenzy. Concord Plaza is a new shopping and entertainment complex planned for the junction of Yan'an Xilu and Nanjing Xilu. It will include a model of the *Titanic* that will sink several times a day for shoppers' amusement. Raffles Plaza is a huge complex being built opposite the Renmin Square metro station. By 2007, if all goes well, the city will also host what developers claim will be the world's tallest building, the World Finance Centre, next to the Jinmao Tower. Another huge 42-storey top-end business, retail and apartment complex called the Summit and the Centre opened in late 2003 on Anfu Lu and Changshu Lu, a block or two south of the Hilton. A new tunnel between Fuxing Lu and Pudong's Zhongyang Lu should open at the end of 2004.

The banks of the Huangpu River are set to see some major changes. Construction will take place for the Shanghai World Expo on both sides of the river, between Nanpu and Lupu Bridges and a new bridge will be built for the 2010 event. The upscale Three on the Bund development project (see p62) will revitalise the southern Bund and the five-year Waitanyuan (Head of the Bund) project is set to redevelop the northern Bund, to complement redevelopment of Suzhou Creek. A new dock is to be built by Star Cruises, catering to up to a million cruise passengers a year. Rumour is that Mandarin Oriental will take over management of the Peace Hotel and that the company behind Hong Kong's famed Peninsula Hotel will develop the site of the former British consulate on the northern Bund.

On the entertainment front, Universal Studios is set to get a jump on its rival Disney by building the first US theme park in China, in the Sanlin area of Pudong. The Formula One grand prix will become an annual fixture from 2004.

Morning sword exercises on the Bund (p61)

Shanghai is investing heavily in the future. Massive freeway projects, metro lines, light rail systems and the US$2 billion Pudong airport are testament to the fact that infrastructure investment in Shanghai between 1994 and 1999 was more than triple the total for the previous 35 years!

The next 20 years will see 11 metro routes and seven light railway lines linking the city centre and Pudong with 11 new satellite cities, all within an hour's commute of Shanghai and joined by a third ring road. Pudong's 22.5km Yanggao Expressway, which currently connects up with the elevated inner ring road, will be joined by the light railway line which will swing over the Huangpu River to form a ring around the city. A high-speed rail link to Beijing will cut the trip down to six hours by around 2007, less if the MagLev train proves its point. There are also big plans to develop Chongming Island, connecting it to the city via a series of underground tunnels and railway lines that will continue into Jiangsu Province.

One of the largest projects in the pipeline is the container port at Luchaogong, accessed by the huge Luyang Bridge (the world's longest), due for completion in 2020.

Arts &
Architecture

Arts & Architecture

ARTS

Shanghai's arts scene is today a pale shadow of the 1930s and even lags behind Beijing when it comes to innovation and experimentation. The city has generally been far more successful at realising epic steel and concrete infrastructure projects than nurturing a dynamic artistic and cultural scene. Ironically, it is Beijing that is more receptive to creative expression and political freedom. Shanghai can be a lonely city for artists.

Top Five Museums

- **Shanghai Museum** (p64) Simply the best museum in China.
- **Shanghai Art Museum** (p63) For Chinese contemporary art.
- **Shanghai Municipal Historical Museum** (p74) For a flavour of old Shanghai.
- **Shanghai Urban Planning Exhibition Hall** (p66) For its absorbing scale model of Shanghai.
- **Shanghai Arts & Crafts Museum** (p69) For its wonderful architecture, not the museum.

LITERATURE

In the 1920s and '30s Shanghai was a publishing industry hub and home to a vibrant literary scene. Protected from Nationalist and warlord censorship by the foreign settlements and invigorated (and appalled) by the city's modernity and foreign influences, Shanghai was host to a golden era in modern Chinese literature.

Mao Dun, an active leftist writer in the 1930s, wrote *Midnight* (Ziye), one of the most famous novels about Shanghai (see the boxed text 'Shanghai Fiction', opposite). Lu Xun, China's greatest modern writer, also lived in Shanghai for a while (for more on Lu Xun, see the boxed text on p79). Ding Ling, whose most famous work is *The Diary of Miss Sophie*, lived in Shanghai, as for a time did the writers Yu Dafu and Ba Jin. Writers were not immune to political dangers; Lu Xun's friend Rou Shi was murdered by the Kuomintang in February 1931.

Eileen Chang (Zhang Ailing, 1920–95) is one of the writers most closely connected to Shanghai, certainly amongst overseas Chinese. Born in Shanghai, she lived in the city only from 1942 to 1948, before moving to Hong Kong and then the USA. Her books are inspired by, and capture the essence of, Shanghai and are full of the city's details and moods. One of her favourite spots for socialising was what is now the Always Café on Nanjing Xilu (see p112). Chang's most famous books include: *The Rouge of the North, The Faded Flower, Red Rose and White Rose, The Golden Lock* and *Love in a Fallen City*.

Shanghainese Wang Anyi is a bestselling author in China, with novels such as *Love on a Barren Mountain, Baotown* and *Song of Everlasting Sorrow*, the last-named detailing the story of a Shanghainese beauty-pageant winner from 1940 to the present. Wang also wrote the script for Chen Kaige's film *Temptress Moon*.

VISUAL ARTS

Shanghai Fine Arts Academy is one of the most important centres of art in the country. One of China's most commercially successful artists is Shanghai's Chen Yifei (www.chenyifei.com), whose oils specialise in nostalgic portraits of Chinese women. One of his paintings sold for more than US$500,000 in the USA, the highest price then paid for any living Chinese artist's work. Chen has recently branched into fashion and film, producing several documentaries on Shanghai.

Contemporary Shanghainese artists include Pu Jie, with his colourful pop-art depictions of Shanghai; Ding Yi, with his weaving-like abstract designs; and Wu Yiming, who creates calmer, more Impressionistic works. Other notables include Zhou Tiehai, a winner of the Chinese Contemporary Art Award, the abstract Shen Fan, and video/installation artists

Shanghai Fiction

- *Candy* (Mian Mian, translated by Andrea Lingenfelter) Modern Shanghai is given a literary voice by writers such as Mian Mian, a former drug addict who writes about complicated sexual affairs, suicide and drug addiction in modern Shanghai. Her other novels *La La La* and *We Are Panic* have not been translated.
- *Death of a Red Heroine* (Qiu Xiaolong) This is a crime novel and also a street-level view of the social changes engulfing Shanghai in 1990. Chief Inspector Chen has a weakness for classic poetry, and his exchanges with his reporter love interest owe more to *The Dream of Red Mansions* than Sherlock Holmes. The author is a prizewinning poet, literary critic and professor of Chinese literature in the US.
- *Empire of the Sun* (JG Ballard) Tells of the author's internment as a child in the Longhua Camp during WWII, subsequently made into a film by Steven Spielberg.
- *Master of Rain* (Tom Bradby) Potboiler detective story set in swinging Shanghai and written by a former ITN newscaster. A naïve British detective investigating the murder of a Russian prostitute stumbles on a trail that leads to the gangster pockmarked Huang. Throw in a Russian love interest, a Chicago detective, a corrupt police department and serial murders, and stir it with a bit of film noir for this take on seedy Shanghai.
- *Midnight* (Mao Dun) In the opening scene of *Midnight*, conservative Confucian, Old Man Wu, visits his son's home in Shanghai. The sight of modern women, including his own daughter-in-law, in high-slit skirts and revealing blouses literally shocks him to death. The novel is a good introduction to the social mores of 1920s Shanghai.
- *Shanghai* (Christopher New) An epic novel tracing several generations of Chinese and expats in old Shanghai.
- *Shanghai '37* (Vicky Baum) A novel set in 1930s Shanghai and climaxing at the Peace Hotel. It draws a thinly veiled depiction of gangster Du Yuesheng.
- *Shanghai Baby* (Wei Hui) A bratty and rather uneven novel, full of sex and self-absorption, drugs and disillusionment, that courts controversy but ultimately lacks substance. The book was banned by the Chinese government and thousands of copies were publicly destroyed.
- *Shanghai: Electric and Lurid City* (Barbara Baker) An excellent anthology of more than 50 passages of writing about Shanghai, from its pretreaty port days to the eve of the 21st century.
- *The Blue House* (Chen Naishan) The author is a keen observer of her native city. In the title story of this collection a young man learns that his grandfather was a prewar steel magnate, the owner of the Blue House. A second story, 'Poor Street', describes a teacher who goes to work in one of the most infamous slums of Shanghai.
- *The Blue Lotus* (Hergé) A favourite with children and adults alike, this 1931 Tintin story sees Tintin rushing around Shanghai in 1931 dodging Japanese spies, bullets and opium traffickers (the Blue Lotus is an opium den), all set against a backdrop of actual events. It sold out in days when finally published in China in 2001.
- *The Distant Land of My Father* (Bo Caldwell) A novel that reads like a biography starts in 1930s Shanghai and traces the life of the narrator, piecing together the story of her father's decision to stay behind in Shanghai after the Japanese invasion, while his daughter and wife move to California. This is a moving portrayal of the relationship between daughter and father, and of betrayal and reconciliation.
- *When We Were Orphans* (Kazuo Ishiguro) Subtle and absorbing portrayal of an English detective who sets out to solve the case of his parents' disappearance in Shanghai, climaxing in war-shattered Hongkou.

Shi Yong and Hu Jieming. Shanghai artists are said to be stylistically more daring and modern, focusing on abstract and avant-garde styles, and thematically less political than their Beijing counterparts.

The southern suburb of Jinshan has its own school of untrained 'peasant' painters, who have been turning out colourful and vibrant paintings for years. Their works have their roots in local embroidery designs and have no perspective. The themes are mostly rural and domestic scenes full of detail of everyday life. You can see a selection of paintings from the Jinshan area in several shops in Yuyuan's **Old Street** (p147), or you can head out to Jinshan itself.

You'll also see a lot of calendar posters from 1920s and '30s Shanghai, started as advertisements by Western tobacco companies and now collected as nostalgia. Most Chinese art of all kinds in Shanghai is bought by foreigners.

Top Five Art Websites

- www.biz-art.com
- www.shanghart.com
- www.artscenechina.com
- www.newchineseart.com
- www.echinaart.com

The **Shanghai Bienniale** (p10) has been held in November every two years since 1996 and brings some interesting exhibits. The main shows are constrained by government cultural controls and it is the fringe shows that have attracted the bulk of the praise and attention in recent years. The city government keeps a tight control on what it calls 'decadent' art forms.

Outside of bienniale years the **Shanghai Art Fair** (p10) is an annual event held in November to bring traditional and modern Western and Chinese art, artists and galleries together. It's open to the public and offers an interesting insight into the current art scene.

Top Five Galleries

- **Art Scene China** (p68) This gallery in the French Concession is complemented by Art Scene Warehouse, part of the new Suzhou Creek Art Centre.
- **ShanghART** (p70)
- **Shanghai Art Museum** (p63)
- **Suzhou Creek Art Centre** (p77)
- **Unique Hill Studio** (p84)

Shanghai's Smaller Galleries

Apart from the major galleries listed individually in the Neighbourhoods chapter (p57) the following smaller galleries often have interesting exhibits. See listings magazines for exhibition details.

Art 4 U Gallery (Map pp244-5; ☎ 6321 8834; www.art4ugallery.net; Room 808, 61 Nanjing Donglu)

Classic Art Gallery (Map pp246-9; ☎ 6433 1939; 108 Shaoxing Lu) Traditional Chinese painting.

Duoyunxuan (Map pp244-5; ☎ 6466 2805; 422 Nanjing Donglu) Several galleries reside in this famous art supplies shop (see p145).

Elegant Art Gallery (Map pp246-9; ☎ 5403 9942; 5 Anfu Lu)

Gang of One Photographs (☎ 6259 9716; 3rd fl, Lane 461, Tianshan Lu, Hongqiao) Works here by excellent local photographer Gang Feng Wang.

Grand Theatre Gallery (Map pp244-5; ☎ 6386 9696; 286 Huangpi Beilu; closed Mondays)

Origin Gallery (Map pp246-9; ☎ 6258 3435; 423 Julu Lu) Photo gallery.

Shanghai Chinese Painting Institute (Shànghǎi Zhōngguó Huàyuàn; Map pp246-9; ☎ 6474 9977; 197 Yueyang Lu) Occasionally has major exhibitions.

Yibo Gallery (Map pp253-4; ☎ 5888 0111; www.yibo-art.com; 198 Huayuan Shiqiao Lu, Pudong)

CINEMA

The first cinema opened up in Shanghai in 1908, but before it reached its glamorous peak, film makers had to convince the distrustful Shanghainese that it was worth their hard-earned dosh. The first cinema owners would therefore run a few minutes of film, cut the reel and go around collecting money from patrons who wanted to see the rest. The Shanghainese soon became hooked and by 1930 the city boasted more than 35 cinemas and 141 film companies. Stars like Marlene Dietrich, Katharine Hepburn, Claudette Colbert and Greta Garbo were household faces in 1930s Shanghai.

China's first-ever film production was shown in Shanghai in 1926. For decades thereafter Shanghai was China's Hollywood and big studios like Mingxing (Star) and Lianhua churned out copies of Western hits, adapted with Chinese flair.

The genre changed in 1932 with the Japanese bombing of Hongkou. As film studios were destroyed and companies lost money they began showing film coverage of the bombing as a last resort; hence, the patriotic film was born. Film makers and left-wing scriptwriters turned to social issues for inspiration and suddenly prostitutes, beggars and factory workers were the characters projected onto the big screen.

This golden era produced its own adored movie stars, such as Ruan Lingyu, Zhou Xuan, Zhao Dan and Shi Hui, who became national celebrities, hounded by the paparazzi 'mosquito press'. The powerful popularity of film hit home when the wedding of 'Butterfly' Wu, revered actress and film icon, eclipsed the wedding of Song Meiling to Chiang Kaishek.

One of the greatest movie icons of the '30s was Ruan Lingyu, 'China's Garbo'. In 1934 she gained fame playing a virtuous prostitute in the silent film *Shennu* (Goddess). Ruan became an even greater icon when, like a Chinese Marilyn Monroe, she committed suicide at age 24 at the peak of her career, much like the novelist she portrayed in her 1935 film *Xin Nuxing* (New Woman).

Zhou Xuan, nicknamed 'Golden Voice', was another of the top actresses and singers from the 1930s and 1940s; her most famous film was *Street Angel* (1934). Zhou died, insane, at the age of 38. *Street Angel* was directed by Yuan Muzhi, who later became the head of the film bureau under the communist regime.

Artist at work, Art Scene China (p68)

One of Shanghai's aspiring actresses who received less critical acclaim was Jiang Qing, who later married Chairman Mao and spearheaded the madness of the Cultural Revolution.

The **Old Film Café** (p78) in north Shanghai shows old Shanghainese films on demand, some with English subtitles, including *New Woman* and others starring Ruan Lingyu.

One classic from the era, the 1937 *Shizi Jietou* (Crossroads), featuring Zhao Dan and Bai Yang, was recently remade as *X-Roads* (2001), starring Zhao Dan's son (Jin Zhao), and directed by Bai Yang's daughter. The new film is interesting for its historical links and juxtaposed images from the original film but it received some pretty bad reviews.

These days more innovative film studios like Xi'an have captured much of the international glory of the so-called fifth generation of directors such as Chen Kaige and Zhang Yimou (the latter produced the stylish *Shanghai Triad* in 1995). Coproduction films have been the most successful. One recent critical success was *The Red Violin*, a coproduction between Canada and the Shanghai Film Studio. Shanghai Film Studio's special effects blockbuster *Crash Landing* was a recent commercial success in China. It is possible to get a tour of the **studio** (Map p257; Caoxi Beilu, south of Xujiahui), but you will have to arrange it in advance with the studio or vi a a travel agency like the China International Travel Service.

Top Five Films

- *Shanghai Express* (1932) One of the world's top-grossing films in 1932/33, this is probably the most famous Shanghai-related movie, though the link is still tenuous. Based on the real-life hijacking of foreigners on a Beijing–Shanghai train in 1923, it won an Oscar for best cinematography and a best-director nomination for Josef von Sternberg, though it created a strong backlash in China. It features Marlene Dietrich purring the immortal and enigmatic line: 'It took more than one man to change my name to Shanghai Lily'.
- *Shanghai Triad* (1995) Zhang Yimou's stylish take on Shanghai's 1930s gangster scene, starring China's most famous art house actress Gong Li.
- *Empire of the Sun* Steven Spielberg's film based on JG Ballard's autobiographical account of his internment in Shanghai as a child during WWII (also see the boxed text 'Shanghai Fiction' p25).
- *Pavilion of Women* Adapted from Pearl Buck's novel and starring Willem Defoe and Luo Yan in a US-Sino coproduction. It was filmed in nearby Suzhou and Zhouzhuang and tells the story of a US missionary who falls in love with the wife of a rich Chinese family. It's not a great film (it's essentially a Chinese melodrama repackaged for English-language consumption) but the sets are sumptuous and the two main actors do a decent job.
- *Suzhou River* (Sūzhōu Hé) Made in 2000 and directed by Ye Lou, another underground film ultimately more successful than *Shanghai Panic*, with touches of Hitchcock and Wong Kar Wai in a haunting tale.

Digital technology is starting to have an effect on avant-garde film making in the city. Andrew Chen's *Shanghai Panic* (Wǒmèn Háipá) is an underground, illegally-shot digital video film made in 2001. It stars Mian Mian (see the boxed text 'Shanghai Fiction' p25) and is adapted from her novel *We Are Panic*. Loosely structured and part improvisation, it follows a group of Shanghai's lost youth, as the sibling-less slackers discuss suicide and sexuality. The docudrama was shown at a few foreign film festivals.

Shanghai's most recent internationally famous actress is Joan Chen (Chen Chong) who started her career at the Shanghai Film Studio in the late 1970s and gained fame in David Lynch's *Twin Peaks*. Shanghai's most famous domestic actress is Liu Xiaoqing.

For a scholarly look at old Shanghai cinema try the book *Cinema and Urban Culture in Shanghai 1922–1943*, edited by Zhang Yingjin.

Foreign Films

Western cinema has been so fixated with Shanghai over the years that Shanghai films are almost a genre unto themselves. In many, Shanghai is merely a backdrop, brought in whenever an element of mystery, allure or just plain sleaze was required. Shanghai never even appears in Hitchcock's *East of Shanghai*, Orson Welles' *Lady from Shanghai* or Charlie Chaplin's *Shanghaied*.

Charlie Chan had a couple of inevitable adventures in a Shanghai about as Chinese as Charlie Chan. Other films that buffs can track down are *The Shanghai Gesture* (1941), directed by Joseph Von Sternberg, starring Gene Tierney and Victor Mature, and *West of Shanghai* (1937), starring Boris Karloff. Then of course there was Madonna and then-husband Sean Penn in 1986's fairly dismal *Shanghai Surprise*.

More recently, British director Michael Winterbottom used Pudong and Sichuan Beilu as a backdrop for his futuristic thriller *Code 46*, starring Tim Robbins. Pudong was also used for *Flatland*, a 22-part TV series featuring Dennis Hopper, set in 2010 Shanghai and filmed entirely in the city.

Shanghai Vice by Phil Agland and Charlotte Ashby is a superb Channel 4 soap opera–style documentary offering an absorbing glimpse into the seedy underside of modern Shanghai and the concerns of local Shanghainese in the late 1990s. It's a must if you can find it.

The Port of Last Resort is another excellent documentary worth tracking down, this time focusing on Shanghai's Jewish history.

CHINESE OPERA

Contemporary Chinese theatre, of which the most famous is Beijing opera, has a continuous history of some 900 years, having evolved from a convergence of comic and balladic traditions in the Northern Song period. From this beginning, Chinese opera has been the meeting ground for a disparate range of forms: acrobatics, martial arts, poetic arias and stylised dance.

There are more than 100 varieties of opera in China today and many are performed in Shanghai. *Huju* or *Shenju* is Shanghainese opera, sometimes called flower drum opera. It is performed in the local dialect and has its origins in the folk songs of Pudong. *Yueju* opera was born in the Shaoxing and Shengxian counties of neighbouring Zhejiang (the ancient state of Yue) in the early 20th century. *Yueju* roles are normally played by women. *Kunju* opera originates from Kunshan, near Suzhou in nearby Jiangsu.

Operas were usually performed by travelling troupes whose social status was very low in traditional Chinese society. Chinese law forbade mixed-sex performances, forcing actors to act out roles of the opposite sex. Opera troupes were frequently associated with homosexuality in the public imagination, contributing further to their 'untouchable' social status.

Formerly, opera was performed mostly on open-air stages in markets, streets, teahouses or temple courtyards. Described by American writer PJ O'Rourke 'as if a truck full of wind chimes collided with a stack of empty drums during a birdcall contest', the shrill singing and loud percussion were designed to be heard over the public throng.

Opera performances usually take place on a bare stage, with the actors taking on stylised stock characters who are instantly recognisable to the audience. Most stories are derived from classical literature and Chinese mythology and tell of disasters, natural calamities, intrigues or rebellions. The musicians usually sit on the stage in plain clothes and play without written scores.

China's most famous 20th-century opera star was Mei Lanfang, who allegedly performed privately for several of Shanghai's gangland bosses in the 1930s.

Other Theatre

The lower Yangzi region has a long tradition of storytelling, farce, comic talk and mimicking, all of which were traditionally performed in teahouses. Yangzhou, Hangzhou and Suzhou all have their own variants. *Pingtan* balladry is a mix of *pínghuà* (Suzhou-style storytelling) and *táncí* (ballad singing), accompanied by the *pípā* (lute) and *sānxián* (banjo). You can hear samples of various Chinese operas and *pingtan* at the Shanghai Municipal Historical Museum in Pudong (p74).

MUSIC

Shanghai had a buzzing live music scene in the 1930s, featuring everything from jazz divas to émigré Russian troubadours, but today it's sadly dominated by Filipino cover bands and saccharine-sweet Canto-pop. Two independent Shanghainese bands worth checking out are Crystal Butterfly and The Honeys; both play occasionally at venues like the Ark (see p130).

Shanghai Music Conservatory is a prestigious clearing house of Chinese talent. One of its most famous former students is Liao Changyong, a world-class baritone who has performed with Placido Domingo, amongst others.

Surprisingly, classical Chinese music is quite hard to find in Shanghai. The *èrhú* is a two-stringed fiddle that is tuned to a low register, providing a soft, melancholy tone. The *húqín* is a higher pitched two-stringed viola. The *yuèqín*, a sort of moon-shaped four-stringed guitar, has a soft tone and is used to support the *èrhú*. Other instruments you may come across are the *shēng* (reed flute), *pípā* (lute), *gǔzhēng* (seven-stringed zither) and *xiāo* (vertical flute).

DANCE

Shanghai's most famous modern dancer is the remarkable Jing Xing, a former colonel in the Chinese army, who became a woman after a sex-change operation in 1995. Jing often performs in Shanghai.

The most famed male dancer is the athletic Huang Doudou who continues to reinvent traditional dance in contemporary styles as part of Shanghai's Song and Dance Ensemble. The city's other famed modern dancer is Hu Jialou, who spent a decade dancing in the US.

EMBROIDERY

Shanghai's finest embroidery can be traced back to the Ming dynasty family of Gu Mingshi, a wealthy official in the imperial court. The finest work, termed *gu* embroidery, came from Gu's eldest son's concubine. As the Gu family declined, the women went commercial and embroidery became a livelihood. At the beginning of the Qing dynasty, Gu's great-granddaughter opened a school to teach the art of embroidery.

Suzhou also has its own style of double-sided *sū* embroidery. Other styles local to Shanghai include embroidered 'paintings' and embroidery using human hair.

ARCHITECTURE

Shanghai's cosmopolitanism is most apparent through its eclectic buildings. A stroll of less than a kilometre can reveal an amazing spread of architectural designs: from Georgian to Gothic, Chicago to neoclassical, Spanish villas to imperial Chinese courtyards. According to Tess Johnston, author of *A Last Look: Western Architecture in Old Shanghai*, 'there is no city in the world today with such a variety of architectural styles'.

Shanghai's Top 10 Buildings

- Jinmao Tower (p73)
- Peace Hotel (p158)
- Park Hotel (p158)
- Hongkong and Shanghai Bank (p88)
- Tomorrow Square (p167)
- Arts & Crafts Museum (p69)
- Ruijin Guest House No 1 Building – Morris Residence (p163)
- Metropole Hotel (p158)
- Hamilton House (p89)
- French apartment block (Map pp246-9; cnr Huaihai Zhonglu & Wukang Lu)

For many, the greatest pleasure in Shanghai is a random wander down the city's side streets, tracking down the ghosts of the past. Like giant skeletons, these buildings are all that remain of old Shanghai and each holds its own tales and history.

CONCESSION ARCHITECTURE

Early architectural construction hit some unusual snags in Shanghai. Because of the lack of qualified architects, some of the earliest Western-style buildings in Shanghai were partially built in Hong Kong, shipped to Shanghai, then assembled on site.

Moreover, the glorious Bund was built (literally and metaphorically) on unstable foundations because of the leaching mud of the Huangpu River. Bund buildings were first built on concrete rafts that were fixed onto wood pilings, which were allowed to sink into the mud. Thus, the bottom entrance step usually originated 2m in the air and sank to ground level with the weight of the building.

In the 1920s the British architectural firm of Palmer & Turner designed many of Shanghai's major buildings (13 buildings on the Bund alone), including the neoclassical Hongkong and Shanghai Bank, the Bank of China, the Peace Hotel, the Yokohama Specie Bank, Grosvenor House (Jinjiang Hotel) and the Customs House, (apparently inspired by the Parthenon). In a remarkable stroke of continuity, the company that shaped so much of 1930s Shanghai has returned to design many of the buildings of the 1990s, including the Harbour Ring Plaza just off Renmin Square.

Old Shanghai's other main architect was Ladislaus Hudec (1893–1958), a Czech who eventually made it to Shanghai in 1918 after escaping en route to a Russian prisoner of war camp in Siberia. Shanghai's American Club, Moore Memorial Church, China United Apartments, the Green House (now Club La Belle), Grand Theatre and Park Hotel (the largest building in the Far East until the 1980s) all owe their creation to Hudec. Fans might want to visit the small exhibition on Hudec on the mezzanine floor of the Park Hotel lobby on Nanjing Xilu.

Many of Shanghai's buildings were constructed in baroque, Neo-Grecian and neoclassical styles to affirm ties with the homelands of the British and French. The 1920s saw the introduction of Art Deco to Shanghai, particularly in theatres, providing a cultural link with New York. The buildings of the 1930s owed more to the USA Chicago style, reflecting rising American power. Fine examples include the Metropole Hotel, Hamilton House, Grosvenor House (Jinjiang Hotel), Broadway Mansions and Picardie Mansions (Hengshan Hotel).

These vast buildings, with their imposing presence, provided a sense of security as well as reflecting the financial optimism of the time. In the end, though, after all the expense and effort, most buildings served their original purpose for only about 15 years before their owners were booted out

Stairway, Peace Hotel (p158)

in 1949. Communism successfully mummified rather than transformed Shanghai, and recently the government has begun to preserve and restore these architectural giants.

Those who are interested in old houses and backstreet architecture should contact the **Shanghai Historic House Association** (SHHA -subscribe@topica.com) for details of its twice-yearly programme of lectures and tours of old Shanghai architecture.

Feng Shui

The ancient Chinese world-views included the belief that the earth, like a human body, has channels or veins, along which benevolent and evil influences flow. This belief, known as *fēngshuǐ* (geomancy), plays an important role in the choice of sites for buildings or tombs and is far from a dead tradition. A feng shui grand master was called in to bless the Jinmao Tower before its opening in 1999.

LONGTANGS

What *hútòngs* are to Beijing, *lòngtángs* (or *nongtangs*) are to Shanghai: back alleys which form whole communities. *Lòngtángs* are Shanghai's major indigenous urban architectural feature.

After the Small Swords Rebellion in 1853, and subsequent civil strife, some 20,000 Chinese fled into the International Settlement. Sensing they could make a quid or two, the British decided to scrap the law forbidding foreigners from owning or subletting houses, and British and French speculators built hundreds of houses in what became Shanghai's biggest real estate boom. The result was the *shíkūmén* (stone gatehouse), a unique mixture of East and West, of interior Chinese courtyard and English terraced housing, which at one stage made up 60% of Shanghai's housing. These were originally designed to house one family, but Shanghai's growth led to sublets of many families, each of which shared a kitchen and outside bathroom to complement the *matang* (chamber pot). For the Shanghainese, a single-family kitchen and separate bedrooms remained a dream until the 1990s.

One preserved, prettified example of the *shíkūmén* is the **Open House museum** (p71) in the Xintiandi complex, though there are hundreds more around town.

MODERN ARCHITECTURE

In a rush towards modernity Shanghai is rapidly deconstructing and reconstructing itself. There is more construction and relative investment now than there ever was in the 1920s. Much of the city resembles a huge building site of ambitious new projects, forested by cranes and fuelled by migrant workers from Sichuan and Anhui.

The results are mixed, but Shanghai has undoubtedly become a test-bed of Western and Chinese architecture. It's interesting to note the completely different styles used to create three theatres. Compare the **Chinese theatre** in the Yuyuan Gardens with the 1930s Art Deco style of the **Lyceum Theatre**, then compare that with the millennial **Shanghai Grand Theatre**.

The Shanghai Grand Theatre, designed by French architect Jean-Marie Charpentier, has an interesting design, incorporating the sweeping eaves of Chinese tradition with a

Architecture Books

- *A Last Look: Western Architecture in Old Shanghai* (Tess Johnston and Deke Erh) Offers a fascinating photographic record of buildings in the city, as do the following two books, both by the same authors. These books are widely available in Shanghai, particularly at the **Old China Hand Reading Room** (p71), but are pricey at around Y450.
- *The Old Villa Hotels of Shanghai* (Tess Johnston and Deke Erh)
- *Frenchtown Shanghai: Western Architecture in Shanghai's Old French Concession* (Tess Johnston and Deke Erh)
- *Shanghai Architecture Guide* (Luigi Novelli) This Italian architect has produced a series of guides to Shanghai's architecture with an emphasis on the city's modern buildings; the merger of Western and Chinese architecture is a major theme.
- *A Tour of Shanghai Historical Architecture* (Shanghai Municipal Tourism Administration) This blue paperback book is excellent for those in search of the remaining islands of colonial architecture but it can be hard to find.

Jinmao Tower

Towering above Pudong like a 21st-century pagoda, the US$540-million Jinmao Tower is the tallest building in the People's Republic of China and, at 420.5m, the fourth-tallest in the world. Designed by the same team that built the Sears Tower in Chicago, the building is highly symbolic. Its 88 floors are auspicious (eight is a lucky number to Chinese) and its 13 bands are linked to Buddhist imagery. Furthermore, the segmented tower is supposed to symbolise bamboo, and also a pen, acting as a counterpoint to the open book–shaped podium. The name Jinmao, meaning 'economy' and 'trade', also carries the additional meanings of 'gold' and 'prosperity'.

futuristic use of plastic and glass. This mix of East and West is nothing new to Shanghai, just look at the Chinese roofs on the otherwise foreign-inspired YMCA and Bank of China buildings.

The architecture of the Shanghai Urban Planning Exhibition Hall echoes that of the Grand Theatre. Its distinguishable roof has four 'florets' to symbolise four budding magnolias, the city's flower.

The buildings in Renmin Square have an interesting layout. The three main buildings lie on an axis cutting through a circle formed on the north by Renmin Park and the south by Renmin Square, creating what some say is the character *zhōng* (centre). All the main buildings face south, in line with Chinese imperial tradition and the tenets of feng shui, which are to create harmony, order and a positive flow of energy. You can find more symbolism at the Shanghai Centre, which was built in the shape of the Chinese character *shān* (mountain).

The Bladerunner-style Pudong skyline forms a modern, ostentatious, hi-tech counterpart to the historic Bund. The gaudy flamboyance of the Shanghai International Convention Centre, with its neoclassical lines and giant glass globes, is rivalled only by the shocking-pink baubles of the Oriental Pearl TV Tower. Only the graceful Jinmao Tower can stand tall with the fine buildings of the Bund, tied as it is to their collective past with its own modern Art Deco twist.

The Shanghai World Finance Building, whose plot stands next to the Jinmao Tower, will total 101 storeys and exceed the height of its tall neighbour by 71.5m. The upper storeys will house a six-star hotel, and a giant vertical hole cored through the top floors will double as the world's highest open-air observation deck and a wind tunnel to alleviate structural stress. Construction was due to start in 2000 but was delayed by funding problems (the estimated cost runs to US$750 million), and is racing other planned building projects in Hong Kong, India, Sao Paolo, Melbourne and Chicago.

TRADITIONAL TEMPLE ARCHITECTURE

Temple architecture in China tends to follow a certain uniformity. There is little external difference between Buddhist, Confucian and Taoist temples, all of which are groups of buildings, arranged in courtyards, aligned on a north–south orientation.

The main entrance complex normally consists of two stone guardian lions, an impressive main gate adorned with calligraphy and two painted celestial guardians. A spirit wall blocks the passage of evil spirits, who can only travel in straight lines.

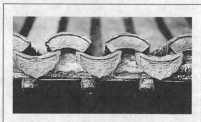

Roof detail, Confucian Temple (p66)

The most striking feature of the Buddhist temple is the pagoda. It was probably introduced from India along with Buddhism in the 1st century. Pagodas were originally built to house relics of the Buddha and later to hold religious artefacts and documents, to commemorate important events, or to store the ashes of the deceased.

Gu lóu (drum towers) and *zhōng lóu* (bell towers) are normally two-storey pavilions whose function is to mark prayer time. The most famous examples of these are at the Longhua Temple (p82).

Food & Drink

Food & Drink

Shanghai offers a dazzling array of food and provides an opportunity for cuisine exploration that should be seized firmly with both chopsticks. Stylish dining is one area where Shanghai leaves Beijing in the dust.

The eastern region of China has long been known as a land of plenty (the 'land of fish and rice') and the quality and variety of fresh produce are reflected in the emphasis put on food. The region is also the source of China's best soy sauces and rice wines.

Eating out in Shanghai is about more than just the food. It is a social lubricant, an opportunity for families to get together, and a chance for the nouveau riche to flaunt their wealth and the nouveau chic to prove their cool. While friends in the West go out for a beer, the Shanghainese will opt for a 'hot and noisy' meal punctuated with increasingly vociferous shots of rice wine. One method of saying 'How are you?' *(nǐ chīfàn le méiyǒu?)* translates literally as 'Have you eaten yet?'

Even if you are a regular at your local Chinese restaurant in London or Sydney you won't necessarily find yourself at home with Chinese cuisine in China. You'll find no fortune cookies or chop suey in Shanghai and only the occasional prawn cracker.

Most top-end Chinese restaurants have some kind of English menu but even these don't include the more interesting dishes. Try out the menu decoder (p41) in this chapter or, even better, go with Chinese friends and let them order. In general, it is always better to eat Chinese food in a group as you'll get a better variety of dishes. The Shanghainese habitually over order. Restaurants often have set meals for a table of 10, which is especially useful if you have to hold a banquet for some bigwig.

CULTURE

ETIQUETTE

There aren't many rules of etiquette attached to Chinese restaurants. In fact you may find that Chinese table manners are very relaxed. Large groups in particular often wreak carnage and desolation wherever they dine.

Everyone gets an individual bowl of rice or a small soup bowl. It's quite acceptable to hold the bowl close to your lips and shovel the contents into your mouth with chopsticks. If the food contains bones, just put them out on the tablecloth or into a separate bowl. Restaurants are prepared – the staff change the tablecloth after each customer leaves.

Remember to fill your neighbours' tea cups when they are empty, as yours will be filled by them. You can thank the pourer by tapping your middle finger on the table gently. On no account serve yourself tea without serving others first. When your teapot needs a refill, signal this to the waiter by taking the lid off the pot.

Chopstick Etiquette

Chopsticks rule in Shanghai so you'd better get practising. If your skills are a little rusty, gain some consolation in the fact that many Shanghainese feel the same confusion when faced with a knife and fork in the town's burgeoning Western restaurants.

The Chinese think nothing of sticking their chopsticks into a communal dish. Nicer restaurants will provide separate serving chopsticks or even spoons; use them if they do so. Pointing your chopsticks at anyone is considered rude.

One other thing worth knowing is that, while you may spit bones onto the floor with impunity or spray your neighbour with rice as you shout across the room with a mouthful of half-eaten food without anyone even noticing, you should never commit the terrible faux pas of sticking your chopsticks into your rice. Two chopsticks stuck vertically into a rice bowl resemble incense sticks in a bowl of ashes and is considered an omen of death.

Chinese toothpick etiquette is similar to that of neighbouring Asian countries. One hand wields the toothpick while the other shields the mouth from prying eyes.

Probably the most important piece of etiquette comes with the bill: although you are expected to try to pay, you shouldn't argue too hard, as the one who extended the invitation will inevitably foot the bill. Going Dutch is unheard of except among the closest of friends and perhaps young Westernised Shanghainese.

One other thing to bear in mind is that restaurant staff get severely aggravated if you stand around the restaurant entrance while checking out the menu. It's best to take a seat even if you're not sure you'll be eating there. You can get up and leave if you don't like the look of the menu.

HOW THE SHANGHAINESE EAT

Chinese meals are social and often very noisy events. Typically, a group of people sit at a round table and order dishes from which everyone partakes; ordering a dish just for yourself would be unthinkable. It's not unusual for one person at the table to order on everyone's behalf.

Epicureans will tell you that the key to ordering is to get a variety and balance of textures, tastes, smells, colours and even temperatures. Most Chinese will order at least one cold dish, a main dish and a watery soup to finish off. Note that both soup and rice are normally served at the end of a meal as fillers, so if you want them to come first you'll have to tell the waiter.

Food and restaurants are subject to Shanghai's faddish whims. One year Hangzhou restaurants will be all the rage, the next it will be Hunanese and half the Hangzhou restaurants from the year before will go bust. When one restaurant gets popular, expect half a dozen copycats to open up in a flash.

There's a definite cachet among Shanghainese when it comes to eating Western food. The Shanghainese cool set is the first in the country to embrace foreign food, whether it be steak or salad, and even cheese and wine.

Most Chinese eat early, often as early as 11am for lunch and 5pm for dinner, but lots of trendy late-night Shanghainese eateries buzz 24 hours. Breakfast is the one meal that foreigners often have problems with. Chinese breakfasts generally include dumplings, *yóutiáo* (fried breadsticks), cold congee, pickles, peanuts and soya bean milk. Bear this in mind before you get too excited about your two-star hotel buffet breakfast. If you can't face this there are several cafés where you can get Western breakfasts. Every mid-range or top-end hotel does a breakfast buffet.

STAPLES
RICE

Rice is an inseparable part of virtually every Chinese meal. The Chinese don't ask 'Have you had your dinner/lunch yet?' but 'Have you eaten rice yet?' Rice comes in lots of different preparations – as a porridge (congee) served with savouries at breakfast, fried with tiny shrimps, pork or vegetables and eaten at lunch or as a snack. But plain steamed white rice – fragrant yet neutral – is what you should order at dinner.

Eggs in soy sauce, a popular street snack

NOODLES

Noodles are thought to have originated in northern China during the Han dynasty (220–206 BC) when the Chinese developed techniques for large-scale flour grinding. Not only were noodles nutritious, cheap and versatile, they were portable and could be stored for long periods. Legend credits Marco Polo with having introduced noodles to Italy in 1295.

Chinese like to eat noodles on birthdays and on the new year, because their long thin shape symbolises longevity. That's why it's bad luck to break noodles before cooking them.

Moslem-style *lā miàn* (pulled noodles) are created when the noodle puller repeatedly stretches a piece of wheat-flour dough, folding it over and stretching again, until a network of noodle strands materialise. Thin, translucent noodles made from rice flour are common in the city's Southeast Asian restaurants.

SOUP

A balanced meal simply must have soup. Traditionally it was the beverage component of the meal; nowadays it shares that role with other liquids. A balanced meal contributes to the balance of Yin and Yang in the body (and thus a body's health) and soup is the main vehicle for the delivery of medicinal and balance-enhancing properties of foods. It gives you heat in winter, keeps you cool in summer.

REGIONAL CUISINES

SHANGHAI

The cuisine of Shanghai is influenced by neighbouring Zhejiang and Jiangsu styles, and is defined, along with Suzhou and Hangzhou cuisines, as Yangzhou or Huaiyang cuisine. It is generally sweeter and oilier than China's other cuisines.

Unsurprisingly, due to its position as a major port and the head of the Yangzi delta Shanghai cuisine features a lot of fish and seafood, especially cod, river eel and shrimp. The word for fish (*yú*) is a homonym for 'plenty' or 'surplus'; fish is a mandatory dish for most banquets and celebrations.

Common Shanghainese fish dishes include *sōngrén yùmǐ* (fish with corn and pine nuts), *guìyú* (steamed mandarin fish), *lúyú* (Songjiang perch), *chāngyú* (pomfret) and *huángyú* (yellow croaker). Fish is usually *qīngzhēng* (steamed) but can be stir-fried, pan-fried or grilled. Both fish and seafood are usually priced by weight, either 50g or 500g.

Squirrel-shaped mandarin fish is a famous dish from Suzhou. The dish dates from a political assassination during the Warring States period, when a dagger was hidden in the thick sauce until the assassin struck.

Several restaurants specialise in *xiánjī* (cold salty chicken), which tastes better than it sounds. *Zuìjī* (drunken chicken) is so called because it is marinated in Shaoxing rice wine. *Shīzitóu* (lion's head) is actually steamed pork meatballs. A variation on the theme is *xièfěn shī tóuzi*, which mixes crab meat with the meatballs. Crab roe dumplings are another Shanghainese luxury. *Bāo* (claypot) dishes are braised for a long time in their own casserole dish.

Vegetarian dishes include shredded pressed bean curd, cabbage in cream sauce, *mèn* (braised) bean curd and various types of mushrooms, including *xiānggū báicài* (mushrooms surrounded by baby bok choy). *Hǔpí jiānjiāo* (tiger skin chillies) is a delicious dish of stir-fried green peppers seared in a wok and served in a sweet chilli sauce. Fried pine nuts and sweet corn is another common Shanghainese dish.

Dazha hairy crabs are a Shanghai speciality between October and December. They are eaten with soy, ginger and vinegar and downed with warm Shaoxing wine. The crab is thought to increase the body's Yin, or coldness, and so rice wine is taken lukewarm to add Yang. Aficionados say that the best crabs come from Yangcheng Lake and are black with hairy feet. Male and female crabs are supposed to be eaten together. They are delicious but can be fiddly to eat. The body opens via a little tab on the underside. Don't eat the gills or the stomach.

HANGZHOU

Part of the 'Eastern School', Hangzhou cuisine is sometimes described as southern food cooked in a northern style and has noticeably less oil than Shanghai cuisine. There's a predominance of fish, shrimp and green vegetables, in fresh and subtle sauces. Longjing shrimp (*lóngjǐng xiārén*) are soaked with Hangzhou's famous longjing tea. *Xīhú chúncài tāng* (West Lake soup) is made with water shield, a green plant that grows in West Lake. *Xīhú tángcù yú* (sweet-and-sour West Lake fish) is another popular dish.

Look out for *Dōngpō ròu* (pork slices), named after the Song dynasty poet Su Dongpo. Flavoured with Shaoxing wine, and cooked and served in a pot, the pork is often quite fatty.

Another local delicacy, apparently a firm favourite with the emperor Qianlong, is *shāguō yútóu dòufu* (earthenware pot fish-head tofu).

Jiàohuà jī (beggar's chicken), also a popular dish, was supposedly created by a pauper who stole a chicken but had no pot to cook it in. Instead, he plucked it, covered it with clay and put it on the fire. These days, the bird is stuffed with mushrooms, pickled Chinese cabbage, herbs and onions, then wrapped in lotus leaves, sealed in clay and baked all day in hot ashes, ending up deliciously crispy.

CANTONESE

This is what non-Chinese consider 'Chinese' food, largely because most émigré restaurateurs originate from Guangdong or Hong Kong. In Shanghai every hotel worth its salt has at least one blowout Cantonese restaurant to cater to its Hong Kong guests.

Cantonese flavours are generally more subtle than other Chinese styles – almost sweet, and there are very few spicy dishes. Sweet-and-sour and oyster sauces are common. The Cantonese are almost religious about the importance of fresh ingredients, which is why so many restaurants are lined with tanks full of finned and shelled creatures.

Expensive dishes – some that are truly tasty, others that appeal more for their 'face' value – include abalone, shark's fin and bird's nest. Pigeon is a Cantonese speciality, served in various ways but most commonly roasted.

Banquets

The banquet is the apex of the Chinese dining experience. Virtually all significant business deals in China are clinched at the banquet table.

Dishes are served in sequence, beginning with cold appetisers and continuing through 10 or more courses. Soup, usually a thin broth to aid digestion, is generally served after the main course.

The idea is to serve or order far more than everyone can eat. Empty bowls imply a stingy host. Rice is considered a cheap filler and rarely appears at a banquet – don't ask for it, as this would imply that the snacks and main courses are insufficient, causing embarrassment to the host.

It's best to wait for some signal from the host before digging in. You will most likely be invited to take the first taste. Often your host will serve it to you, placing a piece of meat, chicken or fish in your bowl. If a whole fish is served, you might be offered the head, the cheeks of which are considered to be the tastiest part. It's OK to decline; someone else will gladly devour the delicacy.

Never drink alone. Imbibing is conducted via toasts, which will usually commence with a general toast by the host, followed by the main guest reply toast, and then settle down to frequent toasts to individuals. A toast is conducted by raising your glass in both hands in the direction of the toastee and crying out *gānbēi*, literally 'dry the glass'. Chinese do not clink glasses. Drain your glass in one hit. It is not unusual for everyone to end up very drunk, though at very formal banquets this is frowned upon. Raising your tea or water glass in a toast is not very respectful so unless you have deep-rooted convictions against alcohol, it's best to drink at least a mouthful.

Don't be late for a formal banquet; it's considered extremely rude. The banquet ends when the food and toasts end – the Chinese don't linger after the meal. You may find yourself being applauded when you enter a large banquet. It is polite to applaud back.

One person (the host) settles the account with the restaurant. Even in the very rare case where the cost is going to be split, this is better done away from the restaurant staff – to pass money to your host in front of others would cause a massive loss of face.

Cantonese dim sum (*diǎnxīn* in Mandarin) are famous and are the speciality of several of Shanghai's restaurants. Apart from *chasiu* (barbecued pork) dumplings, you'll find spring rolls, ho fun noodles (*héfěn* in Mandarin), *wánzi* (fish balls), *zhōu* (congee) and, of course, the acquired taste of chickens' feet.

CHAOZHOU

Named after a coastal area in eastern Guangdong, this is similar to Cantonese cuisine and features squid and lots of other seafood, but with stronger, earthier flavours and richer sauces than Cantonese cuisine. The most famous dishes are some of Chinese food's most expensive – abalone, shark's fin and bird's nest – as well as roast suckling pig and soy goose.

SICHUANESE & HUNANESE

The 'Western School' is the fieriest of all China's cuisines, so take care when ordering. Lethal red chillies (introduced by Spanish traders in the early Qing dynasty), aniseed, peppercorns and pungent *huājiāo* ('flower pepper') are used and dishes are simmered to give the chilli peppers time to work into the food. Meat, particularly in Hunan, is marinated, pickled or otherwise processed before cooking, which is generally by stir- or explode-frying.

Famous dishes include *zhāngchá yāzi* (camphor-smoked duck), *mápō dòufu* (Granny Ma's tofu) and *gōngbǎo jīdīng* (chicken with peanuts). These provinces are a long distance from the coast, so pork, chicken and beef – not seafood – are the staples.

VEGETARIAN

Vegetarianism became something of a snobbish fad in Shanghai in the 1930s, when it was linked to Taoist and Buddhist groups, and then to the underworld. Vegetarian and low-fat food is undergoing a minor revival. Shanghai's monasteries all have good vegetarian restaurants.

The Chinese are masters at adding variety to vegetarian cooking and creating 'mock meat' dishes. Chinese vegetarian food is based on soya bean curd (tofu) to which chefs do some miraculous things. Not only is it made to taste like any food you could possibly think of, it's also made to look like it. A dish that is sculptured to look like spareribs or a chicken can be made from layered pieces of dried bean curd, or fashioned from mashed taro root.

SNACKS

Shanghai has some great snacks (*xiǎo chī* or literally 'little eats') and it's worth trying out as many of them as possible. They are cheap, quick and there's no need to labour through any pesky Chinese menus. What's more, the places to track them down – Shanghai's backstreets – are interesting in themselves.

Look out for *xiǎolóngbaō* (little dragon balls), Shanghai's number one favourite dumpling, which is copied everywhere else in China, but is only true to form here. They are wonderful, but there's an art to eating them – they're full of scalding oil and the interior is hotter than McDonald's apple pies. Tradition actually assigns the invention of the dumpling to Nanxiang, a village north of Shanghai city. Dumplings are normally bought by the *lóng* (steamer basket), though large versions are sold individually for about Y1 each.

Another Shanghainese speciality is the *shēngjiān,* similar to the *bāozi* dumpling but fried in a black pan with a wooden lid. Watch out for the scalding oil. Several Shanghainese restaurants serve *luobocibing* (fried onion cakes), which make a good beer snack.

Shuǐjiǎo are best described as Chinese ravioli, stuffed with meat, spring onion and greens. They are sometimes served by the bowl in a soup, sometimes dry by weight (250g or half a *jin* is normally enough). Locals mix *làjiāo* (chilli), *cù* (vinegar) and *jiàngyóu* (soy sauce) in a little bowl according to taste and dip the ravioli in. Watch out – vinegar and soy sauce look almost identical! The slippery buggers can be tricky to eat with chopsticks so don't wear white as you'll get sprayed in soy whenever you drop them in the bowl. Shuǐjiǎo are often created by family mini-factories – one person stretches the pastry, another makes the filling and a third spoons the filling into the pastry, finishing with a little twist.

Steamed dumplings, are a cheap and tasty snack

Huǒguō (hotpot) is particularly popular in Shanghai in winter. The pot in question is a huge bowl of bubbling, spicy broth into which you dip various skewered vegetables and meats. One reason for its popularity became clear in 1999 when it was revealed that several hotpot restaurants were adding opium poppies to the stock! Mongolian- and Korean-inspired barbecued meats are also popular.

The following is a rundown of the other main street snacks you'll find in Shanghai:

chǎofàn – fried rice

chǎomiàn – fried noodles or 'chow mein', not as popular here as in the West. There is no such thing as 'chop suey' in China.

dàpái miàn – beef noodles with a rib or bone

guōtiē – like a *shuǐjiǎo* but fried in oil

húndun – known in the West as won ton soup, these are small savoury ravioli served by the bowl

jiānbǐng – an egg-and-spring onion omelette made to order on a black hotplate and served folded up with chilli sauce

jīdàn miàn – noodles with egg

mántou – steamed dumplings without filling or taste (and also Chinese slang for a woman's breasts!)

niúròu miàn – beef noodles in a soup.

qìguō – an earthenware pot with a hole in the centre, the soupy contents of which are heated by steam coming up the hole

shāguō – a stewed casserole cooked in an earthenware pot

shāokǎo – an upturned skillet on which you can fry your own meat or vegetables

zhēngjiǎo – a steamed version of a *shuǐjiǎo*

Other street snacks include *chòu* (stinky) tofu, fried tofu, tea eggs (soaked in soy sauce), tofu soaked in soy sauce, and baked sweet potatoes, which can be bought by weight.

Keep an eye open for Thousand Year Eggs – duck eggs that are covered in straw and stored underground for six months (the traditional recipe has them soaked in horses' urine before burial!). The yolk becomes green and the white becomes jelly. More interesting snacks available at markets include chickens' feet, pigs' ears, pigs' trotters and even pigs' faces.

DESSERTS & SWEETS

The Chinese do not generally eat dessert, but fruit is considered to be an appropriate end to a good meal. Western influence has added ice cream to the menu in some up-market establishments, but in general sweet stuff is consumed as snacks and is seldom available in restaurants.

One exception to the rule is caramelised fruits, such as *bāsī pínggǔo* (apple), *bāsī xiāngjiāo* (banana) and even *bāsī tǔdòu* (potato), which you can find in a few restaurants. Other sweeties include *tángyuán* (small, sweet, glutinous balls, traditionally from Ningbo, filled with sugar or bean paste), *bīngshā* (literally 'frozen sand', shaved ice and syrup), *bābaófàn* (a sweet, sticky rice pudding known as Eight Treasure Rice), and various types of steamed buns filled with sweet bean paste.

Bīngtáng húlú (toffee crab apples) and strawberries on a stick are a popular winter treat. Roasted chestnuts are popular over winter and sell for Y10 to Y13 a *jīn. Dànta* (egg tarts) are also popular among Shanghainese. Shanghai's bakeries stock a wide range of Western cakes, various types of cakes stuffed with bean or date paste, and gummy glutinous balls covered in sesame seeds.

Several shops at the Yuyuan Gardens have been selling pear syrup sweets since 1894 but these are generally not to foreigners' tastes.

FRUIT

Shanghai's fruit stalls are well stocked with produce brought from all over the country. November is the best season.

The best fruits are *yòuzi* (pomelos), Fuji apples, pears from Anhui, imported kiwis and bananas from southern China. Mandarins are particularly cheap. Strawberries roll into town around January. Entrepreneurs at the Yuyuan Gardens sell *gānzhezhī* (fresh sugar-cane juice) and *hāmīguā* (slices of Hami melon) on a stick.

DRINKS

Nonalcoholic Drinks

All of the world's major soft-drink producers have plants in Shanghai. Coca-Cola set up its first factory in Shanghai in 1927. Taiwanese and Japanese imports include cold coffee in a can and bottles of delicious iced tea.

Hot tea is normally drunk before or after a meal. There's a wide range of teas available, including *lüchá* (green tea), *mòlihuā* (jasmine), *júhuā chá* (chrysanthemum), *lóngjǐng* (longjing), *wūlóng* (oolong) and *hóng chá* (black tea). In traditional restaurants you will be served tea poured out of a foot-long spout. Bottled ice teas (Y3) are available everywhere and are generally excellent. The Japanese brands Kirin or Suntory are the best.

Shanghai has been hit with coffee-house chic and those watered-down pots of weedy tea that cost next to nothing in the countryside now fetch up to Y40 per pot in Shanghai. A decent cup of coffee is an easy Y30. More often than not a coffee will

Young shop assistant packaging sweets

double your food bill, though some small backstreet Chinese restaurants still serve complimentary tea with a meal. If you're lucky you can find a decent cup of coffee under Y15 and a pot of tea with refills of hot water for under Y12. The only really cheap place to get a hot brew is McDonald's, where a cup of coffee or tea costs around Y4.

Cookery Classes

Cookery classes are held once a month at the Westin. The food on offer varies monthly, from desserts to Italian or Southeast Asian and the quality is very high. The Y350 charge includes the cooking and eating of a three-course lunch. The Portman Ritz-Carlton has a similar deal twice a month for Y328.

Alcoholic Drinks

The most famous domestic brand of beer is Qingdao, originally a German brew, famed for the mineral water used in brewing. The cheapest local brand is Reeb (Lìbō).

Foreign beers have hit China big time and Budweiser (Bǎiwēi) is on its way to dominating China as it does the US. The German beer Becks (Bèikè) has a brewery in China, but though it is very cheap (Y3 per bottle in the supermarket), it is not as good as the European version. The Japanese beers Suntory and Kirin, and Denmark's Carlsberg, all have breweries in Shanghai. Foreign bars have a selection of Bitburger, Guinness, Kilkenny, Coopers, Tetleys and Steinlager, mostly on tap.

Shaoxing rice wine from south of Shanghai is one of many kinds of huángjiǔ. It is traditionally served warm, in a tube.

MENU DECODER
USEFUL WORDS & PHRASES

I don't want MSG.	wǒ bú yào wèijīng	我不要味精
I'm vegetarian.	wǒ chī sù	我吃素
not too spicy	bú yào tài là	不要太辣
(cooked) together	yíkuàir	一块儿
menu	càidān	菜单
bill (check)	mǎi dān/jiézhàng	买单/结帐
set meal (no menu)	tàocān	套餐
let's eat	chī fàn	吃饭
cheers!	gānbēi	干杯
chopsticks	kuàizi	筷子
knife	dāozi	刀子
fork	chāzi	叉子
spoon	tiáogēng/tāngchí	调羹/汤匙
hot	rède	热的
ice cold	bīngde	冰的

RICE DISHES

mǐfàn	米饭	steamed white rice
jīdàn chǎofàn	鸡蛋炒饭	fried rice with egg

SOUP

húndùn tāng	馄饨汤	won ton soup
jīdàn tāng	鸡蛋汤	egg drop soup
sānxiān tāng	三鲜汤	three kinds of seafood soup
suānlà tāng	酸辣汤	hot and sour soup

VEGETABLE DISHES

báicài xiān shuānggū	白菜鲜双菇	bok choy and mushrooms
cuìpí dòufu	脆皮豆腐	crispy skin bean curd
háoyóu xiāngū	蚝油鲜菇	mushrooms in oyster sauce
hēimù'ěr mèn dòufu	黑木耳焖豆腐	bean curd with mushrooms
huǒtuǐ dòufu	火腿豆腐	bean curd stuffed with ham
jiāngzhī qiézi	姜汁茄子	aubergine (eggplant) in ginger sauce
tángcù ǒubǐng	糖醋藕饼	lotus root cakes in sweet-and-sour sauce

SHANGHAINESE DISHES

hǔpíjiānjiāo	虎皮尖椒	tiger skin chillies
jīngcōng ròusī jiá bǐng	京葱肉丝夹饼	soy pork with scallions in pancakes
jīngdū guō páigǔ	京都锅排骨	Mandarin-style pork ribs
sōngrén yùmǐ	松仁玉米	sweet corn and pine nuts
sóngshǔ guìyú	松鼠桂鱼	squirrel-shaped Mandarin fish
sōngzǐ yā	松子鸭	duck with pine nuts
xiāngsū jī	香酥鸡	crispy chicken
xièfěn shīzitóu	蟹粉狮子蝏	lion's head meatballs with crab
yóutiáo niú ròu	油条牛肉	fried dough sticks with beef
zuìjī	醉鸡	drunken chicken

Seafood

chǎo huángshàn	炒黄鳝	fried eel
cōngsū jìyú	葱酥鲫鱼	braised carp with onion
dàzhá xiè	大闸蟹	hairy crabs
fúróng yúpiàn	芙蓉鱼片	fish slices in egg white
guōbā xiārén	锅巴虾仁	shrimp in sizzling rice crust
gānjiān xiǎo huángyú	干煎小黄鱼	dry-fried yellow croaker
jiǔxiāng yúpiàn	酒香鱼片	fish slices in wine
héxiāng báilián	荷香白鲢	lotus-flavoured silver carp
hóngshāo shànyú	红烧鳝鱼	eel soaked in soy sauce
jiāng cōng chǎo xiè	姜葱炒蟹	stir-fried crab with ginger and scallions
mìzhī xūnyú	蜜汁熏鱼	honey-smoked carp
níngshì shànyú	宁式鳝鱼	stir-fried eel with onion
qiézhī yúkuài	茄汁鱼块	fish fillet in tomato sauce
qīngzhēng guìyú	清蒸鳜鱼	steamed Mandarin fish
sōngzǐ guìyú	松子鳜鱼	Mandarin fish with pine nuts
suānlà yóuyú	酸辣鱿鱼	hot-and-sour squid
yóubào xiārén	油爆虾仁	fried shrimp
zhá hēi lǐyú	炸黑鲤鱼	fried black carp
zhá yúwán	炸鱼丸	fish balls

HANGZHOU DISHES

dōngpō bèiròu	东玻焙肉	Dongpo pork
héyè fěnzhēng ròu	荷叶粉蒸肉	steamed pork wrapped in lotus leaf
jiào huā jī	叫化鸡	beggar's chicken
lóngjǐng xiārén	龙井虾仁	stir-fried shrimp with a hint of tea
mìzhī huǒfāng	密汁火方	honeyed ham
shāguō yútóu dòufu	沙锅鱼头豆腐	earthenware pot fish-head tofu
sòngsǎo yú gēng	宋嫂鱼羹	Mandarin fish soup with ham and mushrooms

xīhú chúncài tāng	西湖莼菜汤	West Lake water shield soup
xīhú cùyú	西湖醋鱼	West Lake fish

CANTONESE DISHES

bái zhuó xiā	白灼虾	blanched prawns with shredded scallion
dōngjiāng yán jú jī	东江盐焗鸡	salt-baked chicken
gālí jī	咖喱鸡	curried chicken
háoyóu niúròu	蚝油牛肉	beef with oyster sauce
kǎo rǔzhū	烤乳猪	crispy suckling pig
mìzhī chāshāo	密汁叉烧	roast pork with sweet syrup
shé ròu	蛇肉	snake
tángcù lǐjī/gǔlǎo ròu	糖醋里脊/古老肉	sweet-and-sour pork fillets
tángcù páigǔ	糖醋排骨	sweet-and-sour spare ribs
xiāngsū jī	香酥鸡	crispy chicken

SICHUANESE DISHES

bàngbang jī	棒棒鸡	shredded chicken in a hot pepper-and-sesame sauce
dàsuàn shàn duàn	大蒜鳝段	stewed eel with garlic
gānshāo yán lǐ	干烧岩鲤	stewed carp with ham and hot-and-sweet sauce
gōngbào jīdīng	宫爆鸡丁	spicy chicken with peanuts
huíguō ròu	回锅肉	boiled and stir-fried pork with salty-and-hot sauce
málà dòufu	麻辣豆腐	spicy tofu
shuǐ zhǔ niúròu	水煮牛肉	fried and boiled beef, garlic sprouts and celery
yúxiāng ròusī	鱼香肉丝	'fish-resembling' meat
zhàcài ròusī	榨菜肉丝	stir-fried pork or beef tenderloin with tuber mustard
zhāngchá yāzi	樟茶鸭子	camphor tea duck

HOME-STYLE DISHES

běijīng kǎoyā	北京烤鸭	Beijing duck
biǎndòu ròusī	扁豆肉丝	shredded pork and green beans
guōbā ròupiàn	锅巴肉片	pork and sizzling rice crust
fānqié chǎodàn	番茄炒蛋	egg and tomato
gānbiǎn niúròu sī	干煸牛肉丝	stir-fried beef and chilli
hóngshāo qiézi	红烧茄子	red cooked aubergine
huíguō ròu	回锅肉	double-cooked fatty pork
jiācháng dòufu	家常豆腐	'home-style' tofu
jingjiàng ròusī	精酱肉丝	pork cooked with soy sauce
mù ěr ròu	木耳肉	'wooden ear' mushrooms and pork
níngméng jī	柠檬鸡	lemon chicken
páigǔ	排骨	ribs
qīngjiāo ròu piàn	青椒肉片	pork and green peppers
sùchǎo biǎndòu	素炒扁豆	garlic beans
sùchǎo sùcài	素炒素菜	fried vegetables
tiěbǎn niúròu	铁板牛肉	sizzling beef platter
yángcōng chǎo ròupiàn	洋葱炒肉片	pork and fried onions
yāoguǒ jīdīng	腰果鸡丁	chicken and cashews
yúxiāng qiézi	鱼香茄子	'fish-resembling' aubergine
xiānbèi yāohuā	鲜贝腰花	scallops and kidney

DRINKS

beer	*píjiǔ*	啤酒
Chinese spirits	*báijiǔ*	白酒
Coca-Cola	*kěkǒu kělè*	可口可乐
coconut juice	*yézi zhī*	椰子汁
coffee creamer	*nǎijīng*	奶精
coffee	*kāfēi*	咖啡
milk	*niúnǎi*	牛奶
mineral water	*kuàngquánshuǐ*	矿泉水
red wine	*hóng pútáojiǔ*	红葡萄酒
rice wine	*mǐjiǔ*	米酒
soft drink (soda)	*qìshuǐ*	汽水
soya bean milk	*dòujiāng*	豆浆
tea	*chá*	茶
water (boiled)	*kāi shuǐ*	开水
white wine	*bái pútáojiǔ*	白葡萄酒
yoghurt	*suānnǎi*	酸奶

History

History

PRE-SHANGHAI

Though the earliest imperial records date from the Warring States period (453–221 BC) when the western suburbs of Shanghai belonged to the state of Chu, Neolithic discoveries in Songze, Qingpu County, point to the existence of human settlement in the region 5900 years ago.

Up until the 7th century AD Shanghai itself, then known as Shen or Hu Tu, after the local bamboo fishing traps, was an underdeveloped marshland. In fact, most of eastern modern Shanghai didn't exist until the 17th century, when a complex web of canals was built to drain the region. The early settlement of Shanghai grew up at the confluence of the Shanghai River (long since disappeared) and the Huangpu River.

The migration of Chinese fleeing the Mongols from the north during the Sung dynasty (AD 960–1126) boosted the region's population. This, combined with the silting of the Wusong River, brought about the shift of the regional administrative centre from Qinglong to Shanghai, and in 1291 raised the town up to the status of county seat as part of Jiangsu. In 1553 a wall was erected around Shanghai to defend it against Japanese pirates, and in 1685 a customs house was built, reflecting the growth of local trade. By the late 17th century a population of approximately 50,000 was sustained by cotton production, fishing ports and, due to the city's excellent location at the head of the Yangzi River and its tributaries, trade in silk and tea.

Top Five History Books

- *Shanghai* (Harriet Sergeant) This book is recommended. It is portrait of the city in its heyday combining first-hand accounts with extensive research and lively reconstruction.
- *Shanghai: The Rise and Fall of a Decadent City 1842–1949* (Stella Dong) This is a well-researched, if a bit fruity, look at the city's good old, bad old days.
- *In Search of Old Shanghai* (Pan Ling) A rundown on who was who and what was what back in the bad old days. At 140 pages, it's an easy read and an excellent intro to the city's murky past.
- *Shanghai: Crucible of Modern China* (Betty Peh-T'I Weh) This is a more detailed history of the city until 1943. *Old Shanghai*, by the same author, is a shorter, easier read.
- *Secret War in Shanghai* (Bernard Wasserstein) A denser, sometimes heavy-going look at 'Treachery, subversion and collaboration in the Second World War'. The real joy of the book is its fascinating cast of characters, such as 'abortionist, brothel-owner and sexual extortionist' Dr Albert Miorini, 'monkey expert, narcotics dealer and friend of Errol Flynn' Hermann Erben, the British gun runner General 'One-Arm' Sutton, and 'journalist, aviator and pimp' Hilaire du Berrier.

IT ALL STARTED WITH A LITTLE BIT OF OPIUM

During the early years of the Qing dynasty (1644–1911), the British East India Company and its later incarnations were quietly trading in the only open port to the west, Canton (now Guangzhou), south of Shanghai. British purchases of tea, silk and porcelain far outweighed Chinese purchases of wool and spices, so in the late 18th century the British decided to balance the books by slipping into India for opium to swap for silver to purchase (with a profit) Chinese goods. As the British passion for tea increased so did China's craving for opium. By 1823 the British were swapping roughly 7000 chests of opium annually – with

TIMELINE	Pre-7th century	977	1291
	Early Shanghai, known as Shen, is underdeveloped marshland	Original Longhua Pagoda constructed	Shanghai becomes county seat of Jiangsu

Top Five Shanghai Biographies

- *Life and Death in Shanghai* (Nien Cheng) This is a classic account of the Cultural Revolution and is one of the few biographies with a Shanghai angle.
- *Red Azalea* (Anchee Min) A sometimes racy account of growing up in Shanghai in the 1950s and 1960s amid the turmoil of the Cultural Revolution.
- *Daughter of Shanghai* (Tsai Chin) This book has less to say about Shanghai but is still a good read. Daughter of China's most-famous Beijing opera star, Chin left Shanghai in 1949 and later starred in the film *The World of Suzie Wong* as the original 'China doll' and in the *Joy Luck Club*. This memoir bridges two worlds during two different times.
- *The Life, Loves and Adventures of Emily Hahn* (Ken Cuthbertson) A look at the fascinating life of Emily Hahn, who passed through Shanghai in 1935 (accompanied by her pet gibbon, Mr Mills), got hooked on opium and became the concubine of a Chinese poet.
- *Captive in Shanghai* (Hugh Collar) This is a fascinating personal account of life in the Japanese internment camps in the early 1940s. It's published by Oxford University Press, but is pretty hard to get your hands on.

about 140 pounds of opium per chest, enough to supply one million addicts – compared with 1000 chests in 1773.

In 1825 Emperor Daoguang's census revealed the amount of silver going to the West for Indian opium and, fearing a crippling economy, he appointed Lin Zexu (Commissioner Lin, as he was known to the English) to stop the opium trade. As tensions came to a head in 1839, British merchants were arrested and forced to watch as three million pounds of raw opium were flushed out to sea. Merchants began demanding compensation from the British government. After much negotiation the British gained modified rights to Hong Kong, as well as US$6 million in reparations, but both China and Britain were unhappy with the agreement. In June 1842 the British fleet sailed into the mouth of the Yangzi and took the Wusong Fort, at the mouth of the Huangpu, in a day. Scaling the walls of Shanghai's Old Town, they met with little resistance and went on to take the greater prize of Nanjing. On 29 August 1842 Sir Henry Pottinger signed the Treaty of Nanjing aboard the *Cornwallis* upon the Yangzi River, and China's doors were prised open.

THE ILLEGITIMATE BIRTH OF SHANGHAI

The Treaty of Nanjing stipulated, among other things: peace between China and Britain; security and protection of British persons and property; the opening of Canton, Fuzhou, Xiamen, Ningbo and Shanghai; as well as permission of residence for foreigners and consulates in those cities (for the purpose of trade); fair import and export tariffs; the possession of Hong Kong, and an indemnity of US$18 million. Strangely enough, the trade of opium, legal or otherwise, never entered into the treaty.

Other countries soon followed suit. In July 1844 the Americans adopted the Treaty of Wanghia, which gained them much the same rights as the British and gave US missionaries the right to construct hospitals, churches and cemeteries. Two months later the French took advantage of the existing community of French Jesuits to draw up a similar treaty. In 1843 the first British consul moved into a local house in the Old Town, marking a foreign presence in the city that would last for the next 100 years.

Of the five port cities, Shanghai was the most prosperous due to its superb geographical location, low interference from the Chinese government, and a capitalistic edge. Trade and businesses boomed in Shanghai and by 1850 the foreign settlements housed more than 100 merchants, missionaries and physicians, three quarters of them British. In 1844,

1553	1644	1685	1823
City wall erected around what is now the Old Town	End of Ming dynasty, beginning of Qing dynasty	First customs house built	The British are importing enough opium into China annually to supply one million addicts

Shanghaied

If New York is so good they named it twice, then Shanghai was so bad they made it a verb. To shanghai, or 'render insensible by drugs or opium, and ship on a vessel wanting hands', dates from the habit of press-ganging sailors. Men, many of whom were found drunk in 'Blood Alley' (off modern-day Jinling Lu), were forced onto ships, which then set sail, leaving the comatose sailors no choice but to make up the deficient crew numbers when they sobered up.

44 foreign ships made regular trade with China. By 1849, 133 ships lined her shores and by 1855, 437 foreign ships clogged her ports.

Foreigners were divided into three concessions. The original British Concession more than tripled its size between 1846 and 1848. Bishop William Boone set up a mission in Hangkou a few years later, which founded the city's American Concession, and the French set up their own settlement, known as the French Concession, in 1849. In 1863 the British and Americans merged into a cosy enclave still known as the International Settlement.

The Municipal Council, the members of which were voted on by the business elite, was set up in 1854 to control the British Concession and later the International Settlement, while the French consul-general ran the French *Conseil d'Administration Municipale*. From regulation to sanitation, everything in Shanghai was vested in these foreign oligarchies, a pattern that was to last as long as the settlements. It was not until the early 1920s that Chinese and Japanese (eventually the two largest groups in the settlements) were allowed limited representation on the council.

From the start Shanghai's *raison d'être* was trade. Still sailing to the West were silks, tea and porcelain, and 30,000 chests of opium were being delivered into China annually. Soon great Hong Kong trading houses like Butterfield & Swire and Jardine Matheson set up shop, and trade in opium, silk and tea gradually shifted to textiles, real estate, banking, insurance and shipping. Banks in particular boomed; soon all of China's loans, debts and indemnity payments were funnelled through Shanghai. Buying and selling was handled by Chinese middlemen known as *compradors* (from the Portuguese) from Canton and Ningbo who formed a rare link between the Chinese and foreign worlds. The city attracted immigrants and entrepreneurs from China, and overseas capital and expertise pooled in the burgeoning metropolis.

Gradually sedan chairs and single-wheeled carts gave way to rickshaws and carriages, the former imported from Japan in 1874. Shanghai lurched into the modern age with gaslights (1865), electricity (1882), motorcars (1895), a cinema and an electric tram (1908), and its first bus (1922).

The Manchu gave only cursory glances to the development in Shanghai as all eyes focused on the continued survival of the Qing dynasty.

SHANGHAI'S REBELLIOUS YOUTH

Drenched in opium, sucked dry by local militia, crippled by taxes, and bullied by foreign interests, Shanghai's population was stirring and anti-Manchu rebellions began to erupt. The first major rebellion to affect Shanghai was the Taiping, led by Hong Xiuquan. A failed scholar, Hong Xiuquan claimed to have ascended to heaven and been given a new set of internal organs by a golden-bearded Jehovah, which he used to battle the evil spirits of the world with his elder brother Jesus Christ. The rebels burst out of Jintian village in 1851, swept through Guizhou and ended up taking Nanjing three years later.

An offshoot of the Taipings, the Small Swords Society (Xiǎodāo Hui) entered the Chinese section of Shanghai in 1853 and held it for 18 months before being besieged in the Old Town and then expelled by Manchu and French forces. Fearing the seizure of Shanghai, the

1825	1839	1842	1843–63
Emperor Daoguang appoints 'Commissioner Lin' to stop the opium trade	Chinese destroy three million pounds of opium	British take Shanghai in Opium Wars; Treaty of Nanjing signed	Foreign concessions established

Revolutionary relief on the Customs House (p88)

foreign residents organised the Shanghai Volunteer Corps, a force that would repeatedly protect the interests of foreigners in Shanghai.

The Taipings threatened again in 1860 but were beaten back from Shanghai by the mercenary armies of Frederick Townsend Ward, an American adventurer hired by the Qing government who was eventually killed in Songjiang in 1862. British and Qing forces joined to defeat the rebels, the Europeans preferring to deal with a corrupt and weak Qing government than with a powerful, united China governed by the Taipings.

As rebellions ravaged the countryside hundreds of thousands of refugees poured into the safety of Shanghai's concessions, setting up home alongside the foreigners, sparking a real-estate boom that spurred on Shanghai's rapid urbanisation and made the fortunes of many of Shanghai's entrepreneurs.

As imperial control loosened, the encroaching Western powers moved in to pick off China's colonial 'possessions' in Indo-China and Korea. National humiliation led to the Boxer Rebellion, which was eventually quelled in 1898 by a combined British, US, French, Japanese and Russian force of 20,000 troops. As a result, massive indemnities were strapped on the Qing government. The weakened state of the country, the death of the empress dowager and the legion of conspiring secret societies marked the end of the tottering Qing dynasty. In 1911 representatives from 17 provinces throughout China gathered in Nanjing to establish the Provisional Republican Government of China.

Insular Shanghai carried out business as usual, unaffected by the fall of the Qing or by WWI. As the rest of China fragmented and plunged into darkness, Shanghai emerged as a modern industrial city.

THE BIG CITY

By the first decade of the 20th century Shanghai's population had swelled to one million. As the elite and most cosmopolitan of China's cities, Shanghai attracted capitalists and intellectuals alike, and literature and cinema thrived in the ferment as intellectuals began to ponder the fate of a modern China.

1853	1859	1865	1882
Taiping rebellion rages throughout China unleashing a flood of refugees into Shanghai	More than half of all British troops stationed in Shanghai have venereal disease	Gaslights flicker on in Shanghai	Electricity comes to Shanghai

Shanghai's Russians

In the 1920s and '30s, as China's youth looked to revolutionary Russia for their future, 25,000 White Russians fled for their lives, travelling first to Siberia or Central Asia and then along the railroads to China. Many congregated in Manchuria before being pushed on to Shanghai by the Sino-Japanese War. By 1935 they formed the city's second-largest foreign community after the Japanese.

The refugees scraped the highest rungs of Tsarist society, from generals and aristocrats to poets and princesses, but all had to find a way to survive. The wealthy sold off their jewellery piece by piece. Moscow's musicians played in Shanghai's hotel bands, and ballerinas from St Petersburg quickly learned how to charge by the dance. The men took whatever jobs they could find: as riding instructors or, more commonly, bodyguards, guarding the wealthy against rival gangs and kidnapping.

Ave Joffre (Huaihai Lu) became the heart of the White Russian community, and was lined with Cyrillic signs and cafés serving Shanghai borscht, blinis and black bread. There were Russian cinemas, printing presses and even rival revolutionary and Tsarist newspapers. White Russians kept the Russian diplomats on their toes with their regular attempts to storm the Bolshevik Russian embassy, just north of the Bund.

Yet beneath the glamour was deep despair and poverty. White Russians were stateless and so, unlike other foreigners in Shanghai, were subject to Chinese laws and prisons. Those without money or skills took the city's lowest jobs, or resorted to begging for alms from the Chinese. Others became prostitutes or ended up as drunks lying on street corners. The British looked down on the Russians, believing they 'lowered the tone', but used the men ('real tough nuts') in the Volunteer Corps.

In 1949 the Russians were forced to flee their second communist revolution in 22 years. There are few signs of Mother Russia in Shanghai these days, save for the original Russian embassy, a couple of empty Russian churches (see the French Concession walking tours p92), and the odd Russian cabaret act flirting with the ghosts of the past.

The foreigners had effectively plucked out prime locations and, using their ever-increasing wealth, the result of cheap labour, established exclusive communities designed after their own countries and desirable to their needs.

Exploited in workhouse conditions, crippled by hunger and poverty, sold into slavery and excluded from the city's high life created by the foreigners, the poor of Shanghai had a voracious appetite for radical opinion. Intellectuals and students, provoked by the startling inequalities between rich and poor, were perfect receptacles for the many outside influences circulating in the concessions. The Communist Manifesto was translated into Chinese and swiftly became a hot topic in secret societies. In light of the intense dislike that many Chinese felt for foreigners it seems ironic that fundamental ideals stemmed from overseas inspirations. The first meeting of the Chinese Communist Party (CCP), formed by Marxist groups advised by the Soviet Comintern, took place in Shanghai in 1921. Shanghai, with its large proletariat (30,000 textile workers alone) and student population, had become the communists' hope for revolution, but elsewhere political violence was growing.

In May 1925 resentment spilled over when a Chinese worker was killed in a clash with a Japanese mill manager. In the ensuing demonstrations the British opened fire and nine Chinese were killed. In protest, 150,000 workers went on strike, later seen as a defining moment marking the decline of Western prestige and power.

In 1927 Chiang Kaishek launched his Northern Expedition in an attempt to unite various warlords under a Kuomintang-communist alliance. As the Kuomintang marched on Shanghai, 20,000 Volunteer Corps troops surrounded the settlements with barbed wire. Strikes and a curfew paralysed the city as the Kuomintang (with the help of communist supporters under Zhou Enlai) wrested Shanghai from the Chinese warlord Sun Chaofang.

Kaishek's aim was not focused on the settlements or even the warlords, but rather his erstwhile allies, the communists, whom he then betrayed in an act of breathtaking perfidy.

1895	1908	1911	1912
Motor cars first appear in Shanghai	Electric tramway established	Fall of the Qing dynasty	Modernising republicans pull down Shanghai's ancient city walls

Backed by Shanghai bankers and armed by Shanghai's top gangster Du Yuesheng, Chiang Kaishek armed gangsters, suited them up in Kuomintang uniforms and launched a surprise attack on the striking workers' militia. Du's machine guns were turned on 100,000 workers taking to the streets, killing as many as 5000. In the ensuing period, known as the White Terror, 12,000 communists were executed in three weeks. Zhou Enlai and other communists fled to Wuhan, leaving Shanghai in the hands of the warlords, the wealthy and the Kuomintang.

Nestled safely in a world of selectively structured law and unadulterated capitalism, by the 1930s Shanghai had slammed to the top and was soon to begin its fatal downwards slide. Shanghai had become a modern city equipped with Art Deco cinemas and apartment blocks, the hottest bands and the latest fashions – a place of great energy where 'two cultures met and neither prevailed'. Chinese magazines carried ads for Quaker Oats, Colgate and Kodak, while Chinese girls, dressed in traditional *qipaos* (Chinese-style dresses), advertised American cigarettes. Shanghai's modernity was symbolised by the Bund, Shanghai's Wall Street, a place of feverish trading and an unabashed playground for Western business sophisticates. To this day it remains the city's most eloquent reminder that Shanghai is a very foreign invention.

Earning such labels as 'Paris of the East' and 'Whore of the Orient', the city became an exotic port of call. Flush with foreign cash and requiring neither visa nor passport for

Green Gang Gangsters

In Shanghai's climate of hedonist freedoms, political ambiguities and capitalist free-for-all, it was perhaps inevitable that Shanghai should raise China's most powerful mobsters. Ironically, in 1930s Shanghai the most binding laws were those of the underworld, with their blood oaths, secret signals and strict code of honour. China's modern-day triads and Snakeheads owe much of their form to their Shanghainese predecessors.

One of Shanghai's early gangsters was Huang Jinrong, or 'Pockmarked' Huang, who had the enviable position of being the most powerful gangster in Shanghai, while at the same time holding the highest rank in the French Concession police force.

Another famous underworld figure was Cassia Ma, the Night Soil Queen, who founded a huge empire on the collection of human waste, which was ferried upriver to be sold as fertiliser at a large profit.

The real godfather of the Shanghai underworld, however, was Du Yuesheng, or 'Big-Eared' Du as he was known to anyone brave enough to say it to his face. Born in Pudong, Du soon moved across the river and was recruited into the Green Gang (qīngpāng), where he worked for Huang Jinrong. He gained fame by setting up an early opium cartel with the rival Red Gang and rose through the ranks. By 1927 Du was the head of the Green Gang and in control of the city's prostitution, drug running, protection and labour rackets. Du's special genius was to kidnap the rich and then to negotiate their release, taking half of the ransom money as commission. With an estimated 20,000 men at his beck and call, Du travelled everywhere in a bulletproof sedan like a Chinese Al Capone, protected by armed bodyguards crouched on the running boards.

His control of the labour rackets led to contacts with warlords and politicians. In 1927 Du played a major part in Chiang Kaishek's anticommunist massacre and later became adviser to the Kuomintang. A fervent nationalist, his money supplied the anti-Japanese resistance movement.

Yet Du always seemed to crave respectability. In 1931 he was elected to the Municipal Council and was known for years as the unofficial mayor of Shanghai. He became a Christian halfway through his life and somehow ended up best known as a philanthropist. When the British poet WH Auden visited Shanghai in 1937 Du was head of the Chinese Red Cross!

During the Japanese invasion of Shanghai, Du fled to the city of Chongqing (Chungking). After the war he settled in Hong Kong, where he died, a multimillionaire, in 1951.

1921	1925	1927	1929
Inaugural meeting of the Chinese Communist Party takes place in Shanghai	30 May anti-Western Movement signals decline in Western prestige and power	Anticommunist massacre (the 'White Terror') is unleashed by Chiang Kaishek	Victor Sassoon opens the Peace Hotel

Propaganda poster; see more at the Propaganda Poster Art Centre (p149)

entrance, Shanghai became home to the movers and the shakers, the down-and-out and on-the-run. It offered a place of refuge and a fresh start and rejected no-one. Everyone who came to Shanghai, it was said, had something to hide.

By 1934 the world's fifth-largest city was home to the tallest buildings in Asia, boasting more cars in one city than the whole of China put together, and providing a haven for more than 70,000 foreigners among a population of three million. The city had become three times as crowded as London and the cosmopolitan mix of people was unequalled anywhere in the world. Between 1931 and 1941, 20,000 Jews took refuge in Shanghai, only to be forced into Japanese war ghettos, and to flee again in 1949. By 1935, 25,000 White Russians had flocked to Shanghai, turning the French Concession into Little Moscow. In 1895 the Japanese had gained treaty rights and by 1915 had become Shanghai's largest non-Chinese group, turning Hongkou into a de facto Japanese Concession.

THE DEATH OF OLD SHANGHAI

In 1931 the Japanese invaded Manchuria and Shanghai's Chinese reacted with a boycott of Japanese goods. Two Japanese were killed in scuffles as anti-Japanese sentiment grew and the Japanese seized the opportunity to protect their interests. Warships brought 20,000 Japanese troops, who proceeded to take on the ragtag Chinese 19th Route army. As Japanese bombers razed Zhapei to the ground, 600,000 Chinese refugees fled into the protected International Settlement. After a month of fighting, Zhapei was in ruins and 14,000 lay dead.

By 1937 Sino-Japanese tensions had grown into a full-scale war. Chiang Kaishek took a rare stand in Shanghai and the city bled for it. The Japanese lost 40,000 men, the Chinese anywhere from 100,000 to 250,000. On 14 August, a date that became known as Bloody Saturday, bombs fell onto the foreign concessions for the first time, killing more than 2000

1931	1932	1934	1935
Over 10,000 civilians die fighting the Japanese in Zhapei district	*Shanghai Express* released	Park Hotel built; life expectancy of Chinese in Shanghai is 27 years	Shanghai becomes the world's fifth-largest city; White Russian refugees become second-largest foreign group after the Japanese

Shanghai Vice

Underneath the glitz and glamour of 1930s Shanghai lay a pool of sweat, blood and desperate poverty. In the words of a British resident, Shanghai was violent, disreputable, snobbish, mercenary and corrupt – 'a discredit to all concerned'. 'If God allows Shanghai to endure', said the missionaries, 'He will owe Sodom and Gomorrah an apology'. Others agreed: 'Shanghai is a city of 48-storey skyscrapers built upon 24 layers of hell.'

The city was often a place of horrific cruelty and brutal violence. After the Small Sword Rebellion, 66 heads, even those of elderly women and children, were stuck up on the city walls. In 1927 striking workers were beheaded and their heads put in cages. Up to 80,000 rickshaw pullers worked the littered streets until they dropped while overcrowded factory workers routinely died of lead and mercury poisoning. In 1934 life expectancy of the Chinese in Shanghai stood at 27. In 1937 municipal refuse workers picked up 20,000 corpses off the streets.

Shanghai offered the purely synthetic pleasures of civilisation. Prostitution ran the gamut from the high-class escorts in the clubs of the International Settlement and 'flowers' of the Fuzhou Lu teahouses, to the *yějì*, or 'wild chickens', of Hongkou, who prowled the streets and back alleys. The 'saltwater sisters' from Guangdong specialised in foreigners fresh off the boats. Lowest of the low were the 'nail sheds' of Zhapei. Lists of the city's 100 top-ranking prostitutes were drawn up annually and listed next to the names of 668 brothels, which went by such names as the 'Alley of Concentrated Happiness'.

Prostitution was not the exclusive domain of the Chinese. The traditional roles were reversed when White Russians turned to prostitution and Chinese men could be seen flaunting Western women. An American madam ran Gracie's, the most famous foreign brothel in town, at 52 Jiangsu Lu, in a strip of brothels called The Line.

Linked to prostitution was opium. At the turn of the century Shanghai boasted 1500 opium dens (known locally as 'swallow's nests') and 80 shops openly selling opium. Even some hotels, it is said, supplied heroin on room service, 'served on a tray like afternoon tea'. Opium financed the early British trading houses and most of the buildings on the Bund. Later it funded Chinese gangsters, warlord armies and Kuomintang military expeditions. It was true that the police in the French Concession kept a close eye on the drug trade, but only to ensure that they got a reasonable slice of the profits. Not that there was much they could do even if they had wanted to; it was said that a wanted man in 1930s Shanghai need only pop into the neighbouring concession to avoid a warrant for his arrest.

in separate explosions at the Bund, the Palace Hotel, Great World and Nanjing Lu. Even today it is unclear whether the bombings were a tragic mistake by short-sighted Chinese pilots or a cynical ploy by Chiang Kaishek to drag Western powers into the war. Either way, most foreign residents reacted not by fighting, as they would have done for a colony, but by evacuation. Four million Chinese refugees were not so lucky.

Under Japanese rule the easy glamour of Shanghai's heyday was replaced by a dark cloud of political assassinations, abduction, gun running and fear. Espionage by the Japanese, the nationalists, the British and the Americans for wartime information was rife. The rich were abducted and fleeced. Japanese racketeers set up opium halls in the so-called Badlands in the western outskirts of the city and violent gangs ran rabid. The Kuomintang had long since fled to Chongqing, pulling as much of Shanghai's industry with them down the Yangzi as possible.

By December 1941 the hostilities between Japan and the allied powers had intensified abroad, giving the Japanese incentive to take over the foreign settlements in Shanghai. Suspect foreigners were taken off for interrogation and torture in notorious prisons such as the Bridge House. In early 1943 the Japanese rounded up 7600 allied nationals into eight internment camps. The British and American troops had abandoned Shanghai in 1942 to concentrate their energies elsewhere and the British and American governments, unable to overtake the Japanese, signed over their rights of the foreign settlements to Chiang Kaishek in Chongqing in 1943, bringing to a close a century of foreign influence.

In 1945, following the surrender of the Japanese, the Kuomintang took back the city, fusing the International Settlement and French Concession along with the rest of Shanghai into the Nationalist Administration, closing treaty ports and revoking foreign trading and

1936	1937	1938	1940
Lu Xun dies in Shanghai	Shanghai is taken by Japanese forces; thousands die in bombing raids on the city	20,000 Jews arrive in Shanghai fleeing persecution in Europe	Badlands of Western Shanghai controlled by racketeers and violent gangs

self-governing rights. Once released from their internment a few foreigners tried to sweep out their Tudor homes and carry on, but priorities and politics had shifted. The gangs, con men, dignitaries, merchants, and anyone who could, had already made their escape to Hong Kong. Those who remained had to cope with biting inflation of 1100%.

The Kuomintang-communist alliance, temporarily united against the Japanese, had collapsed by 1941 and as the two returned to internal antagonism, China was in the grip of an all-out civil war. By 1948 the Kuomintang was on the edge of defeat and hundreds of thousands of Kuomintang troops joined sides with the communists. In February 1949 Chiang Kaishek's troops quietly siphoned off 500,000 ounces of the Banks of China's gold reserves into a boat headed for Taiwan. In May Chen Yi led the Red Army troops into Shanghai and by October all the major cities in southern China had fallen to the communists.

In Beijing on 1 October 1949, Mao Zedong stood atop Tiananmen Gate, announced that the Chinese people had stood up, and proclaimed the foundation of the People's Republic of China (PRC). Chiang Kaishek then fled to the island of Formosa (Taiwan), taking with him the entire gold reserves of the country and what was left of his air force and navy, to set up the Republic of China (ROC), naming his new capital Taipei.

THE WORLD HAS LOST OLD SHANGHAI. NO ONE SHOULD THINK THAT ITS PASSING SHOULD BE THE CAUSE OF LAMENTATIONS. ITS PRESENCE FOR A CENTURY OR MORE WAS EVIDENCE OF OPPRESSION, OF CRUELTY AND UNFORGIVABLE DISCRIMINATION. THE FOREIGNERS HAVE LEFT THE SCENE OF THEIR DEBAUCHES. THEIR SPIRITS, I AM SURE, IN GHOSTLY FORAYS MUST BE SEEKING OUT THE SCENES OF THEIR EARTHBOUND JOYS – ALAS, IN VAIN, AS THE LENINIST-MARXIST THOUGHTS OF CHAIRMAN MAO HAVE SWEPT AWAY THE LAST LINGERING WHISPERS OF A HUNDRED YEARS OF SENSUALITY.

Ralph Shaw, 1949

THE PEOPLE'S REPUBLIC

The birth of the PRC marked the end of 105 years of 'the paradise for adventurers'. The PRC dried up 200,000 opium addicts, shut down Shanghai's infamous brothels and re-educated 30,000 prostitutes, eradicated the slums, slowed inflation and eliminated child labour – no easy task. In February 1952, 160,000 workers attended every one of the 3000 meetings held in Shanghai that were designed to denounce the bourgeoisie, with which Shanghai was particularly imbued. The state took over Shanghai's faltering businesses, the racecourse became the obligatory People's Park and Shanghai fell uniformly into the rest of China's modern history. Under Beijing's stern hand, the decadence and splendour faded.

Yet the communists, essentially a peasant regime, remained suspicious of Shanghai. The group lacked the experience necessary to head a big city and they resented Shanghai's former leadership, which they always regarded as a den of foreign imperialist-inspired iniquity, a constant reminder of national humiliation and the former headquarters of Kuomintang.

Perhaps because of this, Shanghai, in its determination to prove communist loyalty, became a hotbed of political extremism and played a major role in the Cultural Revolution, the decade of political turmoil that lasted from 1966 to 1976. Sidelined in Beijing, it was to Shanghai that Mao turned in an attempt to reinvigorate the revolution and claw his way back into power. For most of a decade the city was the power base of the prime movers of the Cultural Revolution, the Gang of Four: Wang Hongwen; Yao Wenyuan (editor of *Shanghai Liberation Army Daily*); Zhang Chunqiao (Shanghai's Director of Propaganda); and Jiang Qing, wife of Mao (and one-time failed Shanghai movie actress known as Lan Ping, who used her position to exact revenge on former colleagues at Shanghai Film Studios). In

1943	1945	1949	May 1949
The end of the formal foreign presence in Shanghai	Japanese surrender	Hyperinflation means that one US dollar is worth six million Chinese dollars	Communists take Shanghai; PRC established

Men study the inscription on the Monument to the People's Heroes, Huangpu Park (p87)

1969 the city was also the launch pad for the campaign to criticise Confucius and Mengzi (Mencius), before the campaign spread nationwide in 1973 and was linked to Lin Biao, Mao's former offsider.

Encouraged by Mao, a rally of a million Red Guards marched through Renmin Square, a force of anarchy that resulted in the ousting of the mayor. Competing Red Guards tried to outdo each other in revolutionary fervour, Shanghainese who had any contacts with foreigners (and who didn't?) were criticised, forced to wear dunce caps, denounced and sometimes killed.

Most extraordinarily, in 1966 a People's Commune, modelled on the Paris Commune of the 19th century, was set up in Shanghai. (The Paris Commune was set up in 1871 and controlled Paris for two months. It planned to introduce socialist reforms such as turning over management of factories to workers' associations.) The Shanghai Commune, headed by Zhang Chunqiao from headquarters in the Peace Hotel, lasted just three weeks before Mao, sensing that the anarchy had gone too far, ordered the army to put an end to it.

As the Cultural Revolution unfolded, between 1966 and 1970, one million of Shanghai's youth were sent to the countryside. Shanghai's industries closed. The Bund was renamed Revolution Blvd and the road opposite the closed Soviet consulate became Anti-Revisionist St. At one point there was even a plan to change the revolutionary red of the city's traffic lights to mean 'go'.

In the revolutionary chaos and a bid to destroy the 'four olds' (old customs, old habits, old culture and old thinking), Chinese religion was devastated. Temples were destroyed, priests were conscripted to make umbrellas, monks were sent to labour in the countryside where they often perished, and believers were prohibited from worship. Posters of Chairman Mao were posted over the doors of the Jing'an Temple to stop Red Guards bursting in (and ripping the icon), St Ignatius Cathedral was desecrated and an image of Mao was

1966–76	1972	1976	1989
Cultural Revolution launched from Shanghai; one million Shanghainese are sent into the countryside	President Nixon visits Shanghai, as China rejoins the world	Death of Mao Zedong	Antigovernment demonstrations in Shanghai's Renmin Square

even painted on the Russian Orthodox Church on Gaolan Lu and remains there to this day (see p92).

In 1976, after the death of Mao, the Gang of Four was overthrown and imprisoned. Accused of everything from forging Mao's statements to hindering earthquake relief efforts, the gang's members were arrested on 6 October 1976 and tried in 1980. Jiang Qing remained unrepentant, hurling abuse at her judges and holding famously to the line that she 'was Chairman Mao's dog – whoever he told me to bite, I bit'. Jiang Qing's death sentence was commuted and she lived under house arrest until 1991, when she committed suicide by hanging.

When the Cultural Revolution lost steam, pragmatists like Zhou Enlai began to look for ways to restore normalcy. In 1972 US President Richard Nixon signed the Shanghai Communique at the Jinjiang Hotel. The agreement provided a foundation for increased trade between the USA and China and marked a turning point in China's foreign relations. With the doors of China reopened to the West, and with Deng Xiaoping at the helm, China set a course of pragmatic reforms towards economic reconstruction, resulting in an annual growth of 9% over the next 15 years.

In communist China, however, the rush of economic reform has generated very little in the way of political reform. Corruption and inflation have between them led to widespread social unrest, which in 1989 resulted in the demonstrations in Tiananmen Square.

The demonstrations overtaking Beijing's Tiananmen Square spread to Shanghai. While students and workers demonstrated, students based at Fudan University constructed their own 'statue of liberty'. The city was threatened with martial law and four days after the massacre in Beijing on 4 June, tanks arrived in Shanghai's Renmin Square. Mayor Zhu Rongji intervened and the momentum petered out after a week or so. Recriminations were swift and several demonstrators were publicly shot.

SHANGHAI REINCARNATE

In 1990 the central government began pouring money into Shanghai. By the mid-1990s more than a quarter (some sources say half) of the world's high-rise cranes could be found looming over Shanghai. As the 20th century drew to a close, the city had built two metro lines, a light railway system, a US$2-billion airport at Pudong, a US$2-billion elevated highway, several convention centres, two giant bridges, several underground tunnels and a whole new city in Pudong.

The government has declared its aim to make Shanghai the financial centre of Asia. Nothing would satisfy the central government more than for Shanghai to replace Hong Kong as China's frontier of the future, swinging the spotlight of attention from the ex-colony on to a home-grown success story. The city is still 20 (officially 10) years behind its southern rival but is catching up so fast that it sometimes appears out of breath.

And yet, as fast as Shanghai strides into the future, its past remains oddly familiar. Joint-venture companies are cautiously returning to claim their former offices; foreign-run bars, restaurants and sporting clubs are back; and Westerners are filing back into expat-centric communities in the International Settlement and French Concession. To the Shanghainese, the Shanghai of the 1930s is dead history, but ghostly images of the past continue to haunt the city as it strives to become a financial, cultural and intellectual hot spot and a major city of the 21st century.

1990	2004–10	2004	2010
Pudong established as a special economic zone, marking the rebirth of the city	Shanghai to host the Chinese Formula One Grand Prix	Shanghai's citizens become the highest paid in China	World Expo in Shanghai

Neighbourhoods

Neighbourhoods

Broadly, central Shanghai is divided into two areas: Pudong (east of the Huangpu River) and Puxi (west of the Huangpu River). The ring road Zhongshan Lu does a long, elliptical loop around the city centre proper. The city centre has two main overpasses: Yan'an Lu running east–west and Chengdu/Chongqing Lu running north–south.

Shanghai has no single focus and the feel of the city still owes much to the original concessions. The Bund is the tourist centrepiece, though not the physical centre of town. West of the Bund is Nanjing Lu, one of Shanghai's main shopping streets.

South of the Bund is the Old Town, a maze of narrow lanes, lined with closely packed houses and laundry hanging from overhead windows. It lies on the southwestern bank of the Huangpu, bounded to the north by Jinling Donglu and to the south by Zhonghua Lu.

West of the old town and hidden in the backstreets north and south of Huaihai Lu, is the former French Concession, with tree-lined streets, 1930s architecture, cafés and bars. Huaihai Lu itself is Shanghai's premier shopping street and is lined with huge department stores. At the western end of the French Concession is Hengshan Lu, where you'll find a major collection of Western restaurants and bars.

As you continue southeast you come to the massive shopping intersection of Xujiahui. Further south is the Shanghai Stadium.

North of the French Concession is the commercial district of Jing'an, with its embassies, malls and top-end hotels focused on bustling Nanjing Xilu and the Shanghai Centre.

West Shanghai is dominated by Hongqiao, an economic zone that is home to several top-end hotels, conference centres and office towers. Further west is Gubei, a Legoland residential area of many expats, and the supermarkets, restaurants and services that cater to them.

North Shanghai includes the Hongkou district in the northeast, the former American and later Japanese-controlled concession. The prestigious Fudan and Tongji universities are here. Northwest is Zhabei district and Shanghai train station; further northeast is the suburban area of Yangpu.

On the east side of the Huangpu is Pudong, a special economic zone of banks, skyscrapers, building sites and new residential complexes, eventually petering out into farmland.

Navigating Shanghai on Foot

The naming of streets in Shanghai once depended on which concession they belonged to, French or English, except for the central area of the city where the streets were given the names of Chinese cities and provinces. While the foreign names have disappeared, streets named after Chinese places have been retained: those named after other Chinese cities are oriented east–west and those named after provinces north–south.

Even so, name changes seem to occur every few hundred metres. The good news is that there is logic to this system as well, and a little basic Chinese will help to make navigating much easier. Many road names are compound words made up of a series of directions that place the road in context with others in the city. Compass directions are particularly common in road names. The directions are:

běi   (north; 北)

nán   (south; 南)

dōng   (east; 东)

xī   (west; 西)

So Dong Lu literally means East Road.

Other words which regularly crop up are *zhōng* (central; 中) and *huán* (ring, as in ring road; 环). If you bring them together with some basic numerals, you could have Dongsanhuan Nanlu, which literally means 'east third ring south road' or the southeastern part of the third ring road.

Pudong is the future of Shanghai. It is made up of various zones such as Liujiazui, which you can see from the Bund, and Jinqiao, home to a small expat community. In the far southeast of Pudong is Pudong international airport, about 40km from the centre of town.

A second (outer) ring road links Hongqiao international airport (in the west of town) with the new Gaoqiao Free Trade Zone, a port on the Yangzi River in Pudong.

ITINERARIES

One Day

The main sightseeing highlight in Shanghai is unquestionably the **Bund** (p61) and you should give yourself a couple of hours to stroll around the area, preferably at night or early morning. For more of a perspective, get sweeping views of the Bund from the Pudong side (take the tourist tunnel or the metro) and visit the **Jinmao Tower** (p73). For something special, eat at **M on the Bund** (p100) if on the Bund, or the **Grand Hyatt** (p164) if in Pudong (reservations advised at both).

Take the metro to **Shanghai Museum** (p64), one of China's finest, which deserves at least a couple of hours. The other great attraction of Shanghai is the **Old Town** (p66), incorporating **Yuyuan Gardens and Bazaar** (p67) and the surrounding teahouses (take a taxi). If you don't like crowds then give this area a miss at the weekends.

Try to save time for one big night out in Shanghai to experience the modern side of the city. Take in the acrobats or a performance at the **Grand Theatre** (p64), try one of the excellent restaurants, then take your pick of the bars and clubs.

Three Days

With more time, budget half a day for your **Shanghai Museum** (p64) visit. After a visit to **Yuyuan Gardens and Bazaar** (p67) in the Old Town, add on a walk to **Dongtai Lu Antique Market** (p148) for some shopping and then take lunch (or dinner) at one of Xintiandi's trendy restaurants. Alternatively, stroll along **Nanjing Lu** (p143) from the **Bund** (p61) to Shanghai Museum to link those two premium sights.

On day two, visit the **Shanghai Art Museum** (p63). To savour a slower-paced Shanghai, fit in a walk through the faded 1930s architecture of the **French Concession backstreets** (p92), where Shanghai still shows its old magic. Perhaps end up at Hengshan Lu (p102) for dinner, or try **1221** (p102) for moderately priced Shanghainese cuisine.

On day three, hop aboard a **boat cruise** (p61) for views of the Bund from the Huangpu River or make it up to the gorgeous **Jinmao Tower** (p73) for the best view of the city. Take a taxi to North Shanghai's old **Jewish quarter** (p79) and maybe grab a meal at the nearby revolving top-floor restaurant of the Ocean Hotel, **Revolving 28** (p113).

ORGANISED TOURS

If you want to see Shanghai in a hurry then the best way is to jump aboard one of the red **Jinjiang tour buses** (🕐 9am-4.15pm; day ticket Y18) that leave every 45 minutes or so from just outside the Garden Hotel on Maoming Nanlu (Map pp246–9). They are comfortable, speedy and cheap. The bus stops at a number of tourist destinations, including Renmin Square, the Oriental Pearl Tower and Nextage Department Store in Pudong, Nanpu Bridge, Yuyuan Gardens and the Bund, and then returns to

Useful Bus Routes

Three useful bus routes for getting around are:

No 3 Travels via Renmin Square to Pudong's Pearl Tower (Y4) and Jinmao Tower (Y4) and on to Jinqiao, Zhangjiang, Sunqiao, Chuansha and Huaxia (Y12). It runs every 30 minutes from 7am to 5.30pm; you can pick it up from the stop just south of the Shanghai Museum on Yan'an Donglu.

No 7 Links the former residences of Song Qingling, Zhou Enlai and Sun Yatsen (Y2).

No 10 Goes to Huaihai Zhonglu, Nanjing Donglu, Sichuan Beilu and Lu Xun Park (Y3). It runs every 15 minutes from 6.30am to 7.30pm.

Top Five Cheap Thrills

Strapped for cash in Shanghai? The following five can be done for free:

- Ascend in the exterior lift to the 42nd floor of the **Jinjiang Tower** (p94) or the 33rd-floor Continental Bar of the **Garden Hotel** (p161) for a cheap adrenaline rush and fine views of Shanghai.
- Take a local ferry across the **Huangpu River** (p72). It's only free west-bound; heading to Pudong you'll have to spoil yourself and splash out eight *máo*.
- Check out the **Bund Historical Museum** (p87) in Huangpu Park. Inside are some fascinating photographs of old Shanghai and interesting historical trivia.
- Hang out in **Fuxing** (p68) or **Lu Xun Park** (p78), where at any time you may come across music, t'ai chi, mah jong, waltzing, therapeutic screaming and fishing.
- Stroll along the **Bund** (p61).

the Jinjiang Hotel. You can get off, go and see the sight, and wait for the next bus to come along and pick you up, using the same ticket.

Comfortable, green **sightseeing buses** (p173) operate from the east end of Shanghai Stadium, and though they primarily serve suburban sightseeing spots, one or two lines pass through points of interest in the city centre. These routes are probably only of interest if you are staying near the stadium, though the Shanghai Stadium metro stop is only a five-minute walk away.

THE BUND & NANJING DONGLU

Eating p99; Shopping p143; Sleeping p157

The Bund (Wàitān in Chinese; pronounced 'bunned' in English) is the most impressive mile in Shanghai. It is a boastful reminder of the city's cosmopolitan and decadent heyday and is the first place to which all visitors to Shanghai gravitate.

Leading off the Bund, by the renowned Peace Hotel, is Nanjing Donglu, the most famous shopping street in China. The best way to experience both areas is on foot; see the Walking Tours chapter (p86) for a selection of three walks in this district.

The streets that lead off the Bund form a gritty commercial district housed in the shells of concession-era buildings, mixed in with a few new apartment complexes. There is some fine architectural exploration to be done here; see the Beyond the Bund walking tour (p89).

Transport

Metro The Bund is a five-minute walk from Henan Zhonglu stop on metro line No 2.

Bus No 42 goes from the Bund at Guangdong Lu to the French Concession, along Huaihai Zhonglu, to Xujiahui and Shanghai Stadium; No 64 goes to Shanghai train station from Beijing Donglu, near Sichuan Zhonglu; Nos 928 and 65 run from Shanghai train station, past Broadway Mansions, along the Bund (Zhongshan Lu) to Shiliupu Wharf and Nanpu Bridge; No 518 runs from Renmin Square to Pudong's Liujiazui.

Ferry Goes to Pudong from the south end of the Bund.

Tourist Tunnel Runs from the Bund to Pudong's Liujiazui, under the Huangpu; Y30/40; see p61 for details.

Tourist 'Train' Runs along the length of Nanjing Donglu's pedestrianised section (Y2).

Top Five the Bund & Nanjing Donglu

- Take a romantic stroll down the **Bund** (below).
- For a flavour of swinging Shanghai, check out the interior of the **Peace Hotel** (p87).
- Experience fine dining at **M on the Bund** (p100) or **Three on the Bund** (p62).
- View the city from the Huangpu River on a **boat or ferry ride** (below).
- Witness the frenzied capitalism (sorry, that's 'socialism with Chinese characteristics') on **Nanjing Donglu** (p143).

THE BUND Map pp244-5
Wàitān

Originally a towpath to pull barges of rice, the Bund gets its Anglo-Indian name from the embankments built up to discourage flooding (a *band* is an embankment in Hindi). The Bund became the seat of foreign power in the early 20th century and provided a grand façade for those arriving in Shanghai by river.

Former HSBC building (foreground) and Customs House, the Bund (p88)

The Bund was once situated only a few feet from the water but in the mid-1990s the road was widened and a 771m-long flood barrier was built (the river now lies above the level of Nanjing Lu due to subsidence). The road that was once jammed with trams and traffic from riverside jetties is now known more prosaically as Zhongshan Yilu, or 'Sun Yatsen Road Section One'.

There are plenty of things to see and do around the Bund: take a boat trip on the Huangpu, enjoy the views of Pudong, visit the Bund Museum or shop at the Friendship Store. These delights are easily combined with an up-close visit to Pudong via the Bund Sightseeing Tunnel or metro from Nanjing Donglu.

The best thing to do is simply stroll and admire the bones of the past. See Walking Tours (p86) for a rundown of the buildings on the Bund. This is a very beautiful area at night.

The ambitious North Bund Development Project is set to revamp the area north of Dianchi Lu to Suzhou Creek over the next few years so expect some changes and disruption in that area.

BUND SIGHTSEEING TUNNEL
Map pp244-5
Wàitān Guānguāng Suìdào
☎ 5888 6000; Y30/40 one way/return;
🕙 9am-9.30pm, until 10.30pm Fri-Sun May-Oct
A strangely pointless attraction, Shanghai's new 'techno tunnel' is best viewed as a convenient way to get across (actually under) the Huangpu River to Pudong, rather than a sight in itself. The 647m of flashing lights are extremely underwhelming, unless of course they manage to induce an epileptic fit in one of your fellow travellers. You can save some money (around Y10) by buying a combination ticket with the sights you want to see in Pudong.

HUANGPU RIVER CRUISE Map pp244-5
☎ 6374 4461; 219-239 Zhongshan Dong Erlu
The Huangpu River offers some remarkable views of the Bund and river-front activity. Tour boats depart from docks on the south end of the Bund, near Jinling Donglu.

Shanghai is one of the world's biggest ports and has been the largest in China since 1852. Today 2000 ocean-going ships and about 15,000 river steamers load and unload here every year. The tour boat passes an enormous variety of craft – freighters, bulk carriers, roll-on roll-off ships, sculling sampans, giant cranes, the occasional junk and Chinese navy vessels

Three on the Bund

3 Zhongshan Dong Erlu

This major new development project in the seven-storey former Union Assurance Co Building (1916) is set to become a new Bund landmark on its opening at the end of 2003. Developed by Handel Lee, creator of Beijing's Courtyard Gallery and designed by architect Michael Graves, the emphasis is very much on top-end lifestyle.

The first two floors of the complex will be taken by luxury retail and design stores, and a Bernardaud café. The 3rd-floor Shanghai Art Gallery looks set to become a leading centre of modern Chinese art. Also featured is an Evian day spa (the first outside France) with an impressive 35m-high western atrium, plus a luxury men's barber shop. The upper four floors of restaurants and bars include top-end Japanese and French restaurants by celebrity chef Jean Georges, the *enfant terrible* of French cooking, plus contemporary Shanghainese cuisine by Jereme Leung in the 5th-floor Whampoa Club. The dazzling rooftop will have a Laris Restaurant and a jazz lounge called the Third Degree. This is just one part of the ambitious North Bund and Suzhou Creek redevelopment, which is set to revitalise the area in the next decade.

(which aren't supposed to be photographed). The 1930s saw the addition of cruise liners and warships.

There are several types of cruises. The one-hour cruise (Y25 to Y35) takes in the Yangpu Bridge; the two-hour cruise (Y45) encompasses both Yangpu and Nanpu Bridges, and a less frequent service heads up to Pudong's Gaoqiao Bridge. The better but more expensive choice is the 3½-hour, 60km round-trip cruise, which takes you up the Huangpu to Wusongkou, the junction with the Yangzi River, and back. Several classes are available for this service, ranging in price from Y35 to Y70; the more expensive tickets include refreshments on the higher deck. Depending on your enthusiasm for loading cranes, the night cruises are more scenic, though the boat traffic during the day is interesting.

The longer boat cruise takes in Suzhou Creek, the International Passenger Terminal, Yangshupu Power Plant, Fuxing Island (site of Chiang Kaishek's last stand), the container port area and Wusongkou (site of the battle between the British and Chinese in 1842 and where the early opium traders unloaded their cargo). You also catch glimpses of Chongming Island and the Baoshan Iron and Steel Complex, the largest in China.

Departure times vary depending on which trip you take, but there are generally morning, afternoon and evening departures for all three categories.

ROOM WITH A VIEW GALLERY

Map pp244-5

☎ 6352 0256; www.topart.cn; 12th fl, 479 Nanjing Donglu

Art critic Wu Liang set up this space on top of a department store to showcase contemporary art and digital videos. There's an image-conscious loft bar attached if you want to make an evening of it. Contact Holly Zhao.

SHANGHAI MUSEUM OF NATURAL HISTORY Map pp244-5

Shànghǎi Zìrán Bówùguǎn

☎ 6321 3548; 260 Yan'an Donglu; admission Y16; 9am-4pm Tue-Sun

This dusty museum, based on the former collection of the British Royal Asiatic Society, consists of a scary assortment of pickled and stuffed animals (including a giant panda and a Yangzi alligator), housed in a draughty old building with bad lighting. Highlights include Chinese mummies unearthed while constructing Dapu Lu, a huge dinosaur skeleton from Sichuan and a Yellow River woolly mammoth. Guides are on hand for free English tours. The museum is midway between the Bund and Renmin Square.

The museum's former chairman, the gangster Du Yuesheng, built the dramatic red brick building across Yan'an Donglu as the Chung Wai Bank (with a private bullet-proof elevator). It served for years as the Shanghai Museum and is now an office block and restaurant.

RENMIN SQUARE AREA

Every communist metropolis worth its salt has an imposing public square at it's heart and Shanghai has Renmin Square (Rénmín Guǎngchǎng; Map pp244-5). Far less austere than Beijing's Tiananmen Square, this is a good place to relax and watch people strolling, flying beautiful kites and even waltzing in front of the musical fountain. It's hard

Top Five Renmin Square Area

- Take in the treasures of the **Shanghai Museum** (p64), arguably Shanghai's finest attraction.
- Enjoy a top-notch performance at the **Shanghai Grand Theatre** (p64).
- Get to grips with modern Chinese art in the wonderfully restored **Shanghai Art Museum** (p63).
- Step inside the elegant **Park Hotel** (p158), one of the 1930s' greatest buildings.
- View the scale model of future Shanghai in the **Urban Planning Exhibition Hall** (p66).

to imagine that in 1966 a million Red Guards marched here, waving Mao's *Little Red Book* and decrying Western bourgeois capitalism. In June 1989 the square was the focus of student demonstrations that echoed those in Beijing. Underneath the square is a huge hidden shopping plaza.

The building anchoring the northwest of the square is the French-designed Shanghai Grand Theatre, Shanghai's premier venue for the arts. Dubbed the 'Crystal Palace', it's particularly brilliant at night. To the northeast of the square is the equally impressive Shanghai Urban Planning Exhibition Hall. Sandwiched between the two is the austere Shanghai Government building.

At the western end of Renmin Square is the tiny but charming **Sanjiao Park** (Sānjiǎo Gōngyuàn; Map pp244-5), where elderly men congregate to admire each other's caged birds. There's also a small goldfish market here.

GREAT WORLD Map pp244-5
Dà Shìjiè
Admission Y30; ◷ **9.30am-6.30pm**
At the corner of Xizang Lu and Yan'an Donglu, Great World was opened in 1917 as a place for

Transport

Metro The Renmin Square/Renmin Park intersection between the Nos 1 and 2 lines is the busiest metro stop in the city. Renmin Square metro exits include the following:

- Renmin Square
- Renmin Dadao
- Fuzhou Lu
- Jiujiang Lu
- New World Department Store & Nanjing Donglu

acrobats and nightclub stars to rival the existing New World on Nanjing Lu. It soon became a centre for the bizarre and the burlesque under the seedy control of the gangster 'Pockmarked' Huang Jinrong in the 1930s before it was commandeered as a refugee centre during WWII.

> **THE ESTABLISHMENT HAD SIX FLOORS TO PROVIDE DISTRACTION FOR THE MILLING CROWD, SIX FLOORS THAT SEETHED WITH LIFE AND ALL THE COMMOTION AND NOISE THAT GO WITH IT, STUDDED WITH EVERY VARIETY OF ENTERTAINMENT CHINESE INGENUITY HAD CONTRIVED.**
> *Joseph von Sternberg, director of the film Shanghai Express, who visited Shanghai in the mid-1930s*

After 1949 the building became a social club (The People's Pleasure Ground), a warehouse and the Municipal Youth Palace. Great World reopened as an entertainment centre in 1987 (see p134) but is a pale reflection of what it was in its heyday. Come here for the history of the place rather than the lacklustre shows.

RENMIN PARK Map pp244-5
Rénmín Gōngyuán
Admission Y2; ◷ **6am-6pm**
Renmin Park is a pleasant place with some nice ponds, an exhibition hall and good views of the surrounding skyscrapers and Park Hotel. The park was built on the site of the old settlement racecourse (built in 1862), which later served as a holding camp during WWII. Saturday sees the place packed with proud parents treating their one child to a ride on the dodgems.

SHANGHAI ART MUSEUM Map pp244-5
Shànghǎi Měishùguǎn
☎ **6327 2829; 325 Nanjing Xilu; adult/student Y20/10;** ◷ **9am-5pm (last entry 4pm)**
This museum, first opened in 1956, moved in 2000 to a stunning new location in the former British racecourse club building and is well worth a visit. The city council deserves much praise for supplying a wide variety of quality Chinese art in a restored and wheelchair-accessible Shanghai monument. The collection ranges from modern oils and pop art to the Shanghai school of traditional Chinese art.

Note the horse-head design on the balustrades and the Art Deco chandeliers, original to the 1933 building. Wheelchairs and prams are available at no charge. Refresh your flagging attention at the neglected but classy café on the 2nd floor. No photos are allowed.

Street sculptures, Nanjing Lu

SHANGHAI GRAND THEATRE
Map pp244-5
Shànghǎi Dà Jùyùan
☎ 6372 8701; http://shimg.163.com;
300 Renmin Dadao

Depending on what's showing, it's often possible to get a tour of the theatre building and its exhibition of musical instruments. Tickets cost Y50 or you can buy a combined Shanghai Museum–Grand Theatre ticket for Y45 from the Shanghai Museum. Either way, you are probably better off spending your money on a performance.

SHANGHAI MUSEUM Map pp244-5
Shànghǎi Bówùguǎn
☎ 6372 3500; 201 Renmin Dadao; adult/student Y20/5; ☺ 9am-5pm Mon-Fri (last entry 4pm), 9am-8pm Sat (local students free 5-7pm)

Originally established in 1952, and totally rebuilt in 1994, this stunning US$700-million museum is symbolic of the many changes that have taken place in Shanghai. Gone are the dry exhibits, yawning security guards and stale air – replaced by excellent spotlighting and state-of-the-art technology. Of the 120,000 displayed items, one-third have never been shown publicly before. While guiding you through the craft of millennia, the museum simultaneously draws you through the pages of Chinese history. Expect to spend half, if not most of, a day here. This museum is one of the highlights of a trip to Shanghai.

Before you go in, take a look at the outside of the building. It was designed to recall an ancient bronze *ding* (a three-legged food vessel used for cooking and serving), and also echoes the shape of a famous bronze mirror from the Han dynasty, exhibited inside the museum. The entrance is to the south and is guarded by a row of lions and mythological beasts.

The most famous collection of the museum is the **Ancient Chinese Bronzes Gallery** (see the boxed text opposite).

Exhibits in the **Ancient Chinese Sculpture Gallery** range from stonework of the Qin and Han dynasties to Buddhist stucco sculpture, which was influenced by Central Asian styles that travelled along the Silk Road. It is interesting to note that sculptures displayed were once

Combination Tickets

You can save a few *kuài* by buying combined tickets for Renmin Square's sights. A ticket covering Shanghai Museum, Shanghai Art Museum and either the Grand Theatre or Urban Planning Exhibition Hall costs Y60 (a saving of Y10). A combined Art Museum and Planning Exhibition Hall ticket costs Y45. Prices may change but the discounts should remain.

almost all painted; only scraps of the paint remain. Images or names of donors were often seen on carvings. The sculptures are mostly of Sakyamuni Buddha, but there are also images of Buddha's disciples (Kasyapa and Ananda), tranquil Bodhisattvas and fierce *lokapalas* (Buddhist protectors).

The **Ancient Chinese Ceramics Gallery** is one of the largest in the museum. Exhibits include 6000-year-old pottery from the Neolithic Songze culture excavated from just outside Shanghai, *sāncăi* (polychrome) pottery of the Tang, and the enormous variety of porcelain ('china') produced by the Qing. There are many pieces from Jingdezhen, one of the most important centres of ceramics work in China, where craftsmen perfected the deep blues of the 15th Yuan dynasty. There are also displays of kilns and the firing process.

On the 3rd floor, the **Chinese Painting Gallery** leads visitors through various styles of Chinese art. The audio guide (see p66) is particularly useful for this section.

The **Calligraphy Gallery** is one of the hardest for foreigners to appreciate, but anyone can enjoy the purely aesthetic quality of the art of Chinese writing. The display covers everything from inscribed bamboo strips and Shang oracle bones to the various scripts such as seal script, official script, and wild cursive script, almost impossible to read even for Chinese, as it misses out many of the strokes.

The **Ancient Chinese Jade Gallery** shows the transformation of the uses of jade from early mystical symbols (such as the *bì*, or jade discs, used to worship heaven), through to later ritual weapons and jewellery. Exhibit No 414 in particular is a remarkable totem, with an engraved phoenix carrying a human head. Bamboo drills, abrasive sand, and garnets crushed in water were used to shape some of the pieces, which date back over 5000 years.

When it comes to the **Coin Gallery** it's tempting to just keep moving. The earliest coins on display have a hole in the middle so they could be carried by string, and some older coins are shaped like keys or knives. There's an interesting collection of coins that were found along the Silk Road but unfortunately there's no English text at present.

The **Ming & Qing Furniture Gallery** features rose and sandalwood furniture of the elegant Ming dynasty and heavier, more ornate examples of the Qing dynasty. Several mock offices and

Bronzes in the Shanghai Museum

The Shanghai Museum is famed worldwide for its bronzes, some of which date from the 21st century BC. The zenith of the production of bronzes was during the late Shang (1700–1100 BC) and early Zhou (1100–221 BC) dynasties, though the Middle Spring and Autumn (722–481 BC) and Warring States (453–221 BC) periods showed a second flowering.

The impressive range of shapes and uses is striking, showing the importance of bronze in ritual ancestor worship and, later, everyday life. Vessels range in shape from a *hu* (wine bottle), *jue* (wine pourer with spout), *gu* (goblet), *bei* (wine jar), *zun* (bowl), *yan* (steamer), *gui* (round food vessel used for rice and grain), *pan* (water vessel), *yi* (square wine vessel) and various wine pots known as *jia, zhi, zun, he* and *you*. The hooks visible on several pots originally held a cloth bag to filter hot wine, one reason why hot-water bowls and steamers are so common.

The most important ritual bronzes are the *dings* (three-legged food vessels used for cooking and serving). The number of dings an official was allowed depended strictly on his imperial rank. Ceremonial bronzes can be huge, such as the 200kg *ding* on display.

The most common form of early decoration is the stylised animal motif, featuring dragons, lions and phoenix. This was replaced in the 10th century BC by zigzags (representing thunder) and cloud designs and later, geometric shapes. Subsequently, decoration spread to fin-like appendages, studs and relief carvings. As bronzes lost their ritual significance, decorative scenes from daily life were introduced. Later still, stamped moulds, lost wax techniques and piece moulds enabled designs to become more complicated.

Remember that the bronzes would originally have been a bright golden colour. It is only oxidisation that has given them a green patina.

An especially creative use of bronze is evident in the *zhong* (bells), each of which produces two notes. Up until the Han dynasty (206 BC–AD 220), bronze bells were China's most important musical instrument; traditional bell concerts are still held occasionally in Shanghai. Other examples of bronze use include 3000-year-old weapons like *dao* (daggers), *yue* (axes), *máo* (spears and swords) forged from two metals. Also shown are bronzes collected from minority nationalities such as the Yi from southwest China, with their characteristic ox motifs, the Ba from Sichuan, the Central Asian Xiongnu (Kushan), with their camel and tiger motifs, and bronze drums from Guangxi.

Ancient Chinese Bronzes in the Shanghai Museum, by Chen Peifen, gives a good rundown on the bronzes on display and is available at the Shanghai Museum bookshop.

reception rooms offer a glimpse of wealthy Chinese home life. For modern versions of Chinese furniture for sale see Shopping (p141).

It's worth saving some energy for the **Minority Nationalities Art Gallery**, one of the most interesting rooms in the museum, as it shows the enormous breadth of China's 56 ethnic groups, totalling some 40 million people. Displays vary from the salmon fish-skin suit of the Hezhenin Heilongjiang, and the furs of the Siberian Oroqen, to the embroidery and batik of Guizhou's Miao and Dong, the Middle-Eastern satin robes of the Uyghurs and the wild hairstyles of the former slave-owning Yi. Handicrafts include Tibetan jewellery, Miao silverware, Uyghur pewter, Yi lacquer work, Tibetan *cham* festival masks and Nuo opera masks from Guizhou.

In addition to the permanent galleries there are also three exhibition halls for temporary displays.

The audio guide (available in eight languages) is well worth the extra Y40. It highlights particularly interesting exhibits and has good gallery overviews and general background information. To rent the guide you need a deposit of Y500, US$40 or your passport. Photos (without a tripod) can be taken in most halls, except those with painting and calligraphy.

The excellent **museum shop** (p146) sells postcards, a series of photo books focusing on individual halls (except bronzes) for Y25 each, and well-made replicas of the museum's exhibits. There are a few overpriced shops and teahouses inside the museum, as well as an attached snack bar and cloakroom.

SHANGHAI URBAN PLANNING EXHIBITION HALL Map pp244-5
Chéngshì Guīhuà Zhǎnshìguǎn

☎ 6318 4477; 100 Renmin Dadao; adult/student Y30/28; 🕙 9am-4pm Wed-Sun

This government building pitches itself as a tourist attraction but essentially it just features enjoyable hi-tech propaganda. The exhibits paint a picture of how Shanghai will develop in the next 20 years (there are plenty of elderly Shanghainese looking to see what will become of their bulldozed houses) and the highlight is definitely the absorbing scale plan of the Shanghai of the future. There are also some interesting photos of 1930s Shanghai, a few interactive displays and a top-floor café. If you need a break, you exit the building through a basement street of mock 1930s cafés.

At the time of research the middle floors were dominated by patriotic Chinese-language displays on the World Expo, due to be held in Shanghai in 2010.

OLD TOWN
Eating p101; Shopping p147

Known in Chinese as Nan Shi (Southern City) and previously as Nan Tao (Southern Market), the Chinese Old Town is the most traditionally Chinese area of Shanghai. Its circular shape reflects the lines of the old 5km-long city walls, erected as protection against Japanese pirates and echoed today by Renmin Lu and Zhonghua Lu. Central Fangbang Zhonglu was once a canal running through the centre of the town from a small harbour at the eastern Dongpu Gate. The city wall was torn down in 1912.

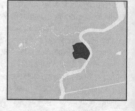

Traditional life remains on show in the Old Town but the old streets are overshadowed in places by towering new apartment blocks and the rampant commercial fallout from Yuyuan Bazaar. Still, if you want to glimpse old Shanghai – that of the Chinese not the foreigners – the backstreets with their crowded lanes, dark alleyways and hanging laundry are the places to explore.

CHENXIANGGE NUNNERY Map pp254-5
Chénxiānggé

Admission Y5; 🕙 7am-4pm

This little-visited complex was once the home of the Pan family (see Yuyuan Gardens & Bazaar, opposite) and has been restored to house around 40 nuns. It's a five-minute walk west of the Yuyuan Gardens.

CONFUCIAN TEMPLE Map pp254-5
Wén Miào

215 Wenmiao Lu; admission Y8; 🕙 9am-5pm

Every Chinese town should have a Confucian Temple, and while this one is nothing special, it's worth a quick visit if you have time to investigate the Old Town (see p96). Parts of the temple date back 700 years but most of it

Transport

Bus No 11 circles the Old Town, following Renmin Lu and Zhonghua Lu; No 66 travels along Henan Lu, connecting the Old Town with Nanjing Donglu; No 930 runs from Renmin Square down Xizang Nanlu to near Dongtai Market and then along Renmin Lu, around the Old Town.

was rebuilt in the Qing period and renovated in 1997.

The buildings include **Zunjing (Respecting Classics) Tower**, the **Dacheng (Great Achievements) Hall** (which served as a hall to pay tribute to Confucius), the **Minglung Hall**, and a hall that was formerly both a Confucian lecture hall and the headquarters of the Small Swords Society. The library for holding Chinese classics doubled as the state library until 1931. The **Kuixing Pavilion** is named after the God of the Literati. Today the halls house a dull exhibition of stones, ink slabs and pyrography.

YUYUAN GARDENS & BAZAAR

Map pp254-5
Yùyuán Shāngshà
Adult/child Y30/10; ☑ 8.30am-5pm

At the northeastern end of the old Chinese city, the Yuyuan Gardens and Bazaar are, while arguably slightly tacky, one of Shanghai's premier sights and worth a visit. Try not to visit on the weekend though, as the crowds can be overpowering.

The Yu Yuan (Yu Gardens) were founded by the Pan family, rich Ming dynasty officials. The gardens took 18 years (1559 to 1577) to be nurtured into existence, only to be ransacked

Top Five Old Town

- Snack on a round of *xiǎolóngbaō* (dumplings) at the **Nanxiang Steamed Bun Restaurant** (p101).
- Visit the traditional Chinese **Yuyuan Gardens** (p67), but avoid the weekends.
- Stroll along the **backstreets** (p95) from Yuyuan to Dongtai Lu Antique Market.
- Check out the cheapest silk in town at the **Dongjiadu Cloth Market** (p147).
- Escape the throngs and take tea at the **Mid-Lake Pavilion Teahouse** (see Pit Stop, below) – overpriced tea but oozing character nonetheless.

during the Opium War in 1842, when British officers were barracked here, and again during the Taiping Rebellion, this time by the French in reprisal for attacks on their nearby concession. Today the gardens have been restored and are a fine example of Ming garden design – if you can see through the crowds. Though the gardens are small they seem much bigger due to an ingenious use of rocks and alcoves. See p180 for more on Chinese gardens. Spring blossoms are particularly lovely in March and April.

Things to look out for include the **Exquisite Jade Rock**, which was destined for the imperial court in Beijing until the boat sank outside Shanghai, and the **Hall of Heralding Spring** (Diǎnchūn Táng), which in 1853 was the headquarters of the Small Swords Society (perhaps one reason why the gardens were spared

Pit Stop

One of the best places to take a break in Yuyuan Bazaar and observe the mob below is in the ornate **Mid-Lake Pavilion Teahouse** (Map pp254-5; ☑ 6am-9.30pm). A pot of black or green tea and all the hot water you can squeeze inside you costs Y20 to Y25 on the ground floor, or Y40 (jasmine) to Y55 (longjing) upstairs, which includes snacks. Get there early in the day for one of the prime window seats. Classical Chinese music (no charge) is performed upstairs on Friday, Saturday and Sunday at 6.30pm and on Monday from 2pm to 5pm.

revolutionary violence in the 1960s). Note also the beautiful stage, with its gilded carved ceiling and excellent acoustics. The two shiny pavilions in the eastern corner were added in 2003.

Next to the entrance to the Yuyuan Gardens is the **Mid-Lake Pavilion Teahouse** (Húxíntíng), once part of the gardens and now one of the most famous teahouses in China, visited by Queen Elizabeth II and Bill Clinton among others. The zigzag causeway is there to thwart spirits (and trap tourists), who can only travel in straight lines. Buy a packet of fish food (Y2) and enjoy the sight of dozens of thrashing koi.

Surrounding all this is the restored **bazaar** area, where more than 100 speciality shops and restaurants jostle over narrow laneways and small squares in a mock 'ye olde Cathay' setting. It's a bit of a Disneyland version of historical China but if you can handle the crowds it's a great stop for lunch and some souvenir shopping (see p147).

Just outside the bazaar is **Old Street** (Laǒ Jiē), known more prosaically as Fangbang Zhonglu, another recently restored street lined with interesting shops and teahouses.

If you can tear yourself away from the shopping frenzy, the Taoist **Temple of the Town Gods** (Chénghuáng Miào; admission Y5), in the southeast of the complex, commemorates an ancient general, Huo Guang, and has some fine carvings on the roof.

FRENCH CONCESSION

Eating p102; Shopping p147; Sleeping p160

The French Concession was once home to the bulk of Shanghai's adventurers, revolutionaries, gangsters, prostitutes and writers, though ironically not many of them were French (the majority of the residents were British, American, White Russian and Chinese). Shanghai's nickname 'Paris of the East' stems largely from the tree-lined avenues, Tudor mansions and French-influenced architecture of this district.

Today the area is still the most graceful part of Shanghai, and the most rewarding district for walks and bike rides. The area also hosts the lion's share of Shanghai's nightlife, restaurants and shopping. The central traffic artery is Huaihai Lu, named after a decisive battle that ended with the communists routing the Kuomintang during the Civil War.

Transport

Metro No 1 line shadows Huaihai Lu and Hengshan Lu, stopping at Huangpi Nanlu, Shaanxi Nanlu, Changshu Lu and at Hengshan Lu.

Bus Services along Huaihai Zhonglu include: No 2 (runs along Huaihai Zhonglu & Hengshan Lu to Xujiahui); No 911 (Hongqiao to the Old Town); No 926 (Shanghai Stadium, Xujiahui & Shanghai Library to Jinling Donglu & the Bund); No 42 (from the Bund at Guangdong Lu via Xiangyang Lu to Xujiahui & Shanghai Stadium); No 831 (Jinling Lu near the Bund to Hongqiao airport); No 920 (from Xujiahui to Shanghai Library, around the Old City then back west along Huaihai Lu).

ART SCENE CHINA Map pp246-9
Yìshùjìng Huàláng
☎ 7437 0631; www.artscenechina.com;
No 8, Lane 37 Fuxing Xilu

Contemporary Chinese art is exhibited in this lovely restored 1930s villa. The previously website-based gallery represents 25 artists whose work ranges from pop art to modern and surreal, plus some inventive reinterpretations of Chinese calligraphy. The gallery is hidden down a quiet alley.

FUXING PARK Map pp246-9
Fùxīng Gōngyuán
Admission Y2; ☉ 6am-6pm

This leafy park, laid out by the French in 1909 and later used by the Japanese as a parade ground in the late 1930s, remains one of the city's most pleasant. It was renamed Fuxing (Revival) after WWII. There is always plenty to

see here – the park is a refuge for the elderly and a practising field for itinerant musicians, t'ai chi masters and some of the weirdest work-outs you'll ever see, from slow motion aerobics to therapeutic screaming. There's always at least one person walking around the park backwards (apparently it's good for your health). You could never look silly here. The busts of Marx and Lenin have weathered the times to carry a certain revolutionary chic these days.

MADAME MAO'S DOWRY Map pp246-9
Máotài Shèjì
☎ 6437 1255; www.madame-maos-dowry.com;
70 Fuxing Xilu; ☉ 10am-6pm

A small gallery/showroom that has wide-ranging exhibitions, with a focus on ceramics and Chinese furniture. Check local press to see what's showing.

Top Five French Concession

- Check out the state of modern art at Shanghai's best art galleries at the **Taikang Lu Art Centre** (p71).
- Walk or bike the wonderful **concession-era backstreets**.
- Browse among the stalls at the city's most popular place for antiques – **Dongtai Lu Antique Market** (p148).
- Eat, drink and be merry in the city's best collection of **restaurants and bars** (p102 & p125).
- Shop till you drop on **Huaihai Zhonglu** (p148), lined with glossy malls and unique shops.

MUSEUM OF PUBLIC SECURITY

Map pp246-9
Shànghǎi Gōng'ān Bówùguǎn
☎ 6472 0256; 518 Ruijin Nanlu; admission Y8;
☺ 9am-4.30pm Mon-Sat
Not quite as dull as it sounds, this museum holds a few gems among the inevitable displays on traffic control. Look out for the gold pistols of Sun Yatsen and 1930s gangster Huang Jinrong amid the fine collection of Al Capone–style machine and pen guns, as well as a collection of hand-painted business cards once used by the city's top prostitutes.

PROPAGANDA POSTER ART CENTRE

Map pp246-9
Xuānchuánhuà Niánhuà Yìshù Zhōngxīn
☎ 6211 1845, 1390 184 1246; Room B-0C, 868
Huashan Lu; admission Y20; ☺ 10am-3pm
A must for fans of heroic socialist art, this small gallery has over 2000 revolutionary propaganda posters dating from the 1950s, '60s and '70s. Many are for sale (see p149), which makes the entry fee a little cheeky. The gallery is particularly hard to find. Check in with the front-gate guards who will telephone to see if anyone's in. Then head around the back of the apartment blocks to Building B and take the lift to the basement. Definitely phone ahead before heading out here.

SHANGHAI ARTS & CRAFTS MUSEUM

Map pp246-9
Shànghǎi Gōngyì Měishù Bówùguǎn
☎ 6431 4074; 9 Fenyang Lu; admission Y8; ☺ 9am-4pm
This arts and crafts institute recently reinvented itself as a museum, highlighting such traditional crafts as embroidery, paper cutting, lacquer work, jade cutting and lantern making. Displays include some impressive socialist realist carvings (including the amazing *Storm on May 30th*), plus the tiniest carving you'll ever see. The original 1930s bathroom is worth a look. It's hard not to suspect that the collections were arranged to herd visitors into the rather

Nanjing Lu's pedestrian strip (p143)

overpriced and tacky ground-floor shops. The highlight of the place is its wonderful architecture. For more information see p93.

SHANGHART Map pp246-9

☎ 6359 3923; www.shanghart.com; 2A Gaolan Lu; ◷ 10am-7pm Fri-Wed, until 10pm Thu

This premier art gallery is the first stop for contemporary Chinese art in Shanghai. It's next to Park 97 restaurant, at the western edge of Fuxing Park.

SITE OF THE 1ST NATIONAL CONGRESS OF THE CCP Map pp246-9
Zhōnggòng Yīdàhuìzhǐ

☎ 5383 2171; 76 Xingye Lu; admission Y3; ◷ 9am-5pm (last entry 4pm)

On 23 July 1921 the Chinese Communist Party (CCP) was founded in this French Concession building (then 106 Rue Wantz), propelling this unassuming *shíkùmén* block into one of Chinese communism's holiest shrines.

There is plenty of Marxist spin in the museum commentary (lots of 'never-ending heroic struggles' and 'anti-feudal democratic revolutions'), just in case you had forgotten that Shanghai is actually part of the world's largest communist country. There's not all that much to see here, but historians will appreciate the site as a defining moment in modern Chinese history.

The first hall paints a fine picture of the foreign settlements before becoming mired in some dull exhibits of early anti-imperial

rebellions. The second hall profiles the founders of the CCP and exhibits early translations of Soviet manifestos. The second building shows the room where the whole Party started, actually the house of one of the delegates, Li Hanjun.

Of the 13 original delegates, only two (one was Mao Zedong) ever worked in the Chinese government. Five were killed before the communists took power and another six either quit the Party or were expelled as traitors.

You must buy your ticket at the northwest corner of the building but enter from the southeast. Marxist stamp collectors will want to peruse the souvenir shop for its complete collection of communist leaders.

SONG QINGLING'S FORMER RESIDENCE Map pp246-9
Sōngqìnglíng Gùjū

☎ 6437 6268; 1843 Huaihai Zhonglu; adult/local students Y8/6; ◷ 9am-5pm

Built in the 1920s by a Greek shipping magnate, this building became home to the wife of Dr Sun Yatsen from 1948 to 1963. Like most former residences the exhibits can be dull unless you are an admirer of Song or of old houses, but the garden of camphor trees is particularly nice. Highlights include the sitting room where Song met Mao Zedong, Zhou Enlai and the writer Guo Moruo, the dining room where she had dinner with Kim Il-sung, and the Soviet limousine presented to her by Stalin.

The Soong Family

The Soongs probably wielded more influence and power over modern China than any other family. The father of the family, Charlie Soong, grew up in Hainan Island and after an American evangelical education he finally settled in Shanghai. He began to print Bibles and money, becoming a wealthy businessman and developing ties with secret societies, during which time he became good friends with Sun Yatsen. Charlie had three daughters and a son.

Soong Ailing married the wealthy HH Kung, a descendant of Confucius, head of the Bank of China and later China's finance minister. (She was also said to be the first Chinese girl in Shanghai to own a bicycle!) Soong Meiling became the third wife of Chiang Kaishek (head of the Kuomintang and future President of China) in 1928. She went to the USA during China's war with Japan and fled to Taiwan with Chiang after the communist victory. Much to the disapproval of her father, Soong Qingling (more commonly known as Song Qingling) married Sun Yatsen, 30 years her elder, studied in Moscow and was the only member of the family to live in China after 1949, until her death in 1981. TV Soong, Charlie's one son, became China's finance minister, premier and the richest man of his generation.

Thus it is said by mainlanders that of the three daughters one loved money (Ailing) and one loved power (Meiling) but only Qingling loved China. Among them, the siblings stewed a heady brew of fascism and communism.

Song Qingling died in Beijing and is buried in Shanghai's **International Cemetery** (Map p256) on Hongqiao Lu, next to her parents' tomb. Her sister Meiling declined the invitation to return to China to attend the funeral; she died in the USA in October 2003, aged 105.

SUN YATSEN'S FORMER RESIDENCE

Map pp246-9

Sūn Zhōngshān Gùjū

☎ 6437 2954; 7 Xianshan Lu; admission Y8;
🕙 9am-4.30pm

China is simply brimming with Sun Yatsen memorabilia, and this is one of his former residences (there are several – he got around). Sun lived here on Rue Molière for six years from 1918 to 1924, supported by overseas Chinese funds. After Sun's death, his wife, Song Qingling (1893–1981), continued to live here until 1937, constantly watched by the Kuomintang plain-clothes police and French police. The two-storey house is set back from the street and is furnished as it was back in Sun's days, though it was looted by the Japanese during WWII. The entry price gets you a brief tour of the house in English.

TAIKANG LU ART CENTRE Map pp246-9

Tàikāng Lù Yìshù Zhōngxīn

Lane 210, Taikang Lu

Shanghai is light on artistic focus, which makes this new arts complex doubly welcome. It's a collection, even a community, of art galleries, studios and shops. The main multistorey warehouse hides a handful of design studios, media companies and home décor boutiques (p147), many of which front the small alley on the eastern side of the building. There is even talk of a kung fu centre, DJ shop and tattoo parlour.

Right on the corner of the alley, at 220 Taikang Lu, the **Pottery Workshop** (☎ 6445 0902; www.ceramics.com.hk) exhibits and sells designer pottery made on site by visiting artists. There's a ceramic studio and two exhibition spaces. It also runs children's and adults' courses in pot throwing (see p204).

Further down the alley is the **Deke Erh Art Centre** (Ěrdōngqiáng Yìshù Zhōngxīn; ☎ 6415 0675; www.han-yuan.com; No 2, Lane 210, Taikang Lu), an impressive warehouse space with ground-floor exhibits and 1st-floor photos. The gallery is owned by local photographer and author Deke Erh, who also runs the **Old China Hand Reading Room** (see Pit Stop below).

Further still along the alley, the **Taikang Art Museum** is a gallery/showroom with changing exhibits in a barn-like space. There are several other galleries in the complex and you can expect more to follow.

Across Taikang Lu from the art centre is a small antique market, which might pick up if

Pit Stop

The Yard in the Taikang Lu Art Centre is a cool courtyard of designer shops that feels very much like Covent Garden's Neal's Yard, before the tourists took over. The **Kommune Café** here has outdoor seating and lots of design and art mags – very kool. It's a good place to grab a coffee or light lunch for around Y25.

On your way to or from the Taikang Lu Art Centre, make a detour to the **Old China Hand Reading Room** (☎ 6473 2526; www.han-yuan.com; 27 Shaoxing Lu), which holds interesting regular exhibits of folk art and photographs. It's run by Deke Erh, a local photographer who also runs the eponymous art centre (see above), and is popular with artsy expats. The café has the cosy feel of a friend's antique parlour, with plenty of old books and magazines to read without any hassle from the staff.

Tree-lined Shaoxing Lu is a peaceful street that also holds several publishing houses and some small art galleries that you could poke around in on a lazy day.

the mostly empty stalls fill up. Half a block east is **Taikang Antique Market** (p150), which has two floors of small antique shops that are worth a sniff around.

XINTIANDI Map pp246-9

Xīntiāndì

www.xintiandi.com; cnr Taicang Lu & Madang Lu

This ambitious new business, entertainment and cultural complex, built by Hong Kong's Shui On Group, has quickly become the city's most stylish collection of restaurants, bars and designer shops. The heart of the complex, just off Huangpi Nanlu, consists of several blocks of renovated (largely rebuilt) traditional *shíkūmén* houses, brought bang up to date with a stylish modern twist. (For more on *shíkūmén* see p31.)

A small museum, the **Shikumen Open House** (admission Y20; 🕙 10am-10pm) depicts traditional life in a 10-room Shanghai *shíkūmén*. Also hidden among the chic restaurants and bars is the small **Central Academy of Fine Arts Gallery** and an even smaller **Postal Museum** next door. Other facilities include **cinemas** (p134), a lakeside park (with a parking lot underneath!) and a residential complex. Several office complexes and hotels will follow in the years, even decades, ahead. Over 3500 families were relocated to create the lakeside park.

ZHOU ENLAI'S FORMER RESIDENCE

Map pp246-9

Jí Zhōu Gōngguǎn

☎ 6473 0420; 73 Sinan Lu; admission Y2; ☻ 9am-4pm

In 1946, Zhou Enlai, the urbane and much-loved first premier of the People's Republic of China (PRC), lived in this former French Concession Spanish villa at 107 (now 73) Sinan Lu. Zhou was then head of the Communist Party's Shanghai office, and spent much of his time giving press conferences and dodging Kuomintang agents who spied on him from across the road.

There's not much to see these days except lots of Spartan beds and stern-looking desks, but the charming neighbourhood, full of lovely old houses, is a great place to wander around. (See the French Concession I walking tour, p92.)

PUDONG

Eating p110; Shopping p151; Sleeping p164

Over 1½ times larger than urban Shanghai itself, the Pudong New Area (Pǔdōng Xīnqū) consists of the entire eastern bank of the Huangpu River. Before 1990 – when development plans were first announced – Pudong constituted 350 sq km of boggy farmland that supplied vegetables to Shanghai's markets. Before that it was home to the godowns (warehouses) and compradors (buyers) of Shanghai's foreign trading companies. Today the only thing sprouting out of the ground are skyscrapers and Pudong has risen to become Shanghai's and China's economic powerhouse. For more information on the zone see p18.

The high-rise area directly across from the Bund is the Liujiazui Finance and Trade Zone, where the Shanghai Stock Exchange is located (the building with the hole in it, not open to visitors). From the unmistakable Oriental Pearl Tower the eight-lane wide Century Ave, modelled on the Champs Elysées in Paris, runs 4.2km to Central Park in the Huamu Tourism Zone. Here you'll find the Shanghai Science & Technology Museum, Pudong's government building and the Eastern Art Centre, set around Century Square. Further out is the huge new International Expo Hall and the MagLev train terminus by the Longyang Lu metro stop.

Pudong is largely home to high-rolling financiers and businesspeople. For the visitor, its main attractions include several huge malls, the tallest building in the PRC, the views back to the Bund and the startling architecture of the area.

Transport

There's now little more than a psychological gap between Pudong and Puxi. If you are headed across the Huangpu River you can choose from the following means of transportation:

Bus No 518 and tunnel bus No 3 *(suìdào sānxiàn)* from opposite the Shanghai Museum to the Jinmao Tower (Y2).

Ferry At Y0.8 this is definitely the cheapest way to cross and as a bonus it offers views of the Bund, though it's a 10-minute walk to the Jinmao Tower on the other side.

Pedestrian tunnel See the Bund section (p61) for details on this train that runs under the Huangpu from the Bund (across from the Peace Hotel) to the Oriental Riverside Hotel in Pudong.

Taxi A taxi ride will cost you around Y25 as you'll have to pay the Y15 tunnel toll heading eastwards.

Tour bus The red Jinjiang sightseeing bus (Y18) or the green sightseeing bus (No 3, Y4) from Shanghai Stadium go to the Oriental Pearl TV Tower.

CENTURY PARK Map pp242-3

Shìjì Gōngyuán

Admission Y10; ☻ 7am-6pm

Come and breathe the air in Shanghai's largest park at the end of Century Ave. The British design incorporates a large central lake, an auditorium and a music fountain, with enough space to really give you the sense that you are out of the city, though it will take a couple more years before the vegetation matures. You can hire tandem bikes (Y20 to Y40) and boats (Y30) by the hour. The spacious paved area between the **Science & Technology Museum** (p75) and the park is great for flying kites and in-line skating.

Top Five Pudong

- Enjoy the classic views of the Bund from **Riverside Park** (see boxed text, p74).
- Take in the scenery from the **Jinmao Tower** (below), a breathtaking building with great views from the 88th floor.
- Splash out in the **Grand Café** (p110) or **Cloud 9 bar** (p129) in the Grand Hyatt.
- Visit the **Municipal Historical Museum** (p74) for a feeling of old Shanghai.
- Form your own opinion of the amazing **architecture** (p31) that shows the future direction of China.

JINMAO TOWER Map pp253-4
Jīnmào Dàshà
☎ 5047 5101; adult/student Y50/25, audio tour Y15; ☺ 8.30am-9pm

Shanghai's most spectacular and beautiful building, visible from almost everywhere in the city, is essentially an office block (owned by the Ministry of Foreign Trade and Economic Cooperation), with the Grand Hyatt renting space from the 54th to 87th floors. The main thing to see if you are not lucky enough to be staying here is the stupendous view from the 340m-high 88th-floor observatory, accessed from the separate podium building to the side of the main tower. Time your visit at dusk for both day and night views and while you're there send a postcard from what is officially the world's highest post office.

A food court and a display featuring the building's remarkable construction process are in the podium next to the main tower. For more on the building see p32.

The Grand Hyatt itself is well worth a visit and offers one of the city's most spectacular splurges; see Eating (p110) for details.

LIUJIAZUI DEVELOPMENT EXHIBITION HALL Map pp253-4
Liùjiāzuǐ Mínsúguǎn
Shiji Dadao; admission Y5; ☺ 8.30am-8pm

This exhibition of photos, folk life and recent development in Pudong, on the edge of Liujiazui Park is mildly interesting but the building itself is the real star. Built in 1914–17 as the residence of a rich merchant, Chen Guichun, it has both a main hall and interior courtyard. It's easily viewed from the outside.

NANPU BRIDGE & YANGPU BRIDGE
Map pp242-3
Nánpǔ Qiáo & Yángpǔ Qiáo
Admission Y5; ☺ 9am-5pm

These two bridges, the world's fourth-longest and longest cable-stayed suspension bridges, respectively, are worth a visit or crossing for the views of the Huangpu and design works. Both bridges have viewing areas, from where you can cross to the other side and take photos.

ORIENTAL ARTS CENTRE Map pp242-3
Dōngfāng Yìshù Zhōngxīn
☎ 6854 0322; to open 2004

Pudong's financial and business emphasis will be given an artistic balance with this arts and cultural centre, featuring a 2000-seat philharmonic orchestra hall, a 300-seat chamber music hall and a 100-seat theatre. The complex is recognisable by its truncated hemispheres, devised by the same French architect who designed Pudong airport. Nearby Century Square is marked by what looks like a giant spinning top or defunct satellite dish.

ORIENTAL PEARL TOWER Map pp253-4
Dōngfāng Míngzhū Guǎngbō Diànshì Tǎ
☎ 5879 8888; ☺ 8am-9.30pm

Love it or hate it, this tripod-shaped, shocking pink, hypodermic syringe of a building has become a symbol of Pudong and of Shanghai's

Oriental Pearl Tower (above)

renaissance, even though, at 468m, the tower has now been both literally and metaphorically eclipsed by the Jinmao Tower. The tower has 11 baubles in total, though only three are currently in use (at 90m, 263m and 350m). The others are up for lease so if you're looking for apartment space with plenty of light...

The tower has a complex ticket system. You can go to the second ball and outdoor viewing platform (Y50); the second ball and the **Municipal Historical Museum** (see below; Y70); or the lower two balls and the museum (Y85). For Y100 you can get to all three balls and for Y150/180 you can enjoy a revolving buffet lunch/dinner in the second ball with free access to all other balls thrown in. Arrive early or you'll have to queue forever for the high-speed elevator.

Boat trips on the Huangpu operate from the Pearl Dock (Mingzhou Mǎtóu), next door to the Oriental Pearl Tower. A 30-minute tour costs Y40 during the day or Y50 at night (7pm & 8pm, May to Sep only). Boats run every hour or so from 10am to 4pm, longer in summer.

SHANGHAI AQUARIUM Map pp253-4
Hǎiyáng Shuǐzúguǎn
☎ 5877 9988; 158 Yincheng Beilu; adult/senior/child Y110/65/70; ☺ 9am-9pm

Education meets entertainment in this slick and impressive China–Singapore joint venture. The statistics speak volumes: 13,000 fish representing 300 species (from sunfish to sea horses, to tiger sharks and endangered Chinese fish) in a range of aquatic environments including the Amazon, the Nile and the deep sea. The 155m-long underwater clear viewing tunnel is particularly awesome. Try to time your visit with one of the fish feedings (currently 10.30am and 3.30pm).

The Disney-style gift shop lets things slip with environmentally unfriendly conch shells for sale. There are plans to introduce group tickets, at Y140 for two people and Y150 for three; otherwise this is a potentially pricey option for a family of four.

SHANGHAI MUNICIPAL HISTORICAL MUSEUM Map pp253-4
Shànghǎi Chéngshí Lìshǐ Fāzhǎn Chénlièguǎn
☎ 5879 8888; admission Y35, audio tour Y30; ☺ 8am-9.30pm

Shanghai has been crying out for a coherent historical museum and now it finally has one, even if it is confined to the basement of the Oriental Pearl Tower. It's a fun and well-produced introduction to old Shanghai, for kids and adults alike.

The exhibits start with some fine old cars (a Buick from the 1940s and then the 1990s) and even an early wheelbarrow taxi, once the main form of public transport in Shanghai. There are plenty of traditional dioramas (that old Chinese museum standby), depicting the Shaoxing wine shops and traditional salted fish shops that existed in real life only a few years ago, but even these are enlivened by a clever use of video and sound. Check out the public phones that you can dial up to listen to old operas. Video screens depict the British race club and local cinema through period film reportage of the city.

Other highlights include the pair of bronze lions that originally guarded the entrance to the Hongkong and Shanghai Bank on the Bund and a period map of the concessions, which shows an amazingly similar road layout to today's. The trip finishes up with scale models of Shanghai's most famous buildings.

Neighbourhoods – Pudong

Size Matters

The main reason to come to Pudong is for the views, and you're spoilt for choice.

The granddaddy of the viewing towers is the **Oriental Pearl Tower** (p73), with views from 263m costing Y50. Whether the tower is worth the cost is debatable. For Y50 you can go to the 420m viewing platform at the top of the **Jinmao Tower** (p73). Even better, you can get a coffee and a free view on the 87th floor of the **Grand Hyatt** (p164), one floor below the observation deck (open only weekday evenings, and during the day on the weekend). There's also the 54th floor of the Grand Hyatt, which has fantastic views both outside and in, looking up at its mind-spinning atrium tower.

Those with vertigo may be satisfied with views of the Bund from the roof garden of the vertically challenged **Shanghai International Exhibition Centre** (Y50; ☺ 8.30am-6pm). For an extra Y50 you can enjoy views while splashing in the gorgeous pool of the **Oriental Riverside Hotel** (p165). You can get similar views for free (or the price of a coffee) at the western end of the **Superbrand Mall** (p151).

The cheapest fix of all comes from **Riverside Park** (Binjiāng Gōngyuán; Map pp253-4), right on the waterfront and currently free of charge. Grab a Starbucks coffee (there's an outlet in the park) and enjoy the early morning views.

Photos aren't allowed but no-one enforces the rule.

SHANGHAI NATURAL WILD INSECT KINGDOM Map pp253-4

Dà Zìrán Yěshēng Künchóng Guàn

☎ 5840 6950; 1 Fenghe Lu, Liujiazui; adult/child Y35/20; 🕙 9am-5pm

Aimed at kids, this collection of creepy-crawlies includes an opportunity to handle some of the hairy monsters. It's one that could be missed unless your kids have a special interest.

SHANGHAI SCIENCE & TECHNOLOGY MUSEUM Map pp242-3

Shànghǎi Kējìguǎn

☎ 6862 0468; 2000 Shiji Dadao; adult/student Y/45; 🕙 9am-5pm, closed Mon

This impressive space-age building aims at providing a fun educational experience but ultimately disappoints. Kids will like the Light of Wisdom hall, with its hands-on science experiments, but in general non-Chinese speakers will find the lack of instructions and English text frustrating. The audiovisual rides (including an earthquake simulator) are fun but draw long queues; the rainforest display is full of fake plastic plants and the upper floors

are still empty. Surprisingly there is nothing on Chinese science and technology (this is after all the land that brought us fireworks and the rudder). The adults' enjoyment will also depend on their threshold for noisy groups of Chinese school kids. Less money, more thought would have worked better.

IMAX films (Y30 to Y40; 45 minutes) show six times a day and there is even a **4D film theatre** (Y30; 17 minutes); book tickets for both in advance. When you need a break there's a good food court for lunch; get your hand stamped with a pass if you want to return to the exhibits.

SHANGHAI WILD ANIMAL PARK
Map p172

Shànghǎi Yěshēng Dòngwùyuán

☎ 5803 6000; Sanzao village, near Nanhui township, Pudong; adult/child Y70/35

At this safari park out in the Boonies (there are wild lions here after all!), you can be driven through open enclosures packed with lions, giraffes and even a white tiger. The park gained notoriety in 1999 when a park worker was mauled to death when he left his vehicle. The easiest way to get here is on sightseeing bus No 2 from Shanghai Stadium (see p173).

Neighbourhoods – Nanjing Xilu & Jing'an

NANJING XILU & JING'AN

Eating p111; Shopping p151; Sleeping p166

The western end of Nanjing Lu is lined with monumental Manhattan-style malls and five-star hotels, both cathedrals to high style and even higher prices. Anchoring the western end is the Shanghai Centre, a focal point for foreign businessmen and tourists alike, with several airline offices, embassies, restaurants, cafés, the Portman Ritz-Carlton, and more. North of Nanjing Xilu is the grittier but interesting Jing'an district, bordered to the north by Suzhou Creek. South is the French Concession (p68).

JADE BUDDHA TEMPLE Map pp250-2

Yùfó Sì

Cnr Anyuan Lu & Jiangning Lu; admission Y10; 🕙 8am-4.30pm; bus 19 from Broadway Mansions, along Tiantong Lu

This active place of worship is one of Shanghai's few Buddhist temples and attracts large numbers of local and overseas Chinese tourists.

Built between 1911 and 1918 in Song dynasty style, the centrepiece is a 2m-high white jade buddha around which the temple was built. The story goes that Hui Gen (Wei Ken), a monk from Putuoshan, travelled to Myanmar (Burma) via Tibet, lugged five jade buddhas back to China and then went off in search of

alms to build a temple for them. Two of the buddhas ended up in Shanghai. This 1.9m-high seated buddha, encrusted with jewels, is

> ## Top Three Nanjing Xilu & Jing'an
>
> - Grab a vegetarian lunch at the **Jade Buddha Temple** (above).
> - Take in an **acrobatic show** (p133) at the Shanghai Centre Theatre.
> - Enjoy a splurge at one of Nanjing Xilu's great **top-end hotels** (p166).

Transport

Metro No 2 line stops at Shimen Yilu, Jing'an Temple and Zhongshan Park, where it connects with the No 3 (Pearl Light Railway) line.

Bus No 19 links the Bund area to the Jade Buddha Temple area; catch it at the intersection of Tiantong Lu and Sichuan Beilu; No 20 runs from Jiujiang Lu, just off the Bund, to Renmin Square, Nanjing Xilu, Yuyuan Lu and Zhongshan Park; No 37 follows a similar route to Jing'an Temple; No 112 zigzags north from the southern end of Renmin Square to Nanjing Xilu, and up Jiangning Lu to the Jade Buddha Temple; No 903 goes from Shanghai train station past the Portman Ritz-Carlton, Hilton and Jianguo hotels.

said to weigh 1000kg. The other prized treasure is a complete set of the Buddhist canon printed from wood blocks in 1890 and stored on either side. There's a cheeky Y5 extra charge to see the jade buddha and no photography is allowed. A smaller 90cm jade buddha from the same shipment reclines on a mahogany couch, facing a much larger stone copy.

The other main halls are the **Heavenly King Hall**, which features the four protector kings and a laughing buddha, the **Grand Hall**, featuring Medicine, Sakyamuni and Amithaba buddhas, with Guanyin behind, and the **Abbot Room**.

Acrobats perform at Shanghai Centre Theatre (p133)

In February the temple is very busy during the Lunar New Year, when some 20,000 Chinese Buddhists throng to pray for prosperity. The surrounding shops can supply everything you need to generate good luck, including bundles of spirit money to burn in incense pots.

The temple, in the northwest of town, is a 20-minute walk from either Shanghai train station or Shimen Yilu metro station.

At lunch time the canteen serves up cheap 100% vegetarian dishes; a nicer vegetarian restaurant on Jiangning Lu that's also run by the temple is worth a try for its fake meat dishes and fruity sanpao tea.

JING'AN TEMPLE Map pp246-9
Jìng'ān Sì
Nanjing Xilu; admission Y5; ⏰ 7.30am-5pm

The Jing'an Temple (Temple of Tranquillity) was originally built in 247 but was largely destroyed in 1851. Khi Vehdu, who ran the Jing'an Temple in the 1930s, was one of the most remarkable figures of the time. The nearly 2m-tall abbot had a large following and each of his seven concubines had a house and a car. At that time the temple was on Bubbling Well Rd, next to the eponymous well, which was walled over in 1919. The temple was eventually divested of its Buddhist statues in the Cultural Revolution and turned into a plastics factory.

Subsequent rebuilding and the almost continuous concrete-based renovations since 1999 have robbed the old complex of much of its charm. Today the temple is of limited interest, except at full moons when the place is packed with worshippers.

Opposite is newly remodelled **Jing'an Park**, formerly Bubbling Park Cemetery, which is worth a stroll. Look out for the copy of the first tram car to travel down Bubbling Well Rd to the Bund, now a coffee bar.

SHANGHAI EXHIBITION CENTRE
Map pp250-2
Shànghǎi Zhǎnlǎn Zhōngxīn

The hulking great monolith of the Shanghai Exhibition Centre can be seen from Nanjing Xilu. It was built as the Palace of Sino-Soviet Friendship, a friendship that soon turned to ideological rivalry and even the brink of war in the 1960s. Architectural buffs will appreciate its monumentality and unsubtle, bold Bolshevik strokes – there was a time when Pudong was set to look like this.

The site of the Exhibition Centre was originally the gardens of the Jewish millionaire Silas Hardoon (see the boxed text opposite).

The Great Jewish Families

The Sassoon family consisted of generations of shrewd businessmen from Baghdad to Bombay, whose achievements brought them wealth, knighthoods, and far-reaching influence. Though it was David Sassoon who initiated cotton trading out of Bombay to China, and son Elias Sassoon who had the ingenuity to buy and build his own warehouses in Shanghai, it was Sir Victor Sassoon who finally amassed the family fortune and enjoyed his wealth during Shanghai's heyday. Victor concentrated his energies on buying up Shanghai's land and building offices, apartments and warehouses. His affairs were plentiful but he remained a bachelor until he finally married his American nurse when he was 70, leaving her his entire fortune. Victor left Shanghai in 1941, returning only briefly after the war to tidy up the business, and then he and his assets relocated to the Bahamas. At one time Victor Sassoon owned an estimated 1900 buildings in Shanghai. Today the Sassoon legacy lives on in the historic Peace Hotel and Sassoon House (known to Sassoon as 'Eve'), now in the Cypress Hotel in Hongqiao, each the site of some infamously raucous Sassoon soirées.

The company of David Sassoon & Sons gave rise to several other notables in Shanghai, among them Silas Hardoon and Elly Kadoorie. Hardoon began his illustrious career as a night watchman and later, in 1880, as manager of David Sassoon & Sons. Two years later he set out in business on his own and promptly went bust. His second independent business venture in 1920 proved successful and Silas Hardoon made a name for himself in real estate. In his father's memory he built the Beth Aharon Synagogue near Suzhou Creek, which later served as a shelter for Polish Jews who had fled Europe. Once a well-respected member of both the French and International Councils, Hardoon's reputation turned scandalous when he took a Eurasian wife, Luo Jialing, and adopted a crowd of multinational children. He then began to study Buddhism. His estate, including the school he had erected (now the grounds of the Shanghai Exhibition Centre) went up in smoke during the Sino-Japanese war. At the time of his death in 1931, he was the richest man in Shanghai.

Like Silas Hardoon, Elly Kadoorie began a career with David Sassoon & Sons in 1880 and he too broke away and amassed a fortune – in real estate, banking, and rubber production. His famous mansion is the result of too much money left in the hands of an unreliable architect; after returning from three years in England, Kadoorie found a 19.5m-high ballroom aglow with 5.4m chandeliers and enough imported marble to warrant the name Marble Hall. Architecture detectives can still visit the staircases and peek at the ballroom of the former mansion, once site of Shanghai's most extravagant balls and now home to the **Children's Palace** (Map pp246-9), at 64 Yan'an Xilu. Kadoorie died the year the communists took power; you can visit his grave in the **International Cemetery** (Map p256) on Hongqiao Lu.

With their immense wealth, Jewish families were pivotal in aiding the thousands of refugees who fled to Shanghai. The Kadoorie family resides in Hong Kong and is still involved in charity work.

Neighbourhoods – North Shanghai

SUZHOU CREEK ART CENTRE Map pp250-2
50 Moganshan Lu

With three galleries now sharing the one complex this centre is worth a visit if you're into contemporary art. **Bizart** (Bǐyì Huàláng; ☎ 6247 0484; 4th fl, Bldg 7) exhibits avant-garde Chinese and foreign art in all media. Viewing is by appointment only, except for exhibitions. At **Eastlink Gallery** (Dōngláng Huàláng; ☎ 6276 9932; eastlink@sh163c.sta .net.cn; 5th fl, Bldg 6) you can find anything from contemporary Chinese and foreign art to video installations. The newest arrival, **Art Scene Warehouse** (Yìshùjǐng Huàláng; ☎ 6277 2499; 2nd fl, Bldg 4; ☺ 10.30am-8pm Tue-Sun) is a chic minimalist warehouse space complementing Art Scene's more intimate gallery in the French Concession (p68). Expect big-scale contemporary and avant-garde Chinese art (and the occasional fashion show) in what is now Shanghai's biggest private gallery.

NORTH SHANGHAI
Eating p113; Shopping p152; Sleeping p167

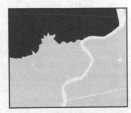

The area of this neighbourhood north of Suzhou Creek was once the American settlement, until it merged into the International Settlement. Originally desirable, by the 1930s the region was one of the poorest parts of Shanghai. It was divided into Hongkou, once known as Little Tokyo because of its 30,000 Japanese residents, and Zhapei, infamous in the 1930s for its factories and slums. The region was torn apart by Sino-Japanese fighting in 1931 when 10,000 civilians were killed in the crossfire.

Today there's not all that much to see in this gritty part of Shanghai but its interesting backstreets offer some good walks. A remnant of the Japanese influence can be seen at the former Japanese Shinto shrine (439 Zhapei Lu). The shrine served as a karaoke bar for a while but was empty at last check. Another interesting building is the **Jingling Church** (Jìnglíng Táng; Map pp244-5; 135 Kunshan Lu), built in 1923, where Chiang Kaishek married Soong Meiling (and where her father was once a pastor). Sichuan Beilu is one of Shanghai's busiest shopping streets.

Transport

Metro The No 3 (Pearl Light Railway) line offers access to Duolun Lu and Lu Xun Park; from the No 1 metro line change at Shanghai train station.
Bus No 21 runs up Sichuan Lu from near the Bund to Lu Xun Park past Duolun Lu; Nos 22, 37 and 921 run up Dongdaming Lu and back down Changyang and Dongchanghzhi Lu; No 934 goes down Changyang Lu to the Bund and Renmin Square.

AURA GALLERY Map pp253-4
Yìàn Huàláng
☎ 6595 0901; www.aura-art.com; 5th fl, 713 Dongdaming Lu; ◷ noon-8pm, closed Mon

This old warehouse space houses changing exhibits by young contemporary Chinese artists and is worth a stop en route to or from the Jewish area. Contact William Zhang. Check magazine listings to see what's on. While you're at it, check to see what's exhibiting at the 3rd-floor **DDM Warehouse** (☎ 3501 3212; ◷ closed Sun).

DUOLUN LU CULTURAL STREET
Map pp242-3
Duōlún Wénhuà Míngrén Jiē
Bus 21 from Suzhou Creek

This recently restored street of fine old houses, just off Sichuan Beilu, was once home to several of China's most famous writers (as well as several Kuomintang generals), when the road was known as Doulean Rd. Today it is lined with art supply stores, curio shops, galleries and teahouses, as well as statues of the writers Lu Xun and Guo Moruo.

The eye-catching cube of the **Shanghai Duolun Museum of Modern Art** at the east end of the street has an impressive three-floor exhibition space but offered few exhibits at the time of research. One unique building is the **Hongde Temple**, at No 59, built in 1928 in a Chinese style as the Great Virtue Church. The lower floor houses temporary craft exhibits, but come Sunday morning, it's worth clambering upstairs to catch a church service (7am and 9.30am).

The main appeal of the street (apart from the galleries and antique shops – see p152) is its various collections. These include: Wang Zaoshi's fabulous **collection of 10,000 Mao badges** (No 183; Y2); the **Haicitang Porcelain Gallery** (No 185) and the **chopsticks collection** (No 191). With a bit of exploration you are bound to dig up some more.

The League of Left-Wing Writers was established down a side alley (then known as Darroch Rd) on 2 March 1930. Today the building serves as a **political museum** (adult/student Y5/3; ◷ 9.30am-4.30pm), worth a look for the architecture alone.

Down another side alley, further along Duolun Lu, is the Jinquan Coin Gallery, located in an old Kuomintang officer's residence. Next door is another architectural hangover, the former Bai Residence. The street ends in the north at the third Kuomintang residence, the almost Islamic-looking Kong Residence.

If you need a break try the **Old Film Café** (☎ 5696 4763; 123 Duolun Lu; coffee Y22-30; ◷ 10am-midnight). Film buffs come here to catch screenings of old Chinese films from the 1920s, '30s and '40s. The walls are decorated with film posters and the rambling upper floors are strewn with copies of old film magazines, books and mementos.

LU XUN PARK Map pp242-3
Lǔ Xùn Gōngyuán
Park: admission Y2; ◷ 6am-6pm; Memorial Hall:
☎ 6306 1181; adult/student Y5/2; ◷ 9am-5pm

This is one of the city's nicest parks, with elderly Chinese practising t'ai chi or ballroom dancing, and even the occasional retired opera singer giving free performances. The Sunday morning

Top Three North Shanghai

- Take a self-guided walking tour through the Jewish district (p79).
- Discover the restored shops and folk collections of Duolun Lu (p78).
- Stray off the beaten track and wander through the traditional backstreets of Hongkou (p58).

Lu Xun

Lu Xun (born Zhou Shuren; 1881–1936) is one of China's most famous writers, and is often regarded as the father of modern Chinese literature. Part of China's May 4 literary movement, his main achievement was to break from the classical literary traditions of the past – unintelligible to most Chinese – to create a modern vernacular literature. He was also a fierce critic of China's social ills, which led to him being canonised by the communist hierarchy even though he was never a member of the Party. Lu Xun's most famous works are *A Madman's Diary, The True Story of Ah Q* and *Kong Yi Ji*. These are presented in two collections: *Call to Arms* and *Wandering*, both of which still make excellent reading. Lu Xun was also famed for promoting woodcuts as a form of mass art.

Apart from the tomb and memorial hall in Lu Xun Park (see below), die-hard fans can visit **Lu Xun's House** (Map pp242-3; No 9, Lane 132, on photogenic Shanying Lu; admission Y4; 9am-4pm), where the writer lived and worked for the last four years of his life (April 1933 to 19 October 1936). Xun had a great fondness for Shanghai and named his son Haiying ('Child of Shanghai'). The house holds a lifeless collection of photographs, letters, manuscripts, furniture and other memorabilia, but few ghosts remain. Look out for the rather morbid calendar and clock showing the date and time of his death.

English corner is one of the largest in Shanghai and a good place to chat to locals in English. You can take boats out onto the small lake.

The park used to be called Hongkou Park but was renamed because it holds the **Tomb of Lu Xun**, moved here from the International Cemetery on the 20th anniversary of his death in 1956. Mao himself inscribed the memorial calligraphy.

The **Lu Xun Memorial Hall** (Lǔ Xùn Jìnìnguǎn) is a state-of-the art museum on the great man. It tries hard, with plenty of videos and wax figures, but you'd have to be a dedicated fan to appreciate the journals, manuscripts and old photos and their socialist spin. The museum bookshop sells collections of Lu Xun's stories in English, French and German.

OHEL MOISHE SYNAGOGUE Map pp253-4
Móxī Huìtáng

☎ 6541 5008; 62 Changyang Lu; admission Y50; 9am-4.30pm Mon-Fri; bus 37, 934 from the Bund

This gutted synagogue (formerly on Ward Rd), was built by the Russian Ashkenazi Jewish community in 1927 and lies in the heart of the 1940s Jewish ghetto (see the boxed text on p80).

There's not much to see in the building except for a few black-and-white pictures. The real reason to come is to take a tour of the surrounding streets with the resident guide Mr Wang. Eighty-four-year-old Wang has lived all his life in Hongkou and can bring alive many of the surrounding sites.

Fish & Bird Market, Zhoushan Lu (p80)

Shanghai's Jews

Shanghai has two centuries of strong Jewish connections. Established Middle-Eastern Sephardic Jewish families like the Hardoons, Ezras, Kadoories and Sassoons built their fortunes in Shanghai, establishing at least seven synagogues and many Jewish hospitals and schools. It was Victor Sassoon who famously remarked: 'There is only one race greater than the Jews and that's the Derby'.

A second group of Jews, this time Ashkenazi, arrived via Siberia, Harbin and Tianjin from Russia after anti-Jewish pogroms in 1906. The biggest influx, however, came between 1933 and 1941, when 30,000 mostly Ashkenazi Jews arrived from Nazi Europe by boat from Italy or by train via Siberia. Many had been issued with visas to cross China by Ho Feng Shan, Chinese consul-general in Vienna, who was recently honoured as the 'Chinese Schindler'.

Shanghai was one of the few safe havens for Jews fleeing the Holocaust in Europe as it required neither passport nor visa to stay. Gestapo agents followed the refugees and in 1942 tried to persuade the Japanese to build death camps on Chongming Island. Instead, in 1943, the Japanese forced Jews to move into a 'Designated Area for Stateless Refugees' in Hongkou.

The Jewish ghetto (stateless Russians didn't have to live here) became home to Jews from all walks of life. It grew to shelter a synagogue, schools, a local paper, hospitals and enough cafés, rooftop gardens and restaurants to gain the epithet 'Little Vienna'. Those Jews who held jobs in the French Concession had to secure passes from the Japanese, specifically the notoriously unpredictable and violent Mr Goya. Poorer refugees were forced to bunk down in cramped hostels known as 'heime', and had to rely on the generosity of others. When the wealthy Anglophile Jewish trading families left in 1941, the situation grew even tighter. Still, the refugees heard of events in distant Europe and realised that they were the lucky ones.

Today there are a few remainders of Jewish life in Shanghai, such as the **Ohel Moishe Synagogue** (p79) and the former Jewish Club (1932) in the grounds of the Shanghai Music Conservatory, where concerts are still performed. A new Museum of Jewish Refugees to China is planned for the site of the former **Ohel Rachel Synagogue** (Map pp250-2; 500 Shanxi Beilu, formerly Seymour Rd). The synagogue was built by Jacob Elias Sassoon in the late 19th century and was recently restored for Hillary Clinton's visit. Nearby are the remains of the school founded on the grounds by Horace Kadoorie.

For information and relatively pricey tours of Jewish Shanghai contact the **Shanghai Jewish Studies Centre** (Map pp246-9; ☎ 5306 0606 ext 2431; Room 352, No 7 – the big building at the end – Lane 622, Huaihai Zhonglu). The centre offers one-day tours of Jewish Shanghai with English- and Hebrew-speaking guides. You can also contact www.chinajewish.org. Mr Wang of the Ohel Moishe Synagogue is another remarkable source of information on the area.

For a mini walking tour of the surrounding streets turn right outside the synagogue, then right again past the former Jewish tenements of Zhoushan Lu, once the commercial heart of the district. At Huoshan Lu turn left to visit Huoshan Park and the memorial plaque erected for the visit of Yitzak Rabin in the late 1990s.

Head back southwest along Huoshan Lu (former Wayside Rd) past the Art Deco façade of the former **Broadway Theatre** (No 49; now the Bailaohui Restaurant), with its rooftop Vienna Café, to the Ocean Hotel. Turn right up Haimen Lu (Muirhead Rd), past Changyang Lu, to what was once a row of Jewish shops and a kosher delicatessen on Haimen Lu, which still has the faded, original painted sign from the 1940s proclaiming 'Horn's Imbiss Stube' and 'Café Atlantis'.

At the top of the road (crossing with Kunming Lu) you'll see the large, renovated **Xiahai Miao Buddhist Monastery**; take a right turn, then another right, down Zhoushan Lu once again, past a small **fish and bird market** on the right and on the left the **Ward Road Jail**, once Shanghai's biggest, to complete the circle back to the synagogue.

HONGQIAO & GUBEI

Eating p113; Shopping p152; Sleeping p168

The western district of Hongqiao is mainly a centre for international commerce and trade exhibitions. There are many office blocks, as well as a few foreign restaurants, hotels and shopping malls. There's some striking modern architecture in the area, especially around New Century Plaza.

Gubei is a new planned community of Legoland-like estates.

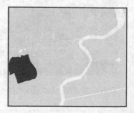

It serves as the residential area for Hong-qiao so has expat-oriented services like art galleries, restaurants and the ever-popular Carrefour megastore.

Further west was once a popular suburban retreat for old Shanghainese. Victor Sassoon had his country villa at what is now the Cypress Hotel and the zoo once served as China's first golf course, in 1917. The district is best known to visitors for its domestic airport and range of furniture and antique stores. Beyond this, the Huqingping Hwy leads out to Dianshan Lake and Zhejiang Province.

Transport

Metro No 2 line currently being extended.
Bus No 911 along Hongqiao Lu to Huaihai Zhonglu and the Old Town; No 831 from Hongqiao airport to Huaihai Zhonglu and the Bund.

Top Three Hongqiao & Gubei

- Browse the furniture shops and warehouses (p152) on a Sunday.
- Stock up at **Carrefour** (p99), Shanghai's best supermarket.
- Enjoy a drink at the **Door** (p129), one of the city's most stylish bars.

AQUARIA 21 Map pp242-3
Dàyáng Hǎidǐ Shìjiè Chángfēng Hǎiyáng Shìjiè

☎ 5281 8888; 451 Daduhe Lu, Changfeng Park, Gate No 4; adult/child over 1m Y80/60

A New Zealand–built and –managed aquarium park that is actually under Yinchu Lake in Changfeng Park. The park follows the course of a river from Peru through Amazonian jungle to the sea. There are also water-life touching tanks, rides and even an aquarium made out of a car, providing loads of fun for children. A neighbouring water-slide park and boating opportunities on Yinchu Lake mean that families can make a nice day of it.

JINGDEZHEN CERAMICS GALLERY
Map pp242-3
Jǐngdézhèn Táocí Yìshù Zhōngxīn

☎ 6385 6238; 1253 Daduhe Lu

This huge gallery features a display of ceramics from the five kilns of the Song dynasty. Among the displays is a huge 3.88m-high vase, said to be the largest in the world, and the giant dragons made of cups and saucers are also eye-catching.

The gallery is in the middle of nowhere in the northwest suburbs. Sightseeing Bus No 6B goes here every 30 minutes from Shanghai Stadium, returning erratically from the opposite side of the street (flag it down). Otherwise, take the metro to Zhongshan Park then take a taxi.

LIU HAISU ART GALLERY Map p256
Liú Hǎisù Měishùguǎn

☎ 6270 1018; 1660 Hongqiao Lu; admission Y5-20 depending on exhibits; ☼ 9am-4pm Tue-Sun

This hulking gallery exhibits works of the eponymous painter, as well as often impressive visiting exhibitions, with the Chine Antiques store (p152) in the lobby.

SHANGHAI ZOO Map pp242-3
Shànghǎi Dòngwùyuàn

☎ 6268 7775; 2381 Hongqiao Lu, cnr Hami Lu; admission Y10, Y25 for special exhibits; ☼ 7am-6pm (last entry 4.30pm); bus 831 from Jinling Lu near the Bund, 505 from Renmin Sq, 911 along Huaihai Lu

If you don't agree with the concept of zoos then this one probably won't convert you. That said, this is one of China's better zoos. All the major African wildlife is represented, but the most interesting animals are probably those endemic to China, such as the red panda, the golden monkeys from Yunnan, and, of course, the pair of giant pandas. Before the first few animals arrived shivering from Yunnan's Xishuangbanna region in 1954, the grounds served as a golf club for the British.

Not far from the zoo, in the grounds of the Cypress Hotel, is the former **Sassoon Mansion**, now the residence of the Norwegian consul-general.

ZHONGSHAN PARK Map pp242-3
Zhōngshān Gōngyuán

780 Changning Lu; Park: admission Y2; Fundazzle: Y25; ☼ 6am-5pm

Known as Jessfield Park to the British, this is a moderately interesting park located in the former 'Badlands' area of 1930s Shanghai. Kids will like Fundazzle (Fāndǒulè), an adventure playground with slides, mazes and tunnels.

Neighbourhoods – Hongqiao & Gubei

Shanghai for Children

Apart from the following sights, shopping malls are generally a hit with their entertainment halls and food courts.

- **Acrobats** (p133) Fun for all the family.
- **Aquaria 21** (p81) or **Shanghai Aquarium** (p74) For an experience both entertaining and educational.
- **Dino Beach** (p82) Waterslides and wave machines are big attractions here.
- **Fundazzle** (p81) An adventure playground with slides, tunnels and mazes, in Zhonghshan Park.

XUJIAHUI & SOUTH SHANGHAI

Eating p114; Shopping p153; Sleeping p169

The Xujiahui area of Shanghai, bordering the western end of the French Concession and known to 1930s expat residents as Ziccawei or Sicawei, was once a thriving Jesuit settlement. Today it's a bustling commercial centre astride the insanely busy five-way intersection (over 10,000 vehicles funnel through Xujiahui each hour), and home to some of Shanghai's biggest department stores and entertainment complexes. To the north-east is the pleasant new Xujiahui Park; south are the sports facilities of Shanghai Stadium.

The cultural heart of south Shanghai has long been the Longhua Temple but these days the main landmark is the huge Shanghai Stadium sports complex by the inner ring road. There aren't too many reasons to come all the way down here, except perhaps to catch one of the sightseeing buses by the stadium or take the kids to one of the amusement parks in the southern suburbs.

Transport

Metro No 1 line and No 3 (Pearl Light Railway) lines run through the district. Xujiahui and Shanghai Stadium stops are on the No 1 line. The No 3 line stops at Caoxi Lu, near Shanghai Stadium.

DINO BEACH

Rèdài Fēngbào

☎ 6478 3333; 78 Xinzhen Lu; adult Y30 Tue, Y60 Mon, Wed-Fri, Y80 Sat & Sun, children ½ price; ⏰ 9am-9pm, Jun-Sep

Way down south in Minhang district, this popular summer place has a beach, a wave pool, water slides and tube hire to beat the summer heat, but can be heaving at the weekends.

GUILIN PARK Map pp242-3

Guìlín Gōngyuán

Caobao Lu

This park probably isn't worth a special visit but it's a pleasant enough place. It's famous for its spring blossoms and because it houses the former (1932) residence of the gangster 'Pock-marked' Huang Jinrong, now a teahouse.

HOKKAIDO INDOOR SKI SLOPE

☎ 5485 3428; 1835 Qixing Lu, Xinzhuang; admission Y100 Mon-Fri/Y120 Sat & Sun for 1st 90 min then Y60/72 per hr

The latest must-have accoutrement of modern Shanghai living is apparently…snow! The slope is aimed at first-timers so don't expect anything overly long or steep. Snowboard lessons are available here at the **Burton Snowboard School** (☎ 6431 9738; www.wildrampage.com). To get there take the metro to Xinzhuang and hop in a taxi or shuttle bus.

JINJIANG AMUSEMENT PARK

Map p172

Jīnjiāng Lèyuán

☎ 6468 0844; 201 Hongmei Lu; admission Y60

Roller coasters, rides and a huge Ferris wheel are all here in this amusement park, near Minhang metro station.

LONGHUA TEMPLE & PAGODA

Map pp242-3

Lónghuá Tǎ

Admission Y6; ⏰ 7am-4pm; bus 44 from Xujiahui

Southwest of central Shanghai, close to the Huangpu River, here is the oldest and largest monastery in Shanghai. It's said to date from the

Top Three Xujiahui & South Shanghai

- Watch Shanghai's middle classes at play in Xujiahui's giant malls (p82).
- Catch a concert or football match at **Shanghai Stadium** (p135).
- Attend a mass at **St Ignatius Cathedral** (p84).

10th century, when the King of Wu built it for his mother. Built in the Song style but renovated in Guangxu's reign of the Qing, it has recently been restored several times for tourism. The 'longhua' refers to the pipal tree under which Buddha achieved enlightenment.

There are five main halls, starting with the **Laughing Buddha Hall**. To either side of the entrance are a bell and a drum tower. The temple is famed for its 6500kg bell, which was cast in 1894. To strike the bell is auspicious, at least for the temple, which charges Y10 for three strikes. If you've got a handy Y360, 108 strikes are thought to be even more auspicious. There are several side buildings to explore, including the **Thousand Arhat Hall** (an arhat is one of Buddha's disciples), with one bearded arhat attempting what looks suspiciously like a Mexican wave.

The proletariat temple canteen serves up cheap 100% vegetarian dishes at lunch time (try the Y8 *luóhàn miàn* if you like mushrooms); the restaurant in the adjoining Longhua Hotel serves upscale variants (Y20 to Y28 per dish).

The nearby seven-storey, 44m-high **Longhua Pagoda** was originally built in 977. It has been reconstructed many times, most recently in 1952. A tourism complex along the lines of the Yuyuan Bazaar has recently been built around the pagoda.

Longhua stages traditional celebrations during New Year (both Western and Chinese) and during its temple fair in April, when folk performers, dragon dances and snack sellers descend on the place en masse.

MARTYRS MEMORIAL Map p257
Lièshí Língyuán
Admission Y1, memorial hall: Y5; 9am-4pm
Next to the Longhua Temple, this rambling park marks the site of an old Kuomintang prison, where 800 communists, intellectuals and political agitators were executed between 1928 and 1937. You can take a bizarre underground tunnel to the original jailhouse (some

people might find the tunnel a bit creepy). Fans of Socialist Realist art will get a kick out of the epic sculptures, others will be easily bored. This is one of the few places in Shanghai where you'll be reminded that China is actually after all a communist country. During WWII this area was a Japanese internment camp and airfield, as depicted in the JG Ballard novel and Spielberg film *Empire of the Sun*.

SHANGHAI BOTANICAL GARDENS
Map pp242-3
Shànghǎi Zhíwùyuán
6451 2269; 1111 Longwu Lu; admission Y8; 8am-5pm, longer in summer
About 2km southwest of the Longhua Pagoda are the Shanghai Botanical Gardens. Though parts are sparse and neglected, there are some beautiful green areas in which to sit and enjoy the quiet if you need to escape Shanghai's concrete jungle; the gardens on the southwest side are particularly nice, as are the bonsals of the Penjing 'potted landscape' Garden. A new exhibition greenhouse offers a chance to get close to tropical flora (admission Y40).

The northern side has a dusty memorial temple, originally built in 1728. It's dedicated to Huang Daopo, who supposedly kick-started

Carving, Longhua Temple (opposite)

Xu Guangqi

Xujiahui ('the Xu family gathering') is named after Xu Guangqi (1562–1633), a Chinese renaissance man. Xu was an early student of astronomy, agronomy and the calendar and he established a meteorological observatory that relayed its information to the tower on the Bund. He was then converted to Catholicism by Mateo Ricci and was baptised with the name Paul. He became a high official in the Ming court and bequeathed land to found a Jesuit community, which eventually led to the construction of St Ignatius Cathedral. Xu's tomb can still be visited in nearby **Guangqi Park** (Map p257), next to the modern-day Shanghai Meteorological Department, and stands as an inspirational symbol of Shanghai's openness to accept foreign ideas.

Shanghai's cotton industry by bringing the knowledge of spinning and weaving to the region from Hainan Island.

ST IGNATIUS CATHEDRAL Map p257
Tiānzhǔjiào Táng
158 Puxi Lu
St Ignatius Cathedral (1904), restored after its 50m Gothic spires were lopped off by Red Guards, is open once again for Catholic worship. Up to 2500 Chinese Catholics cram into the impressive church at Easter, making it the second-most important Catholic spot in eastern China, after Sheshan Cathedral, just outside the city.

The yellow building across Caoxi Beilu was once part of the Jesuit settlement. The old convent across the road has since gone.

The cathedral is a short walk south of the Xujiahui metro station (metro exit 3). Services are held weekdays at 6.15am and 7am, Saturday at 6pm and Sunday at 5.30am, 6am, 7am, 8am and 6pm.

UNIQUE HILL STUDIO Map p257
☎ 5410 4815; Room 301, Tianlong Apt,
907 Tianyueqiao Lu
You'd never guess there was a gallery hidden in this anonymous apartment block southeast of Shanghai Stadium. The changing exhibits are strong on Old Shanghai memorabilia, such as cigarette posters and period photos. Check listings magazines to see what's on before heading out here.

Chinese Christians

Shanghai has at least 140,000 Catholics, largely due to its history of Jesuit communities. **St Ignatius Cathedral** (above) is the largest in the city, though **Sheshan Cathedral** (p174) is the seat of the Bishop of Shanghai. At both locations you'll be faced with the unexpected sight of Chinese kneeling at confessionals and praying to statues of the Virgin Mary. There is much friction between the government and the Chinese Catholic Church because the church refuses to disown the Pope as its leader. Nor does China's one-child policy sit well with the Catholic stand on abortion. (In 1973 a nationwide birth-control programme was instituted, with each couple permitted to have just one child in order to limit population growth.) For this reason, the Vatican maintains diplomatic relations with Taiwan, much to China's consternation.

To see or take part in prayer, Catholics can visit the **Christ the King Church** (Map pp246-9; cnr Julu & Maoming Lu) or St Ignatius Cathedral. Protestants can visit the **Community Church** (Map pp246-9; Hengshan Lu).

Walking Tours

Walking Tours

THE BUND

This walk reveals the architectural glories of the Bund, Shanghai's most impressive mile. To walk it in one go, cross Suzhou Creek over Garden Bridge, work your way down the east side of Zhongshan Dong Yilu and either view the buildings from a distance or cross the underpass for a closer view. The walk is just as enjoyable during the day or at night, when the buildings are closed but the Bund is spectacularly lit.

At the northern end of the Bund, on the north bank of Suzhou Creek, is **Broadway Mansions**, built in 1934 as an exclusive apartment block. The Foreign Correspondents' Club occupied the 9th floor in the 1930s and used its fine views to report the Japanese bombing of the city in 1937. The building became the headquarters of the Japanese army during WWII. At one time the US military lived on the lower floors.

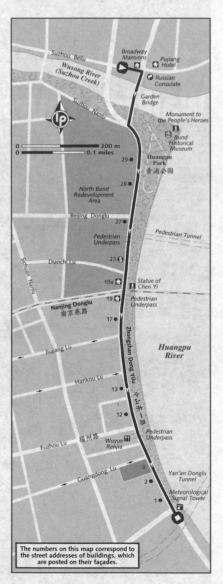

Walk Facts

Start Broadway Mansions
End Yan'an Donglu

Just east of here, along the old Broadway is the **Russian consulate**, the only consulate currently occupying its original location. The building first served as the Soviet consulate, then a seamen's club, before becoming the Soviet consulate again in 1987, and then finally the Russian consulate. Previously there was a string of other consulates in this area, including American, German and Japanese.

Behind the consulate is the **Pujiang Hotel**, Shanghai's backpacker favourite. The hotel opened in 1846 as Astor House, the first hotel in Shanghai, and later became the Richard Hotel. The hotel claims that it was the site of the first electric light and telephone line in Shanghai. In 1990 China's first stock exchange was set up here in the former ballroom, until its move to Pudong in 1998.

Heading south over Suzhou Creek you will cross **Garden Bridge** (Wàibáidù Qiáo), built in 1906 in place of an earlier wooden bridge. In 1937 the bridge marked the de facto border between the International Settlement and Japanese-occupied Hongkou and Zhapei.

Huangpu Park (Huángpú Gōngyuán), the first park in Shanghai, was laid out by a Scottish gardener shipped out especially for that purpose. Today the park holds an uninspiring **Monument to the People's Heroes**, which offers some of the best photo opportunities of Pudong. Underneath the monument is the **Bund Historical Museum** (Wàitān Lìshǐ Jìniànguǎn; admission free; ⏰9am-4.15pm), which is worth a stop for its great old photos of the Bund. Turn left at the entrance to go chronologically. The socialist sculpture at the entrance of Huangpu Park was built on the site of the old British bandstand.

No Dogs or Chinese

Huangpu Park was the site of the infamous (and legendary) sign that forbade entry to 'dogs or Chinese'. In fact there never was such a sign, though the spirit of the law certainly existed. The first of the five park regulations adopted in 1916 forbade the entry of dogs and bicycles; a separate regulation later denied entry to Chinese, except for Chinese nannies, servants and friends of foreigners. The regulation was finally rescinded in 1928 but has since become a powerful symbol of Shanghai's semicolonial rule.

Continuing south down the Bund (at No 29) you pass the former **British consulate** (1873), the earliest building on the Bund. The imposing building is now a government department.

Further down, at No 28, is the **Glen Line Building**, with the radio antenna on top. At No 27 is the former headquarters of early opium traders Jardine Matheson, which became one of Shanghai's great hongs (trading houses). According to Tess Johnston in her book *The Last Colonies*, in 1941 the British embassy occupied the top floor and faced (presumably with a glare) the German embassy, across the road in the Glen Line Building! The building was later taken over by the Japanese navy and after that hosted the US consulate for a while.

The imposing **Bank of China** building, at No 23, was commissioned by director HH Kung, and was built in 1937 with specific instructions that it should be higher than the adjacent Cathay Hotel. The building is a strange architectural mishmash, designed in a New York/Chicago style and later topped with a blue Chinese roof to make the building appear more patriotic.

Next door to the Bank of China, at No 19a, the famous **Peace Hotel** (1926–29) was once the most luxurious hotel in the Far East and is still an Art Deco masterpiece. The hotel was built as the Cathay by Victor Sassoon, and originally occupied only the 4th to 7th floors of the Sassoon house. The guest list included Charlie Chaplin, George Bernard Shaw and Noel Coward, who wrote *Private Lives* here in four days in 1930 when he had the flu. Sassoon himself spent weekdays in his personal suite on the top floor with its unsurpassed 360-degree views. You can just imagine him standing there, lording over the Bund. The suite later became a bankers' club.

Even if you are not staying at the Peace Hotel you can look around the wonderful lobby (only half its original size) and visit the famous ballroom with its sprung floor. The main east entrance (next to the Citibank sign) is no longer in use but there are still some nice Art Deco touches around it. Now, as in the 1930s, banks make up part of the lower floor. The hotel was renamed the Peace Hotel in 1956. The Gang of Four used the hotel as an operations base during the Cultural Revolution.

Opposite and part of the Peace Hotel is the pink and white **Palace Hotel** (1906), No 19, one of the oldest buildings on the Bund. A plaque commemorates the International Opium Commission, which was held here in 1909. The once-famous rooftop garden is no more. Stray Chinese bombs (aimed at Japanese warships in the Huangpu) crashed through the roof of the hotel and outside the Peace Hotel in 1937, killing 720 passers-by.

Across the road from the Peace Hotel is a **statue of Chen Yi**, Shanghai's first mayor, that bears more than a passing resemblance to Mao. The plinth previously held a statue of Sir Harry Parkes, British Envoy to China (1882–85), erected in 1890 and torn down by the Japanese in 1941 to be used as scrap metal in the war effort.

Further south, at No 17, is the former home of the **North China Daily News**. Known as the 'Old Lady of the Bund' the *News* ran from 1864 to 1951 as the main English-language newspaper in China and the mouthpiece of the municipality commission. Look above the central windows for the paper's motto. Huge Atlas figures support the roof. Today the building is once again home to American Insurance International, the first of the Bund's original

Imposing entrance of the Customs House (below)

tenants (who left en masse in 1949) to return to its former home. Other Bund fixtures are being sold off and will no doubt be similarly dusted off and cleaned up. The current building was completed in 1923.

Three buildings down, at No 13, stands the **Customs House** built in 1925 as one of the most important buildings on the Bund. On top of the building is a clock face and 'Big Ching', the bell that was modelled on Big Ben. The bell was dismantled in the Cultural Revolution and replaced by loudspeakers that blasted out revolutionary slogans and songs. The clockworks were restored in 1986 for the visit of Queen Elizabeth II.

A statue of Robert Hart, early Inspector of Customs for the Chinese Imperial Customs Service, stood outside the Customs House until the Japanese dismantled it during WWII. Born in Portadown in Northern Ireland, Hart reorganised the Chinese customs service during his 48 years employ there and helped with reforms of the Qing bureaucracy. As a result he won the rare respect and friendship of Chinese and the position of the most influential foreigner in China. The previous Customs House was a Tudor mansion built on the remains of a Chinese-style building, which was itself destroyed by the Small Swords Rebellion in 1853. The original customs jetty stood across from the building, on the Huangpu River.

Next door to the Customs House is No 12, the grandest building on the Bund, the former **Hongkong and Shanghai Banking Corporation (HSBC) building**. The bank was established in Hong Kong in 1864 and in Shanghai in 1865 to finance trade and it soon became one of the richest in Shanghai, arranging the indemnity paid after the Boxer Rebellion. When the current building was constructed in 1923 it was the second-largest bank in the world and 'the finest building east of Suez'. The bronze lions that once guarded the entrance and were rubbed shiny by superstitious Chinese can now be found in the Municipal Historical Museum (p74) in Pudong.

Until 1995 the building held the offices of the municipal government before they moved to Renmin Park; it now holds the Pudong Development Bank and several

Pit Stop

If you need a break, try **Bonomi Café** (p101) inside the HSBC building (enter through the right side entrance). For a special meal with views of the Bund try **M on the Bund** (p100) just off the Bund. For a simple lunch of Suzhou-style noodles try **Wuyue Renjia** (p109) down the side of the Royal Thai consulate.

offices. Enter and marvel at the beautiful mosaic ceiling, featuring the 12 zodiac signs and the world's eight great banking centres.

At No 3 is **Three on the Bund**, an impressive new restaurant and retail development (p62).

The **Shanghai Club** (1911), the city's best-known bastion of British snobbery, stood at No 2 on the Bund. The club had 20 rooms for residents, but its most famous accoutrement was the bar, which at 33m was said to be the longest in the world. Foreign businessmen would sit here according to rank (no Chinese or women were allowed in the club), with the taipans closest to the view of the Bund. The building is now empty and awaiting re-development after a short spell as the Dongfeng Hotel (a seamen's hostel) with, much to its embarrassment, a KFC in the old bar. These days the modern-day variants of the club's creaking leather chairs, ironed newspapers and expensive cigars are more likely to be spotted in the Portman Ritz-Carlton or the American Club. Next door, and the last building on the Bund proper was No 1, the **McBain Building** or Asiatic Petroleum Building, built in 1915 in the neoclassical style.

Just across from the overpass you can see the 49m-tall **Meteorological Signal Tower** (admission free) originally built in 1908 opposite the French consulate and, in 1993, moved 22m north as part of the revamping of the Bund. Today it houses a small collection of old prints of the Bund and a replica 1855 map of the Bund. Views from the roof are excellent if you can persuade the guard to let you up there.

By the overpass you'll find Yan'an Donglu, once a canal and later filled in to become Ave Edward VII, the dividing line between the International Settlement and the French Concession. South of here the Bund was known as the Quai de France. A block south, Jinling Lu is the former Rue du Consulat, where the French embassy once stood.

BEYOND THE BUND

This walk takes you parallel to the crowds of the Bund, from south to north, through the lost architecture of the International Settlement. It can be tacked neatly on to the end of the Bund walking tour.

Walk Facts
Start Yan'an Donglu
End The North Bund

Start at the crossing of the Yan'an Donglu overpass and the Bund (near the Manabe Café). Head south from the overpass and turn right into Jinling Lu. At Sichuan Nanlu take a short detour left to the spires of **St Joseph's Church 1** at No 36, consecrated in 1862 and now surrounded by a school through which you can gain access.

From here head north on Sichuan Nanlu, under the overpass, for about two blocks. On the left you'll find the smoky old **Club de Shanghai 1920 2**. On the corner with Guangdong Lu, look for No 93; the former **Golden Cage 3**, once home to the captive concubines of a colourful Chinese entrepreneur. Peek in at the wonderful floor, gold ceiling mosaics and stained-glass windows.

Continuing up Sichuan Nanlu for 50m, Alley 126 on the right conceals a beautiful old brick *shíkùmén* (stone gatehouse). Look out also for the building at No 133 Sichuan Nanlu (Xinhua Bookstore offices) and its original faded sign announcing 'Imperial Chemical (China) Ltd'. At Fuzhou Lu turn right (east) and take a look at the **Tudor building 4** at No 44, the former offices of Calbeck Macgregor & Co, wine importers and agents in the 1930s for Martini & Rossi, Johnny Walker and others.

Backtrack west along Fuzhou Lu until you reach the corner of Fuzhou Lu and Jiangxi Nanlu, where you'll find the matching architecture of the **Hamilton House 5** (south) and the **Metropole Hotel 6** (north; see also p158), both built around 1934. The former was commissioned by David Sassoon and built by Palmer & Turner as an apartment complex. Both buildings had terraced rooftop gardens.

The best view is from the old **Municipal Council building 7**, the squat building on the northwest corner. The Bund Historical Museum (p87) has a wonderful photo of the building in the early 1950s when it was covered with a huge portrait of Mao. Government departments now occupy this whole block.

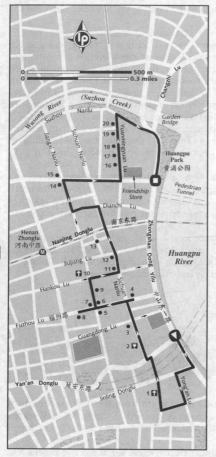

Fifty metres west is the former **American Club 8** at 209 Fuzhou Lu, built in 1924 in the American Georgian style with dark bricks imported from the USA. It's now the People's Court; an irony considering much of Fuzhou Lu west of this point was once lined with brothels, gambling houses and opium dens.

Head back to the Metropole Hotel and turn north past the **Bank of Communications 9**, at 200 Jiangxi Nanlu (you can go in to marvel at the marble interior), to the corner with Hankou Lu. The red brick building on the northwest corner is the Trinity Cathedral (1869), known to Chinese as the Hóng Miào, or **Red Temple 10**. Its tall steeple has long since gone.

Head east on Hankou Lu, once a street of publishers and presses. At the corner with Sichuan Lu lies the elegant portico of the **Guangdong Development Bank 11**, formerly the Joint Savings Society Bank (1928) and designed by Ladislaus Hudec (see p30 for more on the man). Across the street is an intriguing building with '1908' carved out underneath the lovely lintel.

One block north along Sichuan Lu is Jiujiang Lu, an old banking street, where you can see the **Bank of East Asia 12**, formerly the Continental Bank, on the southwest corner. Continue north past the **Zhongyang Market 13** on the left and look out for the charming pale green and then blue brick buildings ahead at the junction with Nanjing Donglu.

Continue north on Sichuan Lu to a collection of old red brick buildings darkened by pollution and perpetually strung, it seems, with enormous underpants. Turn left onto Dianchi Lu until you hit Jiangxi Nanlu (there's a nice Art Deco bank on the corner) and turn north past Ningbo Lu until you get to several impressive buildings – one is the **Electric Power Co 14**, another the **Everbright Bank 15** – at the junction with Beijing Donglu.

Head east past a graceful but woefully neglected building with beautiful balconies at 190 Beijing Donglu. When you get to the Friendship Store (there are toilets on the 2nd floor), either pop in for some shopping or turn north for, you guessed it, some nice **old buildings 16–20**, this time on Yuanmingyuan Lu, one of the least-touched streets in Shanghai. From here, head along Suzhou Nanlu to the Bund.

NANJING LU

China's Oxford St or Fifth Ave, Nanjing Lu is the most famous shopping street in China, with a reputed 1.7 million visitors per day on the weekend. Known to the Chinese as the *da malu,* or Great Horse Rd, it was famously classified in 1937 as one of the seven most interesting roads in the world. A large section was pedestrianised in 1999 so it's now a much more enjoyable place to stroll.

The eastern stretch of the road is of minor interest, though there are some nice architectural touches if you look up, particularly at the crossing with Sichuan Nanlu. One thing you might not have been expecting is the sex shop, diagonally across the road from the Peace Hotel. No 181, at the corner with Jiangxi Nanlu is the impressive Art Deco former **Shanghai Electric Power Building** 1. The crossing with Henan Lu was once home to Shanghai's first racecourse (opened 1862).

Walk Facts

Start Peace Hotel, Nanjing Donglu
End Shanghai Art Museum, cnr Huangpi Beilu

Nanjing Lu was once lined with specialist shops but only a few remain. Look out for **Duoyunxuan** 2 (422 Nanjing Donglu; no English sign), a painting and calligraphy supplies shop which dates from 1900, and **Shaowansheng** (No 414), a venerable local food store that specialises in local sweets and cured meats (even dried pigs' faces) from Shanghai, Shaoxing and Ningbo.

At No 429 is the former **Sincere** 3, the first department store on Nanjing Lu (1917), which got its name because it was the first store to introduce fixed prices. In 1937 a misguided Chinese or Japanese bomb fell on the store, leaving 100 dead and 600 wounded in the wreckage.

As you continue along Nanjing Donglu you will pass many of the great department stores of the 1930s. At No 635 is the Hualian Commercial Building, formerly **Wing On** 4 (1918). Wing On recently opened a new department store on Nanjing Lu, this time at the western end.

The No 1 Provisions Store, at No 720, was formerly the **Sun Sun Store** 5, built in 1926. Just as today, old Shanghai's department stores used whatever gimmicks to win customers, offering live bands and at one time even a dwarf to get attention. Sun Sun went as far as installing a 6th-floor radio studio where customers could watch local stars perform. Brave the crowds to check out the amazing variety of dried mushrooms, ginseng and sea cucumber, the latter priced at Y3400 (US$425) per 500g!

Further on, the corner of Guizhou Lu marks the site of the notorious 30 May Massacre of 1925, when a dozen or so unarmed Chinese were killed by British police during anti-Japanese protests.

At No 800, the No 1 Department Store (p146), formerly **Sun Company** 6, opened in 1936 and was the first store on the road to boast an escalator, 30 years before the first of these arrived in Hong Kong. For years the store has been the largest in China and still is, in its most recent reincarnation in Pudong. The next mammoth store is **New World**, originally built in 1915 as an amusement centre.

Just off Nanjing Donglu, at the intersection of Xizang Lu and Jiujiang Lu is **Mu'en Church** 7, formerly the Moore Memorial Church. Sunday services are still held at 7.30am, 9.30am, 2pm and 7pm.

From here Nanjing Donglu becomes Nanjing Xilu (former Bubbling Well Rd) and curves around the former racecourse, which covered what is now Renmin Square and Renmin Park.

The **Pacific Hotel** 8, formerly the China United Apartment Building, has some lovely details in its entrance lobby.

The dark brown building at No 170 is the **Park Hotel** 9 (p158), originally built as a bank in 1934; with 22 floors it was the highest building in the Far East in the 1930s. The top-floor restaurant (whose roof once slid back so that guests could wine and dine under the stars) and dance floor are still there. The lobby is worth a quick look.

The nearby **Grand Theatre 10** isn't up to much today but was the best theatre in Shanghai at the time of opening in 1933. It had 2000 sofa-style seats equipped with earphones for simultaneous translation.

The walk finishes at the junction of Nanjing Donglu and Huangpi Beilu. Here you'll find the old racecourse grandstand, which is now the **Shanghai Art Museum 11** (p63). From here you can head east to Renmin Square, or branch off west to the Jiangyin Lu Bird & Flower Market.

FRENCH CONCESSION I

The French Concession's grand avenues and impressive architecture provide fabulous inspiration for walks. From Huangpi Lu metro station head south down Huangpi Nanlu. When you cross Taicang Lu pause to look at the old brick building at **No 127 1**,

Walk Facts

Start Huangpi Lu metro station
End Hengshan Lu

where Mao and the other communist delegates stayed (in a girls' dormitory) while attending the first Communist Party congress. Continue south past the renovated *shíkūméns* of the **Xintiandi complex**. At Xingye Lu turn right and visit the site of the **1st National Congress of the CCP 2** (p70).

From here head west, across Chongqing Nanlu and along Nanchang Lu. At café-lined Yandang Lu head south and pass through Fuxing Park (p68). Exit at the west side passing the very chic café Park 97 (p127), and continue west along Gaolan Lu to get a look at the former Russian Orthodox **St Nicholas Church 3**. The church was built in 1933 in dedication to the murdered Tsar of Russia, and now houses the Ashanti Dome restaurant. Note the icon of Chairman Mao painted by a caretaker during the Cultural Revolution (when it was a washing machine cooperative) to protect the church. Outside dining times the staff will normally let you in to see the upper floor dome and restored frescoes.

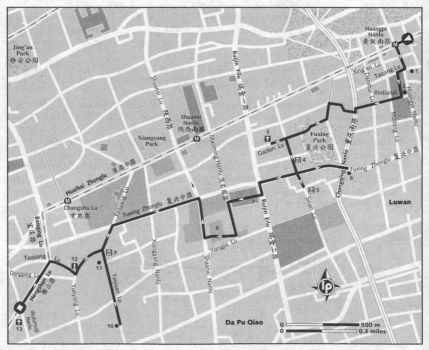

Walking Tours – French Concession I

Sun Yatsen immortalised in the garden of his former home (below)

From here walk south down Sinan Lu (formerly Rue Massenet) past the former residences of **Sun Yatsen 4** and **Zhou Enlai 5**. This precinct is lined with beautiful old residences.

If you're interested, at the corner of Fuxing Zhonglu (formerly Rue Lafayette) you can walk a block east to see the apartment block on the southeast corner which was once home to US communist sympathiser and journalist **Agnes Smedley 6**. Otherwise, back at the corner of Fuxing Zhonglu and Sinan Lu, head west to Ruijin Erlu (formerly Route des Soeurs) and then south to the **Ruijin Guest House 7**. This is the former Morris estate, home to Mohowk Morris, the founder of the *North China Daily News*, and his sons Harry and Hayley, who were famous racehorse and dog owners. You can stroll around the complex. The beautiful but pricey Face bar (p127) will tempt if you are in need of liquid refreshment. Chen Yi, the first mayor of Shanghai, once used this building as an office.

From here walk through the complex to the western exit on Maoming Nanlu (formerly Rue Cardinal Mercier), currently Shanghai's premier bar strip. When the bars start to peter out take an alley west which leads into a huge **flower market 8** in what is Cultural Square. This was once the site of the Canidrome, the French dog track, which opened in 1928 to a capacity crowd of 50,000.

From here head north to Fuxing Zhonglu, then west and take a left to Fenyang Lu (formerly Route Pichon). One block south of here is the wonderful building of the **Shanghai Arts & Crafts Museum 9** (p69), built in 1905 as the residence of a high-ranking French Concession official and later home to Chen Yi.

Just south of here is the Shanghai Ear, Nose and Throat Hospital, once the beautiful **Shanghai Jewish Hospital 10**. History buffs can continue five minutes down Taiyuan Lu to the **Taiyuan Villa 11**, where General Marshall, US mediator between Mao and Chiang Kaishek, resided between 1945 and 1949.

Alternatively, head west along Fenyang past the statue of **Pushkin 12**, erected by White Russians on the centenary of Pushkin's death in 1937, smashed by Red Guards in 1966 and rebuilt in 1987. Continue along Dongping Lu to No 9, once the residence of Chiang Kaishek, and later, Jiang Qing (Mao's wife).

You are now at Hengshan Lu (formerly Ave Petain), Shanghai's premier strip of foreign restaurants. Here at No 53 you'll find the English-style **Community Church 13**, built in 1924 as the largest Christian church in Shanghai and later turned into a gym during the Cultural Revolution. Sunday services (☎ 6437 6576) are at 7.30am, 10am and 7pm in Chinese and at 4pm in English. The imposing building opposite the church is the former American School. The stately nearby 41 Hengshan Lu is a luxury serviced apartment block, home to Shanghai's latest batch of foreign taipans.

From here you can get a meal at Yang's, Bai's or one of the Western restaurants on Hengshan Lu (p125), or take the metro home.

FRENCH CONCESSION II

From Shaanxi Nanlu metro station head north up Maoming Nanlu to the **Garden Hotel 1**, originally constructed as the French Club, or Cercle Sportif Français, in 1926. The club was subsequently used by the US army in the 1940s before being converted to the People's Cultural Palace after Liberation. Mao stayed in the building in 1959. The eastern entrance of the hotel features a gold mosaic statuary niche and the original staircase

Walk Facts

Start Shaanxi Nanlu metro station
End Hilton Hotel

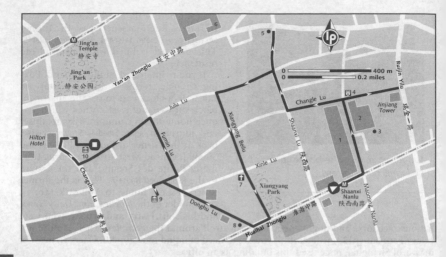

leading up to the ballroom with its beautiful, stained-glass ceiling piece. On the 2nd floor, the columns are capped with nude reliefs, concealed during the Cultural Revolution and now unveiled in their former splendour. The former Art Deco pool is now the Oasis Café, but in summertime the 3rd-floor terrace allows lovely views of the garden and the eastern window lintel.

To the east of the Garden Hotel is the **Jinjiang Hotel** 2 (p162). The north block, built as the Cathay Mansions in 1929, was where Zhou Enlai and President Nixon signed the Shanghai Communique in 1972, marking China's return to the world community after the isolation of the Cultural Revolution. Shanghai's diplomatic community was held under house arrest in the building in 1941 when the Japanese took control of the city. To the south is **Grosvenor House** 3, a plush 1930s apartment block.

Continue north to Changle Lu and you'll see the **Lyceum Theatre** 4, once home to the British Amateur Dramatic Club (built 1931) and now an unremarkable cinema. From here you can take a detour one block east to the Jinjiang Tower and take the external lift to the 41st floor for great views of the city.

Heading back west along Changle Lu, turn right up Shaanxi Lu (formerly Ave Roi Albert) to **Moller House** 5, at No 30, one of the most fantastic buildings built in the 1930s (1938). The Scandinavian-influenced gothic peaks could double as the Munsters' holiday home. The Swedish owner, Eric Moller, was the owner of Moller Line and was a huge racing fan. Previously home to the Communist Youth League, the building now houses a hotel, the Hengshan Moller Villa (p161), so you can pop in and admire the wood panelling. The **Shanghai Exhibition Centre** 6 is nearby on Yan'an Zhonglu.

Head back south, go one block west at Changle Lu and then head south down Xiangyang Beilu. On the corner with Xinle Lu is the lovely blue-domed **Orthodox Russian Mission Church** 7 (1934). The church now houses a restaurant, after years hosting an ungodly securities exchange. Next door, the Grape Restaurant (p108), is a good place to grab lunch if you're hungry.

Head down to busy Huaihai Zhonglu (formerly Ave Joffre, named after the commander of the French army in WWI), past the entrance to Xiangyang Park, a haven for elderly chess players, and turn right to Donghu Lu. Here at the corner, hidden behind elegant Art Deco gates, is the **former house of the gangster Du Yuesheng** 8, which at one time also served as an opium warehouse, movie studio and part of the American consulate.

From here, head up Donghu Lu to the junction and take Changle Lu. Hidden down lane No 637 Changle Lu, at No 24, is the **Chinese Printed Blue Nankeen Exhibition Hall** 9, which is worth a visit if you are a fan of Shanghai's famous blue cloth (p148).

Head north up Fumin Lu and take a left into Julu Lu, Shanghai's late-night bar strip, and then turn right into Changshu Lu. At Lane No 303 Huashan Lu take a look at No 16, the **former residence of Cai Yuanpei** 10 (admission Y5; ☉ 9am-4pm), an early-20th-century intellectual,

Top Five Markets

Shanghai doesn't have the best markets in China but a few are worth a visit. The following are ranked in order of interest:

- **Dongtai Lu Antique Market** (p148; Map pp254-5) Antiques old and new make this a fun place to shop, where the French Concession meets the Old Town.
- **Flower, Bird, Fish & Insect Market** (p96; Map pp254-5) Near Dongtai Lu Antique Market, creepy crickets, bug-eyed goldfish and chattering birds rule the roost here.
- **Jiangyin Lu Bird & Flower Market** (Map pp244-5; east end of Renmin Sq) Check out the traditional architecture of the school at No 101 and the small indoor market at No 150.
- **Cultural Square Flower Market** (p93; Map pp246-9) Shanghai's sweetest-smelling and most colourful market between Maoming Nanlu and Shaanxi Nanlu, near Yongjia Lu – but slated for demolition.
- **New Shanghai Metropolis Flower Market** (Map pp244-5) Not as pleasant as the Cultural Square market, but it's the biggest in town, with 350 stalls. Located behind Shanghai No 1 Department Store on Xizang Zhonglu.

educator and reformist. The picturesque lane is full of beautiful old houses. Here you are opposite the Hilton, where you can take a taxi home or step in for a break.

OLD TOWN

The Old Town is a fascinating place in which to wander and though it holds its secrets well, propinquity dictates that life is often on display in the streets. It's common to see people emptying their chamber pots (few houses have flush toilets here), airing duvets, playing cards and sunning themselves

Walk Facts

Start Fangbang Zhonglu, on the south side of Yuyuan Bazaar
End The city's Islam centre

in winter. At every turn you might hear the hiss of a wok, dodge a pole of drying laundry, or marvel at gutted ducks strung up for curing – though giant housing blocks now pressure the old lanes from all directions.

From the southern entry to the Yuyuan Bazaar head east along Fangbang Zhonglu, once a canal, past an old **stage 1** to several traditional inns, selling snacks and tubes of warmed *huángjiǔ* (Shaoxing rice wine). One of the nicest of these is the **Shenyonghe Inn 2**.

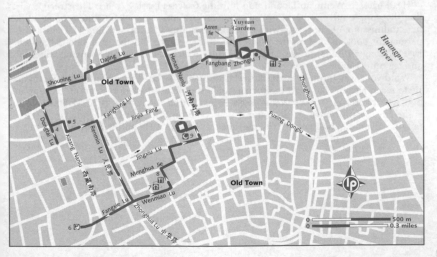

Seafood for sale, Flower, Bird, Fish & Insect Market, Old Town (see right)

Further along the road is the pastel-blue building of a traditional Chinese medicine clinic. From here you can explore any of the surrounding alleys like Anren Jie or Danfeng Jie, before heading back along Fangbang Zhonglu (also known as Old St) to Henan Nanlu. See p147 for details of shops along this street.

From this corner head north a block to Dajing Lu, once a centre of opium dens, now a vibrant produce market. At the west end of the market is the **Dajingge 3** (built 1815), which contains the only preserved section of the 5km-long city walls. The walls were built in 1553 to protect the city against pirates but were torn down in 1912. Admission to the gateway and its (Chinese only) displays on the history of the Old Town is Y5. Look out for the nearby shops selling oil and alcohol in traditional old jars.

From here head south, then west to Xizang Nanlu, where you can take a look at **Dongtai Lu Antique Market 4**, Shanghai's most interesting 'antiques' market. On the eastern side of the road is the **Flower, Bird, Fish & Insect Market 5**, which provides a fascinating stroll among bird and cricket cages, fish aquariums and garden supplies.

Head back to Renmin Lu, where you can either take Fangbang Lu back to Yuyuan Gardens, take bus No 911 to Huaihai Zhonglu, or continue south, following the course of the former city walls.

At Wenmiao Lu take a five-minute diversion west to visit the **Baiyun (White Cloud) Taoist Temple 6** (Báiyún Guān; admission Y2) on Xilinhou Lu; the temple was the birthplace of the Quanzhen sect of Taoism. Built in 1873, there's not much to see except the statue by the entrance, which seems to be giving the finger to anyone who enters! The temple has been sidelined by recent apartment tower construction. If you are lucky you'll get to hear Taoist music played by priests.

Head back to Wenmiao Lu and pop into the **Confucian Temple 7** (p66). The streets encircling the temple offer some nice views. Sunday attracts a popular Chinese book market here (admission Y1) in fitting with the temple's status as a former library. There's also a permanent book market on the north side of the temple. On the west side is the **Kongyiji Jiujia 8** (Kǒngyǐjī Jiǔjiā), a great traditional inn, which serves cheap Shaoxing wine, food and tea until 10pm.

Wind your way through the back streets of Menghua Jie, Zhuangjia Jie and Xicangqiao Jie to reach Henan Nanlu. At the corner you'll see a Hui Moslem restaurant, recognisable by its Arabic script. The **Xiaotaoyuan Mosque 9**, just round the corner at 52 Xiaotaoyuan Lu, is the city's main centre of Islam and if you come on Friday at lunch time you'll see the faithful streaming in to prayer. The mosque was built in 1917 and is named after a nearby peach garden. From here you can head back to Fangbang Zhonglu.

Eating

Eating

Beijing may be the political heart of China but it's Shanghai where China's culinary revolution is unfolding. When it comes to stylish and cutting-edge cuisine Shanghai leaves Beijing in the dust. It's a full-time (but highly enjoyable) job keeping up with all the new restaurants that spring up daily around town. To catch up with the current favourites see the various listings magazines or the annual *Shanghai Restaurant Guide* (Y50), published by *That's Shanghai*.

If you are looking for a quick authentic meal, Shanghai's side streets are lined with snack stalls and small restaurants serving cheap, local food, though you'll need the Chinese menu decoder in the Food & Drink chapter (p33) to make sense of most menus. You can fill up at these cheap eats for well under Y30 per person.

Fast-food outlets in both genuine and counterfeit form cater to the masses everywhere, and there are countless branches of KFC (Kěndéjī), Pizza Hut (Bìshèngkè) and McDonald's (Màidānglǎo), plus Subway, TCBY, Taco Bell Grande, Häagen-Dazs and even a Kenny Rogers' Roasters! Subway costs Y14 to Y26 for a 6- to 12-inch sandwich; Pizza Hut Y45 to Y85 for a 9- to 12-inch pizza.

A favourite with teen urbanites are the city's food courts, which can be found in most department stores. They may not offer *haute cuisine* but they do provide an opportunity to sample a range of food without having to navigate a Chinese menu; just prepay with a magnetic card, point at the dim sum, noodles, curry dishes or drinks and remember to redeem the excess afterwards. Make sure the hot dishes are steaming or prepared fresh for you.

Moving up a culinary rung, Shanghai's restaurants offer an amazing variety of cuisines, from Hangzhou to Hunanese, Thai to teppanyaki. 'Asian fusion', a much over-used concept, is currently all the rage, though the one thing that links all of Shanghai's better restaurants is an impeccable sense of style and interior design. As with most things Shanghainese, looking good is an essential part of the package.

At the top end you can expect to pay from Y200 per meal, more if you dress it up with drinks and appetisers, which is still pretty good value by international standards. Many mid-range and top-end restaurants serve particularly good-value lunch specials so you can save money by eating heavy for lunch and light for dinner.

There are great restaurants all over town but if you simply can't make up your mind where to go, you're bound to find something at Xintiandi, where a couple of dozen stylish restaurants and bars await your custom, along with a row of taxis to take you back home.

Some Shanghai restaurants have several branches around town. They include Itoya, Gino's, Simply Thai, Bi Feng Tang, Pizza Italia and Lulu's. To find the one nearest to you check under Eating in the index (p238).

For a rundown of the food on offer and some cultural pointers on what to expect dining out in Shanghai see the Food & Drink chapter (p33). For information on tipping practices see the Directory (p216).

Best Splurge

- **T8** (p107) For when you need to impress.
- Martinis in the **Glamour Bar** (p125) followed by dinner at **M on the Bund** (p100) and then back to the Glamour Bar.
- Cocktails at the **Face** (p127) followed by dinner at **Lan Na Thai** (p104) or **Hazara** (p104).
- Anything in the **Grand Hyatt** (p110) but remember to gaze at your date not the jaw-dropping window views.
- Sunday brunch at the **Portman Ritz-Carlton** (p167).

Self-catering

Shanghai has over 5000 convenience stores, most of them 24-hour; the most prevalent are Lawson, Kedi and Allday. Seven-Elevens are expected to arrive en masse in 2005. A step up are the growing number of local supermarkets such as Hualian, Lianhua, Homegain (Jiādélì) and Tops (Dǐngdǐngxiān). Short-term visitors will find most of what they need here, though long-term visitors will need to look elsewhere for breads, dairy products, wine and meats. One convenient place is the supermarket in the basement of the Parkson department store at Huaihai Lu and Shaanxi Nanlu. There's a smaller supermarket in the basement of the Westgate Mall.

ALL CHINA NATIVE PRODUCTS & SPECIALTY FOODS Map pp250-2
Quánguótǔ Tèchǎn Shípǐn Gōngsī
451 Huaihai Lu
This old-timer stocks more than 5000 speciality foods from around China.

BAUERNSTUBE Map p256
☎ 6275 8888; Sheraton Grand Taipingyang;
5 Zunyi Nanlu
Probably the best cheeses, cakes, bread and meats in Shanghai, with a central European twist, and there's a little café attached. There are other good hotel delis at the Westin and Hilton hotels.

CARREFOUR Map p256
Jiālèfú
Shuisheng Lu, Gubei; ⌚ 8.30am-10pm
The French chain is currently the only foreign supermarket that actually turns a profit and at weekends the place is packed, largely because prices are the same as those in Chinese supermarkets. You can find everything from imported wines to French bread. There are branches south of the city at the **Friendship South store** (☎ 3412 4688; 7388 Huimin Lu) and east of the city in **Jinqiao** (☎ 5899 1899; 279 Biyun Lu).

CITY SUPERMARKET Map pp250-2
Chéngshì Chāoshì
☎ 6279 8018; Shanghai Centre, Nanjing Xilu;
deliveries all branches ☎ 6391 0765
For the imported goodies you just can't get anywhere else, at a price. The Shanghai Centre branch has 50% off bakery items after 7pm. The branch at **Times Square** (Map pp254-5; ☎ 6267 4248; basement, 99 Huaihai Zhonglu) has a good deli with some of the cheapest brewed coffee in town (Y8). Gubei expats can visit the branch at **Hongqiao** (Map pp242-3; ☎ 6446 1110; 3211 Hongmei Lu). There is also a free delivery service.

CROISSANT DE FRANCE
Map pp244-5   Bakery
Kèsòng
Cheap breakfasts are best done DIY in Shanghai and this chain is handy for its freshly baked croissants (most branches have recently stopped

Top Five Delivery
- **Yellow Submarine** (Huángse Qián Shuǐ Tǐng; Gubei ☎ 6401 2774, Pudong ☎ 5843 1113) Free delivery of its excellent pizzas and subs until midnight. A 10-inch pizza with unlimited toppings costs Y54; a 6-inch torpedo costs Y22.
- **Sherpa** (☎ 6209 6209; www.sherpa.com.cn) delivers from over 20 restaurants around town until 10pm for a charge of around Y15, depending on the distance. See the website for menus.
- **Melrose Pizza** (Měiluōsī; ☎ 6467 7114) Free pizza delivery until 2am. There are branches at **1 Tongren Lu** (Map pp250-2), **207 Maoming Nanlu** (Map pp246-9), **838 Hengshan Lu** (Map pp246-9) and next to the Intercontinental Hotel on Zhangyang Lu in **Pudong** (Map pp242-3). You can also get a traditional diner-style breakfast at Mike's Diner at the Maoming Nanlu branch.
- **Pizza Hut** (Gubei delivery ☎ 6867 1100)
- **Montrose Wine** (www.montrosechina.com) A wide range of plonk delivered right to your doorstep in case you're not in a fit state to drive.

serving coffee, which is a shame). There's a branch on Jiangxi Zhonglu near Nanjing Donglu, and another at the corner of Sichuan Nanlu and Jinling Donglu, a block from the Bund.

GLENMORE DELI Map pp242-3
Xǐyì Shípǐn Shānghǎng
☎ 6464 8665; www.chinadeli.com; 196 Guyi Lu, off Wuzhong Lu; ⌚ 9am-10pm
Another expat favourite, its door is disguised in a wild yellow mural. It stocks hard-to-find goodies like Vegemite, sun-dried tomatoes and Australian meats and wines.

THE BUND & NANJING DONGLU
Fast-food joints are sprinkled liberally around the Bund and Nanjing Donglu to cater to the endless stream of disoriented tourists and exhausted shoppers. There's also a scattering of famous old restaurants that are worth trying at least once. The Bund is set to be thrust into the culinary spotlight with the opening of the much-lauded Jean Georges and Laris by 2004, joining M on the Bund as the classiest joints in town. Over in

Renmin Square, **Kathleen's Fifth** (☎ 6327 0004; 325 Nanjing Xilu) is set to open in 2004 on the roof of the Shanghai Art Museum (entrance next to the Grand Theatre), promising fine views of Shanghai's central skyline.

JUELIN RESTAURANT
Map pp244-5   *Vegetarian*
Juélín Shūshíchù
☎ 6326 0115; 250 Jinling Donglu; dishes Y16-22;
🕑 11am-1.30pm, 5pm-7.30pm
One of Shanghai's most famous vegetarian restaurants, it's divided like most of the city's older restaurants into a cheap fly-blown ground level and a pricier upper floor. Dining hours are limited so get there early.

M ON THE BUND
Map pp244-5   *Continental/Modern*
☎ 6350 9988; www.m-onthebund.com; 7th fl, 20 Guangdong Lu; dinner mains Y160-220, 2-/3-course set lunch Y98/118
Michelle Garnaut has taken her renowned skills from Hong Kong's M on the Fringe to create this modern Shanghai icon, where the city elite and local foodies congregate to schmooze over a modern and eclectic range of dishes. How about oysters warmed with spinach, bacon and hollandaise sauce or the signature leg of lamb, followed by a traditional-style Sussex Pond lemon pudding

Outdoor dining at M on the Bund (above)

or the much-touted M pavlova? Oh, yes. And there's the magnificent terrace view of the Bund (diners only, reservations essential), one of the city's best. If you don't feel like dinner, it's worth having a drink at least (there's a fine selection of wines).

M also serves a weekend brunch (Y198 two courses, Y218 three courses; 11.30am to 3pm), a fine Sunday afternoon tea of scones and clotted cream (Y88; 3.30pm to 5.30pm) and special post-theatre menus for major events. It's also *the* place to admire the Bund fireworks on National Day or Chinese New Year. Expect to blow around Y300 a head here.

PREGO Map pp244-5   *Italian*
☎ 6335 1888; Westin Hotel, 2nd fl, 88 Henan Zhonglu; mains Y100-150
The Westin's flagship restaurant offers homemade pasta and pizzas perked up by dishes like beef carpaccio and mussel stew with garlic bread, or fettucine with Maine lobster and saffron (Y112). Sit in the bright and buzzy main hall, pick up some culinary tips at the open-plan kitchen, or just pop in for an espresso at the to-die-for dessert bar (Y48). Purists will enjoy the 50 types of grappa.

WANG BAOHE RESTAURANT
Map pp244-5   *Crab*
Wáng Bǎohé Jiǔjiā
☎ 6320 7609; 603 Fuzhou Lu; crab meals Y200
This 250-year-old restaurant claims to be the oldest in Shanghai. It specialises in extravagant crab dishes, from crab-roe dumplings to whole hairy crabs, all washed down with the Wang Baohe's own special Shaoxing-style wine, none of which comes cheap.

XINYA Map pp244-5   *Cantonese*
Xīnyǎ Cháguǎn
☎ 6322 4393; 719 Nanjing Donglu; dishes Y18-50
It's refreshing to see a Shanghai restaurant that has avoided the temptation to go all chic and minimalist. Xinya (Sunya in Cantonese) is a huge restaurant dating from 1927, now adjoining the Ramada Plaza. The 2nd floor serves dim sum during the day, while other floors serve good value à la carte Cantonese cuisine. Try the roasted crispy duck (Y75) and the trusty beef in oyster sauce or be more adventurous with the stewed snake in a secret recipe. The English menu smooths things along.

Eating – The Bund & Nanjing Donglu

Food Streets

For all kinds of restaurants at all kinds of budgets, Shanghai has several streets devoted almost exclusively to the art of feeding your face.

- **Zhapu Lu** (Map pp244-5; bus 55) Close to the Pujiang Hotel, with dozens of restaurants. Even if you don't eat here, check out the great aquariums at Nos 88 and 324.
- **Huanghe Lu** (Map pp244-5) Behind the Park Hotel and just off Nanjing Donglu, this is another busy street, though restaurant touts can be pushy here.
- **Yunnan Lu** (Map pp244-5) Houses some interesting speciality restaurants. Gigantic **Xiao Shaoxing**, at No 118, specialises in cold boiled chicken, while **Xiao Jinling**, at No 28, specialises in salted duck. You can also get Beijing duck, Moslem noodles and Uyghur kebabs here.
- **Wujiang Lu Snack Food Street** (Map pp250-2) A less famous collection of cheap restaurants off Nanjing Xilu. There's nothing special here but there are lots of cheap (Chinese menu only) places.
- **Grand Gateway** (Map p257) A food street of sorts, it includes branches of **Wujing Tang, Ajisen Ramen, Gino Café, Pizza Hut** and the demonically tasty **Kyros Kebab**. Next door is a huge collection of restaurants called the **Hongji Free Plaza**.

Cheap Eats

BONOMI CAFÉ Map pp244-5   *Café*
Bōnuòmi Kāfēidiàn

☎ 6329 7506; Room 226, 12 Zhongshan Dongyilu; coffee Y25-32

Bonomi is an Italian chain that has cleverly set up shop in some of Shanghai's best locations. Our favourite is here on the Bund, hidden in the Whitehall-like corridors of the former building of the HSBC. Take a rousing espresso (Y15) onto the superb terrace and pick from an array of Italian drinks, sandwiches and cakes. Very cool.

DONGHAI CAFÉ Map pp244-5   *Café*
Dōnghǎi Kāfēiguǎn

☎ 6321 1940; 145 Nanjing Donglu; coffee Y12

At last, a place with reasonably priced coffee within reach of the Bund! If you're trekking up and down Nanjing Donglu on a budget the Donghai is a real lifesaver. Downstairs serves decent coffee (and even beer) and there are also cheap set meals. Upstairs is more comfortable but a tad more expensive.

XINGHUA LOU Map pp244-5   *Cantonese*
Xìnghuā Lóu

☎ 6355 3777; 343 Fuzhou Lu; dim sum Y5-10, dishes Y20-40

This old-school dinosaur has been pumping out quality Cantonese dishes and dim sum since the reign of Emperor Xianfeng. There is something for everyone here, with a bakery selling savoury dumplings, a ground-floor canteen serving oily hot-and-sour soup (Y5) and Cantonese dim sum (like *shāomài* – meat-filled pockets of noodle dough) and an upper-floor

restaurant offering reasonably priced Cantonese food. Ask for the English menu.

OLD TOWN

The Yuyuan Gardens and Bazaar area offers excellent snack food, a couple of famous old restaurants and branches of most major chains.

GREEN WAVE GALLERY
Map pp254-5   *Chinese*
Lǜbōlàng Jiǔlóu

☎ 6328 0602; Yuyuan Bazaar; dim sum sets Y50 or Y100

Tour groups flock to this traditional building, partly because of its location overlooking the Mid-Lake Pavilion Teahouse, and partly because the décor and views fit the quintessential image of old China (ah, mastaaah...). The food's not bad but is pricey for what is only marginally better than that served downstairs by street vendors. There's one advantage though: the English menu.

NANXIANG STEAMED BUN
RESTAURANT Map pp254-5   *Snacks*
Nánxiáng Mántoúdiàn

378 Fuyou Lu, Yuyuan Bazaar; dumplings Y8

You can spot this place by the queues of salivating Chinese outside, waiting impatiently for the city's most famous *xiǎolóngbāo* (see p38), made by an assembly line of white-coated Chinese matrons. Join the masses and grab a takeaway or try your luck for an upstairs table, with its bustling dim sum trolleys and fine views of the Mid-Lake Pavilion Teahouse. You won't even get near the place on the weekends.

Uyghur & Muslim Food

Most of Shanghai's Muslim restaurants are run by Uyghurs – Central Asians from the Xinjiang region of western China. A tasty alternative to the seafood and sweetness of Shanghainese cuisine, Xinjiang dishes consist of lots of mutton (though chicken and beef dishes are available), peppers, potatoes, spices, and delicious nan (flat bread). Shanghai's other main Muslim food is that of the Hui, represented in Shanghai by Lanzhou-style noodles. Uyghurs have largely cornered the lucrative street-corner mutton kebab trade.

One good reason to try a Uyghur restaurant is to savour the conspicuously non-Han Chinese atmosphere. Recordings of swirling Central Asian lute music complement the Arabic calligraphy on the walls and meals are washed down with a *piala* (bowl) of Central Asian green tea *(kok chai)*.

Try *shashlyk* (shish kebabs), *suoman* (delicious fried noodle squares) or *laghman* (long noodles). Vegetarians should ask for *goshtsiz* (without meat). To avoid mutton overdose, try the generally excellent *chon tashlick tokhor* (Chinese: *dàpánjī* – fried chicken, peppers and potatoes). Fancier places sell fruity Xinjiang wines like Loulan (named after a ruined Silk Road city).

The main **Uyghur restaurant ghetto** (Map pp244-5; Xinjiang restaurants) has traditionally been Zhejiang Zhonglu, between Guangdong Lu and Yan'an Donglu, though recent deconstruction has reduced the quarter to a fraction of its former self and what remains is still under threat. Most call themselves the 'Xinjiang Restaurant', or Xinjiang Mussulman Ashkanas in Uyghur.

Our favourite Uyghur restaurants in town are:

Afanti Restaurant (p113)

Pamir Restaurant (Pami'er Cānting; Map pp246-9; Fumin Lu) Below street level, recognisable by shouts from Uygur kebabmeisters, the Pamir does decent kebabs, nan and more, washed down by a Xinjiang beer.

Taklamakan Restaurant (Map pp253-4) Authentic but sometimes glum place with good barbecued lamb (Y22) and *dàpánjī* (Y45), with a German and English menu. It's near the Ocean Hotel.

FRENCH CONCESSION

From department store restaurants to restored old villas, the French Concession holds Shanghai's widest selection of restaurants, from French to Thai, catering to anyone's wildest culinary fantasies.

1001 NIGHTS

Map pp246-9   *Lebanese/Middle Eastern*
☎ 6473 1178; www.1001nights.com.cn; 4 Hengshan Lu; mezes Y25-40, mains Y60-70; ☺ belly dancers 8-11pm
The stars of the show here (apart from the Uyghur belly dancers, of course) are the mezes and salads, with everything from tabouleh to baba ganoush. Heavier fare stretches to grilled meats and couscous but leave space for a baklava, Turkish coffee and a toke on the hookah (hubble-bubble) to round the evening off. Bismillah!

1221 Map pp242-3   *Shanghainese*
☎ 6213 2441; 1221 Yan'an Xilu
No-one has a bad thing to say about this stylish expat favourite. Meat dishes cost around Y28 to Y38, and the plentiful eel, shrimp and squid dishes are around twice this. The crispy duck (Y48) is excellent, as are the drunken chicken and *yóutiáo niǔròu* (beef with dough

strips). The pan-fried sticky rice and sweet bean paste (from the dim sum menu) makes a good dessert. It's also worth ordering the eight-fragrance tea just to watch it served spectacularly out of 60cm-long spouts. The service is excellent.

1931 Map pp246-9   *Café*
☎ 6472 5264; 112 Maoming Lu; coffee Y30
This small, warm café, outfitted with a 1930s theme, is one of the nicest places for a break. There are set meals for around Y60 that come with soup and fruit and give you a half-price drink, plus good, if somewhat pricey, Shanghainese snacks.

BACI/TOKIO JOE'S

Map pp246-9   *Italian/Japanese*
☎ 5383 2208; www.lankwaifong.com; 2 Gaolan Lu; pasta Y90-110
Fashionable people and fashionable food are the hallmarks of these two restaurants, which along with a bar and the California Club (p129) make up Park 97 (p127), the Shanghai incarnation of Hong Kong's 1997 Group. Baci in particular is classy without being flash (so rare in Shanghai), with crisp linen and a décor

Nanxiang Steamed Bun Restaurant (p101)

of cream and dark brown. Upmarket Italian dishes are the order of the day here; try the tagliatelle with soft-shell crabs in fresh tomato and thyme sauce (Y113), rounded off by home-made pistachio and hazelnut ice cream with chocolate sauce. Remember to ask for the daily specials. The outside seating by the entrance to Fuxing Park is glorious in summer.

The other half of this slightly schizophrenic place is Tokio Joe's, a tiny Japanese place heavy on the sushi and sashimi (Y40 to Y80).

BAOLUO JIULOU

Map pp246-9   *Shanghainese*
Bǎoluō Jiǔlóu
☎ 5403 7239; 271 Fumin Lu; dishes Y20-50
Once you've mastered the basics of a Chinese menu, gather up a boisterous bunch of friends and join the Shanghainese night owls who queue down the street all through the night to get into this amazingly busy place. It's open 24 hours and is always packed; a great place to get a feel for Shanghai's famous buzz. Try the excellent *rùishi niúpái* (Swiss steak), *géli shīzitóu* (lion's head with clams) or *shī tóuzi* (mandarin fish). There's no English menu.

CAFÉ MONTMARTRE Map pp246-9 *French*
Mèngmàntè Xīcānguǎn
☎ 5404 7658; 55 Xiangyang Nanlu
After dodging the fake-Rolex sellers in neigh-bouring Xiangyang Market, take refuge in this

arrondissement hideaway, serving up such Gallic gastronomic goodies as *moules frites* (mussels and fries, Y68), house foie gras, ba-guettes, crepes and quiche. The décor is pure French brasserie, with café tables, a downstairs bar for a reviving espresso or aperitif and an upstairs terrace overlooking the market; all in all a fine place to smoke, gesticulate wildly and discuss existentialism. Blackboards spell out the plats du jour.

COFFEE CLUB Map pp254-5 *Café/Western*
☎ 5382 8370; 8 Jinan Lu; mains Y50, coffee from Y22
The sofa-lined windows make this bright and breezy place particularly popular with expats who live in the nearby Somerset Mansions. Meals range from Italian to Malaysian, with crepes and iced coffees for dessert. This is also a good place for a wide range of break-fasts (7am to noon), including Belgian waffles (Y29). It also serves hard-to-find decaf coffee and sells coffee beans. Happy hour (buy one get one free) runs from 5pm to 8pm (7pm for cocktails). This is the only place in Shanghai to try 'lees' fruit beers from Montreal, aged in the bottle without additives or pasteurisation.

DISHUIDONG Map pp246-9 *Hunanese*
Dīshuǐdòng
☎ 6253 2689; 2nd fl, 56 Maoming Nanlu;
mains Y28-45
Shanghai's favourite Hunanese restaurant is surprisingly downhome (with waitresses decked

out in Hunanese blue cloth) but serves up killer cuisine. Try the *làzi jīdīng* (fried chicken with chilli) or one of the excellent claypot dishes and brace yourself for a chilli onslaught. Milder dishes include the wonderful spare ribs or braised spring chicken with ginger (Y38), plus the crowd-pleasing caramelised bananas for dessert. You'll need to line up plenty of cold beers to cool the palate. There's an English menu, though as ever, the Chinese version offers more range. Booking is advised.

FRAGRANT CAMPHOR GARDEN

Map pp246-9   *Teahouse*
Xiāngzhāng Yuán
10 Hengshan Lu
Flagship branch of the Harn Sheh chain of Taiwanese-style teahouses, which feature a cornucopia of bizarre and delicious beverages for around Y35 a pop. The décor is great, as are the smoothies. There are more happening branches around town, in the **French Concession** (Map pp246-9; 2A Hengshan Lu & at 758 Huaihai Lu) and at **Xujiahui** (Map p257; Grand Gateway).

GUYI HUNAN RESTAURANT

Map pp246-9   *Hunanese*
Gǔyì Xiángwèinng
☎ 6249 5628; 89 Fumin Lu; dishes Y20-40
While the Guyi is certainly more stylish than Dishuidong, controversy rages over which has the better food. Skip the copious bullfrog dishes for a trusty *làzi jīdīng* (Y24) or one of the *pīngguǒ* (personal hotpot) dishes but beware; the heat builds slowly so take things easy. There are also several of the obligatory Mao-inspired dishes. Book ahead for one of the coveted window tables.

HAZARA Map pp246-9   *Indian*
Hāzālā Cāntīng
☎ 6466 4328; www.face-shanghai.com; Bldg 4, Ruijin Guest House, 118 Ruijin Erlu; mains Y70-90
Spoil yourself with a drink in the next-door Face bar and then spin a coin. Heads and you'll get excellent north Indian dishes from the *tandoor* (clay oven) or *handi* (brass pot) in an exotic and intimate Middle Eastern–style tent. Tails gets you great Thai food in the upstairs **Lan Na Thai** (below).

HOT POT KING Map pp246-9   *Hot Pot*
Láifú Lóu
☎ 5403 0410; 1066 Huaihai Zhonglu
A steamy place that's a great bet in winter, with an English menu.

INDIAN KITCHEN Map pp246-9   *Indian*
Yìndù Xiǎochú
☎ 6473 1517; 572 Yongjia Lu; dishes Y20-30, set lunches Y18-50; metro Hengshan Lu
You'll have to follow your nose through the French Concession backstreets to track down this top-notch neighbourhood curry house, which is packed at weekends with Brits desperate for a chicken balti. The great-value set lunches come with a Tiger beer.

ITOYA Map pp246-9   *Japanese*
Yìténgjiā
☎ 5382 5757; 3rd fl, Shanghai Central Plaza, 381 Huaihai Zhonglu; sets Y50-70, mains Y50-80
A popular chain that is recommended for its set lunch specials (Y50) and other sets, from grilled eel to sushi or sukiyaki, all served with salad, miso soup, pickles and snacks. Otherwise the sushi is around Y25 to Y55. There are several locations across town, including **Kerry Centre** (Map pp250-2; ☎ 5298 57777; 1515 Nanjing Xilu), **Maxdo Centre** (Map p256; cnr Xingi Lu & Xanxia Lu, Hongqiao) and the **Jianguo Hotel** (Map p257; ☎ 6481 0177; 439 Caoxi Beilu just south of Xujiahui).

KEVEN CAFÉ

Map pp246-9   *Breakfast/American*
Kǎwén Kāfēi
☎ 6433 5564; 525 Hengshan Lu
Serves reasonably priced breakfasts all day, as well as soups and sandwiches, for just under Y50. Drinks will double the bill.

LAN NA THAI Map pp246-9   *Thai*
Lánnàtàiguó Cāntīng
☎ 6466 4328; www.face-shanghai.com; Bldg 4, Ruijin Guest House, 118 Ruijin Erlu; mains Y70-130
Upstairs from the Face bar, the sensuous wood-carvings and cobalt-blue walls make this one of the most beautiful and stylish restaurants in town. It's a favourite for high-flyers who can afford the great Thai salads (try the lemon grass shrimp salad), green curries and subtle desserts, like the crunchy water chestnut in dough in chilled coconut milk with jackfruit. Eat here in mid-April for a special Song Kran festival menu.

NEPALI KITCHEN Map pp246-9   *Nepalese*
Nípōěr Cāntīng
☎ 5404 5077; 178 Xinle Lu; lunch specials Y20-30, evening set meals Y60-75
Reminisce about that Himalayan trek over a

plate of Tibetan *momos* (meat or vegetable dumplings; Y30) amid prayer flags in this homey, lodge-like place. For a more laid-back meal head upstairs, take your shoes off and recline on traditional cushions, surrounded by colourful *thangkas* and paper lamps. Prices are higher than the Annapurna Circuit but then you're not just eating dahl bhat... Evening set meals are a good bet, with traditional Nepali dishes such as *sekuwa* (grilled beef) and *sikarni* (yoghurt).

OOEDO Map pp246-9 *Japanese*
Dàjiānghù

☎ 6467 3332; 30 Donghu Lu; buffet Y200

One of the best of Shanghai's many Japanese restaurants is Ooedo for its delicious all-you-can-eat sushi, sake and tempura buffet.

PATIALA PEARL Map pp246-9 *Indian*
Pàdàilā Yìndù Cāntīng

☎ 6467 6277; 155 Changshu Lu; mains Y50-90, lunch/dinner specials Y48/88

You're spoilt for choice in Indian restaurants in Shanghai but this is one of the best (*Shanghai Talk* magazine recently declared that here is the 'best curry in Shanghai'). The décor is fairly plain, with only an open kitchen to divert the eye from the fine curries. Try a *malai murg* (chicken in a creamy sauce) or vegetarian *kofta dilbahar* (cottage cheese and potato with fruits and tomato gravy; Y38), and soothe the spices with a Masala tea, lassi (Y25) or kulfi (with pistachio and saffron). Like most Indian restaurants it really stings you with the rice (Y20 to Y40).

PAULANER BRÄUHAUS
Map pp246-9 *German*
Bǎojiānà Cāntīng

☎ 6474 5700; 150 Fenyang Lu

This wildly popular place brews its own beer (p126) and packs in the (mostly Chinese) crowds every night of the week, despite the near stratospheric prices (a fact that leaves all other bar and restaurant owners scratching their heads). Table-shaking specials like the German sausage platter (Y130) and Bavarian pork knuckle (Y160) will leave vegetarians plenty of room for an apfelstrudel (Y40). Sunday brings a buffet brunch (Y160; 11.30am to 4.30pm). A second branch and a deli has opened in **Xintiandi** (☎ 6320 3935), with pleasant outdoor seating.

PEOPLE 6 Map pp246-9 *Chinese*
☎ 6466 0505; 150 Yueyang Lu; mains Y30-50

Number 6 is a similar deal to No 7 (see below),

but in the southern French Concession, offering fine café-style window seating or upstairs dining with a bird's eye view down on the bar. The tables lend themselves to intimate dinners rather than large groups. Swipe your hand through the metal cube to open the *Star Trek*–like door and congratulate yourself on being in the know.

PEOPLE 7 Map pp246-9 *Chinese*
☎ 5404 0707; 805 Julu Lu; mains Y30-50

Most mortals can't even open the front door in this beyond-cool restaurant and bar, let alone find the toilet! Once you do get in (we're not saying how...) you first see a great bar area of back-lit glass, designer bamboo and comfy white chairs – perfect for an intimate tryst or a Japanese cocktail. After all the ultracool minimalist concrete and chrome, the food seems almost incidental. The menu is unadventurous but familiar, with Beijing duck, chicken in lemon sauce, garlic sea bass, crispy chicken with onion sauce and a few Japanese-influenced dishes. Portions are on the small side but the chic comes at a surprisingly reasonable price.

PUNJABI Map pp246-9 *Indian*
☎ 6472 5464; 2nd fl, 102 Xiangyang Lu

The main reason to come to Punjabi is the Y68 evening (5pm to 11pm) all-you-can-eat curries and all-you-can-drink Qingdao beer (lunch Y45), certainly one of the best deals in town. The large hall is better suited to groups than couples, despite the pukka Hindi music, and is bound to kick-start a good boys' night out.

QUANJUDE Map pp246-9 *Beijing duck*
Quánjùdé

☎ 6433 7286; 786 Huaihai Zhonglu

A branch of the famous Beijing duck restaurant chain, offering more than 100 dishes made from every conceivable part of a duck's anatomy. The big draw of course is the Beijing duck, served with pancakes and hoi sin sauce (and finally a soup) for Y168. You can choose your own duck by marking it with a honey pen if you want to pay for that privilege. Fried scorpions with duck liver (Y58) are another speciality for the brave. Takeaway duck without all the trimmings costs Y98. The chain boasts that is has served up over two million ducks.

SASHA'S Map pp246-9 *Continental*
☎ 6474 6166; House 11, 9 Dongping Lu; mains Y95-170, set meals Y188-255

This restaurant is ensconced in a house that was once part of the Soong family complex and later used by Jiang Qing as a base for Beijing opera. Sasha's is famed for its great outside summer barbecue (Y138; evenings May to September), carvery (Y250; Thursday to Sunday) and Sunday brunch (year-round). The homey ground-floor pub has draught Guinness, Becks, Beamish, Boddingtons and Tetleys at Y50 a pint, a Friday night happy hour and plenty of comfy leather chairs.

SHINTORI 02 Map pp246-9 *Japanese*
Xīndùlǐ

☎ 5404 5252; 803 Julu Lu; mains Y60-80;
🕓 dinner only

Once you've found out how to get into People 7 and been suitably impressed, head into this restaurant next door and prepare for your jaw to drop, again. The warehouse-industrial-chic interior resembles a set from a Peter Greenway film, from the eye-catching open kitchen that looks like it should house Hannibal Lector to the sleek staff running around like an army of black ninja. The menu is equally witty; the cold soba noodles come in a bowl made of real ice. The green tea tiramisu may well be the ultimate Shanghai fusion dish.

SIMPLY THAI Map pp246-9 *Thai*
☎ 6445 9551; 5C Dongping Lu; mains Y50-60

Everyone raves about this intimate and unpretentious place for its delicious, inexpensive Thai food and pleasant outdoor seating. Lunch specials are particularly good value. There are less intimate branches in **Pudong** (Map pp253-4; 5th fl, Superbrand Mall) and **Xintiandi** (Map pp246-9; Simply Café).

SPICE MARKET Map pp254-5 *Southeast Asian*
Dōngnányà Cāntīng

☎ 6384 6838; 8 Jinan Lu; set lunch Y35, mains Y30-60

The unbeatable value five-course Malaysian, Thai or Indonesian set lunches are the draw here. Thai dishes are authentically fiery, with sweet tamarind sauce to cool the mouth, and there are lots of lime, coconut and satay tastes. The décor is divided into traditional Thai, Singapore and Malay seating.

The evening à la carte menu is a *Who's Who* of Asian dishes, from pad thai to nasi goreng, along with more interesting fare like the pomelo, chicken and chilli salad (Y35) and grilled whole fish with chilli, dry shrimps and coconut stuffing (Y60). Five-course dinners cost Y88. You can save more money on a bucket of beer (five bottles) for Y135.

TGIF Map pp246-9 *American*
Xīngqīwǔ Cāntīng

☎ 6473 4602; 10 Hengshan Lu; mains Y145-195

Since when are burgers at the top end of the price scale? Since they hit Shanghai with imported beers and beef. TGIF serves up predictable steaks, ribs and burgers, with happy hour drink and food specials (4pm to 7pm).

VEGETARIAN LIFESTYLE
Map pp254-5 *Chinese/Vegetarian*
Zǎozishù

☎ 5306 8000; 77 Songshan Lu

For light and healthy Chinese vegetarian food, lacking the oil that blights so many Shanghainese restaurants, try this bright place, just off the eastern end of Huaihai Zhonglu. There's an English menu.

WUNINOSACHI Map pp246-9 *Japanese*
Hǎizhīxīn

☎ 6445 3406; 402 Shaanxi Nanlu

This easily missable place is very popular, largely for its Y150 all-you-can-eat-and-drink sushi-and-sake deals (make a reservation). Like most Japanese restaurants in Shanghai there's no English sign and the entrance is totally innocuous; look for the black grilles. There's another branch at **169 Xinle Lu**.

XIAN YUE HIEN
Map pp246-9 *Shanghainese, Cantonese*
Shēn'àoxuān Jiǔlóu

☎ 6251 1166; 849 Huashan Lu; dishes Y20-40, specialities Y100

The Ding Xing garden, originally built for the concubine of a Qing dynasty mandarin, is now reserved for retired Communist Party cadres so the only way you'll get a peek is to eat at this bustling restaurant. The English picture menu is a help, with a good range of Shanghainese and Cantonese dishes like chicken with chestnut casserole (Y28), lion's head meatballs with crab roe (Y56) or spare ribs in honey sauce (Y32), but the real draw is the dim sum, served overlooking the lawn on mornings and afternoons.

Xintiandi

This upscale plaza in the French Concession quickly became the epicentre of upscale Shanghai dining when it opened in 2001. There are dozens of chic restaurants and bars here so take your pick; only the best are listed here. It's particularly popular with Hong Kongers. The northern block houses the densest concentration of

Buffet Blowouts

Shanghai's big hotels offer some of the city's best splurges, often at surprisingly reasonable rates. Specials change monthly so check out local listing magazines and the *Shanghai Star* for a rundown of current deals.

For a grand Sunday brunch, the **Portman Ritz-Carlton's Tea Garden** (p167) has an unlimited Moët & Chandon champagne-and-jazz brunch (Y360; 11.30am to 2.30pm), which features lobster, smoked salmon, sushi, imported cheeses, pistachio soufflé, Belgian waffles, French pastries...well, you get the picture. More affordable brunch options include **Sheraton Grand Taipingyang** (p169; with free-flowing champagne Y188), **Four Seasons** (p166; Y295) and the **Westin** (p159; with/without champagne Y262/195). **M on the Bund** (p100), **T8** (p107) and **Sasha's** (p105) also offer Sunday brunches.

High tea (most 3pm to 6pm) is another must-do Shanghai decadence. Good places include the Four Seasons, **Novotel Atlantis** (p165; Y68) and **Grand Hyatt** (p110; Y100) but again, the most decadent of all is the Portman Ritz-Carlton's high tea, either Chinese style with dim sum and green tea or Western style with scones, strawberries and a glass of Moët & Chandon, all to the soothing sounds of a string quartet.

Other options include the excellent value all-you-can-eat weekday dim sum at the **Sheraton** (Y88), Four Seasons, **Crowne Plaza** (p166; Y68) or the Novotel's **Art 50 revolving restaurant** (with 2 glasses of beer Y78). There are seafood buffets at **Art 50** (Y188) and the **Pudong Shangrila** (p165; Y218; ☺ Friday night). Finally, the **Sofitel** (p159) has a German buffet every Saturday for Y168, which includes all the microbrewed German beer that you can pump down your throat.

Remember that all hotel prices tag on an extra 15% service charge.

---

expense accounts in the city, but the prices drop rapidly as you make your way south to the chains. There are also some lovely summer cafés and a popular Starbucks.

KABB Map pp246-9 *American*
☎ 3307 0798; 5 North Block, Xintiandi, 181 Taicang Lu

For those times when the desire to chew becomes overpowering, this smart American bar/grill hits the spot, delivering authentic American-portioned comfort food at mid-range prices. There's a good selection of main course salads, burgers and Tex-Mex and good lunch specials, including soup and salad combos. Staff recommend the chicken feta pasta with sun-dried tomato (Y75).

The outdoor café-style seating is particularly popular for a slower-paced Sunday brunch, when the menu stretches to French toast with banana, walnut syrup and eggs Benedict, all with unlimited coffee.

The bar also has a pleasant buzz to it, with a good wine list (wine of the month Y180 a bottle) and mix-it-yourself Bloody Marys.

T8 Map pp246-9 *Continental/Fusion*
☎ 6355 8999; 8 North Block, Xintiandi, 181 Taicang Lu; mains Y200, 2-/3-course set lunch Mon, Wed-Fri Y158/198; ☺ closed Tue lunch

Recently voted one of the best 50 restaurants in the world by *Conde Nast* magazine, T8 is giving M on the Bund a run for its money as the most lauded restaurant in Shanghai. The food can best be described as 'modern Mediterranean fusion with Asian influences', with subtle flavours and excellent presentation. Our slow-cooked lamb and Sichuan high pie with yellow coriander bisque (Y198) had a perfect crust, a dense filling and was topped with caramelised onions.

The dark seductive interior is just as impressive; antique Chinese cabinets contrast with the stylish round tables and bright open-plan kitchen. Symbolism is rife, from the feng shui–driven entrance to the eight (an auspicious number) goldfish in the tank.

The bar and comfortable lounge area are great for a drink and dinner is served until 11.30pm so it's perfect for a late meal. Dress to impress. The **weekend brunch** (2/3 courses Y188/228) is served with sparkling wine in the upper-floor Indonesian-style members' club. This is modern cuisine so don't expect any sides.

VA BENE Map pp246-9 *Italian*
☎ 6311 2211; House 7, North Block, Xintiandi, 181 Taicang Lu; mains Y100-150, 2-course set lunch Y148

Xintiandi's northern end is packed with top-end places and this is another super-trendy place, with an emphasis this time on basil and olive oil. The interior has an opera-set feel, with lots of terracottas, yellows and browns, and there's nice conservatory seating. As ever, the *primo piatti* offer the most interesting combinations: crepes with ricotta cheese, spinach, cream and cantarelle sauce; risotto with Gorgonzola cheese, asparagus and sun-dried tomato or the Gorgonzola cheese and

The bar at T8 restaurant (p107).

smoked salmon pizza. For a pre-meal drink or post-meal cigar, head upstairs to the lush sofa-lined Va Va Room bar/lounge.

Cheap Eats

BAI'S RESTAURANT

Map pp246-9   *Shanghainese*
Báijiā Cānshì
☎ 6437 6915; No 12, Lane 189, Wanping Lu; dishes Y15-25

Hidden down another backstreet off Hengshan Lu is this small, clean, family-style restaurant with tasty Shanghainese food and an English menu. The *hǔpí jiānjiāo* (tiger skin chillies) are mild and sweet and there are plenty of affordable delicacies like the *cháozhou tóngbǎi xiè* (baked crab, onion and green pepper). The *suànxiāng bàngbànggǔ* (fried pork ribs in garlic) are a house speciality but a little overpriced (Y9 each).

DÉLIFRANCE Map pp246-9   *Sandwiches*
☎ 5382 5171; Central Plaza, 381 Huaihai Zhonglu

Fans of the Hong Kong version might be a little disappointed with this one but for Shanghai office workers and Huaihai Lu shoppers this brasserie-style sandwich and coffee shop is a blessing (think gleaming brass and Edith Piaf on the stereo). Coffee, soup and sandwich lunch specials go for Y28 to Y35. It's also a great place for coffee and cakes, plus it's the only place in town to get a chicken curry baguette.

FENGYU SHENGJIAN Map pp246-9   *Snacks*
Fēngyù Shēngjiān
41 Ruijin Erlu, cnr Nanchang Lu

Don't let the Stalinist service and orange plastic seats put you off at this nondescript canteen, as it turns out some of the best shrimp and pork *shēngjiān* (fried dumplings) in town for a bargain Y2.50, plus a range of other snacks.

GAOLI Map pp246-9   *Korean*
Gāolì Jiǔjiā
☎ 6431 5236; No 1, Lane 181, Wuyuan Lu; meals Y20-40

A cheap hole-in-the-wall Korean barbecue *shāokǎo* place that is popular with the local students.

GINO CAFÉ Map pp246-9   *Italian/Café*
Jìnuò Yìdàlì Tǐxián Cāntīng
Parkson department store, 918 Huaihai Zhonglu

For cheap, no-frills Italian food this popular chain features good-value lunch specials of chicken, pasta or pizza, with cappuccino. There are two branches at **Xujiahui** (Map p257; Grand Gateway & 33 Caoxi Beilu), other branches at **Gubei** (Map p256), **Hongqiao** (Map p256; Friendship Shopping Centre) and on **Nanjing Donglu** (Map pp244-5; 66 Nanjing Donglu).

GINO GOURMET Map pp246-9   *Italian/Café*
Jìnuò Měishì
☎ 5306 7370; 158 Chengdu Nanlu

A step up from Gino Café and from the same company, offering excellent value seven-course meals for Y58, or a 6-inch pizza with soup/salad, dessert and coffee for Y38, which is pretty much what most other places charge for the coffee alone.

GRAPE RESTAURANT

Map pp246-9   *Chinese/Shanghainese*
Pútáo Yuán
☎ 6472 0486; 55 Xinle Lu; dishes Y15-25

One of the most enduring private Chinese restaurants from the 1980s, the reliable Grape still packs in the crowds at its bright premises beside the old Orthodox church at the junction with Xiangyang Lu. Try the delicious *yóutiáo chǎoniúròu* (dough sticks with beef).

MEGABITE Map pp246-9   *Food Court*
Dàshídài

283 Huaihai Zhonglu

One of the more popular food courts, in the basement of the Hong Kong Plaza, serving up all the fast-food favourites. There is another branch at **Metro City** (Map p257) with endless varieties of Chinese food, teppanyaki, crepes, fruit, ice cream and pots of tea.

PIZZA ITALIA Map pp246-9   *Pizza/Delivery*
Yìdàlì Bǐsà

☎ 6473 9994; www.pizzaitalia.com.cn;
1111 Huaihai Zhonglu

The best value 12-inch pizza in town weighs in at only Y45 to Y55, or Y10 per slice, cooked in ovens specially imported from Italy. There's a branch in **Pudong** (Map pp253-4; ☎ 6209 4720; 5th fl, Superbrand Mall) and a takeaway stall in **Gubei** (Map p256; ☎ 6209 4720; C6 Rotterdam Garden, 18 Shuicheng Nanlu). It also offers a free delivery service; see the website for an on-line menu.

STARBUCKS Map pp246-9   *Café*
☎ 5465 2377; 559 Nanchang Lu; coffee Y12-18

The granddaddy of American coffee houses has finally arrived in Shanghai with a caffeine-fuelled wallop. The ambition is to wean the Chinese masses from tea leaf to coffee bean and, in Shanghai at least, the latter is winning the caffeine war. There are currently 21 branches, including this one, with more appearing weekly. All are smoke-free and all offer wireless broadband Internet access with your coffee.

WUYUE RENJIA Map pp246-9   *Noodles*
Wùyuè Rénjiā

No 10, Lane 706, Huaihai Zhonglu; noodles Y10-15

Hidden down a backstreet off Huaihai Zhonglu, and at a handful of other locations, this chain serves up cheap bowls of Suzhou-style noodles in a very civilised 'old Cathay' atmosphere, with Chinese opera and folk tunes in the background. Some branches have no English menu but you can't really go wrong here. Choose between *tāng* (soupy) or *bān* (dry) noodles; in either case the flavouring comes on a side plate. The excellent *xiābào shànbèi miàn* comes with shrimp and fried eels in an oniony fish soup (Y16).

There are several other branches across town, including one hidden down a backstreet at **595 Nanjing Xilu** (Map pp250-2), another just off the Bund (Map pp244-5), between the Thai consulate and Fuzhou Lu, and one on **Taikang Lu** (Map pp246–7).

XIANZONGLIN Map pp246-9   *Teahouse*
Xiānzōnglín

671 Huaihai Lu; drinks Y16

A modern chain that incorporates a fun teahouse/treehouse design, substituting swings for seats. The place has cheapish drinks and specialises in Taiwanese favourites like *zhēnzhū chá* (pearl sago tea) and fruity apple, passion fruit and lemon teas. There are many copycat places around town; look for the rabbit logo.

YANG'S KITCHEN
Map pp246-9   *Chinese/Shanghainese*
Yángjiā Chúfáng

☎ 6431 3028; 9 Hengshan Lu, Lane 3

For good, reasonably priced Chinese food and a non-scary English menu, Yang's can't be beaten. The *níngméngmì jiānruǎnjī* (lemon chicken) for Y22 is delicious and the *ròumò qiéguā jiābǐng* (stewed eggplant with pork mince), which you roll up in little pancakes, is out of this world. The crispy duck (half a duck Y28) is also a winner, as is the *xièfěn dòufu* (crab meat and tofu Y42). It's down a small lane just off Hengshan Lu. Tea and snacks will push your meal up by Y9.

YUAN YUAN Map pp250-2   *Chinese*
Yuányuán Fàndiàn

195 Chengde Lu

A typical home-style Chinese restaurant, this place is like thousands of others in the city, except that for some reason it's got an English menu. It's cheap, tasty and worth a stop if you are at the western end of Nanjing Xilu.

ZENTRAL Map pp254-5   *Health/Sandwich Bar*
Shànqù

☎ 6374 5815; www.zentral.com.cn;
567 Huangpi Nanlu; set meals Y15-18

If you crave an alternative to oily Shanghainese fry-ups but your wallet is as empty as your stomach, Zentral is your best bet. There are cheap lunch sets, good smoothies, brown rice, sugar-free desserts and Y10 cappuccino. The menu even offers the paranoid a breakdown of the calories and fat content of each dish. The food itself is unremarkable but the location is useful, there is a comfy sofa and it delivers.

Eating – French Concession

PUDONG
GRAND HYATT

Map pp253-4   *Italian/Japanese/International*
Jīnmaò Kǎiyuè Dàjiǔdiàn
☎ 5830 3338; Jinmao Tower, Zhongyang Dadao

If it's a special night out with a view you're after, the restaurants at the Grand Hyatt really can't be beaten. 'On 56' is a collection of four restaurants and a wine bar on the 56th floor. **Cucina** (mains Y100) has wonderful Italian dishes from Campania, breads and pizzas fresh from the oven, and the open-plan kitchen lets you keep an eye on preparation. **Grill** (steaks Y230-300) offers fine imported meats and seafood. The Japanese **Kobachi** features sushi, sashimi and yakimori. **Canton**, the stylish Cantonese restaurant, is the flagship and features afternoon dim sum. The breathtaking atrium is a great place to meet. Highest views come from the 86th floor Shanghainese restaurant.

The **Grand Café** (buffet Y198-228) offers stunning views through its glass walls, and a good-value buffet, which allows you to choose a main course and have it prepared fresh in the show kitchen. If you're going to spend Y40 on a coffee in some crummy Shanghai café, you might as well make an afternoon of it here for the all-you-can-manage weekend high tea for Y100.

Weekends bring a minimum charge of between Y90 to Y100 to all the Hyatt's restaurants. To reserve a table by the window in any of these restaurants, book well in advance.

LULU RESTAURANT

Map pp253-4   *Shanghainese*
Lǔlǔ Jiǔjiā
☎ 5882 6679; 2nd fl, China Merchants Tower, 161 Liujiazui Donglu; dishes Y12-30, seafood Y70

Out in Pudong, one of your best bets for decent Shanghainese cuisine. You'll find all your Shanghainese favourites, including *xièfěn shīzi tóu* (crab and pork meatballs, Y15 each). There are branches in **Gubei** (Map p256; ☎ 6270 6679; 336 Shuicheng Nanlu) and behind the **Jīng'an Temple** (Map pp250-2; ☎ 5882 6689; 161 Yuyuan Lu). The most stylish and spectacular of all takes up most of the 5th floor in **Plaza 66** (Map pp250-2; ☎ 6288 1179; 1266 Nanjing Xilu) and is the epitome of stylish, modern Shanghai. It's perfect for a trendy group meal blowout.

Cheap Eats
ALI BABA'S Map pp253-4   *Turkish*
☎ 5878 9745; Unit 57, 17 Yincheng Xilu; set lunch Y30, dinner buffet Y68

One of dozens of restaurants in the Liujiazui Food Corner complex, the Iskender kebab (Y38) here is hard to beat, with döner meat on bread with tomato sauce and yoghurt. There are also good-value lunch and dinner buffets in the larger of the two branches here, plus evening belly dancing (from 7pm to 9pm).

FOOD COURT LIVE Map pp253-4 *Food Court*
Zhongyang Dadao, next to Jinmao Tower; meals to Y20

In the basement, serving the hordes headed up to the top-floor viewing platform. Chinese fast-food stalls specialise in claypot dishes, Hainan chicken, Cantonese barbecue, wok and noodle dishes, and set meals.

THAI THAI Map pp253-4   *Thai*
Superbrand Mall, Liujiazui Lu; dishes Y19-22, set meals Y35

For a cheap meal in the Superbrand Mall, this bright and cheap stop is a step above the rest of the fast-food court. Dishes like *tom kah gai* (coconut, lemon grass and chicken soup) and green curry are small but come with rice and

---

Top Five Vegetarian/Health Food Restaurants

- **Zentral** (p109) Cheap low-fat lunches on the run.
- **Tiffin** (Map pp246-9; ☎ 6391 0639; 3rd fl, Shanghai Central Plaza, 111 Huaihai Zhonglu; dishes Y25-50) Take a break when shopping the malls on Huaihai Zhonglu. Vegetarian Chinese food with a twist here, such as the salt- and MSG-free baked green pepper with potatoes and cheese, or the smoked tofu. Makes for a good shopping rendezvous for the health conscious.
- **Vegetarian Lifestyle** (p106) Chinese food without the oil or MSG.
- **Temple Restaurants** at **Longhua Temple** (p82) or **Jade Buddha Temple** (p75) Because they've been doing this for hundreds of years.
- **Element Fresh** (p111) Snappy gourmet sandwiches and killer smoothies.

carry enough chilli and lemon grass to bring back memories of sweaty meals in Thailand. Add a papaya salad for Y12 or try the set meals.

NANJING XILU & JING'AN

Business lunches and after-dinner drinks are the rule here, with a concentration of expat restaurants around the Shanghai Centre, some flashy Chinese joints in some even flashier malls and even a sprinkle of historic Shanghai restaurants.

BALI LAGUNA Map pp246-9 *Indonesian*
☎ 6248 6970; 189 Huashan Lu

The lakeside setting in Jing'an Park is tropical enough but wait until you get into the open long-house interior, decked out in dark wood and rattan. Waiters in sarongs serve up excellent seafood curry in a fresh pineapple, *gado gado* (vegetable salad with peanut sauce) and *kalio daging* (beef in coconut milk, lemon grass and curry sauce). The full bar makes this also a great place for a drink.

BRASIL STEAKHOUSE
Map pp250-2 *South American*
Bāxī Shāokǎowū
☎ 6255 9898; 1649 Nanjing Xilu;
lunch/dinner buffet Y55/66

A wildly popular barbecue buffet that serves up all-you-can-handle grilled Argentine-style meats with a salad bar. There is a second Brasil Steakhouse opposite **Shanghai Library** (Map pp246-9; ☎ 6437 7288; 1582 Huaihai Zhonglu).

ELEMENT FRESH
Map pp250-2 *Sandwiches/American*
Yuánsù Cāntīng
☎ 6279 8682; Shanghai Centre, 1376 Nanjing Xilu;
sandwiches Y35-75, lunch mains Y60-90,
dinner mains Y80-180

There aren't many places for a decent sandwich in Shanghai so this light-lunch spot is a welcome addition. The focus is on fresh, healthy sandwiches and salads; vegetarians may well faint with excitement at the roasted eggplant on walnut bread with mozzarella and olives. Then there are lots of fresh juices, imaginative smoothies and the best-value coffee around. The décor is bright and stylish, with a small bar and comfy sofas. Mornings bring big breakfast sets (Y50 to Y60) with pancakes and French toast, while evenings offer

after-work drinks and heavier meals. There's a take-away service.

GONGDELIN Map pp250-2 *Vegetarian*
Gōngdélín Shūshíchù
☎ 6327 0218; 445 Nanjing Xilu; dishes Y16-32

This place, Shanghai's most famous vegetarian restaurant has been open since 1922 but these days it's most popular with out-of-towners. All the food is designed to resemble meat, and is convincingly prepared. The food and atmosphere are well worth exploring, even if you are not a vegetarian, though the English menu is poor. Upstairs is more traditional and pricier.

GREEN WILLOW VILLAGE
RESTAURANT Map pp250-2 *Yangzhou*
Lûyáng Jiǔjiā
☎ 6258 4422; 763 Nanjing Xilu; dishes Y20-50

Established in 1936, this stalwart offers Chuanyang cuisine – a mix of Sichuan and Yangzhou cuisine – along with some 'medicinal' dishes (food specifically designed to aid certain ailments, according to Chinese belief). There's an English menu but, if you can read it, the Chinese menu has greater variety and a better selection of the cheaper dishes. Regulars recommend the crispy duck *(xiāngsū yā)* at Y29 for half a duck.

JIANGNANCUN Map pp250-2 *Hangzhou*
Jiāngnáncūn Jiǔjiā
☎ 6317 5059; 3rd fl, 1033 Chang'an Lu, cnr Tianmu Lu;
dishes Y20-40

A five-minute walk from Shanghai train station, this cavernous place is so popular that somehow it fills up every night. It serves up Hangzhou specialities such as *xīhú cùyú* (sweet-and-sour West Lake fish), longjing shrimp (Y98), water shield soup (Y16), and *hángzhōu juànjī* (Hangzhou chicken), actually a meatless dish made with bamboo shoots. The restaurant has an English menu.

MALONE'S AMERICAN CAFÉ
Map pp250-2 *American*
Mǎlóng Měishì Jiǔlóu
☎ 6289 4830; 257 Tongren Lu; mains Y60-90

This American-style bar/grill is popular with the bearded and bellied in search of beer and Malone's 30 kinds of burgers. House specials spread to the Thai chicken wrap, a range of Tex-Mex and a Sunday roast (Y108; 6pm to 11pm). The happy hour (5pm to 8pm), live music (from 10pm) and comedy nights (p133) add to the frat-boy atmosphere.

MEILONGZHEN Map pp250-2 *Chinese*
Měilóngzhèn
☎ 6253 5353; No 22, Lane 1081, Nanjing Xilu;
dishes Y30-50
Shanghai has a host of famous local restaurants, none more so than this fantastic old building, which has been churning out food since the 1930s. The rooms once housed the Shanghai Communist Party headquarters but are now bedecked in Chinese woodcarvings and huge lamps. The house speciality is Meilongzhen special chicken, though the menu is also heavy on fish, seafood and the occasional snake, mixing Sichuanese, Huaiyang and Shanghainese tastes.

TONY ROMA'S Map pp250-2 *American*
☎ 6279 7129; Shanghai Centre, 1376 Nanjing Xilu;
ribs Y130-150
A branch of the famous US chain known for its fine ribs, but also burgers (Y85) and other heavy grill combos (Y150 to Y170). It's a shame the décor is so dull.

ZEN Map pp250-2 *Cantonese*
Cǎidiégǎn Jiǔjiā
☎ 6288 1141; 5th fl, Plaza 66, 1266 Nanjing Xilu;
dishes Y30-70
OK, so this place is in a shopping mall but don't run off screaming just yet. Trendy Zen is actually bright, airy and stylish, arched around the horseshoe-end of Plaza 66, giving some tables a great night-time view of the Shanghai Exhibition Hall. The menu has lots of choice

among the shark's fin and abalone and prices are reasonable (dishes come in half or full servings). Favourites include the sautéed chicken with ginger and spring onion in clam sauce (Y98) and the baked chicken in rock salt.

Cheap Eats

ALWAYS CAFÉ Map pp250-2 *International*
☎ 6247 8333; 1528 Nanjing Xilu; dinner mains Y40-50
We could tell you about the burgers, Mexican melts and Asian dishes here but what draws the regulars to Always are the excellent-value set lunch specials with coffee for Y20 (11.30am to 5pm) and the buy-one-get-one-free happy hour (5pm to 8pm). At last, reasonable prices in Shanghai! The more-varied dinner menu features chef salads, quiche Lorraine and tacos for around Y50 – and don't forget the apple pie (Y38). Street-side seating and a vaguely continental European café-bar feel bring a warm and cosy atmosphere and a loyal clientele.

BI FENG TANG Map pp250-2 *Dim Sum*
Bì Fēng Táng
☎ 6279 0738; 1333 Nanjing Xilu
This is an incredibly popular place that serves cheap dim sum snacks like shrimp dumplings, honeyed pork and egg tarts for Y13 to Y25, as well as coffee and cheap Budweiser. This Nanjing Xilu branch, across from the Shanghai Centre, has an English menu on request and plenty of fine outdoor seating when the weather is good. Other popular branches are at 1 Dapu Lu (Map pp246-9; ☎ 5396 1328), Gubei

One of several popular Bi Feng Tang branches (above)

Top Four Asian Fast Food

The food isn't gourmet but it's fast, tasty and cheap. Eat with the masses – the Party will be proud.

- **Wujing Tang** (Map p257) A Taiwanese chain that serves up good noodles for around Y20, with a wide range of fruit juices. Branches in **Metro City** and **Grand Gateway**, both in Xujiahui.
- **Ajisen Ramen** (Wèiqiān Lāmiàn; Map p246-9; ☎ 6372 5547; 518 Huaihai Lu) Also known as 1000 Taste Noodles, has very tasty Japanese noodles (Y12 to Y20) served in wonderful wooden bowls, and good set meals with lots of side dishes. It's a bustling place with good service. There are branches in **Grand Gateway** (Map p257; Xujiahui) and on **Nanjing Donglu**.
- **Yonghe** (Yŏnghé; Map p254-5; Lippo Plaza) There are two Chinese chains called Yonghe, one with a logo that's part Colonel Sanders, part Chairman Mao. Both serve up Chinese snacks and noodles 24 hours a day. One of the better branches is at **Lippo Plaza** on Huaihai Lu.
- **Mos Burger** (Mòshì Hànbǎo) A Japanese chain offering a mix of teppanyaki burgers, noodles and conveyer-belt sushi (noodles Y18 to Y25). The picture menu makes ordering easy. There are branches in **Yuyuan Bazaar** (Map pp254-5), the **French Concession** (Map pp246-9; cnr Huaihai Zhonglu & Shaanxi Nanlu), and at dozens of other places across town.

(Map p256; ☎ 6208 6388; 37 Shuicheng Nanlu) and the bustling 24-hour **175 Changle Lu** (Map pp246-9; ☎ 6467 0628).

TACO POPO Map pp250-2 *Mexican*
☎ 6279 4820; 265 Tongren Lu; dishes Y10-15
Grab a stool if you're lucky at this hole-in-the-wall diner for trailer-home tacos and cheap burritos, tacos and enchiladas. It's great for a pit stop between clubs or beer runs. A sit-down version above **Judy's Too** (Map pp246-9; Maoming Lu) is open late weekends.

NORTH SHANGHAI

AFANTI RESTAURANT Map pp242-3 *Uyghur*
Āfàntí Shíchéng
☎ 6555 9604; 775 Quyang Lu; mains Y30;
bus 503 to/from Renmin Sq
Discerning fans of Uyghur cuisine will want to head out here to the northern Boonies for some of the city's best Central Asian food in a friendly and authentic environment. The *dàpánjī* is great as is the *gosh gorma* (Chinese: *chǎo kǎoròu* – fried mutton) and the camel and horse meat from the Yili Valley on the border with Kazakhstan. There is Uyghur music and dance in the evenings, plus an English menu.

The restaurant is in the basement of the Tianshan Hotel, next to the Silk Road Hotel; look for the building with the golden domes.

LE BOUCHON Map pp246-9 *French*
☎ 6225 7088; 1455 Wuding Xilu
Francophiles should make a beeline for a tasty in the middle of nowhere in northwestern

Shanghai. There are daily specials and a good selection of French wine.

MÜNCHENER FREIHEIT
Map pp242-3 *German*
☎ 6598 8103; 192 Chifeng Lu; mains Y30-48
Cheapest German cuisine in town, popular with students from Fudan and Tongji universities, serving solid meals like sausages, sauerkraut and potato salad, Bavarian pork knuckle or *leberkäse* (meatloaf), washed down by draught Hofbräu München (Y58 a pitcher) or bottled Erdinger Weisbier (Y30). Also on offer are salads, pasta and pizza dishes.

REVOLVING 28
Map pp253-4 *Chinese/Sichuanese*
☎ 6545 8888; www.oceanhotel-sh.com; 1171 Dongdaming Lu; mains Y30-90; bus 921, 22, 37
The revolving top floor of the Ocean Hotel has some of Shanghai's best views, taking in both Pudong and the Bund. The competent Sichuanese dishes aren't expensive and it also sells cheap snacks outside main meal times. A two-hour meal gives you a complete revolution of the city.

HONGQIAO & GUBEI

FOLK RESTAURANT Map p256 *Shanghainese*
Xiānqiángfáng
☎ 6295 1717; 1468 Hongqiao Lu; mains Y30-50
Another place worth a visit for its beautiful atmosphere more than its food, housed in a Tudor-style building stuffed full of Chinese antiques. Standard Shanghainese dishes, including pork wrapped in pancakes and Ganjiang smoked duck (Y48) are on offer in a hefty

English menu made of bamboo. There's another designer location in the **French Concession** (Map pp246–7; ☎ 5383 9893; 171 Nanchang Lu); the writer Guo Muruo once lived across the road.

FRANKIE'S PLACE

Map p256   *Singapore/Malaysian*
Fǎlánjī Cāntīng
☎ 6209 1955; 1477 Gubei Lu; mains Y20-40

Frankie's is a bright and friendly place. It's a bit out of the way, which makes it most popular with local Gubei residents and grocery shoppers headed to or from nearby Carrefour. Weekday set lunches feature excellent laksa, Hainanese chicken or *bak kut teh* (pork ribs) and cost just Y20, with one drink included. Dinner dishes stretch to beef rendang, or chicken with lime leaves, plus a good range of cheaper veg options like *rojak* (Malay salad) or Malaysian vegetable curry. Frankie tends to move location frequently so double-check by phone.

XUJIAHUI & SOUTH SHANGHAI

Food courts galore cater to Xujiahui's hardened shoppers but there are also some good restaurants nearby, particularly on Tianyueqiao Lu.

SHANGHAI UNCLE Map p257   *Shanghainese*
Shànghǎi Āshū
☎ 6464 6430; 211 Tianyueqiao Lu; dishes Y28-80

This is what Shanghai is all about; stylish, smart, bustling and just a little brash. Dishes are more interesting than the standard, from the baked eel (Y60) to the pine-nut coated ribs (Y68) and presentation is top-notch. It's such a popular mix, in fact, that uncle has opened several other branches around town.

OLD STATION RESTAURANT

Map p257   *Shanghainese*
Shànghǎi Lǎozhàn
☎ 6427 2233; 201 Caoxi Beilu; dishes Y26-80

With crisp linen and a sharp colonial façade, this restaurant serves meals that are classier than most of the alternative fare around Xujiahui. There's something for everyone on the English menu, from the twice-cooked crispy duck (Y48) to the eggplant and salty fish casserole (Y22) and prices are reasonable. Train buffs should phone ahead to book a table inside one of the two period railway cars.

1 *Riverside walkway along the Bund (p61)* 2 *A tour boat on the Huangpu River (p61) passes the Convention Centre* 3 *Monument to the People's Heroes, Huangpu Park (p87)* 4 *Statue of Chen Yi (p87) the Bund*

1 Shanghai Grand Theatre (p64)
2 Shanghai architecture (p29)
3 The latest mobile phone, a must-have accessory (p15) 4 Shanghai Stadium (p135)

1 Bright lights of Nanjing Lu
(p60) 2 High fashion on Huaihai
Zhonglu (p147) 3 Eyes on fashion,
Nanjing Lu (p143) 4 Shanghai
souvenirs

1 Late-night music, Julu Lu (p127)
2 Kaleidoscopic light display, Nan-jing Lu (p60) 3 Café chic, Xintiandi complex (p71) 4 Outdoor band performance, Jing'an Park (p76)

1 Street game of checkers
2 Picturesque 1930s architecture, French Concession (p92)
3 Resident, Old Town (p66)
4 Traditional rooftop ornamentation, Old Town

1 The man himself, Confucian Temple (p66), Old Town
2 Performer prepares for a show, Shanghai Grand Theatre (p64)
3 Early-morning t'ai chi, Renmin Park (p63) 4 Acrobats, Shanghai Centre Theatre (p133)

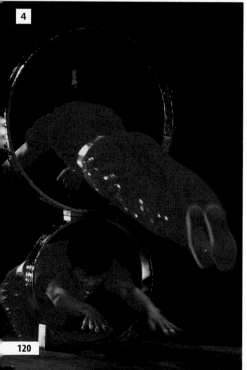

1 *Decorative knots – traditional handicrafts used to express good wishes* 2 *Confucian Temple (p66), Old Town* 3 *Ingredients for traditional Chinese medicines* 4 *Goldfish (koi), symbolising wealth*

鮮 肉 月 饼

每只1元

1 Street stall (p38) selling pastries
2 Sweet shop temptations
3 Freshwater lobsters 4 Toffee crab
apples (p40)

北 京 冰 糖 葫

Entertainment

Entertainment

PERHAPS IN NO OTHER CITY DOES SO MUCH HUMAN ENERGY GO INTO THE SEARCH FOR AMUSEMENT AS AMONG THE FOREIGN POPULATION OF SHANGHAI

Journalist George Sokolsky, 1930s

Shanghai is fast emerging as the most spiritually polluted city in China. All the old evils (and a few new ones) are creeping back, with a vengeance. Over the last couple of years there's been an explosion of nightlife options, offering everything from the marginally sleazy to ultrachic. None of it comes cheaply, however. A night on the town in Shanghai is now comparable to a night out in Hong Kong or Taipei.

Shanghai maintains a spirited rivalry with Beijing for the title of China's most cultured city and has attracted some big names in the last few years. Its fabulous new Grand Theatre has hosted Jose Carreras, Britain's Royal Opera and the Royal Ballet. Broadway shows like *Les Misérables* and *Cats* have recently started playing to Chinese audiences for the first time.

The Shanghai International Festival of Arts features a variety of performances, with past years bringing everything from *La Traviata* and the Kirov Ballet to Tibetan opera and Japanese pop. This annual festival, held in November in conjunction with the Shanghai Art Fair and Asia Music Festival, forms one of the highlights of Shanghai's cultural calendar.

Most Western festivities are also celebrated where you'd most expect them: St Patrick's Day at O'Malley's; Oktoberfest at Paulaner Bräuhaus; 4th July at any American restaurant.

Add to this a small but thriving club scene and a never-ending series of locally organised events (anything from Mardi Gras parties to booze cruises on the Huangpu River) and you end up with the nation's most exciting entertainment scene. Shanghai reveals a hedonism that most people never dreamed existed in communist China.

Tickets

Tickets for most of Shanghai's cultural events can be purchased at the **Shanghai Cultural Information & Booking Centre** (Map pp250-2; ☎ 6217 2426; www.culture.sh.cn in Chinese; 272 Fengxian Lu), behind Westgate Mall. It often has tickets when other places have sold out. The office carries a monthly English-language *Calendar of Performances in Shanghai*, though you can find the same information in the local press.

Shanghai Centre Theatre (Map pp250-2; ☎ 6279 8600, 6279 8663; theatre@shanghaicentre .com; 376 Nanjing Xilu; ⏱ 9am-7.45pm) also sells tickets for most local performances around Shanghai.

Beijing-based www.webtix.com.cn is due to add Shanghai to its on-line ticket agency. Two Chinese-language ticket booking websites are www.tickets.com.cn and www.piao.com.cn.

PUBS & BARS

Shanghai's pub and bar scene offers a lot to choose from and new places keep cropping up as older places close down. *That's Shanghai* keeps its finger on the pulse of Shanghai's nightlife, so check for the hot spots, which come and go according to Shanghai's notoriously fickle crowd.

One thing stays the same, however; drinks at most of the popular bars in Shanghai are expensive, starting at around Y35 for a bottle of beer or Y40 for a draught. So if you're

Top Five Performing Arts Venues

- **Shanghai Grand Theatre** (p132) For big shows and classical music.
- **Shanghai Centre Theatre** (p133) The most popular acrobats in town.
- **Cotton Club** (p131) Shanghai's most reliable venue for live jazz.
- **Jing'an Hotel** (p131) For its bargain Sunday evening chamber music.
- **Glamour Bar** (opposite) Chamber music or cabaret over a martini or two.

looking to save money, down a few stiff ones at the local corner stall before venturing into bars, or order drinks with your meal – alcohol in restaurants is usually much cheaper than in bars. Most places have some kind of happy hour from around 5pm to 8pm.

Different areas of the city peak at staggered times: Hengshan Lu's restaurants and bars take an after-work and after-dinner crowd early in the evening until midnight; Maoming Nanlu is busiest from midnight until around 2am. At the weekends many head for a club in the wee hours, while the hard core finish off a late night at Julu Lu around 5am. If you can pull an all-nighter, it's interesting to see the city's late-night side.

THE BUND

Like business districts in most cities, the area around the Bund empties early but there are still a few places to get a drink after enjoying a stroll along the Huangpu. After all, the Bund's buildings do look great lit up at night, as does futuristic Pudong across the river.

GLAMOUR BAR Map pp244-5
☎ 6350 9988; www.m-onthebund.com; 7th fl, 20 Guangdong Lu
Perfect for a predinner cocktail or post-Bund nightcap, the Glamour Bar at M on the Bund mixes sophisticated silvers and golds with updated Art Deco to create a sense of 1930s Hollywood glamour. The bar is on the top floor of the former Nissan Shipping Building (1927) so the night-time views of the Bund are wonderful. Evenings also bring sophisticated music,

with a jazzy cabaret feel that borders on the avant-garde, several times a month (Y120 minimum; from 10pm). There is also monthly chamber music (p131). Then there's the late-night bar and dessert menu until 11.30pm.

The Y68 minimum will get you one cocktail. Martinis are the drink of choice, or try a Shanghai Sunset – Cointreau, bitters and orange juice. Lovely, darling!

NOAH'S BAR Map pp244-5
☎ 6323 7869; 6th fl, 37 Fuzhou Lu; local beer Y15, imported Y30
The crummy lift up to this bar on the top floor of the **Captain Hostel** (p160) won't impress your date but the rooftop views of Pudong just might make up for it. There's outdoor and indoor seating, big portions of American food and a large screen for movies.

PEACE HOTEL Map pp244-5
☎ 6321 6888; 20 Nanjing Donglu; ☺ until 11pm
The top floor of the Peace Hotel gets you close to the views Victor Sassoon enjoyed in the 1930s and makes a fine place to wind down on a summer afternoon or evening. The entry fee of Y50 (plus 15%) – effectively a minimum charge – includes a beer, coffee or soft drink.

FRENCH CONCESSION
Hengshan Lu
BENI'S BAR Map pp246-9
Bèiní Kāfēiwū
☎ 6433 5964; 705 Yongjia Lu; beer Y20
A neighbourhood bar at the southern end of the Hengshan strip that is less expat-oriented than the rest of Hengshan Lu.

BLARNEY STONE Map pp246-9
☎ 6415 7496; 5A Dongping Lu
More intimate than O'Malley's, this Irish pub is the closest thing to a local, except that the beer's more expensive (Y65). For your money you get Guinness and Kilkenny on tap, British

Jazz at the Peace Hotel (p131)

newspapers on the bar and BBC World or live football on the TV. You won't find many locals in this local but it is one of the friendliest places in Shanghai and if you are new in town you'll doubtless strike up a conversation with one of the expat regulars. Otherwise, there are live Irish music evenings from 8pm and a pool table upstairs. Food runs to Irish stew or a Dublin fry-up of sausage, bacon and mushroom. Shangwho? Don't be put off by the drawn shutters; it's open.

O'MALLEY'S Map pp246-9
Oūmǎlì Cāntīng
☎ 6474 4533; 42 Taojiang Lu; Guinness/Kilkenny Y60
O'Malley's raised the standards of beer drinking considerably when it introduced draught Guinness and Kilkenny beers to Shanghai residents in the mid-1990s. It still remains one of the most popular expat places to hang out, either on the large lawn in good weather, or in the typical old-world pub atmosphere inside. There's live Irish music from around 8.30pm to 11.30pm, and plenty of U2 and Cranberries on the stereo at other times. It's not cheap, though. The pub also cooks up meals like Irish stew, rack of veal, and steak and chips for equally hefty prices (around Y170).

PAULANER BRÄUHAUS Map pp246-9
Bǎojiánà Cāntīng
☎ 6474 5700; 150 Fenyang Lu
It's Oktoberfest every night of the week in this grandmeister of Shanghai microbreweries, set in a glitzy three-storey, Munich-style beer hall converted from an old Chinese mansion, with stained glass borrowed from German churches. The Chinese staff are decked out in ill-fitting lederhosen, making it all a bit surreal, but it's very popular with well-heeled Chinese and the nightly Filipino bands get the place buzzing. Lager and dark wheat beer, brewed according to original 16th-century recipes, cost from Y60 for a small (0.3L) glass to a whopping Y105 for a litre, which means you'll only have change left for a freshly baked pretzel (Y8) or pickings from the late-night snack menu (11pm to 1am).

Maoming Lu
This street has become a night-time magnet. During the week the place is a quiet mix of bars, cafés and restaurants, but every weekend the bars turn into clubs and crowds spill out into the streets. On Saturday nights it's not uncommon for people to grab a cold beer from nearby Lawson's convenience store and join the street party. See Clubs (p129) for details of late-night dancing options. Places come and go every six months, so expect things to be different, though even if the venues change, more often than not the locations remain the same. There are continual rumours that the street (at least the western side) will be redeveloped soon, in which case all will change.

AMBER Map pp246-9
☎ 6466 5224; 184 Maoming Lu
Part bar, part club, the tracks at Amber go beyond the norm, ranging from drum 'n' bass and African drumming to world fusion and even Chinese reggae! Monday is ladies' night, Tuesday gets your taxi fare back, Wednesday is hip-hop, and there are other drink specials.

BLUE FROG Map pp246-9
Lánwā
☎ 6445 6634; 207-223 Maoming Lu; beer Y35, shots Y30
Good bar food, classy décor and a comfy upstairs lounge raise this place a notch above the other Maoming dives. Wednesday is 'martini and a manicure' night, there's folk music on Thursday and sleepy Sunday brings out the board games. Stagger your way through all 100 shots and you'll get your name on the wall and a shot a day for life. Plus the logo's cute. Cheap drinks on Tuesday.

BUDDHA BAR Map pp246-9
☎ 6473 7988; 172 Maoming Nanlu
No relation to the Parisian original (and its endless ambient CD mixes), the Buddha Bar gets going after midnight.

JUDY'S TOO Map pp246-9
☎ 6548 1001; 176 Maoming Lu
Sitting somewhere between a bar and a club, Judy's has been going for ages and is still one of Shanghai's most popular places. Sunday is movie night, Tuesday there's live music from 10pm, Wednesday is ladies' night from 9pm and Thursday is '80s night. Happy hour runs from 7pm to 10pm, when drinks are Y20. At weekends the place goes mad. Beers cost around Y35. On the 2nd floor is Taco Popo, a Mexican restaurant.

MANHATTAN BAR Map pp246-9
☎ 6467 0284; 207 Maoming Lu

Relocated from Julu Lu, the Manhattan is the golden oldie of late-night venues and a popular retreat after weekend clubbing. The daily happy hour (7pm to 10pm) gives you one free beer for every one you buy and offers Y10 shots.

WOODSTOCK BAR Map pp246-9
☎ 6473 4807; 180 Maoming Lu

Another long-time stalwart of Shanghai's debauched late-night scene, Woodstock has also relocated from its former location on Julu Lu. Strong on cheap beers and bar girls, if there's nothing going on there are always half a dozen options next door.

Julu Lu

Prostitution is illegal in China, therefore there are no prostitutes in Shanghai... But if there were anything close you'd find them on Julu Lu, so be careful with whom you schmooze. Located near the Hilton, the seedy and the upmarket happily coexist here. It's quite remarkable that the whole street hasn't been closed down. Aside from the sleaze, Julu Lu's strip of bars is also the haunt of the late-night crowd; it gets going well after midnight and continues until dawn. Places change frequently; just dig around for what's new on the Lu.

BADLANDS Map pp246-9
☎ 6466 7788; 895 Julu Lu

A fine place to drift away into margarita-ville. As well as margaritas, it serves cold Corona (Y35), two-for-one tequila on weekends after 9pm, and plenty of nachos and burritos (Y50 to Y75) to line the gut. There's also an eclectic jukebox.

GOODFELLAS Map pp246-9
☎ 6467 0775; 907 Julu Lu

A long-time spit-and-sawdust party place, with cheap drinks before 10pm.

OLD MANHATTAN BAR Map pp246-9
☎ 6248 2777; 231 Huashan Lu

The first expat pub in Shanghai and still pulling in the Hilton overflow. Just around the corner from Julu Lu.

Other French Concession Bars

BONNE SANTÉ Map pp254-5
☎ 6384 2906; 8 Jinan Lu

This wine bar close to Huaihai Lu is at the base of the Somerset Residence. The monthly wine tastings are a highlight.

EDDY'S BAR Map pp246-9
☎ 6282 0521; 1877 Huaihai Zhonglu; drinks Y15-20

A gay-friendly bar/café that occasionally pushes the envelope with drag acts. For the latest gay venues look for the cryptic comments in local listings magazines.

FACE Map pp246-9
☎ 6466 4328; www.face-shanghai.com; Bldg 1, Ruijin Guest House, 18 Ruijin Erlu; beer Y50-55, cocktails Y50-60

A strong contender for most beautiful bar in Shanghai, on the ground floor of a wonderful old building, the Face has antique Chinese opium beds set against lush and warm persimmon-coloured walls. Prices aren't cheap but there's nowhere better to take a date or laze in front of the manicured lawn on a summer's afternoon. Drinks of choice include draught Tetleys or Hoegaarten, plus great cocktails (try the chocolate mint martini). Bar snacks come from the attached **Lan Na Thai** (p104) and **Hazara** (p104) restaurants, so stretch to Thai fish cakes and chicken tikka. Don't forget the 10% service charge.

KIWI BAR Map pp246-9
☎ 6407 3861; 88 Guangyuan Xilu; beer Y20

Cheap drinks all the time, random free rounds of tequila shots and alcoholic management make this rowdy but friendly local a great place to get buzzed without having to cash a fistful of travellers cheques. Draught and bottled Steinlager and meat pies reflect the Kiwi management. As the Kiwi manager (recognisable by his consistent lack of any kind of shirt) says, 'It's a privilege if you get barred from the Kiwi'.

PARK 97 Map pp246-9
☎ 6318 0785; 2 Gaolan Lu

Dress up, for this is another chic place for a drink. Classically stylish rather than gimmicky, it's always full of interesting beautiful people. Added attractions include two excellent restaurants (**Tokio Joe's** and **Baci** – see p102), Sunday brunch specials, great outdoor summer

Live music at a Julu Lu nightclub (p127)

seating bordering Fuxing Park and the best Bloody Marys in Shanghai. One of a growing number of places to offer sake cocktails; try the Sakanta (sake, strawberry liqueur, sours mix and fresh strawberries Y55), or there are champagne cocktails, a range of grappa and draught Tetleys. Happy hour (5pm to 8pm) has cheap house drinks.

SHANGHAI SALLY'S Map pp246-9
Shànghǎi Gùxiāng
☎ 5382 0738; 4 Xiangshan Lu
This old French Concession stalwart is one of the oldest expat bars in town, imitating a British pub with darts (Tuesday) and pool competitions (Thursday), bangers and mash (Y60), and draught Guinness and Tetleys. Downstairs there is a clubby lounge space, the Underground, which has comfy sofas and dance floors. The British management has moved on and recent changes have proved confusing, serving up jazz (including some interesting funked-up erhu music) next to nights devoted to hip-hop (Wednesday) and even chess (quiet Mondays). We'll see... Happy hour (4pm to 9pm) has Y20 beer and women get cheap drinks (Y10) on Tuesday.

TIME PASSAGE Map pp246-9
Zuótiān Jīntiān Míngtiān
☎ 6240 2588; No 183, Lane 1038, Huashan Lu
The only bar in Shanghai (apart from Noah's, maybe) that has a backpacker feel. Drinks and

food start at Y15, and there's a selection of books and plenty of interesting things on the walls to look at.

NANJING XILU
A more sedate mainstream and business-types bar scene can be found on Nanjing Xilu, catering to the expat crowd at the Shanghai Centre.

LONG BAR Map pp250-2
☎ 6279 8268; Shanghai Centre, 1376 Nanjing Xi Lu
This bar is named after that of the former British Club, supposedly the longest bar in the world in the 1930s. Now in the Shanghai Centre, the bar is still popular with expat businessmen. It has draught Guinness and Kilkenny (Y60 a pint), plenty of specials (50% off a selected menu item every day) and happy hours (weekdays 5pm to 8pm; weekends 3pm to 8pm).

PUDONG
GRAND HYATT Map pp253-4
Zhongyang Dadao
As with most things Hyatt, the Grand has some of the city's most elegant bars. These places make a great splurge for special occasions and for the extra few *kuài* you'll feel like you're, literally, in heaven. And when you want to move on, **Pu-J's** (p130) club is just next door.

Cloud 9, on the 87th floor, gets you as high as you can legally get in a Shanghai bar, featuring unbeatable views and excellent Asian tapas. It's open weekday evenings and during the day at weekends.

The **Piano Bar**, on the 53rd floor, is more sedate and decadent, with suede walls, cosy sofas, opium beds (for drinking, not smoking) and 1930s jazz classics on the piano. Next door, the more austere **Bar Twist** serves martinis to a younger set.

OTHER AREAS
DOOR Map p256
☎ 6295 3737; 1468 Hongqiao Lu
Anyone with a flair for interior design should make a beeline for this very stylish bar above the Hongqiao branch of **Folk Restaurant** (p113). The Chinese band plays Western music on Chinese instruments (weekends from 8pm).

TOP OF THE WORLD Map p257
☎ 6426 6888; Regal Shanghai East Asia Hotel, Tianyueqiao Lu
A bar perched in the roof of Shanghai Stadium, with a great view of the stadium interior, really has to be a sports bar. It has English sport on the TV, pool tables, and a daily happy hour (5pm to 8pm), half-price draughts on Monday and all-day happy hour on Sunday. There's a Y300 cover charge for the bird's-eye view when events are staged in the stadium below.

CLUBS
Shanghai is beginning to attract some top-notch DJs from abroad and there are a lot of popular dance venues, making it one of the hippest clubbing destinations in Asia. Smaller clubs have parties with cheap drinks and specials every couple of weeks; look out for fliers and adverts in local magazines. Things can be quiet during the week but the music is often more interesting at these times.

CALIFORNIA CLUB Map pp246-9
☎ 6318 0785; 2 Gaolan Lu; ⏱ 9pm-2am, until 4am weekends
Small dance space with a 2nd-floor chill-out lounge plays house and the occasional '80s nights, with visiting DJs and special events. Part of **Park 97** (p127), on popular nights entry is sometimes limited to members only.

CLUB LA BELLE Map pp250-2
☎ 6247 5559; www.labelle-shanghai.com; 2nd fl, 333 Tongren Lu; beer Y45, mains Y150-200; ⏱ closed Sunday
Set in a 1938 villa, the **Green House** (p30), designed by Hudec, and previously owned by the family of architect IM Pei, is a restaurant that turns into a lounge club as soon as the after-dinner coffee gets cold (10pm). Lots of guest DJs from abroad pick up the action (Ben Watt of Everything But the Girl fame played here during our visit) with some disco, old school and hip-hop, though at other times you might have to settle for some (gulp!) Elton John and a glitter ball. There is a nice outdoor sundeck for summer lazing. Chill out in the afternoon with DJ'd lounge music and two-for-one drinks. Downstairs is the swish Cantonese **Mandarin Sky**, which is the place for pre-clubbing dim sum.

GUANDII Map pp246-9
☎ 6372 6020; Fuxing Park
A stylish, beautiful club for stylish, beautiful people.

LOFT Map pp246-9
☎ 5386 6268; www.fusionclub.com.cn; 323 Fuxing Zhonglu; cocktail Y50, beer Y35-40
An impressive complex in a converted old cinema that is versatile enough for all your moods, whether you want to eat, drink or dance. The very cool dance space on the top floor is sufficiently large to give you some curtained privacy away from the sweaty mass and there's a fine outdoor space in summer. There's no cover charge on regular nights. The dance floor overlooks a lower-floor wine bar called the **White Room**; painfully chic, with lots of glass, chrome and cream sofas, and wine bottles displayed in glass racks. The Japanese design influence is confirmed by the sake by the pot (Y75 to Y95) and yakitori bar snacks. Lastly there's a (groan, not another...) ground-floor Asian fusion restaurant called the **Kitchen** (mains Y60-90), with weekday lunch specials for Y60.

PARAMOUNT Map pp250-2
☎ 6249 8866; www.sh-paramount.com; 218 Yuyuan Lu; minimum charge Y70, 2nd-fl lunch buffet Y58-68, afternoon dancing Y40
For something a little more nostalgic, this renovated old theatre (the Paramount was the biggest nightclub in the 1930s) has fused karaoke bars with an old-time dinner/dance hall

to make something quintessentially Shanghainese. The 4th-floor restaurant and 2nd-floor karaoke lounges both have dance floors where you can foxtrot to a live band from 7.15pm (Shanghainese jazz from 9.30pm). It's a bit bizarre but might be of interest if you're intent on capturing some of the flavour of the 1930s (a sense of humour helps too).

PEGASUS Map pp254-5
☎ 5385 8189; 2nd fl, Golden Bell Plaza, 98 Huaihai Zhonglu

Shanghai's latest hi-tech disco, ultramodern and techno, but with a touch more class than **Real Love** or **Rojam**, both listed below.

PU-J'S Map pp253-4
☎ 5049 1234 ext 8731

A chic club out in Pudong, part of, but not in, the Grand Hyatt, on the 3rd floor of the adjoining podium building. The club has two music venues, one of which features Shanghai's famous jazz vocalist Coco, cigars, wine and a decadent atmosphere. The other has live bands from the USA and elsewhere, and a dance floor. In between is a chic tapas bar. A cover charge of Y100 at weekends gets you into both places and includes one standard drink (around Y40 each). It's open to 2am at weekends; dress up.

REAL LOVE Map pp246-9
Zhēn Ài
☎ 6474 6380; 10 Hengshan Lu

Shanghai's busiest disco at the time of writing; the Y40 weekend cover charge (Y30 weekdays) includes one drink.

ROJAM DISCO Map pp246-9
☎ 6390 7181, www.rojam.com; 4th fl, Hong Kong Plaza, 283 Huaihai Zhonglu

A huge place, popular with local clubbers and great for observing Shanghai's moneyed youth at play. It packs in 1500 people at weekends. Charges run from Y40 to Y60.

YY'S Map pp246-9
☎ 6466 4098; 125 Nanchang Lu

It's not as popular as it once was but things still get going after midnight in this long-running favourite. Owner Kenny has made a few changes to the basement club recently and it remains a busy weekend joint. During the day, or to catch your breath, you can enjoy a drink in the cool bar upstairs.

MUSIC
ROCK & POP

Shanghai has a lamentable live music scene. Although the Asian Music Festival brings Chinese bands into Shanghai every November, most bars feature nothing more exciting than a Filipino cover band, carrying on a tradition that once again dates from the 1930s.

There are occasional gigs at the Shanghai Grand Stage (inside Shanghai Stadium), yet these are mostly sappy Cantonese crooners or plastic pop stars. Once in a while decent bands arrive from Beijing and even the occasional foreign megastar like Whitney Houston jets through on an Asian tour (the Rolling Stones cancelled their Shanghai gig during the SARS epidemic in 2003). Check *That's Shanghai* to see who's playing. O'Malley's (p126) and Blarney Stone (p125) have live Irish music nightly from 9pm to 11.30pm.

ARK HOUSE Map pp246-9
Yàkē Yīnyuè Cāntīng
☎ 6326 8008; House 15, North Block, Xintiandi, Lane 181, Taicang Lu

A long-overdue venue for underground Chinese bands, ranging from pop to Chinese punk, generally with an alternative edge. Even the occasional British band lands up here. Gigs get going on Friday and Saturday from 9.30pm. There's a cover charge of Y30 to Y50.

PLANET MUSIC PUB Map pp246-9
☎ 6472 0023; No 200, Lane 210, Taikang Lu

If you are feeling bold on a Saturday night try this grungy bar next to the **Taikang Lu Art Centre** (p71) for a more underground, alternative sound.

JAZZ & BLUES

Shanghai has a long tradition of jazz, dating from the 1920s when Russian and Filipino bands jammed together in the French Concession. The International Jazz Festival, featuring artists like David Sanchez, is part of the annual International Festival of Arts.

Two of Shanghai's most famous jazz vocalists are Coco, a man who often dresses as a woman, and Shadow, a woman who often dresses as a man. Both sing an excellent range of jazz standards, Broadway numbers, old Chinese songs and the occasional original composition. Coco often haunts the **Cotton Club** (below) or **Pu-J's** (opposite); check listings.

Apart from the places below you'll find fairly tame jazz in the top-end hotels, particularly the Hilton's top-floor Penthouse bar, the Portman Ritz-Carlton bar and the Niche Bar at the Westin. Drinks are around Y60 and Monday is the day of rest.

CJW Map pp246-9
☎ 6385 6677; House 2, North Block, Xintiandi
Cigar Jazz and Wine (CJW) is an über-chic locale, with a professional international jazz band nightly. It's more about the look than the sound here.

COTTON CLUB Map pp246-9
Miánhuā Jùlèbù
☎ 6437 7110; 1428 Huaihai Lu
One of the best and longest-running bars for live jazz, this comfortable, unassuming place features blues bands on Friday and Saturday from around 10pm and more laid-back jazz the rest of the week. Tuesday is open-mike night and on Monday the place is as quiet as a mouse. The crowd here is younger than the more-portly hotel jazz scene.

HOUSE OF BLUES & JAZZ Map pp246-9
☎ 6437 5280; 158 Maoming Lu
This restaurant and bar is for serious jazz lovers. The owner, a Chinese TV celebrity, has plastered the walls with old photos of jazz legends. The in-house band delivers live music from 10pm to 1am. Sunday night is a free-for-all jam, and Monday is quiet. At other times, there are recorded classics. Upstairs offers Western and Chinese food.

JAZZ 37 Map pp250-2
☎ 6256 8888; 500 Weihai Lu
Terrific views and a stylish bar on the top floor of the **Four Seasons Hotel** (p166) add to the smoothness of this lounge-scene jazz (from 9pm Monday to Saturday). There's no cover charge but the drinks are pricey at around Y60.

PEACE HOTEL Map pp244-5
Hépíng Fàndiàn
☎ 6321 6888; fax 6329 0300; 20 Nanjing Donglu
Shanghai's most famous hotel features Shanghai's most famous jazz band, an ancient (all over the age of 70) jazz sextet that has been churning out nostalgic covers like 'Summertime' and 'Moon River' since time immemorial. It's a tourist favourite but it's debatable whether it's worth the Y42 cover charge (plus pricey drinks). From 8pm.

CLASSICAL MUSIC
Along with Beijing, Shanghai is one of the great cultural centres of China. The Shanghai Symphony Orchestra (conductor Chen Xieyang), Shanghai Broadcast Symphony Orchestra and Shanghai Philharmonic Orchestra regularly perform classical music. For traditional Chinese music, look out for the Shanghai Traditional Chinese Music Ensemble. The *Shanghai Star* lists weekly music events.

CONSERVATORY OF MUSIC Map pp246-9
Yīnyuè Xuéyuàn
☎ 6431 0334; 20 Fenyang Lu
The auditorium in this complex off Huaihai Zhonglu holds classical music performances on Sunday evenings at 7pm during term time. Tickets are cheap (around Y20) and the performers are often the stars of the future.

GLAMOUR BAR Map pp244-5
☎ 6350 9988; www.m-onthebund.com;
7th fl, 20 Guangdong Lu
This classy bar features monthly chamber music by members of the Shanghai Symphony Orchestra. Performances fall on the last Sunday of the month, cost Y50 (students Y20) and start at 5pm. See the Glamour Bar listing on p125 for more details.

JING'AN HOTEL Map pp246-9
☎ 6248 1888 ext 687; 370 Huashan Lu
Chamber music is played every Sunday night at 8pm at the hotel's San Diego Hall. Tickets are a steal at Y20.

JINJIANG HOTEL Map pp246-9
☎ 6258 2582; 59 Maoming Nanlu
Holds a classical concert every Sunday at 2pm in the Grand Hall. Tickets cost Y50 and include refreshments.

SHANGHAI CONCERT HALL Map pp244-5
Shànghǎi Yīnyuè Tīng
☎ 6386 9153; 523 Yan'an Donglu
In 2003, the Shanghai government picked up and moved this classic building (all 5650 tons

Tomorrow Square, left (p167) and Shanghai Grand Theatre (below)

of it) 66m away from busy Yan'an Donglu to a quieter park-side location. This wasn't the first time a Shanghai landmark has been shifted (the Bund Meteorological Tower was moved in the 1990s) but this time the relocation actually cost more than building a brand-new concert hall. When the hall reopens in early 2004 it should once again host smaller-scale (and cheaper) concerts by local and international musicians, particularly soloists. The theatre normally posts a bilingual programme outside its ticket office. Chinese architects built the hall in 1930 as the Nanking Theatre.

SHANGHAI GRAND THEATRE Map pp244-5
Shànghǎi Dàjùyuàn

☎ 6372 8701; www.shgtheatre.com;
300 Renmin Dadao

Shanghai's premier venue for national and international opera, ballet, music and drama, hosting everything from *Cats* to Chinese ballet. Ticket prices generally range from Y100 to Y500.

THEATRES

The Shanghai Opera House, Shanghai Ballet Troupe and Shanghai Theatre Academy all present traditional Chinese drama and opera and interpretations of Western opera, ballet and theatre. Shanghai Grand Theatre

(above) and Shanghai Centre Theatre (opposite) are the premier venues. Several smaller theatres hold interesting performances, normally in Chinese only but sometimes with English subtitles. Shanghai has already hosted *Les Misérables* and *Cats*. *Phantom of the Opera* is expected to arrive in 2004.

LYCEUM THEATRE Map pp246-9
Lánxīn Dàjùyuàn

☎ 6256 4631; 57 Maoming Nanlu

Completed in 1930, this theatre is one of the oldest in Shanghai and once housed the British-run Shanghai Amateur Dramatic Society. Now all manner of acts perform here, including drama, magic, dance, movies and acrobatics. The theatre is currently under renovation, which hopefully will preserve its Art Deco charms.

MAJESTIC THEATRE Map pp250-2
Měiqí Dàjùyuàn

☎ 6258 6493; 66 Jiangning Lu

This is another venue for local drama productions, as well as occasional ballet.

SHANGHAI ARTS THEATRE Map pp250-2
Yìhǎi Jùyuàn

☎ 6256 8282; 466 Jiangning Lu

An eclectic mixture of drama and live music north of Nanjing Xilu.

SHANGHAI DRAMATIC ARTS CENTRE
Map pp246-9
Shànghǎi Huàjù Yìshù Zhōngxīn
☎ 6473 4567; 288 Anfu Lu

A good place to look for interesting Chinese drama. If the production is a wipe-out you can always take consolation in the nice old villa-style buildings of the complex.

SHANGHAI THEATRE ACADEMY
Map pp246-9
Shànghǎi Xìjù Xuéyuàn
☎ 6248 2920; 630 Huashan Lu

Stages interesting plays in its Experimental Theatre.

YUNFENG THEATRE
Map pp250-2
Yúnfēng Jùchǎng
☎ 6253 3669; 1700 Beijing Xilu

A minor stage near the Jing'an Temple, which puts on occasional Chinese-oriented musicals and drama.

COMEDY CLUBS

Malone's (p111) hosts the China Comedy Club (www .chinacomedyclub.com; admission Y200) in its 3rd-floor bar on Friday and Saturday nights. Sets get going at 9pm. The acts are generally high-quality British comedians on an Asian tour.

O'Malley's (p126) occasionally hosts the Punchline Comedy Club (www.punchlinecomedy .com; tickets Y220).

OPERA
CHINESE OPERA

Beijing and local operas are almost exclusively performed in Chinese and are therefore pretty inaccessible to most foreigners. There are, however, several local opera troupes such as the Shanghai Peking Opera House and the Shanghai Local Opera School, which are worth seeing, if only for the spectacle and costumes. Larger venues like the Shanghai Grand Theatre occasionally stage high-profile Chinese operas such as the amazingly popular *Dream of the Red Mansions*.

KUN OPERA HOUSE
Map pp246-9
Shànghǎi Kūnjùtuán
Shaoxing Lu

Occasional Kun and other styles of opera are performed in this backstreet old-time theatre.

YIFU THEATRE
Map pp244-5
Yìfū Wǔtái
☎ 6351 4668; 701 Fuzhou Lu

Formerly the Tianchan Stage, this local theatre, a block east of Renmin Square, is recognisable by the huge opera mask above the entrance. The theatre presents a popular programme of local operas, farce, Yue opera and Beijing opera, as well as touring operas from Anhui and Fujian. A standing Beijing opera performs at weekends at 1.30pm.

WESTERN OPERA

In recent years, the Shanghai Grand Theatre (opposite) has hosted Carreras, Domingo and Pavarotti (separately) and productions of *Aida* and *La Traviata*. Tickets range from Y100 to Y500 and local restaurants often host special post-theatre dinners.

BALLET

The main hall of the Shanghai Grand Theatre (opposite) has seen the State Kremlin Ballet and Britain's Royal Ballet. The Majestic (opposite) has smaller performances, as well as folk dances from all over China.

ACROBATICS

Chinese acrobatic troupes are among the best in the world, and Shanghai is a good place to see a performance.

SHANGHAI CENTRE THEATRE
Map pp250-2
Shànghǎi Shāngchéng Jùyuàn
☎ 6279 8663; 1376 Nanjing Xilu

Shanghai Acrobatics Troupe (*Shànghǎi Zájì Tuán*) has popular performances here most nights at 7.30pm. It's a short but fun show and is high on the to-do list of most first-time visitors. Tickets sell for Y50, Y80 and Y100. Buy them a couple of days in advance from the ticket office at the entrance to the Shanghai Centre.

Big-name music and drama performances also sometimes fill this premier hall.

SHANGHAI CIRCUS WORLD
Map pp242-3
Shànghǎi Mǎxìchéng
☎ 6652 2395; 2266 Gonghexin Lu; bus 46 & 916 from Renmin Sq, 95 from Shanghai train station

If the Shanghai Centre has no performances when you're in town consider schlepping out to the far northern outskirts of town to this impressive complex. Stars include a Uyghur tightrope walker and, unfortunately, a performing panda named Ying Ying. Shows start at 7.30pm; tickets cost Y50, Y80, Y100, Y150 and Y280.

CINEMAS

Beijing allows about 30 foreign (read Hollywood) movies per year, with more appearing every year. Over 150 films are screened at the annual week-long Shanghai International Film Festival (www.siff.com) in June, though Cannes doesn't need to worry about the competition quite yet.

Foreign movies are generally dubbed into Chinese but there are exceptions: it always pays to call ahead and double-check the language being screened. Listings magazines like *That's Shanghai* advertise film schedules.

Tickets for the better cinemas cost Y40 to Y50, down to Y20 for morning shows.

Maria's Choice (mariaschoice-subscribe@topica.com) is a private film club that arranges screenings of independent Chinese films with English subtitles at Kodak Cinema World. Sign up for an email list update of screenings.

Shanghai Science & Technology Museum (p75) has an IMAX cinema and there are plans to build more in Shanghai, probably near Renmin Square, as part of a rumoured 10-screen multiplex cinema.

Otherwise, most expats and Chinese invest in a VCD (video CD) player, which opens up a far wider choice of films at a fraction of the price (VCDs cost about Y15 each to buy, half this if pirated). Be aware that if you are found packing your weight's worth of pirate VCDs back to your home country they will be confiscated.

ENTERTAINMENT CENTRES

The city's major shopping centres offer a whole range of diversions, from cafés and restaurants to entertainment complexes. These can prove a godsend if you have kids (or a spouse) who start to yawn and roll their eyes as soon as you step into a shop.

Xujiahui boasts several entertainment centres and promises more to come. The basement of **Metro City** (Map p257; exit 9 of the Xujiahui station) has Sega machines, air hockey and pool tables and **Grand Gateway** (Map p257) has a host of hi-tech toys. **Superbrand Mall** (Map pp253-4; Pudong) plans to introduce an array of virtual reality simulators second only to NASA. Most (very short) games cost around Y3.

GREAT WORLD Map pp244-5
Dà Shìjiè
☎ 6374 6703; 1 Xizang Nanlu; admission Y30
For more traditional entertainment, check out this wedding-cake building near Renmin Square, which was once the famous and salacious Great World of pre-1949 Shanghai (p63).

Movie Screenings for Foreigners

The following cinemas show Western movies in the original language and Chinese movies with English subtitles.

Golden Cinema Haixing (Map pp246-9; ☎ 6418 7034; www.hotcinema.com; 4th fl, Haixing Plaza, 1 Ruijin Nanlu)

Kodak Cinema World (Map p257; ☎ 6426 8181; http://cinemaworld.kodak.com; 5th fl, Metro City, 1111 Zhaojiabang Lu, Xujiahui)

Paradise Cinema City (Map p257; ☎ 6407 1165; 6th fl, Grand Gateway, Xujiahui)

Shanghai Film Art Centre (Map pp246-9; ☎ 6280 6088; 160 Xinhua Lu) The main venue for the Shanghai International Film Festival, with a branch in Pudong at Nextage department store (Map pp253-4).

Studio City (Map pp250-2; ☎ 6218 2173; 10th fl, Westgate Mall, 1038 Nanjing Xilu)

UME (Ultimate Movie Experience) Cinemaplex (Map pp246-9; ☎ 6373 3333; 4th fl, Xintiandi; tickets Y60) Six cinemas and comfy sofas here.

Yonglegong (Paradise) Cinema (Map pp246-9; ☎ 6431 2961; 308 Anfu Lu)

Screenings of foreign films are also held at **Alliance Française** (☎ 6357 5388, www.alliancefrancaise.org.cn; 6th fl, 297 Wusong Lu; bus 55), which shows French films (in French) on Friday at 6.30pm; admission Y10 and the **German Centre** (☎ 6501 5100; www.germancentreshanghai.com; 1233 Siping Lu; bus 55, 61), showing films in German every Wednesday at 7pm.

Entertainment at Great World (opposite)

There's a potpourri of performances available on different stages, including Shaoxing opera, nationalities' song and dance, acrobatics, comedy sketches, films, magic, a Guinness World Records display, distorting mirrors and a teahouse. Performances go on all day but peter out after 6pm.

SPECTATOR SPORTS

Shanghai Stadium (Map p257) seats 80,000 spectators for major sports events (football is the most popular) and occasional soft-rock concerts. Manchester United played Shanghai's Shenhua football team here in July 1999. Tickets range from Y20 to Y100, depending on the event. The best views of the ground come from the Top of the World bar (p129), though a cover charge is generally introduced whenever there is an event.

Shanghai Shenhua, coached by a Yugoslavian manager, is the city's top team and local matches are played in the Hongkou Stadium (Map pp242-3) in north Shanghai.

Shanghai's local basketball team is the Shanghai Sharks, who won the national championship in 2002 under the leadership of star player Yao Ming (all 226cm of him). Yao moved to the NBA's Houston Rockets in 2002 and is currently one of the hottest sports stars in America, endorsing everything from Visa cards to Gatorade, without speaking any English!

If tennis is your thing, the annual Shanghai Open (p10) attracts many top tennis players (Michael Chang is a local favourite, rivalled only by Anna Kournikova who reached the final in 2002).

One of Shanghai's top sporting events is the Shanghai International Marathon (p11), which dodges traffic every November.

Formula One comes to Shanghai in 2004, and a grand prix circuit is currently being built in the Anting district northwest of the city. Races are screened live at many bars across town.

HEALTH & FITNESS

The active lifestyle is starting to catch on in Shanghai, with flash gyms popping out of the ground everywhere, but the Chinese favourites, badminton and table tennis, still rule the day. There are many expat clubs, ranging from squash to softball, karate, darts, Frisbee, basketball and even scuba diving and expat Brits still play cricket in Shanghai like they first did in 1858. See local listings magazines for contact details, as these change frequently.

BADMINTON

There are public badminton (yǔmáo qiú) courts at Shanghai Stadium (above), located just east of the gymnasium. Otherwise, play Chinese-style in any street that has plenty of traffic.

BOWLING

There are more than 2000 tenpin bowling (bǎolín) alleys in Shanghai, in hotels, entertainment centres and even department stores. Costs at the cheaper places range from Y6 to Y15 per person per game, depending upon the time of day; shoe hire is extra.

BUNGEE JUMPING

Yes, you can bungee jump in Shanghai, or to be more specific, off the roof of Shanghai Stadium. The jump is organised by the Extreme Sports Centre (☎ 6426 5535), a Sino-US joint venture. A 70m jump costs Y180, which works out at around Y40 per second.

Alternatively, you can do a reverse bungee (in which you're yanked upwards into the sky) for Y150, or try the Sky Glider (a bit like freefall hang-gliding) for Y100. Masochists can try all three jumps for Y300 and you'll even get a certificate (to prove that you are insane). If you need a witness, Y30 gets a friend in, plus a Coke and a snack.

The jump site is accessed through the lobby of the **Regal Shanghai East Asia Hotel** (Map p257). Jumps take place daily from 1.30pm to 9pm.

CYCLING

Shanghai's mad traffic can make cycling the city's most stressful, if not potentially lethal, activity (second to the bungee jump, of course). However, the French Concession offers some charming areas for biking and the ambitious can make longer excursions out of the city to places like Sheshan and even Suzhou. See the Excursions chapter (p171) for details of these destinations.

The Shanghai Bike Club is an expat group that organises rides every Sunday from Gubei. Check the latest *That's Shanghai* magazine for contact details.

BOHDI BIKES Map pp242-3

☎ 3226 0020; www.bohdi.com.cn; Room 406, No 59, Alley 710 Dingxi Lu

Bohdi's sells its own top-end US mountain bikes, rents bikes (Y150 per day) and has information on bike trips in the area.

GIANT BIKES Map pp246-9
743 Jianguo Xulu, cnr Hengshan Lu

Offers a good selection of its own brand of Taiwanese mountain and other bikes for sale.

WOLF'S MOUNTAIN BIKE CLUB
☎ 6472 9325; wolfs@263.net

Wolf's runs popular excursions around town and can find every kind of widget or accessory you may need. Contact the owner Lao Wang. Check listings magazines for current contact details.

GOLF

Golf in China is the preserve of businesspeople and the new elite. Add to this the fact that Shanghai's golf clubs are aimed squarely at the Japanese and it's no surprise that golfing is one of the city's most expensive pastimes. See the boxed text below for details.

GYMS

Most top-end hotels provide gyms free for their guests with steep membership for everyone else. If you're not a fitness guru but just like to pop into a gym now and again, the one at the **Oriental Riverside Hotel**

Golf for Visitors

The following clubs are open to nonmembers and charge from US$50 to US$100 for 18 holes and a caddy, more at weekends when reservations are a must.

Binhai Golf Club (☎ 5830 6811, 5805 8888; Binhai, Nanhui, near Pudong airport) Shanghai's only 54-hole golf course.

Grand Shanghai International Golf & Country Club (☎ 6210 3350; Zhengyi village, Kunshan, Jiangsu)

Hongqiao Golf Club (☎ 6401 6666; 567 Hongxu Lu, Hongqiao) In the west of town.

Shanghai International Golf & Country Club (☎ 5972 8111; sigc@sh163a.sta.net.cn; Xinyang village, Zhujiajiao, Qingpu County, 40km west of Shanghai) Designed by Robert Trent Jones Jr; for members and guests only.

Shanghai Links (☎ 5897 5899, 5897 7946; 1600 Linbai Lu, Chuansha, Pudong) Course designed by Jack Nicklaus.

Tianma Golf & Country Club (☎ 5766 2686; www.uecidomain.com/tianma; Sheshan, Songjiang)

Tomson Golf Club (Map pp242-3; ☎ 5833 8888; 1 Longdong Lu, near Century Park, Pudong) The closest 18 holes to town. **Hotel Intercontinental Pudong** (p165) can book for guests.

There are several driving ranges visitors can use if you want to polish up your swing.

East Asia Golf Club (☎ 6433 1198; 135 Jianguo Xilu)

Liujiazui Golf Club (Map pp253-4; ☎ 5882 9028; 501 Yincheng Lu, Pudong) Big hitters staying in the Grand Hyatt can simply walk out of the hotel to this enclosed driving range next door.

Shanghai Grasslands Golf Club (☎ 5976 1111; 1366 Sanyiba Hwy, Xujing, Qingpu) Southwest of Shanghai.

(p165) in Pudong charges non-guests Y50 per visit to use the gym or Y100 to use its fabulous swimming pool. The **Crowne-Plaza Shanghai** (p166) offers a temporary membership, which includes use of the gym, sauna and pool for Y180, which is good value for Shanghai. Most gyms are open from 6am to 11pm. If you are a member of a branch elsewhere or even overseas you can generally use the other gyms free of charge.

The following are a few good gyms with memberships for six months or one year. Some also offer short-term rates.

ALEXANDER CITY CLUB Map pp246-9
☎ 5358 1188; www.aforme.com; Xintiandi, South Block, 6-7, Lane 123 Xingye Lu
One of the flashiest and most expensive gyms, with plenty of space. The superb facilities include a pool, juice bar, spinning studio, spa, Thai restaurant, plus a squash court that is the wrong size! Part of a Taiwanese chain, it will set you back Y300 for 30 visits or Y7200 for annual membership.

BODY TECH GYM Map pp246-9
☎ 6281 5639; 387 Panyu Lu
A large range of muscle-toning and cardio machines is available here, plus free weights, personal trainers, lots of aerobic and other classes, and a sauna. The equipment is good even if the décor is tired. A six-month/year membership is discounted to Y2000/3000. Off-peak memberships (9am to 5pm only) cost Y1500/2000.

CLARK HATCH FITNESS CENTRE
Map pp246-9
☎ 6212 9998; Radisson Plaza Hotel, 78 Xingguo Lu
Facilities here include a heated pool, aerobics, yoga and t'ai chi classes, a bowling alley, a spa, trainers and a squash court. One month's membership costs Y1200.

FITNESS FIRST Map pp250-2
☎ 6288 0152; www.fitnessfirst.com.hk; Plaza 66, 1266 Nanjing Xilu; 6.30am-11pm Mon-Fri, 7am-10pm Sat & Sun
Another chain, in the flash basement of Plaza 66 mall, facilities include exercise studios, a large range of fitness equipment and a sauna. It offers classes and personal training, massage and aromatherapy. Membership (six months minimum) is around Y3400/5000 off-peak/peak hours.

GOLD'S GYM Map pp250-2
☎ 6279 2000; 258 Tongren Lu
This huge US franchise is for those who perhaps take their fitness more seriously than their wallet. Annual membership is Y3000 (Y2000 off-peak) and the facilities and classes are among the best in Shanghai. Body pump, yoga and kick-boxing classes cost extra. A month's membership is Y800. There's a branch in **Pudong** (Map pp253-4; ☎ 588 1616; 55 Changyi Lu).

GUBEI GYM CLUB Map p256
☎ 2219 5818; 59 Ronghua Xilu
Away from the city centre, this gym is only practical for local and expat residents. Facilities include a sparse gym, swimming pool, tennis courts, squash court, bowling alley, sauna, shooting range and there are aerobics classes. Annual memberships range from Y7000 to Y10,000 but you can get good-value cards for 10 hours of swimming/tennis/squash for Y500/350/400. One-time fees for the same cost Y70/70/60.

KERRY GYM Map pp250-2
☎ 6279 4625; 1515 Nanjing Xilu
Memberships for three/six/12 months cost Y4000/7000/13,000 or Y2500/4500/8000 at off-peak hours (9am to 5pm weekdays, 9am to noon Saturday).

MEGAFIT Map pp246-9
☎ 5383 6633; www.megafitchina.com; 398 Huaihai Zhonglu, opposite Shanghai Central Plaza
This mid-price gym has memberships for Y500 a month, Y2888 per year.

PHYSICAL FITNESS Map p257
☎ 6426 8282; Metro City, Xujiahui
With another branch at **Hong Kong Plaza** (Map pp246-9; ☎ 6390 8890; 283 Huaihai Zhonglu), members can use either gym for a monthly fee of Y300 or Y230 off peak. Longer memberships have a joining fee.

STAR GYM Map pp250-2
☎ 5228 3818; 428 Jiangning Lu; 6am-11pm
Spacious with good facilities, there is a nice public pool (Y20 per visit), aerobics and spin classes, sauna and bowling. Annual memberships cost Y3600 for unlimited use, or Y1800 if you only visit weekdays before 5pm. A month's pass is Y900, or get a package of 10/20 visits for Y800/1300.

TOPFORM HEALTH CLUB Map p257

☎ 6426 6888; Regal East Asia Hotel, 800 Lingling Lu
Memberships for three/six/12 months cost Y1000/1800/2700 for off-peak times (6.30am to 5pm Monday to Friday) and get you cardio and muscle-toning machines, two aerobic classes weekly, sauna, whirlpool and very friendly staff. Unlimited memberships for one/three/six/12 months cost Y800/1700/2800/4200.

HASH HOUSE HARRIERS

This eccentric expat organisation ('drinkers with a running problem') originated with the British in Malaysia. The Shanghai chapter organises runs most Sunday afternoons, followed by a meal and plenty of beers. Check www.shanghaihhh.com or listings magazines for details.

Serious runners might be interested in the Shanghai Marathon (p11) held annually around November.

KARTING

DISC KART Map pp250-2

Díshìkǎ Sàichēguǎn

☎ 6277 5641; 326 Aomen Lu, northern Shanghai
This is the largest go-cart track in town, at least until the Formula One circuit is built in 2004... It costs Y35 for eight minutes' driving off-peak (2pm to 8.30pm Monday to Friday and midnight to 4am), or Y50 at other times (8.30pm to midnight weekdays and 2pm to midnight weekends). Regulars buy a Y300 ticket to get a 20% discount on prices. There's a bar, and credit cards are accepted. You'll have to search for this place, hidden down a deserted alley at the junction of Aomen Lu and Jiangning Lu.

MARTIAL ARTS

LONGWU INTERNATIONAL KUNG FU CENTRE Map pp246-9

☎ 5465 0047; 215 Shanxi Nanlu
Coaches from Shanghai's martial arts team take classes in Chinese martial arts and kung fu. A free trial class is offered each evening.

WUSHU CENTRE Map pp250-2

☎ 6215 3599; 595 Nanjing Xilu
The centre runs courses in various martial arts including karate, though normally in Chinese only.

MASSAGE & SPAS

In China, massage is traditionally performed by the blind and is closely linked to the same Chinese system of the body's pressure points that acupuncture relies on. There are over 40 massage centres in Shanghai, almost all of them legitimate. For more details see the boxed text opposite.

PAINTBALL

WEICHENG PAINTBALL CENTRE Map pp242-3

Wěichéng Cǎidàn Shèjìfáng

☎ 5252 0278; Zhongshan Park; ⊗ 8.30am-4.30pm
The place to get kitted up and vent your frustrations. The highly cathartic experience costs Y40.

POOL & BILLIARDS

Shooting some stick comes free at Shanghai Sally's (p128), O'Malley's (p126), Face (p127) and Malone's (p111) though you'll pay for it through the cost of beers. Shanghai Sally's has pool competitions on Thursday nights.

Metro City (Map p257; Xujiahui) has snooker and pool tables costing Y20 to Y60 per hour, depending on the time of day.

Shanghai's biggest pool hall, at the east end of Shanghai Stadium (Map p257), is open 24 hours. Before noon a game of pool costs Y15, rising to Y25 from noon to 6pm, or Y30 from 6pm to 2am. Depending on the time of day, billiards cost from Y20 to Y40.

ROCK CLIMBING

MASTERHAND CLIMBING CLUB Map pp242-3

☎ 5696 6657; Hongkou Stadium, 21 Upper Stand, 444 Dongjiangwan Lu; ⊗ 10am-10pm
With a similar setup to Ozark (below), the indoor wall costs Y40 without time limit.

OZARK CLIMBING CENTRE Map pp250-2

☎ 6226 6825; 1 Jiangsu Lu; ⊗ 10am-10pm
Located in north Shanghai, Ozark has several 12m and 15m beginner, speed and competition walls. Unlimited climbing costs Y40 Monday to Thursday and Y50 at other times, plus Y3 for shoes and Y5 for a safety belt (the best Y5 you'll ever spend). Climbs for children cost Y35, whatever the day. Wear loose-fitting clothes.

Because You Deserve It!

To revive flagging energy before you tackle more of swinging Shanghai, indulge in a massage or spa. Results guaranteed! Ask locals for advice or try the centres listed here.

Dragonfly (Map pp246-9; ☎ 5405 0008; 20 Donghu Lu; ⏰ 11am-2am) Designer massage centre that offers Chinese finger massage, Japanese-style shiatsu and foot massage in soothing surroundings for around Y120 per hour, with discounts from 11am to 4pm.

Funing Massage Centre of Blind Person (Map pp246-9; ☎ 6437 8378; 597 Fuxing Zhonglu; ⏰ noon-2am) Is next-door to the Thumbpoint and offers a similar deal.

Green Massage (Map pp254-5; ☎ 5386 0222; 58 Taicang Lu; ⏰ 11am-2am) Aromatherapy and Chinese foot massage for around Y90.

Thumbpoint Pressure Centre of Blind Person (Map pp246-9; ☎ 6473 2634; 597 Fuxing Zhonglu; ⏰ noon-2am) Offers 45-minute massages for Y40, or an hour-long foot massage for Y60. Discounts of around 20% are given if you buy a block of 10 hours.

Spas are the latest rage to sweep through Shanghai. From seaweed body masks to a G5 massage designed to break down fatty deposits, the following places offer some privileged pampering, at a cost. A Y1000 package at the Hilton's 4th-floor spa or the Westin's Banyan Tree makes for a great splurge or gift.

Bali Spa (p165; Novotel Atlantis) Hot stone and Indonesian scent massages (Y350 per hour)

Banyan Tree (p159; Westin) A range of two- or three-hour Thai and Balinese massage sessions from Y1000 to Y2000. Staff recommend a sensual apple or black sesame body scrub, followed by a melon and aloe facial scrub, topped off with a honey cucumber mask. Oh yeah... you know you want it...

Spa (p162; Hilton) Clinical Chinese and Swedish massage, with Shanghainese *(tuina)* pressure-point therapy, reflexology, reiki and hydrotherapy, or try a sea-salt and lavender rub.

RUGBY

Local heroes the Shanghai Hairy Crabs take on expat rivals like Beijing's Foreign Devils. Practices are held every Saturday afternoon at the Shanghai Football Club ground opposite Carrefour in Pudong's Jinqiao district. Check www.shanghaifootballclub.com or magazine listings for contact details.

SCUBA DIVING

Yes, you can learn to dive in Shanghai, though your open water dives are thankfully not in the East China Sea. **Aquaria 21** (p81) offers PADI courses and even shark dives in its aquarium (Y600 a dive).

SQUASH

The squash *(xiǎo xiàngpí qiú)* courts at the **Hotel Equatorial** (Map pp246-9; ☎ 6248 1688; 65 Yan'an Xilu) can be rented for Y80 per hour, plus Y15 per person entrance fee, and Y30 for a racquet. The **JC Mandarin** (p166) charges a flat Y100 per hour for the squash court and rents racquets for Y30 per hour. If you're in town for a while, consider joining a squash league from one of the local magazine listings.

SWIMMING

All the top-end hotels have pools; though if swimming is your thing and you're coming in winter make sure your hotel has an indoor pool.

ORIENTAL RIVERSIDE HOTEL Map pp253-4
☎ 5037 0000; hotel@shicc.net;
2727 Binjiang Dadao, Pudong

The great circular pool here is enclosed in a glass dome with views of the Bund. Pool entry costs Y100 for non-guests.

SHANGHAI SWIMMING POOL Map p257
Nanatorium; ☎ 6438 2372; www.ssc.sh.cn;
near Shanghai Stadium

The pool is open to the public from 7am to 9am and 1pm to 9pm on weekdays and from 9am to 9pm (Y20 to Y25) at weekends. You can get a monthly card for Y300. A shop next door sells swimming costumes.

TENNIS

There are several places to play tennis *(wǎng qiú)*, though you'll need your own racquets. Reservations are suggested for the weekend.

In south Shanghai, **public tennis courts** (Map p257; about 500m southwest of Shanghai Stadium) cost Y20 to Y35 per hour from 6am to 8am on weekdays/weekends and Y60/80 at night.

INTERNATIONAL TENNIS CENTRE

Map pp246-9

☎ 6415 5588; rieah@prodigychina.com; 516 Hengshan Lu

Part of the Regal International East Asia Hotel (p163) this is probably the best tennis facility in Shanghai but it's open to members and hotel guests only and fees are steep.

XIANXIA TENNIS CENTRE Map p256

Xianxia Wǎngqiú Zhōngxīn

☎ 6262 8327; 1885 Hongqiao Lu

This is a premier site, though it's quite far from the centre. Weekday costs are Y40/80 per hour for daytime/evening play or Y60/100 on weekends, with racquet hire at Y30. Courts are a little cheaper between 6am and 8am. Reception is in the north side of the tennis stadium.

WATER SPORTS

Shanghai Boat and Yacht Club www.shanghaibyc.org has six boats and organises outings at the Dongxing International Yacht Club on Dianshan Lake, about 50 minutes drive from Shanghai along the Huqing Expressway. Members currently meet at 10am Sunday at Sasha's (p105); nonmembers are welcome to tag along for a sail. Boats and jet skis are available for hire at the yacht club. The club might move to the Aquatics Water Sports Centre, on the northeast shore of the lake, currently a training institute.

The main place for powerboat fun is the pricey **Suzhou Taihu Mercury Club & Marina** (www .mercurymarinechina.com) on Tai Lake, a couple of hours west of town, where you'll find mostly moneyed locals. Groups can hire houseboats here just as the expats of the 1930s did.

For something more physical, try competitive **dragon-boat racing**, held on Sunday at Dianshan Lake. Outings costs around Y50 for boat hire and transport from Gubei. See www.shanglong.gmxhome.de for details.

YOGA

Y+ Map pp246-9

☎ 6433 4330; www.yplus.com.cn; 299 Fuxing Xilu

The first yoga centre in Shanghai offers a full range of classes in Ashtanga yoga for both men and women, along with hot (Bikram) yoga, which takes place in a heated room to aid stretching and toning. Beginners are welcome. The very nice centre is part of a redesigned merchant's complex that will include a bar and restaurant. There are plans to introduce kids' yoga and Pilates classes, plus workshops on topics such as proper eating for exercise, and massage for stress release. Rates are around Y100 per class.

Shopping

Shopping

Shanghai is well known among Chinese as *the* place to shop in China. Ever since the 1930s the city has boasted the cream of China's department stores and today Shanghai is fast rivalling Hong Kong as a shopper's heaven. Nanjing Lu and Huaihai Lu have always been the busiest shopping streets, but now it seems almost every side street is devoted to the art of retail therapy. Bring some extra spending money; you'll need it.

If you're in town for just a couple of days head to Dongtai Lu Antique Market for interesting souvenirs and to Xiangyang Market for cheap knock-offs and cheap CDs. Nanjing Donglu is worth a stroll for its silk shops and sense of history (see p90) and Huaihai Zhonglu or Nanjing Xilu are worth a look for their insights into the moneyed Shanghainese.

If wandering aimlessly for miles poking into every boutique is your shopping style then stick to Nanjing Lu and Huaihai Lu, where you will find Western, Japanese and Chinese clothing boutiques wedged between the major department stores. If you shop purely out of necessity, the department stores listed in this chapter carry nearly everything, including the items sold in the jammed boutiques.

Shopping Tips

Most shops in this chapter are open from 10am to 9pm, though government-run stores often close at 6pm. Yuyuan Bazaar and Dongtai Lu Antique Market are both best visited early in the day.

In most shops, after you've selected an item the sales assistant will write a ticket, then send you to the cashier, who will collect your money and send you right back to the salesperson,

Haggling

While prices in formal stores are supposed to be standardised, it never hurts to ask for a discount. In the markets, haggling over prices is all part of the shopping experience. In fact, many vendors are genuinely upset when shoppers refuse to partake in the haggling game.

The most common method of haggling is for vendor to display the price on a calculator, hand the calculator to you, you punch in 25% to 30% of the asked price, the vendor shakes their head and emits a cry that suggests you just insulted their ancestors, comes down a little, passes the calculator back to you and so on until the price comes down about 50%. At Xiangyang Market you may have to pay around 60% of the asked price, while vendors at the Dongtai Lu Antique Market and Yuyuan Bazaar will often drop as low as 30% of the original price. A lot of vendors have learned to say 'final price', but this rarely holds true.

Another method for the less patient is to offer around 35% to 40% of the asking price and when it is refused, smile, shrug and walk away to a nearby stall selling exactly the same thing. Nine times out of 10 the vendor will chase you down and agree to your price, but you could walk away empty-handed.

A few key points to remember will keep haggling from turning into arguing. First of all, try to get the vendor alone; saving face is of utmost importance in China and if you have an audience you'll never get the price you are seeking. If people gather around, bow out and go back later.

Secondly, try to smile throughout the entire process. Smiling will keep the negotiations light even if you can't come to an agreement. Rolling your eyes in disgust, shaking your head and getting angry are sure ways to ruin the deal and to jack up the price for the next customer.

Finally, remember that Y10 is just over US$1 and probably worth spending if you are taken with the item. If negotiating in pidgin Chinese, be very careful of similar-sounding numbers, like 14 *(shísì)* and 40 *(sìshí)*, and 108 *(yìbàilíngbā)* and 180 *(yìbàibā)*, as these offer great potential for misunderstanding, deliberate or otherwise. Note that Chinese shops advertise the final sale price, and it is marked as a proportion; thus 20% discount will be marked as 打8折.

Ultimately, you get ripped off only if you end up buying something you didn't really want in the first place.

who will have your items bagged. It rarely happens that the wrong item ends up in the bag, but you should always check.

Most department stores will exchange items with a receipt, though smaller shops and markets have an 'every sale is final' clause. To save yourself a headache, make sure you scrutinise the item carefully and try on clothing before buying. Also make sure you have a legible receipt and get a business card.

Shipping & Customs

Most reputable shops will take care of insurance, customs and shipping for larger items, though find out first exactly what the dealer covers. Separate charges may materialise for handling, packaging, customs duty and quarantine, driving the shipping charges above the price of the item! Also consider how much it will cost to get the goods from the shipping port to your home.

Technically, nothing over 200 years old can be taken out of China, but few antiques in Shanghai are really this old. If you are buying a reproduction, make sure the dealer provides paperwork stating that it is not an antique. Dealers should also provide the proper receipts and paperwork for any antiques. Keep the receipts along with the business card of the dealer, just in case.

Shipping clothing, curios and household items on your own is generally not a problem and China Post has an excellent packing system for airmailing light items.

THE BUND & NANJING DONGLU

Nanjing Lu has been known for centuries as China's golden mile. In the 1920s the department stores Sincere, Wing On, Sun Sun and Da Sun imported luxury goods from Paris, London and New York. Once supreme, it's now looking a bit frayed and has slipped a few notches compared with the emerging luxury option of Huaihai Lu and other shopping areas. However, Nanjing Lu still attracts millions of Chinese tourists and shoppers with its imported brands, eateries, and traditional Chinese shops.

Mercifully, a pedestrian strip has been established from Xizang Lu, just east of Renmin Park, to Henan Lu, allowing shoppers to browse without the hassles of traffic. A toy train (Y2) runs from one end of the strip to the other. Most shops on Nanjing Lu are Chinese department stores, with a few foreign brands throw in, and a good hunt can lead to some bargains. The **Hualian department store** (Map pp244-5; 635 Nanjing Donglu, formerly No 10, and before that Wing On) and the No 1 Department Store at 830 Nanjing Donglu, are fascinating places to browse if you can stand the crowds.

AMERICA'S EYES   *Spectacles*
Multiple locations
With outlets all over town, this chain has several branches on **Nanjing Donglu** (Map pp244-5;

Shopping Streets

In the tradition of an Asian bazaar, Shanghai still has concentrations of goods in specific streets.

Changle Lu & Maoming Nanlu (Map pp246-9)
Women's Chinese clothing and tailoring

Shaanxi Lu (Map pp246-9) Shoes

Dongtai Lu (Map pp254-5) Antiques

Fuzhou Lu (Map pp244-5) The traditional art supplies, bookshop and brothel street of Shanghai (the brothels have gone)

Taikang Lu (Map pp246-9) Galleries and design studios

Maoming Nanlu (Map pp246-9) Chinese dresses, blue cloth

Changshu Lu (Map pp246-9) Chinese clothing stores

Fenyang Lu (Map pp246-9) Musical instruments, serving the nearby music conservatory (there's even a Steinway & Sons branch)

Yishan Lu (Map p257) Home design

Top Five Shopping Venues

- **Dongtai Lu Antique Market** (p148) Curios and souvenirs
- **Xiangyang Market** (p150) Knock-offs, clothes & DVDs
- **Yuyuan Bazaar** (p147) Souvenirs and crafts
- **Dongjiadu Cloth Market** (p147) Cheap silk brocade, cashmere and more
- **Fuyou Antique Market** (p147) Antiques, early mornings at weekends

Best Buys

SEEKERS OF CURIOS ARE WARNED THAT MANY OF THOSE TO BE FOUND IN THE CHINESE CITY ARE EXCELLENT IMITATIONS OF THE AUTHENTIC ARTICLE.

All About Shanghai; A Standard Guidebook, 1934

All Chinese products and popular souvenirs eventually find their way to Shanghai, and the city is rapidly beginning to resemble one giant shopping centre. The following is a rundown of the city's best buys.

Antiques are the most popular purchases but genuine antiques are not as abundant as dealers would like us to believe. 'Antique' usually refers to items at least 50 years old; in Shanghai the majority of goods have been leached from the countryside, artificially antiqued, refurbished and sold at astoundingly high prices. Until recently antiques were required to have a red-wax seal affixed; though customs seem to have loosened up on this, you may still see antiques with globs of wax stuck to them. Most 'antiques' have been refurbished so look carefully to see how much of the piece is original. For antique furniture see Hongqiao & Gubei later in this chapter (p152).

Silk is an excellent buy, with brocade a fraction of the price it is abroad. If you are heading to Suzhou you can pick up silk there (see p183). Eastern China is famous for its *gu* and *su* embroidery (see p29). Very fine embroidery is rare today but you may still find some pleasing pieces; check for fine filament and invisible needle marks.

Pearls from Tai Lake can be a good buy but you need to know what you are looking at. There are several ways to check for fakes: if you rub the pearl along your teeth you should feel a grating; a fake pearl will turn black when you put a flame to it.

Clothes can be a good buy, though sizing appears to be random so try on anything before you buy it. If you are on the small side you will undoubtedly find bargains in some of the Chinese department stores. Xiangyang Market is a knock-off paradise.

Qipaos, the beautiful Chinese-style dresses, also known as cheongsams, started as Manchurian dresses, gained popularity during the Manchu Qing dynasty and later, the swinging 1930s. They are now firmly back in fashion. Most department stores have small collections of *qipaos* for around Y900. For gorgeous, unique and sometimes more-expensive styles there are several small boutiques on Changle Lu, between Maoming Lu and Shanxi Lu; many of these shops will custom-tailor.

Also popular, and increasingly chic in Shanghai, is the *mián'ǎo* (padded jacket). The jackets known as 'Chairman Mao' jackets in the West are known in China as *zhōngshān zhuāng* ('Sun Yatsen' jackets). Also look out for *dùdōu*, skimpy silk halter tops that are really Chinese negligees.

If one thing is connected with China in Western minds it's **tea and teapots**. The dark-coloured Yixing ware is the most valued of all teapots in China. Prices range from Y10 for mass-produced pots on bargain tables at Yuyuan Bazaar, to Y20,000 in exclusive teashops. Check for a snug-fitting lid, and if you can, a non-drip spout.

If you are setting up home in Shanghai, household appliances, crockery, bedding and furniture can be found in most department stores, as well as in Carrefour. The recent boom in apartment buying has fuelled a mad growth in DIY shops, ranging from chic boutiques to huge hyperstores like Home Mart or the British giant B&Q. American giant Wal-Mart is due to land in Shanghai's northern suburbs in 2005.

Unless you're a big Mariah Carey or Kenny G fan you won't be spoiled for choice for Western **music** in Shanghai, so you are better off bringing favourites from home or buying in Hong Kong. Shanghai can be a good place to stock up on Chinese music, though. Domestic tapes are cheap at Y7; imported classical music CDs sell for around Y130. Hustlers sell (illegal) pirated music CDs and DVDs around town for Y8.

China produces lovely **musical instruments**, such as the *èrhú* (vertical fiddle), *pípa* (lute) and *gǔzhēng* (zither). For both Chinese and Western musical instruments try the various shops on Fenyang Lu, catering to students attending the Conservatory of Music. Other places include the **Shanghai Musical Instrument Factory Store** (Map pp244-5; 114 Nanjing Donglu), or the 5th floor of **No 1 Department Store** (p146). Stalls at Yuyuan Bazaar sell traditional egg-shaped wooden instruments known as *xūn*.

one is next to the Sofitel Hyland Hotel), as well as Xujiahui's **Grand Gateway** and **Metro City** (Map p257), on **Huaihai Zhonglu** (Map pp246-9; 1002 Huaihai Zhonglu, next to Xiangyang Park) and on **Nanjing Xilu** (Map pp250-2; opposite CITIC Square). For prices well below those at home the staff can grind a pair of lenses in a few hours, following a prescription, your spec-tacles, or an on-the-spot eye test. Different specials are featured every month.

CENTRE OF TEA FROM HOME & ABROAD Map pp244-5 *Tea*
137 Daming Lu
Sells more than 1000 different local and imported teas, near the Pujiang Hotel.

D-MALL & HONG KONG SHOPPING
PLAZA Map pp244-5   *Mall/Clothes*
Dǐměi Gòuwù Zhōngxīn
Located under Renmin Park (access through
Renmin Square station), D-mall and Hong
Kong Shopping Plaza are a merging maze of
boutiques with mid- and low-end Japanese,
Chinese and Western styles, refreshingly dif-
ferent from the repeats along Nanjing Lu and
Huaihai Lu. Prices are much more affordable
(and negotiable) than elsewhere.

DUOYUNXUAN ART SHOP
Map pp244-5   *Art*
☎ 6360 6475; 422 Nanjing Donglu
A multistorey traditional-looking building (no
English sign) that has an excellent selection
of art and calligraphy supplies. The 2nd floor
is one of the best places for heavy art books,
both international and Chinese, and the 3rd
floor houses antiques, galleries and some
framed embroidery.

FLOWER MARKET   *Flowers*
Cnr Beijing Lu & Xizang Lu
Shanghai buys and sells US$120 million worth
of flowers every year and this, the biggest
flower market in Shanghai, is where much of
the handling goes on. It's worth a visit if you're
into horticulture but it's not as colourful as the
Cultural Square Flower Market (p148).

FOREIGN LANGUAGES BOOKSTORE
Map pp244-5   *Books*
☎ 6322 3200; 390 Fuzhou Lu; 🕙 9.30am-6pm until
7pm weekends
This is the city's main source for English-
language books. The 1st floor has a good range
of cards, maps and books on Shanghai and the
4th floor, known as Shanghai Book Traders, has
a surprisingly wide range of imported books
and novels, including Lonely Planet guides
and phrasebooks. Prices are a little higher than
you'll find abroad. There are smaller branches in
Gubei (Map p256; SBT Bookstore; 71 Shuicheng
Nanlu), in Xujiahui (Map p257; 50 Hongqiao Lu)
and on Huashan Lu (Map pp246-9; between the
Hilton & Equatorial hotels).

FRIENDSHIP STORE Map pp244-5   *Souvenirs*
☎ 5308 0600; 40 Beijing Donglu
If you can't stand crowds or if you are hopeless
at haggling, this government-run giant is a good
place to browse at your leisure. What used to
be a prestigious store open only to foreigners
and the party elite is now a department store
open to the masses but particularly aimed at
tour groups bussed in from the nearby Bund.
Fixed prices are marked in both RMB and US
dollars, and give an idea of ballpark figures if
you plan to haggle elsewhere. The store has a
good bookshop, carpets, antiques and some
nice shadow puppets, as well as a money exchange (open until 9.30pm). A separate annexe

Exotic blooms, Flower Market (above)

northeast of the main building houses more carpets, antiques and furniture. There are plans to relocate as part of the North Bund Development Project, though there is no firm new location at present.

GUAN LONG CAMERA SHOP
Map pp244-5   *Photography*
190 Nanjing Donglu
Shanghai's foremost photographic supplies shop for all kinds of film and processing and almost any camera accessory you could ask for, at prices slightly higher than other camera shops in town. There's a smaller branch at 227 Jinling Donglu, just west of Henan Lu.

HAISHANG QINGHUAI ALLEY
Map pp244-5   *Curios*
61 Nanjing Donglu
If you have some time to kill after mooching around the Bund, head down the escalators on the south side of Nanjing Donglu, not far from the Peace Hotel, into this underground collection of stalls. It's a bit hit and miss, with a lot of teenage tat and kitsch crafts but you might just find something unique here. Check out stalls B040 for antique Chinese newspapers, B085 for embroidery and B153 for hand and thumb painting.

JINGUAN SILK & WOOLLEN STORE
Map pp244-5   *Silk*
373 Nanjing Donglu
A popular stop for silk, brocade and cashmere. Brocade costs around Y63 per metre.

LAOKAFOOK SILK & WOOLLEN STORE Map pp244-5   *Silk*
257 Nanjing Donglu
Another place to compare silk styles and prices, along with the nearby Silk King and Jinguan stores mentioned in this section.

NO 1 DEPARTMENT STORE
Map pp244-5   *Department Store*
Nanjing Donglu
Worth a visit from an anthropological viewpoint, if nothing else. This is the quintessential Chinese department store, averaging 150,000 shoppers a day over 12 levels of merchandise. The 5th floor has gifts and souvenirs.

SHANGHAI ANTIQUE & CURIO STORE
Map pp244-5   *Antiques/Curios*
☎ 6321 5868; 192-246 Guangdong Lu
A government-run shop that takes up an en-

tire block and offers some interesting smaller items. The complex includes the Jinghua Art Auction Co.

SHANGHAI DRAMA COSTUME & ACCESSORIES SHOP Map pp244-5   *Clothes*
Xìjú Fúzhuāng Yòngpǐn Chǎng
181 Henan Zhonglu
This is the place for all your fake beard needs (Y40), plus opera headdresses and platform stage shoes. For very reasonable prices this opera shop also has nice silk pyjamas, embroidered bags and heavily embroidered robes. It's a great place to kit up for a fancy dress party!

SHANGHAI MUSEUM ART STORE
Map pp244-5   *Art/Ceramics*
201 Renmin Dadao
Attached to the Shanghai Museum, this high-priced but high-quality store offers some variety from the same old tourist hash; it's definitely worth a visit if you are in the museum. Apart from the excellent range of books on Chinese art, architecture, ceramics and calligraphy there is a good selection of quality cards, prints and slides. The annex shop sells fine imitations of some of the ceramic pieces on display in the Zande Lou Ceramics Gallery (as well as scarves and bags) but these come at a hefty whack, starting at about US$100. The store has it's own currency exchange.

SHANGHAI ZHEJIANG TEA STORE
Map pp244-5   *Tea*
333 Fujian Zhonglu
Conveniently located on the corner of Nanjing Donglu, selling all kinds of tea from Anhui to Zhejiang.

SILK KING Map pp244-5   *Silk*
66 Nanjing Donglu
The city's largest fabric chain offer silks at Y68 to Y88 per metre (depending on the width) and can custom-tailor a *qipao* for around Y400, plus the price of the brocade (count on about 4m). There are also some off-the-rack clothes. If custom-tailoring, expect a three- to 10-day wait, at least two fittings and a fee of around Y600 to Y1200, including the fabric, though rush jobs are possible in 24 hours. There are branches across Shanghai, including one on **Nanjing Xilu** (Map pp250-2; 819 Nanjing Xilu) and two on **Huaihai Zhonglu** (Map pp246-9; at No 550 opposite Isetan & No 1226).

OLD TOWN

Though it wasn't originally set up as a shopping district, **Yuyuan Bazaar** (Map pp254-5) has become exactly that. All souvenirs can be found here, along with some alleged antiques and some interesting shops specialising in things like fans, scissors and walking sticks. Others carve chops while a row of craftsmen paint calligraphy, make shadow puppets and cut onlookers' profiles from thin sheets of paper. Pearls from Jiangsu's Tai Lake are sold everywhere and can be a good buy if you have a good eye. Prices are generally tripled, even in the department stores and salespeople can be pushy, but if you enjoy haggling you can come home loaded with teapots, silks, pearls, chops, jade, blue cloth and a few dubious curios.

DONGJIADU CLOTH MARKET
Map pp242-3   *Cloth/Silk*
Dongjiadu Lu
The cheapest place for cloth in Shanghai. The row of shops facing the main street concentrates on silk brocades at Y30 per metre, or rayons at Y15 per metre. Stalls inside sell every other fabric you could want, including cashmere. Several good tailors here will make anything from a Western suit to a *qipao*. The location on the southeast edge of the old town is a bit inconvenient. Buses run north–south to/from the Bund, or take a taxi.

FUYOU ANTIQUE MARKET
Map pp254-5   *Antiques/Souvenirs*
459 Fangbang Zhonglu
There's a permanent antique market here on the 1st and 2nd floors, but the place really gets humming on Sunday morning from dawn onwards, when sellers from the countryside fill up all four floors. The range is good, but again, there's a lot of rubbish so you need a shrewd eye if you don't want to pay too much over the odds.

OLD STREET Map pp254-5   *Crafts/Souvenirs*
Lǎo Jiē
Fangbang Zhonglu
This remodelled street is lined with specialist tourist shops, selling everything from Jinshan-style folk paintings (Nos 436, 372, 411), old photographs of Shanghai (No 346), calligraphy (No 424), woodcuts (No 413), blue cloth (No 438), old bank notes (Nos 428 & 423) and buddhas (No 349). There are also various shops

selling temple deities and a range of accessories that will come in handy when worshipping your ancestors.

OLD TOWN GOD TEMPLE ANTIQUE
MARKET Map pp254-5   *Antiques*
Lǎochéng Huángmiào Gǔwàn Shìchǎng
Huabao Bldg, Yuyuan Bazaar
The basement of the Huabao Building, slap bang in the centre of the bazaar, houses a collection of established antique shops, with an emphasis on antique watches, carved wood and pottery. These are the kind of antique stalls that accept all major credit cards. The upper floors of the building are strong on Chinese dresses, silk and scarves, though the sales staff can be a bit pushy and you need to haggle.

FRENCH CONCESSION

Huaihai Lu in the French Concession area is definitely *the* modern shopping street in Shanghai. Shops start in the east (near Huangpi Lu metro) with a succession of towering department stores that are bursting through the ground at an alarming rate. From here, Dongtai Lu Antique Market and Xintiandi are only a short walk away. The central section, east of Isetan, is mostly local brand stores, concentrating on fashion and fast food. Yangdang Lu, a pleasant pedestrian street running off Huaihai Zhonglu, has some nice small boutiques and outdoor cafés that offer a pleasant break from the mayhem, particularly in summer. The Benetton store at 651 Huaihai Zhonglu is said to be the world's largest.

Remember to peek down the side streets like Shaanxi Nanlu, Maoming Nanlu and Changshu Lu, which are strong on dress shops, shoes and fashion.

Shops start to peter out west of Xiangyang Market, though there are several home-furnishing stores here. The west end at the corner of Changshu Lu (Changshu Lu metro station) is anchored by Maison Mode.

ARTS CRAFT STORE OF THE CHINESE NATIONALITIES
Map pp246-9   *Tailoring/Clothes*
73 Yandang Lu
Ignore the confusing name; this unassuming dress shop specialises in excellent tailoring. You can get an expertly tailored *qipao* in five days starting at Y1000.

Huaihai Lu Department Stores

There are too many department stores to mention on Huaihai Lu but the following are worth a look. Almost all have a food court and entertainment arcade on the upper floors and the top floors often have bargain tables.

Hong Kong Plaza (Map pp246-9) Has a Megabite food court in the basement, Rojam disco on the top floor as well as a sparse selection of boutiques.

Isetan (Map pp246-9) Six floors of great brand-name shopping.

New Hualian Commercial Building (Map pp246-9) The place to go for kids, with brands like Cherokee, Sesame Street and Pooh, as well as Lego and Silverlit, spread out over three floors.

Pacific Department Store (Map pp246-9) A pleasant store where you can find everything from baby strollers to air-conditioners, as well as foreign and upscale Asian brand-name clothing. Strong on bargain close outs.

Parkson (Bǎishèng Gòuwù Zhōngxīn; Map pp246-9) Mid-priced foreign (Nike, Elle, Esprit, Revlon) and upscale Chinese brands. The basement has a well-stocked supermarket with foreign goodies and access to Shanxi metro station. The ground floor has an ATM.

Shanghai Central Plaza (Map pp246-9) Loads of upscale clothes stores, plus a Délifrance (see p108), DHL, Starbucks and hair and nail salons. The basement connects to the Huangpi Nanlu metro station.

Times Square (Map pp254-5) Upscale mall anchored by Lane Crawford and featuring all the glossies – Dolce & Gabanna, Gucci etc, plus designer Walter Ma. The 4th floor has a decent outdoor sports collection with genuine North Face and Marmot hiking gear.

CHINESE PRINTED BLUE NANKEEN EXHIBITION HALL Map pp246-9 *Cloth*
Zhōngguó Lányìn Huābù Guǎn
No 24, Lane 637, Changle Lu; ☺ 9am-4.30pm
Follow the blue signs through a maze of courtyards until you see bolts of blue cloth drying in the yard. Originally produced in Jiangsu, Zhejiang and Guizhou provinces, this blue-and-white cotton fabric (sometimes called blue calico) is similar to batik, coloured using a starch-resist method and indigo dye bath. As it has become more and more popular, manufacturers have started block-printing bolts of cloth, which are often inferior to the handmade pieces. This museum/shop, started by the Japanese artist Kubo Mase, displays and sells items made by hand from the cloth, right down to the buttons. It has been in business for 20 years, takes pride in quality, and does not give discounts. You can visit as part of the French Concession II walking tour (p94).

CULTURAL SQUARE FLOWER MARKET Map pp246-9 *Flower Market*
162 Shaanxi Nanlu
The city's most colourful and fragrant city block houses everything green, from cut flowers and bonsai to gardening supplies. The flower shops spill out onto Shaanxi Nanlu. It's worth a visit to see the range of Chinese blooms before the entire block is demolished and redeveloped (see p93).

DONGTAI LU ANTIQUE MARKET
Map pp254-5 *Antiques/Curios*
A block west of Xizang Nanlu, this market street of over 100 stalls spreads over both Dongtai Lu and Liuhe Lu. It is the most popular market in Shanghai, for both expats and visitors. The 'antique' stalls sell some interesting items among the inevitable Mao memorabilia, including ceramics, 'antique' posters, pocket watches, paintings and a host of other collectables. Several shops specialise in 'antique' pieces collected from the countryside, such as the tiny embroidered shoes made for women with bound feet.

Haggle hard here as it's all vastly overpriced – prices fold to half almost immediately. If you wander around you will see the same stuff at a variety of prices, as a lot of it is mass-produced for the market. Only about 5% of the items sold here really qualify as antique. However if you like the look of something and can get a fair price for it, buy it for what it is and not as an antique. Larger antique shops are tucked behind the rows of stalls.

FUXING WEST Map pp246-9 *Home Design*
☎ 6431 8019; 299-2 Fuxing Xilu
Hand-embroidered items adapted into a modern design is the angle here, so expect plenty of stylish cushions and throws. It's part of 'Passage Fuxing', a renovated 1932 silk-trading house that also houses the Y+ yoga centre (see

p140) and a new fusion restaurant that boasts an excellent rooftop terrace. More boutiques are planned to create a small-scale, alternative version of Xintiandi.

GE TANG Map pp254-5 *Furniture/Antiques*
☎ 6384 6388, 6326 3355; www.getang.com; Liuhekou Lu
A small shop just off Dongtai Lu Antique Market, negotiable and friendly, with an emphasis on furniture. It also has a larger shop at 8 Huqingping Hwy, Hongqiao.

GOLDEN DRAGON Map pp246-9 *Silk*
☎ 6473 6691; 145 Maoming Nanlu
Another good place for silk and brocade at reasonable prices.

LU Map pp246-9 *Clothes*
☎ 6467 9803; 124 Maoming Nanlu
An unusual little boutique that specialises in 1930s nostalgia and Art Deco style with a modern twist; strong on clothes and shoes.

LUO BEN Map pp246-9 *Outdoor Gear*
☎ 6433 4932; 293 Fuzing Xilu
Stocks imported Patagonia and Snow Peak gear, rucksacks, hiking boots and cycling gear (the French owner has cycled thousands of miles across China and Tibet – it's his bike hanging in the store). The cosy loft space aims to become a focal point for Chinese adventure travel information, with a small café and top-floor lounge.

LYCEUM JEWELLERY & ANTIQUE STORE Map pp246-9 *Antiques/Curios*
☎ 6255 1667; 398 Changle Lu
Not the first place you'd come for antiques but if you have time to dig around, this store occasionally has some very nice pieces amid a whole lot of junk.

MAISON MODE Map pp246-9 *Fashion*
☎ 6431 0100; 1312 Huaihai Zhonglu
A designer mall that houses your major wallet drainers – Bally, Prada, Cartier, Gucci, as well as a basement branch of **Simply Life** (p150). Press your face up against the glass longingly and then head to Xiangyang Market for a cut-price knock-off.

MANDARAVA Map pp246-9 *Carpets*
☎ 6215 4233; 38 Maoming Nanlu; ❐ 11am-9pm
Walking into this shop is like entering an Aladdin's cave piled high with quality kilims

Coins, Dongtai Lu Antique Market (opposite)

and tribal carpets from Afghanistan, Iran and Turkmenistan.

NEW RAY PHOTO MAKING LTD
Map pp246-9 *Photography*
☎ 6433 0101; 1650 Huaihai Zhonglu
Near the Shanghai Library, New Ray offers an excellent slide-processing service at slightly lower rates than Guan Long (p146).

PASSEPARTOUT Map pp246-9 *Ethnic/Crafts*
108 Changshu Lu
The side streets off Huaihai Lu hide niche stores like this one, which sells ethnic items like Tibetan jewellery, scarves and clothes that are currently so popular with young Chinese trendies. Next door is 1001 Nights, which sells 'Silk Road' copperware and jewellery; a few doors down is Made in Heaven, for more jewellery.

PROPAGANDA POSTER ART CENTRE
Map pp246-9 *Posters*
Xuānchuánhuà Niánhuà Yìshù Zhōngxīn
☎ 6211 1845, 1390 184 1246; Room B-0C, 868 Huashan Lu; adult Y20; ❐ 10am-3pm
If socialist art is your thing, check out this gallery, where many propaganda posters from

the Cultural Revolution are for sale. See p69 for more details.

SHANGHAI HARVEST STUDIO

Map pp246-9 *Crafts*
☎ 6473 4566; harveststudio108@sina.com; Room 118, No 3 Bldg, 210 Taikang Lu

Part of the trendy Taikang Lu art scene, this boutique sells interesting Miao embroidery, either as traditional clothing or modern hybrid wallets and scarves. The Miao are an ethnic group in Guizhou province with strong links to Thailand's Hmong people. For details of Miao embroidery classes run at the studio see p204.

SHANGHAI TANG

Map pp246-9 *Fashion/Design*
www.shanghaitang.com; 127 Maoming Nanlu

In 2003, David Tang's branch of East meets West fashion and design finally made it to the town it's named after.

SHANGHAI YUANYOU CULTURE & ART CO LTD

Map pp246-9 *Antiques/Furniture/Carpets*
☎ 6248 3469; 340 Huashan Lu; ⏰ 9.30am-10pm

A tourist-oriented shop near the Hilton that sells smaller items amongst the furniture and carpets.

SIMPLY LIFE Map pp246-9 *Home Design*
☎ 3307 0178; www.simplylife-sh.com; 8, No 1, Xintiandi, 181 Taicang Lu

The flagship store of this interior design chain is in Xintiandi, with smaller branches on **Dongping Lu** (Map pp246-9), on **Huaihai Zhonglu** (Map pp246-9; Maison Mode basement) and at Pudong airport (domestic departure hall). It's strong on pottery, vases and embroidery but prices are fairly high. There are several other design stores in Xintiandi, on the northern and western sides.

TAIKANG ANTIQUE MARKET

Map pp246-9 *Antiques/Curios*
Taikang Gǔwán Shìchǎng

There's no tourist hassle at this collection of 50-odd antique shops; in fact it can be hard to get anyone's attention through the haze of cigarette smoke and clack of mah jong tiles. The stalls are heavy on porcelain and are mostly aimed at local Chinese. Shop A-01 has some interesting historical pieces, including revolutionary slides from the 1960s.

TAIKANG LU ART CENTRE

Map pp246-9 *Home Design*
Lane 210, Taikang Lu

This design and art centre is a focus for fashion and home design shops (see p71 for more details). Shops worth a lazy meander for home décor and design accessories include Jooi Design (Room 201, 2nd floor central block), Tiramisu (Room 401) for its clothes, L'Atelier Mandarine (Room 318) and Antique Home Design (Room 111), as well as the ground-floor **Harvest Studio** (above). The central block is known as the 'International Artist Factory', which sounds like an early Pink Floyd track.

TOTS – THE ORIGINAL TOY STORE

Map pp246-9 *Toys*
☎ 6358 1109; 77 Ruijin Erlu

This is one Shanghai's smallest but best kids' stores, with thought-provoking puzzles, educational toys and games and some craft displays. There's a branch in the **Gubei Shopping Centre** (Map p256; Hongqiao).

WEALD OUTFITTER

Map pp246-9 *Outdoor Gear*
☎ 6372 4180; 22 Chongqing Nanlu

A good-quality but sparse collection of tents, packs, climbing and outdoor gear, including Teva sandals and Timberland boots.

XIANGYANG MARKET

Map pp246-9 *Clothes Market*
Huaihai Zhonglu

This large open-air market is not as rewarding to explore as its famous predecessor Huating Market, which closed in 2001, but it's still the second-most-popular market in town with visitors, after Dongtai Lu. Travellers are drawn in search of bargain fakes and knock-offs, from the Hard Rock Cafe Shanghai T-shirts to North Face coats and Prada bags. Some garments are so obviously fake that they carry three different designer labels on one sleeve! Others may have been manufacturers' samples that never made it to the big world – even the vendors don't know the difference sometimes.

Despite the misleading labels, some items are decent quality in their own right. Check every zip and snap and try the rub test to make sure the dye doesn't rub off onto your fingers – we once had a friend leave a streak of blue while swishing down the ski slopes in a fake North Face jacket. Make sure clothing fits (there are no returns here) and remember to haggle...hard. The pesky fake-Rolex sellers and DVD lurkers can be irritating. If an item proves to be truly defective you can state your case at a little complaints office by the north entrance.

ZHENJIANZHAI ANTIQUE SHOP

Map pp246-9   *Antiques/Curios*
☎ 5404 2024; 98 Wuyuan Lu
More crusty back room than glossy antique hall, this small space has so many curios strewn about it's hard to tell what's for sale. It makes for great lurkers discovery.

PUDONG

As the district hots up, more and more strip malls and department stores are bound to make their debut along Pudong Nanlu and Central Ave. Further out, several remote megastores (like Carrefour) cater to the growing Pudong expat community.

NEXTAGE Map pp253-4   *Department Store*
Yaohan
☎ 5830 1111; 501 Zhangyang Lu
Asia's largest department store (second in size only to Macy's in New York), on the corner of Pudong Lu and Zhangyang Lu, offers 150 retail outlets selling from 100,000 sq metres of floor space. The 10-storey monster is owned by Shanghai No 1 Department Store. Across the street, Times Square sells mostly Chinese labels.

SUPERBRAND MALL Map pp253-4   *Mall*
Zhèngdà Guǎngchǎng
☎ 6887 78888; 168 Liujiazui Xilu
A year after opening, the upper floors of Shanghai's largest mall remain deserted and the 8th floor multiplex cinema and entertainment zones haven't yet materialised. The mall is Thai-owned and anchored by the Lotus department store, so it's not surprising that the 5th-floor food court includes several Thai restaurants and a Thai import food shop. Free buses run from the store to various parts of Shanghai. The restaurants and cafés in the west end offer great views over to the Bund.

NANJING XILU & JING'AN

Nanjing Xilu, the western section of Nanjing Lu, is more upscale and elitist than the eastern end. There are still plenty of small boutiques aimed at local shoppers but the most obvious icons of consumerism are the huge glossy malls full of luxury items most Shanghainese only dream about being able to afford.

CHINA NATIONAL PUBLICATIONS
IMPORT & EXPORT CO Map pp250-2   *Music*
☎ 6215 0555; 555 Wuding Lu
Shanghai's oldest CD shop is a bit out of the way but it has one of the city's best collections of imported classical music (and art books) and will order anything you want.

CITIC SQUARE   *Mall/Fashion*
☎ 6218 0180; 1168 Nanjing Xilu
This hi-tech mall is a strange affair, where Alfred Dunhill rubs shoulders with Ronald McDonald, and the Chinese staff at Kenny Roger's Roasters greet you in wide-brimmed cowboy hats. The huge mall has a strong emphasis on high-end clothes.

JINGDEZHEN PORCELAIN ARTWARE
Map pp250-2   *Porcelain*
☎ 6253 0885; 1175 Nanjing Xilu cnr Shaanxi Lu
One of the best places for traditional and modern porcelain. Credit cards are accepted and it can handle shipping. It also has a centre in the northwestern suburbs, accessible by sightseeing bus No 6B from Shanghai Stadium. See the Neighbourhoods chapter (p81) for more details.

OZARK Map pp250-2   *Outdoor Gear*
☎ 6226 6825; 1 Jiangsu Lu
Sells its own brand rucksacks, Gore-Tex jackets and climbing accessories. Part of Ozark Climbing Centre (p138) in the northwest of town.

PLAZA 66 Map pp250-2   *Mall/Fashion*
☎ 3210 4566; 1266 Nanjing Xilu
Cartier, Lagerfeld and Dior rule the roost here, though the minimalist window displays are so exclusive that the shops rarely actually see any shoppers. The restaurants are top-notch, including a huge Lulu Restaurant, Zen Cantonese and Coconut Bistro. Marvel at the model jet suspended from the ceiling above the tasty ground-floor café offerings.

WESTGATE MALL Map pp250-2   *Mall*
Méilóngzhèn Guǎngchǎng
☎ 6272 1111; 1038 Nanjing Xilu
A favourite among expats, the Westgate mall and office tower is attached to another branch of Isetan, a Watson's, a 5th-floor sports hall and a good basement supermarket. Labels include Versace and Burberry and there are occasional exhibitions or fashion shows in the main atrium. Nearby are branches of Benetton and Esprit.

ZHANG'S TEXTILES Map pp250-2 *Crafts*

☎ 6279 8587; Suite 202A, Shanghai Centre, 1376 Nanjing Xilu

The Shanghai Centre address means this top-end shop caters to flush expats, offering a sublime collection of antique and framed embroidery, from dragon robes to shoes for bound feet. It has a sister store in Beijing.

NORTH SHANGHAI

DUOLUN LU CULTURAL STREET

Map pp242-3 *Collectables*

Duolun Lu, off Sichuan Beilu; East Baoxing Lu light rail (No 3)

This rehabilitated pedestrian street in the north of town has a nice collection of curio and specialist shops, offering such offbeat gems as collectable revolutionary comic books, Tibetan 'zee' stones and antique radios. Visit No 166 Duolun Lu for a collection of shadow puppets, No 91 for stamps and No 106 for teapots. No 181 has a great collection of revolutionary nostalgia from the Cultural Revolution, strong on posters and old 45s. For more on Duolun Lu see p78.

HONGQIAO & GUBEI

The west of town has a few department stores catering to the expat residents of nearby Gubei and by far the city's best selection of antique furniture shops, many of which can direct you to even larger warehouses further west on the Huqingping Hwy. Antique (more commonly 'antiqued') furniture is big business in Shanghai these days. The shops listed in this section all offer a certificate of authenticity, accept credit cards and can handle shipping and customs.

AMBIANCE Map p256 *Home Design*

☎ 6219 3474; 1438 Hongqiao Lu

Chinese, Filipino, Thai and Indian home accessories here form part of 'Antiques Alley' (see Jinjiu Antique Furniture below). Ask the owner, Maureen, about handicraft classes (see p203).

CHINE ANTIQUES

Map p256 *Furniture/Antiques*

☎ 6270 1023; 1660 Hongqiao Lu

In business for over 10 years, this is one of the glossiest antique stores, with prices at the higher end of the spectrum. This branch

is at the **Liu Haisu Art Gallery** (p81) and there's a warehouse on the western outskirts. A small branch office in the **French Concession** (Map pp254-5; ☎ 6387 4100; 38 Liuhekou Lu, just off Dongtai Lu) can direct you to another warehouse a couple of minutes' walk away.

FRIENDSHIP SHOPPING CENTRE

Map p256 *Department Store/Books*

Hóngqiáo Yǒuyì Shāngchéng

☎ 6270 0000; 26 Xianxia Lu, Hongqiao

Alongside the clothes shops and supermarket is a small but well-stocked bookshop with a good range of magazines, tourist books and postcards, plus jazz and classical music CDs.

GUYI ANTIQUE

Map pp242-3 *Furniture/Antiques*

☎ 6406 9157; 1058 Wuzhong Lu

A small shop with manageable furniture pieces and antiques, that are more interesting than your average altar table; with the requisite warehouse in the western suburbs.

HENRY ANTIQUE WAREHOUSE

Map pp242-3 *Furniture/Antiques*

☎ 6401 0831; www.h-antique.com; 8 Hongzhong Lu

This large warehouse, with over 2000 high-quality pieces, both large and small, is a good first stop. It's down a small alley and is clearly signposted. The Traditional Furniture research department of Tongji University is based here.

HONGQIAO PARKSON

Map p256 *Department Store*

Zunyi Lu

A branch of the popular department store, with a food court, cinema (mostly Chinese language), basement supermarket and several restaurants, including the Coffee Bean & Tea Leaf, Kyros Kebab and Zen, all bustling at lunch with local office workers.

JINJIU ANTIQUE FURNITURE

Map p256 *Furniture/Antiques*

☎ 6278 9656; www.jinjiufurniture.com; 1438 Hongqiao Lu

Four warehouses of furniture and lovely Chinese screens, combined with two other furniture and design shops make this 'Antiques Alley' a good one-stop destination. There are more reproductions than antiques.

Bustling Yuyuan Bazaar (p147)

JUST ANTIQUE & CLASSICAL
FURNITURE Map p256   *Furniture/Antiques*
☎ 6209 4862; 1438 Hongqiao Lu
Owner Benny Lok from Hong Kong offers antiques but specialises in custom-made quality reproduction furniture, with a factory in the western suburbs.

SHANXI ANTIQUES
Map p256   *Furniture/Antiques*
☎ 6401 0056; 731 Hongxu Lu
Furniture and antiques from the 'yellow earth' province of Shanxi, plus some Mongolian chests, are the specialities here. The best pieces are in the upper-storey building at the back.

YIXINYUAN (ALEX'S) ANTIQUE SHOP
Map p256   *Furniture/Antiques*
☎ 6242 3067; 1970 Hongqiao Lu
This shop has a polished showroom and a giant warehouse of things waiting to be stripped.

ZHONG ZHONG JIA YUAN ANTIQUE
FURNITURE Map pp242-3 *Furniture/Antiques*
☎ 6406 4066; 3050 Hechuan Lu
More pieces under one roof here than anyone can take the time for; ask to see all the rooms (about 15!), including the unrestored pieces in the warehouse. This must be the largest collec-

tion of wooden screens in Shanghai. The sales staff are slicker and prices slightly higher than some other places in town.

XUJIAHUI & SOUTH SHANGHAI
Easily accessible by metro, Xujiahui has six giant department stores looming over its insanely busy intersection. It is easier to get to the department stores by using the underground metro walkways than to cross the congested streets.

GRAND GATEWAY
Map p257   *Department Store*
Gǎnghuì Guǎngchǎng
☎ 6407 0111
This is China's second-largest mall, with 250 outlets. The basement has a supermarket, the 6th floor has an Internet café and plenty of entertainment options to keep the nonshoppers happy. The complex also houses about 30 restaurants. The shops are good quality midrange Chinese brands. For tennis racquets, sports gear and even the odd tent try Sport City in the basement.

HUI JIN DEPARTMENT STORE
Map p257   *Department Store*
This often-overlooked store is worth a look for sales on Chinese and foreign brand names; the basement has a decent supermarket with

some imported items. Next door is **Shanghai No 6 Department Store** (Dìliù Bǎihuò), which is popular with the locals and thus usually crowded.

IKEA Map p257 *Home Design*
Yíjiā Jiājū
Caoxi Beilu
This is the yellow and blue Swedish company's largest store in Asia, recently opened southeast of Shanghai Stadium. The complex includes a Swedish restaurant, a kids' play centre and acres of self-assembly pine furniture. It is jammed with Shanghainese decorating their first-ever houses.

METRO CITY Map p257 *Computers*
Half of this mall is about technology, selling electronics, computers and software; the other half is all about fun, with a good arcade and food court, a branch of **Physical Fitness gym** (p137) and **Kodak Cinema World** (p134).

ORIENT SHOPPING CENTRE
Map p257 *Department Store*
☎ 6487 0000
Another mall for Chinese and lesser-Western brands and decent household items. The basement supermarket has a great selection of chocolate, ice cream, coffee and alcohol.

PACIFIC DEPARTMENT STORE
Map p257 *Department Store*
Tàipíngyáng Bǎihuò
Not as flash as the Grand Gateway but still packed with some very decent brands that are continually on sale. The 8th floor has video games and a food court.

PACIFIC DIGITAL PLAZA
Map p257 *Computers*
Tàipíngyáng Diànnǎosì
Due to high import tariffs there are few computer bargains to be had in Shanghai. Prices are similar to those in the USA and warranties

are practically unheard of. But if you do need some technology, this warren of shops is jammed full of computers, laptops, MP3 players, flat-screen monitors and more. Remember to check that the port is adaptable to the voltage in your home country.

SHANGHAI JADE CARVING FACTORY
Map p257 *Jade*
☎ 6436 2660; 33 Caobao Lu
You'd have to be pretty dedicated to make it out to this standard tour-group stop but it can be a good place to learn more about the carving process.

Clothing Sizes
Measurements approximate only, try before you buy

Women's Clothing

Aus/UK	8	10	12	14	16	18
Europe	36	38	40	42	44	46
Japan	5	7	9	11	13	15
USA	6	8	10	12	14	16

Women's Shoes

Aus/USA	5	6	7	8	9	10
Europe	35	36	37	38	39	40
France only	35	36	38	39	40	42
Japan	22	23	24	25	26	27
UK	3½	4½	5½	6½	7½	8½

Men's Clothing

Aus	92	96	100	104	108	112
Europe	46	48	50	52	54	56
Japan	S		M	M		L
UK/USA	35	36	37	38	39	40

Men's Shirts (Collar Sizes)

Aus/Japan	38	39	40	41	42	43
Europe	38	39	40	41	42	43
UK/USA	15	15½	16	16½	17	17½

Men's Shoes

Aus/UK	7	8	9	10	11	12
Europe	41	42	43	44½	46	47
Japan	26	27	27½	28	29	30
USA	7½	8½	9½	10½	11½	12½

Sleeping

Sleeping

Shanghai boasts more than 100 star-rated hotels, including 21 five-star hotels, and more are popping up daily. Most are aimed squarely at business travellers, with a glut of four- and five-star places but a surprising dearth of international-standard three-star options.

The vast majority of Shanghai's hotels are identical mid-range joints, and there's little to choose between them, except location. Short-stay tourists may prefer to be based on Nanjing Donglu or near the Bund, while business visitors will need to be based wherever their business takes them, often in Hongqiao or Pudong. Location near a metro station is a definite advantage for getting around the city. The best budget deals are on the fringes of town, but this isn't as bad as it sounds if you are within walking distance of a metro station (most common in the south of the city).

Top-end hotels generally fall into two categories: the historic villa hotels of old Shanghai and the slick modern towers of new Shanghai, bursting with modern amenities. Business travellers will probably opt for modern facilities like the Portman Ritz-Carlton, Hilton or the imposing Grand Hyatt in Pudong. Those with a sense of history might want to stay at one of the more urbane options, like the Ruijin Guest House or Peace Hotel, where they can wrap themselves in nostalgia.

Most top hotels have executive or club floors aimed at business travellers where an extra US$20 to US$40 gets you separate check-in, a dedicated lounge with complimentary drinks and use of a meeting room for an hour or so.

Although top-end hotels usually list their rates in US dollars you always have to pay in RMB. Almost all hotels change money for guests and most mid-range and top-end places accept credit cards. We list standard room rates here, though deluxe and suite rooms are often available. All hotel rooms are subject to a 10% or 15% service charge, but many cheaper hotels don't bother to charge this. People's Republic of China (PRC) residents often get special rates.

When you check into a hotel you will have to fill in a registration form, a copy of which will be sent to the local Public Security Bureau (PSB; Gōngānjú) office.

Rates & Discounts

Apart from dormitory beds at around US$7, there's not much in Shanghai below around US$30 for a double room. If you're landing at the airport, try the **tourist office** (☎ 6268 8899) in the international arrivals hall. It has a list of hotels offering discounts.

With so much competition around, few hotels in Shanghai actually charge the full rack rate, though prices have crept up in recent years, particularly for two- and three-star hotels. Outside peak times (May to September and Chinese New Year) you can normally get a discount of 30% to 40% if you ask, though it's important to ask if the discounted price includes tax, as this will eat up 10% or 15% of your discount. Newly opened hotels offer particularly good deals. You should also be able to negotiate a better rate for a longer stay, especially at top-end hotels. In this book we list the rack rate and then the best discount we were offered in April (mid-season). Discounted rates might be a little cheaper in the dead of winter.

It's also worth knowing that travel agencies and websites can get you sizable discounts at the top-end hotels. Sites like www.sino-hotel.com, www.shanghai-hotel.net, www.shanghaihotels.com.cn and www.asia-hotels.com offer reviews and advanced booking at good discounted rates. The

The Big Players

Bookings for many of the multinational chains are made by the mother corporation; Starwood (www.starwood.com) for the Sheraton, Westin and St Regis; Marriott (www.marriott.com) for the Marriott Courtyard, JW and Renaissance hotels; Accor (www.accor.com) for Novotel and Sofitel; and Intercontinental (www.ichotelsgroup.com) for Holiday Inn, Intercontinental and Crowne Plaza hotels.

special Internet rates offered by hotels are normally much the same as the discounted rate offered to walk-in guests.

For an explanation of the symbols used in this chapter to describe room type see the Quick Reference page on the inside front cover.

Long-term Rentals

There are several distinct types of longer-term accommodation in Shanghai. One thing common to all is the need to register with the local PSB. Now that the distinction between foreigner and local Chinese accommodation has been abolished, rents have started to fall.

The cheapest way to stay in Shanghai is to share a flat or rent local accommodation from a Chinese landlord. Classified ads in *That's Shanghai* and others advertise apartments or flat-shares. While the average monthly rent for Chinese in Shanghai is around Y2 per sq metre, foreigners will be lucky to get by with any apartment less than US$400 per month.

Most expat residents who work in Shanghai rent a serviced apartment. These run the gamut from towering apartment blocks in the centre of town to villa-style communities out in Pudong and Gubei, where you can forget that you are in China. Most serviced apartments offer hotel-style facilities such as a clubroom, a gym, and a maid service. Shanghai currently has a glut of these blocks and prices have been falling in the last couple of years. In general, rents vary from US$1000 to US$5000 per month for a two-bedroom apartment.

It is even possible to stay in an old-style Shanghai house. Though the idea of a Tudor house in a secluded French Concession backstreet sounds fine, what you gain in style you often lose in suspect electricity and plumbing, poor heating and a continual need for renovations. You won't save any money by choosing an old house, either. Locals have cottoned on that foreigners like the older houses and most rents run from US$1000 to US$3000 per month.

If you want to actually buy a place you definitely need a property agent to help you through the legal minefield. Foreigners can indeed purchase detached houses in Shanghai but are not yet allowed to buy semi detached houses or apartments.

THE BUND & NANJING DONGLU

This is probably the most popular location for tourists, close to the historic highlights of the Bund and views of Pudong. Hotels on Nanjing Donglu are right in the heart of the commercial action and can be a bit noisy but are close to the metro line, which makes getting anywhere else in town a breeze. A **Howard Johnson Plaza Hotel** (Gujiā Dàjiǔdiàn; Map pp244-5) and Le Meridien are due to open on Nanjing Donglu in 2004.

Top Five Historic Hotels

- **Ruijin Guest House** (p163) The former Morris residence, with a lovely garden setting and excellent restaurants.
- **Xingguo Hotel** (p163) Musty garden villas frequented by the ghosts of British taipans and Chinese Communist leaders, now a five-star Radisson hotel.
- **Hengshan Moller Villa** (p161) *Adam's Family*–inspired whimsy, with many original features intact.
- **Peace Hotel** (p158) Victor Sassoon's showpiece on the Bund sums up swinging Shanghai more than any other.
- **Garden Hotel** (p161) Former Cercle Français Sportif, with some lovely Art Deco touches.

Hengshan Moller Villa (p161)

BROADWAY MANSIONS Map pp244-5
Shànghǎi Dàshà

☎ 6324 6260; fax 6306 5147; www.broadwaymansions
.com; 20 Suzhou Beilu; d Y960-1080, discount of 30%
Across Suzhou Creek from the Bund is this classic building, with dominant views over the north Bund, the Huangpu River and Pudong. It was built in the 1930s as an apartment block and was later used to house American officers after WWII. The rooms are looking a bit tired these days, especially the bathrooms which are crying out for a renovation, but the views are great. The more expensive doubles have better views on the higher floors. Make sure you ask for a room facing the Bund.

CENTRAL HOTEL Map pp244-5
Wángbǎohé Dàjiǔdiàn

☎ 5396 5000; www.centralhotelshanghai.com;
555 Jiujiang Lu; d US$180, discounted to US$86
A modern hotel in an excellent location built by the group that owns the Wang Baohe restaurant (see p100).

METROPOLE HOTEL Map pp244-5
Xinchéng Fàndiàn

☎ 6321 3030; fax 6321 7365; 180 Jiangxi Zhonglu;
d Y500-700
A couple of blocks from the Bund, the Metropole was one of Shanghai's most glamorous hotels in the 1930s. A few Art Deco touches remain but the interior now feels more like a standard smoky Chinese hotel, though the façade is as grand as ever. The rooms are fairly spacious but the plumbing is slightly suspect, and it's a little overpriced.

NANJING HOTEL Map pp244-5
Nánjīng Fàndiàn

☎ 6322 2888; 200 Shanxi Nanlu; d Y330-450,
discounted by 20%
Newly renovated modern doubles make this hotel quite good value, especially as it's just off Nanjing Donglu.

NEW ASIA HOTEL Map pp244-5
Xīnyà Dàjiǔdiàn

☎ 6324 2210; fax 6356 6816; 422 Tiantong Lu;
d/superior Y330-400/540, discounted to d/superior
Y298/398
Near the main post office in Hongkou, on the grittier side of Suzhou Creek but also within walking distance of the Bund, this 1930s-era building is a decent choice. Extensive renovations inside have taken away some of its historical feel but the old B&W photos in the lobby add some charm. Doubles can be a little dark but are decent value; modern superior rooms are more spacious and less smoky. It's near the Sichuan Beilu shopping district.

PACIFIC HOTEL Map pp244-5
Jīnmén Dàjiǔdiàn

☎ 6327 6226; fax 6372 3634; 104 Nanjing Xilu;
s/d from US$55/70-120, discount of 30%
Just east of the Park Hotel, this overlooked hotel has a small but opulent foyer with some nice Art Deco details and is cheaper than the Park.

PARK HOTEL Map pp244-5
Guójì Fàndiàn

☎ 6327 5225; fax 6327 6958; 170 Nanjing Xilu;
s/d from US$80/150, discounted to s/d Y550/880
Erected in 1934, the Park is one of Shanghai's best examples of Art Deco architecture from the city's cultural peak. Recent renovations have robbed the interior of some of its old-world appeal but those who know their history will still be charmed by the ghosts of the past. Rooms are comfortable and the service is efficient. Book ahead to get a fine view of Nanjing Lu and Renmin Park. For more details on this hotel see p91.

PEACE HOTEL Map pp244-5
Hépíng Fàndiàn

☎ 6321 6888; www.shanghaipeacehotel.com;
20 Nanjing Donglu; s/d US$120/160-220, discount of
25-40%
If there's one place left in Shanghai that will give you a sense of the past it's this, the old Cathay, which still rises majestically from the Bund. The sumptuous lobby is one of the best examples of an Art Deco interior left in Shanghai. The national deluxe suites (US$520) are laid out in 1930s Art Deco style to represent the concessions of the time. Some travellers have rightly pointed out, however, that in terms of service, this hotel is way overpriced and that it's perhaps better to visit than stay in. Discounts knock doubles down to around US$115 in spring and US$80 in winter. Only three of the standard rooms have a view of Nanjing Lu (only suites view the Bund) so book ahead. For more on the history of the hotel see the Bund walking tour (p87). See the Entertainment chapter for details of the top-floor bar (p125) and the hotel's famous jazz band (p131).

PEACE PALACE HOTEL Map pp244-5

Hépíng Huìzhōng Fàndiàn

☎ 6329 1888; 23 Nanjing Donglu; s/d US$120/160-220, discount of 25-40%

Across from and part of the Peace Hotel, this older annexe has similar rates, dipping as low as Y700 for a double in winter. It's often referred to as the Peace Hotel South.

RAMADA PLAZA Map pp244-5

Nán Xīnyà Huáměidá Dàjiŭdiàn

☎ 6350 0000; www.ramadainternationalhotel.com; 700 Jiujiang Lu; d from US$150, discount of 25%

Formerly the Grand Nation, the new Ramada offers tourists a great location. The gaudy faux lobby feels worryingly like a shopping mall but the impressive hidden inner atrium makes up for that. Rooms are modern and pleasant as you would expect for this new hotel, though the service isn't up to scratch yet. The hotel has a Thai and Western restaurant, a China Eastern office and Club Ramada fills the upper floors, though gym facilities aren't up to much, if that's important to you.

SEAGULL HOTEL Map pp253-4

Hǎi'ōu Fàndiàn

☎ 6325 1500; www.seagull-hotel.com; 60 Huangpu Lu; d/sightseeing rooms US$99/150, discounted to US$70/105

The Seagull was originally built near the Pujiang Hotel as part of the Seamen's Club but the prime location made upscale renovations inevitable. Sightseeing rooms have awesome views of the Bund but you pay for the view with smaller than average rooms. There's a fine open-air riverside café, open to all. The central Bund is a 10-minute walk over Suzhou Bridge.

SEVENTH HEAVEN HOTEL Map pp244-5

Qīzhòngtiān Bīnguǎn

☎ 6322 0777 ext 701; fax 6351 7193; 627 Nanjing Donglu; s/d from Y280/340, discount of 20%

It might not look much from the outside but this good-value hotel is right in the thick of things on Nanjing Donglu, to the west of Century Square, inside the Overseas Clothing store (look up to see the sign). Rooms are small but clean. Reception is on the 7th floor.

SHANGHAI RAILWAY HOTEL

Map pp244-5

Shànghǎi Tiědào Bīnguǎn

☎ 6322 6633; 160 Guizhou Lu; s/d/tr Y280/360/480

Another passable budget hotel just off Nanjing

Park Hotel (opposite)

Donglu, this isn't bad value, though some rooms have no windows.

SOFITEL HYLAND HOTEL Map pp244-5

Hǎilún Bīnguǎn

☎ 6351 5888; sofitel@hyland-shanghai.com; 505 Nanjing Donglu; s/d from US$170/190, discount of 40%

A favourite tourist option right in the centre of the Nanjing Donglu shopping frenzy, this is a dependable and solid choice, run by the French Accor group. French and German cuisine (and home-brewed beer) are served at Le Pub 505.

WESTIN SHANGHAI Map pp244-5

Wēisītīng Dàfàndiàn

☎ 6335 1888, reservations ☎ 1-800-WESTIN-1 in the US or Canada; www.westin.com/shanghai; 88 Henan Zhonglu; d US$320, discount of 40-50%

A stylish new arrival, a couple of blocks from the Bund and near the old town, the Westin ranks as the best in this area. It is part of the Bund Centre, with its characteristic lotus-bud top. Top-of-the-line facilities include the Thai-style Banyan Tree spa, an import food store and deli and the excellent EEST (Asian) and Prego (Italian) restaurants. All rooms come with rainforest shower heads, broadband Internet access and a fax machine.

159

YANGTZE HOTEL Map pp244-5
Yángzǐ Fàndiàn

☎ 6351 7880; www.e-yangtze.com; 740 Hankou Lu;
s/d/tr Y450/680-780/780-880, discount of 30%

The Yangtze was built in 1934 and the exterior, including the wonderful Art Nouveau balconies, is largely unchanged. However, the inside is more of a standard Chinese hotel, with faded décor, the faint aroma of cigarette smoke and dim lights. Still, singles are good value, there's a nice café and most rooms come with a balcony (though these are currently noisy due to a nearby construction site). 'A' rooms are bigger and better. The hotel is just off Nanjing Donglu, behind the Protestant church that faces Renmin Park.

Cheap Sleeps
CAPTAIN HOSTEL Map pp244-5
Chuáncháng Qīngnián Jiǔdiàn

☎ 6325 5053; www.captainhostel.com.cn; 37 Fuzhou Lu; dm/r Y55/330-400, discount of 20%

Affiliated to Youth Hostels International (YHI), this hostel is more central than the Pujiang, in an old Art Deco building a stone's throw from the Bund. Dorms are clean and fresh with maritime-inspired bunk beds and personal lockers. The clean communal bathrooms have 24-hour hot water. The rooms with private bathroom rank as some of the best value in Shanghai.

Budget facilities include a useful notice board, free use of a microwave and washing machine. It's also one of the few places in town offering bike hire (Y10 for four hours then Y2 per hour). The top-floor Noah's Bar has cheap beers and fine views. Minor quibbles are the expensive Internet and crummy lift. A YHI card gets you a Y5 discount.

CHUNSHENJIANG HOTEL Map pp244-5
Chūnshēnjiāng Bīnguǎn

☎ 6351 5710; 626 Nanjing Donglu; d Y300-330

Another mid-range option nearby, at the corner of Zhejiang Lu. Corner rooms have fine views of Nanjing Lu's neon glare but can be noisy. The entrance is set back from the road, so you'll have to look for the sign.

EAST ASIA HOTEL Map pp244-5
Dōngyà Fàndiàn

☎ 6322 3223; 680 Nanjing Donglu; d Y380-580, discounted to s/d Y280/340-420

A central budget choice. Access is through a clothes store and by lift to the 2nd floor.

NEW ASIA STAR DAFANG HOTEL
Map pp244-5
Dàfàng Fàndiàn

☎ 6326 0505; fax 6311 4542; 33 Fujian Lu;
s/d Y248/278-298, discount of 15%

This friendly and modern hotel's location tucked away from the fashionable districts, but still fairly close to the Bund, makes it quite a good deal. The rooms facing Fujian Lu are noisy (there's a bus stop just outside the hotel). Rooms facing inwards are smaller, cheaper and quieter; the higher floor rooms are generally best. There are a few family rooms that come with a double and single bed. The hotel is just south of the Yan'an Donglu overpass.

PUJIANG HOTEL Map pp244-5
Pǔjiāng Fàndiàn

☎ 6324 6388; fax 6324 3179; www.pujianghotel.com;
15 Huangpu Lu; dm/r Y55/from Y330, 4-/5-bed Y330/350

This distinguished old gentleman is for those mindful of their máo – it's central (only a short walk to the Bund), has loads of style and the rooms are vast. Built in 1846 as the Astor House, this was Shanghai's first hotel and the management claims that Albert Einstein and Charlie Chaplin stayed here (though presumably not in the dorm rooms). The upstairs galleries look like they belong in a Victorian asylum and the thick lacquered walls, high ceilings and winding corridors add to the general boarding-school feel but there's a nobility about the place that makes the dorm beds a bargain. Backpacker facilities include a washing machine in the upstairs bar; put a load in and grab a cheap beer (Y10) and a nightly movie at 7pm. The hotel has recently started calling itself Astor House once again.

FRENCH CONCESSION
Leafy, tree-lined streets, excellent restaurants and good shopping make this the most aesthetically pleasing district in which to be based. It also has the largest collection of historic villa hotels.

DONGHU HOTEL Map pp246-9
Dōnghú Bīnguǎn

☎ 6415 8158; www.donghuhotel.com; 70 Donghu Lu; s/d from US$90/110, discounted to Y550/680, old block d Y600

Set back off Huaihai Zhonglu, the Donghu consists of two blocks. The newer block, on the south side of the road, has smaller but newer

Pujiang Hotel (opposite)

rooms. The old block across the road is more 1950s Soviet socialist than 1930s swinging Shanghai but the rooms are spacious, clean and quiet and some have a garden view.

GARDEN HOTEL Map pp246-9
Huāyuá Fàndiàn
☎ 6415 1111; www.gardenhotelshanghai.com; 58 Maoming Nanlu; d US$250-310, discounted to US$170-190

The elegant Japanese-run Okura Garden boasts nice grounds on the site of the old French Club and an excellent location, across from the Jinjiang Hotel and near Huaihai Zhonglu. See the French Concession II walking tour (p93) for more on the hotel's history. An extra US$20 on the room rate gets you a garden view. There's an indoor pool, a French café and a top-end Japanese restaurant. Blue dots on the employees' uniforms show their language ability, with three stars the best.

HENGSHAN HOTEL Map pp246-9
Héngshān Bīnguǎn
☎ 6437 7050; hshs@81890.net; 534 Hengshan Lu; standard US$88, superior US$100-115, discount of 15-25%

These former 1930s Picardie Apartments still hold a few hints of their original interior Art Deco charm. The quality has been raised a bit recently, with a nice ground-floor restaurant (Planet Shanghai), particularly nice bathrooms and some classy architectural touches. The location is good, between the Hengshan Lu restaurant strip and Xujiahui shopping centre. The cheapest standard rooms are small and may require you to walk up one or two flights of stairs.

HENGSHAN MOLLER VILLA Map pp246-9
Héngshān Mǎlè Biéshù Fàndiàn
☎ 6247 8881; fax 6289 1020; 30 Shanxi Nanlu; old house s US$95, new block standard US$80, old building business room US$180, 15% discount

The wacky architecture of Moller House, one of the most fantastic buildings in Shanghai, was off-limits for years until 2002, when the Hengshan group renovated it as a peaceful boutique hotel. The main Moller building has only business rooms and two single rooms; the standard rooms are in the dull, new block next door. Most features of the main house rooms are original, from the wood panelling and staircases to the fireplaces. Singles are small but fair value; business rooms are much larger and come with a huge balcony that

The foyer, Hengshan Moller Villa (p161)

overlooks the garden. There's an atmospheric but pricey bar. See the French Concession II walking tour p94 for details of the house.

HILTON HOTEL Map pp246-9
Jìng`ān Xīĕrdùn Fàndiàn
☎ 6248 0000; www.hilton.com; 250 Huashan Lu; r from US$230, discount of 35%
This old-timer is still holding its own. Facilities include an indoor swimming pool, tennis and squash courts. Food isn't a problem, with Italian, Sichuanese, Cantonese and Shanghainese restaurants plus a popular Atrium café, 39th-floor Penthouse Bar and a good bakery and deli. Tense after a long business meeting? Get a quick stress release massage in the new spa for Y260.

JIANGONG JINJIANG HOTEL
Map pp246-9
Jiàngōng Jīnjiāng Dàjiŭdiàn
☎ 6415 5688; fax 6472 2827; 691 Jianguo Xilu; d US$90-108, discounted to Y638-688

A good location just off Hengshan Lu, a small gym, Shanghainese cuisine and one of the city's few Ningbo restaurants make this a good choice. Rooms are spacious if a little plain; ask for a renovated room. The upper floors give nice views over the city.

JINCHEN HOTEL Map pp246-9
Jīnchén Dàjiŭdiàn
☎ 6471 7000; 795-809 Huaihai Zhonglu; s/d from Y288/328
Shopaholics who are up against the clock can stumble out of the Jinchen into the heart of Huaihai Lu's shopping strip for optimum shopping efficiency.

JINJIANG HOTEL Map pp246-9
Jīnjiāng Fàndiàn
☎ 6258 2582; fax 6472 5588; 59 Maoming Nanlu; Cathay Bldg s/d US$155/165, discounted to Y880, Jin Nan Bldg d Y450, Grosvenor Villa d US$200, discount of 30%
This historic complex underwent massive renovations in 1999. It consists of the main

Georgian-style Cathay Building, the cheaper Jin Nan Building and the lavish Grosvenor Villa (Guìbīn Loú), in the southernmost part of the complex. All rooms include access to the gym and indoor pool. The hotel stages classical music concerts on Sunday (see p131 for details).

MASON HOTEL Map pp246-9
Měichén Dàjiǔdiàn
☎ 6466 2020; 935 Huaihai Zhonglu; s/d Y750/900, discounted to Y600/720

There aren't many boutique hotels in Shanghai and this small and intimate hotel, next to Printemps department store and the metro stop, is one of them. The 120 bright and spacious rooms are arranged around a snappy enclosed courtyard, plus there's a 2nd floor lounge, a rooftop beer garden and a Starbucks. The rooms overlooking Huaihai Lu are a bit noisy.

RADISSON PLAZA XINGGUO HOTEL
Map pp246-9
Xìngguó Bīnguǎn
☎ 6212 9998, toll free reservation in China 800-3333 3333; www.radissonasiapacific.com; 78 Xingguo Lu; s/d US$220/240, discounted to US$138/158, garden villas from US$75-120, discounted to US$68-105

The Radisson has upgraded the former Xingguo Hotel, adding a Clark Hatch gym and pool, a nice lounge, squash court and a restrained elegance. What hasn't changed are the lovely gardens and sense of oasis. The pub has a half-priced happy hour between 5pm and 9pm and live music from 9.30pm. An extra US$20 gets you a garden view.

Four of the seven villas set in the manicured grounds are rented out by the attached **Xingguo Hotel** (☎ 6212 9070; fax 6251 2145), which has a separate reception. Part of the complex was built for the Butterfield & Swire Company in the 1920s; interestingly, the building's architect never saw the finished product. Building No 1 (Room 103) was one of Mao's favourite places to stay. Room décor is suitably old fashioned (you can still picture Mao briefing Zhou Enlai in the *en suite* meeting rooms), but rates give access to the Radisson's modern facilities.

REGAL INTERNATIONAL EAST ASIA HOTEL Map pp246-9
Fùháo Huánqiú Dōngyà Jiǔdiàn
☎ 6415 5588; rieah@prodigychina.com; 516 Hengshan Lu; d from US$200, discounted to US$90

The gym and sports facilities at this marbly five-star pad are some of the best in Shanghai.

RUIJIN GUEST HOUSE Map pp246-9
Ruìjīn Bīnguǎn
☎ 6472 5222; www.shedi.net.cn/outedi/ruijin; 118 Ruijin Erlu; s/d US$85/150, discounted to Y500/840

Another historic option, the Ruijin has elegant grounds and a series of old mansions converted into rooms. Building No 1 was the former Morris estate (see p93) and communist stalwarts Liu Shaoqi, Zhou Enlai and even Ho Chi Minh all stayed here at some point. Some of Shanghai's most romantic and stylish restaurants are nestled in the gardens. The website offers good on-line discounts.

TAIYUAN VILLA Map pp246-9
Tàiyuán Biéshù
☎ 6471 6688; fax 6471 2618; 160 Taiyuan Lu; d Y300-Y450

The Ruijin Guest House also runs this villa, in a separate location but still in the French Concession. The peaceful complex includes the historic former residence of General Marshall (see p93), where rooms hit the Y1000 to Y1200 mark. Most rooms have been modernised.

Cheap Sleeps
CONSERVATORY OF MUSIC GUEST HOUSE Map pp246-9
Yīnyuè Xuéyuàn Wàibīn Zhāodàisuǒ
☎ 6437 2577; 20 Fenyang Lu; d shared/private bathroom Y100/200

This old budget stand-by has a great location off Huaihai Zhonglu. The pleasant strains of music practice waft around the campus courtyards, giving the surroundings a civilised air. The snag? It's often fully booked in summer so it's essential to ring ahead or come with a contingency plan. The cheapest rough-and-ready doubles include a fan and access to a clean, shared bathroom. Nicer standard doubles with private bathroom have carpet and air-con. Some floors are noisier than others; the 2nd floor is probably the best if you get the choice. This guesthouse is a short walk from the Changshu Lu metro station; to find it, walk through the entrance to the conservatory, left around the curve past a green villa. There's a washing machine on the 3rd floor. Classical music performances are held in the auditorium during term time; see p131 for details.

EDUCATION HOTEL Map pp246-9
Jiàoyù Bīnguǎn

☎ 6466 0500; fax 6466 3149; 3 Fenyang Lu; r Y380 discounted to Y300 with tax & breakfast

A slightly smoky and noisy hotel frequented by Chinese businessmen, this wouldn't be a bad bet if it weren't for the noisy building site nearby. Still, it's the cheapest hotel in the district.

PUDONG

Hotels in Pudong cater mostly to business people but it's not a bad tourist option if you are based in the Liujiazui district as you are only a metro ride away from the Bund.

COURTYARD BY MARRIOTT Map pp242-3
Qílǔ Wànyí Dàjiǔdiàn

☎ 68886 7886; www.marriott.com; 838 Dongfang Lu; d US$180, discount of 50%

A fairly unremarkable new hotel, a notice-able notch below the other four-star places, but with good-value weekend rates of Y500. There's a Thai restaurant in Spices Café, dim sum in Chinese, broadband Internet and a small gym but no views.

GRAND HYATT Map pp253-4
Jīnmaò Kāiyuè Dàjiǔdiàn

☎ 5830 3338; shanghai.hyatt.com; d from US$320, discounted to US$148 in winter, US$188 in spring

This is one of the brightest stars on the Shang-hai hotel horizon. Not the place for those with a fear of heights, the Hyatt starts on the 54th floor of the Jinmao Tower and goes up another 33 storeys; everywhere from the hair salon to the bathtubs has stunning views. Described as 'contemporary Art Deco with Chinese touches', the hotel is very much design-led, with endless attention to detail – from the original art on the walls to the custom-made

The Grand Hyatt, Jingmao Tower (see left)

glassware. The rooms are packed to the steel rafters with hi-tech gadgets such as TV Inter-net access, fog-free mirrors, three-jet showers and sensor reading lamps. Add US$15 to the room base rate for a Bund view and another US$45 to make that a breathtaking corner window room. For business travellers, the Regency Club offers meeting rooms, separate check-in, free breakfast, tea and snacks, all for an extra US$20.

World's Highest Bubble Bath

The Grand Hyatt is the highest hotel above ground level in the world (not the world's tallest hotel – that accolade goes to a hotel in Dubai), and so begins an endless line of somewhat pointless superlatives – the highest gym above ground level, the world's highest minibar etc. The hotel also boasts the world's longest laundry chute (420 vertical metres) and an impressive 61 elevators, which shoot high rollers up into the air at 9m/second. The interior atrium is the world's tallest at an impressive 33 storeys, and only *starts* on the 55th floor. It's hard not to believe that the post office on the 88th floor wasn't put there deliberately to make it the world's highest.

To ensure its stability in Pudong's boggy soil, the building rests on 429 steel pipes rammed 65m into the ground. Still, in case of a freak typhoon you'll need to hold on to your coffee; the pinnacle is designed to swing a stomach-churning 75cm.

HOLIDAY INN PUDONG Map pp242-3
Pǔdōng Jiàrì Jiǔdiàn

☎ 5830 6666; www.holiday-inn.com; 899 Dongfang
Lu; d Y15 00, discount of 20-30%

Another standard option, with a fitness centre,
indoor swimming pool, Mediterranean restaurant and Flanagan's Bar.

HOTEL INTERCONTINENTAL
PUDONG Map pp242-3
Xīnyà Tāngchén Zhōujì Dàjiǔdiàn

☎ 5831 8888; www.intercontinental.com; 777
Zhangyang Lu; d superior/deluxe US$280/290, discount
of 50%

The former Asia Thompson, in the heart of
Pudong near the Nextage department store,
is more sombre than Pudong's other hotels
but the facilities are up to par, with an indoor
pool, decent bar, sushi and Chinese restaurants and western buffet and a casual noodle
bar. Guests get temporary membership of
the Asia Thompson Golf Course, a 20-minute
drive away.

HOTEL NIKKO PUDONG Map pp242-3
Zhōngyóu Rìháng Dàjiǔdiàn

☎ 6875 8888; sales@nikkopudong.com;
969 Dongfang Lu; d US$170, discount of 40%

Part of the sleek Japanese chain, with an indoor
swimming pool, several Japanese and Korean
restaurants (including one on the 31st floor)
and a Starbucks.

ORIENTAL RIVERSIDE HOTEL Map pp253-4
Dōngfāng Bīnjiāng Dàjiǔdiàn

☎ 5037 0000, hotel@shicc.net; 2727 Binjiang Dadao;
d US$210, discounted to US$110

Instantly recognisable for its gaudy glass
globes, the Oriental Riverside is situated on
the east bank of the Huangpu facing the Bund
and attached to the Shanghai International
Convention Centre. Facilities include a 9th-
floor swimming pool and health club and an
11th-floor bar with panoramic river and Bund
views. An extra US$30 will get you a room
with a Bund view (worth it); another US$10
gets you a deluxe room. The spacious rooms
are used mostly by conventions but it's not a
bad tourist choice, close to the Bund and
Pudong sights without the noise and traffic,
and with the metro and tourist tunnel nearby.
The best rooms are on the 6th floor; it's a
shame there are no balconies.

NOVOTEL ATLANTIS Map pp242-3
Hǎishén Nuòfútè Dàjiǔdiàn

☎ 5036 6666; www.novotel.com; 728 Pudong Dadao;
d US$150, spring discount of 40%

There's nothing stuffy at this bright and breezy
modern hotel, from the open business centre
in the lobby lounge to the in-room pizza
delivery (until 11pm). Strong points include
the women-only floor, the kids' play areas and
activities, the Bali spa and in-room broadband
Internet access. Get a high floor for the views.
Restaurants include a top-floor revolving restaurant with art exhibits, Olive's for Italian and
Mediterranean cuisine, and a 'fusion Shanghainese' restaurant.

PUDONG SHANGRILA Map pp253-4
Pǔdōng Xiānggélìlā Dàjiǔdiàn

☎ 6882 6888; slpu@shangri-la.com; 33 Fucheng Lu;
d from US$150

The Shangrila is a solid luxury choice in the
heart of Liujiazui. Avoid a north-facing room
as your window will be taken up by the Superbrand Mall. An extra US$20 gets you a view of
the Bund, which is worth it. Facilities include
an indoor pool, tennis court, deli and BATS bar.
The lobby window offers some of the finest
views of the Bund.

RAMADA PLAZA PUDONG
Pǔdōng Huáměidá Dàjiǔdiàn

☎ 5055 4666; www.ramadaplazapd.com;
18 Xin Jinqiao Lu; d US$128

Be warned, this one's in the middle of nowhere, way out in far eastern Pudong, which
is great if you are working in the nearby Jinqiao
zone or at the airport, but not if you want to
explore the city centre.

SOFITEL JINJIANG ORIENTAL
PUDONG Map pp242-3
Dōng Jǐnjiāng Dàjiǔdiàn

☎ 5050 4888; reservation@sofiteljjoriental.com;
889 Yanggao Nanlu; d from US$111

The second Sofitel in Shanghai has a pool, gym
and five places to eat, including a 46th-floor
revolving French restaurant.

ST REGIS SHANGHAI Map pp242-3
Ruìjí Hóngtǎ Dàjiǔdiàn

☎ 5050 4567; www.stregis.com/shanghai; 889 Dongfang Lu; d US$320, discounted to US$140 at weekends

This latest offering in beyond-luxury mixes hi-
tech (Bose radios, broadband Internet) with
old-style service. The 24-hour personal butlers

will record your pillow preference for your next visit just before fixing your laptop. This hotel, which boasts the largest standard hotel rooms in Shanghai, was built to resemble a red pagoda building owned by the parent Yunnanese tobacco company. If you've had a long flight try the anti-jet lag pressure massage (Y400, 60 minutes) or the special hot stone massage.

The décor is contemporary, stylish and warm, as is the excellent Italian restaurant Danielli's. Unlike other hotels in Shanghai, all guests can use the executive club facilities.

NANJING XILU & JING'AN

The business and shopping district of Jing'an, focused around bustling Nanjing Xilu, is deservedly popular among businesspeople. It has a useful location halfway between the Bund and Hongqiao, it's close to the major office towers and embassies, with good restaurants nearby and easy access to the metro. If you are looking for more of a deal on your room rate, there are several three-star hotels near the Shanghai train station which offer good value. It's not a bad place to be based as it's near the starting point of the metro line but the railway neighbourhood isn't the best and can be noisy, so check for double-glazing.

CROWNE PLAZA SHANGHAI
Map pp246-9
Yínxíng Huángguān Jiǔdiàn
☎ 6280 8888; www.shanghai.crowneplaza.com; 400 Panyu Lu; s/d US$210/230, discounted by 50%
A dependable but unexciting modern option, popular with foreign tourists. The location is pleasant, off tree-lined and historic Xinhua Lu, but is a bit out of the way between the French Concession and Hongqiao. There are Cantonese, Italian and Shanghainese restaurants (with a good steak and seafood buffet), a fitness centre, Charlie's Bar (happy hour daily 4pm to 8pm) and a gift shop that stocks the British papers. Schedules for the cinema next door are posted inside the hotel.

EAST CHINA HOTEL Map pp250-2
Huádōng Dàjiǔdiàn
☎ 6317 8000; fax 6317 6678; 111 Tianmu Xilu; d Y780-880, discounted to Y380-480
The rooms here are decent if you are arriving

late or departing early by train. There are a few unadvertised economy standard rooms for Y330.

FOUR SEASONS Map pp250-2
☎ 6256 8888; www.fourseasons.com; 500 Weihai Lu; d from US$300, weekend discounts of 33%
The new Four Seasons is a very classy place with a lobby decorated with huge art works, warm golden tones and 5m-tall palm trees. The simple but elegant rooms come with voicemail and 24-hour butler service. An extra US$10 gets you a deluxe room; a premier double is only US$40 more. Restaurants include one of best steak houses in Shanghai, plus Shanghainese, Cantonese and a top floor jazz bar.

HOLIDAY INN DOWNTOWN Map pp250-2
Shànghǎi Guǎngchǎng Chángchéng Jiàrì Jiǔdiàn
☎ 6353 8008; www.holiday-inn.com; 285 Tianmu Xilu & 585 Hengfeng Lu; d US$140, discounted to Y790
Near the train station (and so not downtown at all), this bizarrely structured hotel consists of two wings in separate buildings. Room rates are the same in both wings and include breakfast and service charge. The Great Wall wing has the larger fitness centre and the deluxe rooms. Rooms are double-glazed but the area can still be noisy. There's one room adapted for people with disabilities.

JC MANDARIN SHANGHAI Map pp250-2
Shànghǎi Jīnwénhúa Dàjiǔdiàn
☎ 6279 1888; www.jcmandarin.com; 1225 Nanjing Xilu; s/d US$210/230, discounted to US$136/146
Peer pressure amongst the overcrowded five-star hotels of Shanghai has resulted in a giant overhaul to this already impressive hotel that will see new restaurants and a new lobby. Facilities include tennis and squash courts and an indoor pool. The hotel was built on the ruins of the old 1930s Burlington Hotel.

JINGTAI HOTEL Map pp250-2
Jīngtài Dàjiǔdiàn
☎ 6272 2222; fax 6218 4778; 178 Taixing Lu; d Y680-780, discounted to Y476-544
This professional hotel has well-trained staff, comfortable, clean rooms and a great location, just off Nanjing Xilu and near the metro. There are also a few unadvertised economy rooms for Y580, discounted to Y380, though they have no windows and can feel a bit

claustrophobic. Rooms are slightly smaller on the Nanjing Xilu side.

JW MARRIOTT TOMORROW SQUARE
Map pp250-2
Míngtiān Guǎngchǎng JW Wànyí Jiǔdiàn
☎ 6360 0503, toll free 10 800-8520469;
www.marriott.com; 399 Nanjing Xilu
This new top-end tower should push Shanghai's luxury offerings to even greater heights. Expect rooms from the 30th to 50th floors, executive apartments, a Mandara spa and Californian grill to open in late 2003. Take that, Grand Hyatt!

LIANG'AN HOTEL Map pp250-2
Liáng'ān Dàfàndiàn
☎ 6353 2222; www.lianganhotel.com; 920 Changan Lu; s Y398, d Y398-548, discounted to s Y248, d Y298-368
A modern giant located near a street full of cheap restaurants and prostitutes – so watch your step. The 8th-floor rooms are the cheapest.

PORTMAN RITZ-CARLTON Map pp250-2
Bōtèmàn Lìjiā Jiǔdiàn
☎ 6279 8888; www.ritzcarlton.com; 1376 Nanjing Xilu; s/d US$320/340, discount of 50%
Renovated in 1999 at the cost of US$30 million and part of the massive Shanghai Centre, this is the cream of the crop in Puxi and the biggest expat hang-out since the Peace Hotel c1931. Top-notch facilities include the 7th-floor health club with swimming pools, squash courts, tennis courts and a top-of-the-line gym. Phone ahead and they'll even run a Chinese herbal bath for your arrival (for an extra US$20).

ZHAO'AN HOTEL Map pp250-2
Zhào'ān Jiǔdiàn
☎ 6317 2221; fax 6317 0338; 195 Hengtong Lu; d Y498-588, discounted to Y350-450
The location close to the metro stop makes for easy transport, and the helpful staff, pleasant, bright rooms and clean bathrooms make this a decent choice for a reasonable price. Deluxe rooms are much more spacious.

ZHONGYA HOTEL Map pp250-2
Zhōngyà Fàndiàn
☎ 6317 2317; www.zhongyahotel.com; 330 Meiyuan Lu; d from Y378, discounted to Y286
Just across the road from the East China Hotel, this is comparable but cheaper, with a bowling alley and small fitness centre. Pricier

rooms are often a good deal as they are discounted by 50%. The hotel claims to have nonsmoking and rooms suitable for people with disabilities.

NORTH SHANGHAI
There are several good-value budget options a little out of the way in the northwest of town. There's no metro out here but it's only a short Y10 to Y15 taxi ride to the Bund.

OCEAN HOTEL Map pp253-4
Yuǎnyáng Bīnguǎn
☎ 6545 8888; www.oceanhotel-sh.com; 1171 Dongdaming Lu; d from US$110, discounted to US$77
It's all about the views here at this otherwise rather inconveniently located hotel. The revolving restaurant on the 28th floor has good views of the Bund and Huangpu and rooms go up to the 25th floor. An extra US$10 gets you views of the Huangpu, US$20 gives you Bund views and deluxe rooms have a view of Pudong. There's also a 24-hour café and good Chinese and Japanese restaurants.

SHANGHAI E-BEST HOTEL Map pp253-4
Shànghǎi Yìbǎi Jiārì Jiǔdiàn
☎ 6595 1818; fax 6595 3093; 687 Dongdaming Lu; s/d Y198/228-288, view d Y408-428
This new hotel in Hongkou has a range of cheapish rooms. The cheapest singles have no external windows and are a bit claustrophobic. Nicer superior doubles are more spacious, with river-view rooms on the 5th floor. Rooms are clean and fresh with wooden floors but have irritatingly dim lighting.

Cheap Sleeps
CHANGYANG HOTEL Map pp242-3
Chángyáng Fàndiàn
☎ 6543 4890; fax 6543 0986; 1800 Changyang Lu; d Y210-270; bus 22, 934 from the Bund
Furthest out of all. Dated but clean doubles vary in price, depending on how much sun the room gets.

DAMING FOUNTAIN GARDEN HOTEL
Map pp253-4
Dàmíng Xīngyuàn Jiǔdiàn
☎ 6537 3399; daming@sfc.com.cn; 1191 Dongdaming Lu; s/d Y359/459, discounted to Y228/278
This new hotel was offering good-value introductory rates in 2003, the cheapest during the

week. It's next to the Ocean Hotel and has even better views. The top-floor Western restaurant and bar has excellent views over the Huangpu and very reasonable prices (set meals Y48, Y15 beer), with a happy hour from 5pm to 8pm.

DONGHONG HOTEL Map pp253-4
Dōnghóng Dàjiǔdiàn

☎ 6545 5008; fax 6545 5034; 1161 Dongdaming Lu; s Y210-245, d from Y300, with breakfast

If the Daming is full try this place, part of the same building as the Ocean Hotel (see p167). It's a cheaper, two-star option popular with local businessmen; lots of different room types.

LINTONG HOTEL Map pp253-4
Líntóng Bīnguǎn

☎ 6546 5060; fax 6537 3903; 188 Lintong Lu; d Y280-320, discounted to Y220-240, tr Y298 (Y268)

The location near the old Jewish area is inconvenient for sure, but also interesting, with lots of scope for local exploration on foot. The rooms are good value.

SHIZEYUAN HOTEL Map pp242-3
Shīzéyuán Bīnguǎn

☎ 6546 6008; fax 6546 7524; 999 Changyang Lu; d Y198-228

Good-value and spotless doubles, with rates depending on the height of the floor. It's popular with Chinese visitors.

HONGQIAO & GUBEI

There's a cluster of hotels in Hongqiao aimed at expats and businesspeople working in the area. The zone is close to Hongqiao airport but a long way from Pudong airport.

CYPRESS HOTEL Map pp242-3
Lóngbǎi Fàndiàn

☎ 6268 8868; cypress@stn.sh.cn; 2419 Hongqiao Lu; d US$160, discounted to US$98

Out in the Boonies but with a pleasant garden and a health club with a driving range, tennis and squash courts and an indoor pool.

GALAXY HOTEL Map p256
Yínhé Bīnguǎn

☎ 6275 5888; www.galaxyhotel.com; 888 Zhongshan Xilu; d Y1400-1600, discounted to Y800-850

This is straight old-school, with lots of marble,

a night club and Japanese and Korean restaurants catering to the Asian groups and businessmen. There are cheap lunch-time specials in the lobby restaurant. The only hotel in town to admit to having a 'Mexican suite'.

GUBEI GARDEN HOTEL Map p256
Gubeiwan Dàjiǔdiàn

☎ 5257 4888; fax 6295 8277; 1446 Hongqiao Lu; d Y620, discount of 25%

New in 2003, this small, stylish hotel has a boutique hotel feel, with bright, nonsmoking rooms and a ladies-only floor. The twin rooms are much bigger than the singles and cost the same price.

HONGQIAO STATE GUEST HOUSE
Map p256
Hóngqiáo Yíng Bīnguǎn

☎ 6219 8855; fax 6275 3903; 1591 Hongqiao Lu; d from US$100

You used to have to be a Communist party bigwig to get into the gardens and villas of this secluded hotel but now the front gates are open to all. Facilities include a gym and an outdoor pool.

MARRIOTT HOTEL HONGQIAO
Map pp242-3
Wànyí Hóngqiáo Dàjiǔdiàn

☎ 6237 6000; www.marriott.com; 2270 Hongqiao Lu

The excessive use of marble doesn't lend much intimacy here but the business clientele likes the voicemail, pool, tennis court, steakhouse and sports bar (happy hour 5pm to 8pm, with free finger food). Gift-certificate packages can bring rates down to Y680 for a double.

RAINBOW HOTEL Map p256
Hóngqiáo Bīnguǎn

☎ 6275 3388; www.shanghai.net.rainbow; 2000 Yan'an Beilu; d Y1300-1500, discounted to Y650-750

Good value if you get the discounts, this place is heavily oriented towards Japanese and Korean businessmen and offers an indoor swimming pool and gym.

RENAISSANCE YANGTZE SHANGHAI
Map p256
Yángzijiāng Wànlì Dàjiǔdiàn

☎ 6275 0000; yangtze@prodigycn.com; 2099 Yan'an Xilu; d US$109, discounted to US$105 at weekends

Another top-end place, next to the Sheraton, aimed at top-end business trips. The Dynasty and Chaozhou Garden restaurants are particularly good. A second Renaissance opened in Pudong in late 2003.

SHERATON GRAND TAIPINGYANG

Map p256

Xǐlái Dēngháodá Tàipíngyáng Dàfàndiàn

☎ 6275 8888; sheratongrand@uninet.com.cn; 5 Zunyi Nanlu; s/d US$210/230, discount of 40%

Sheraton took over the former Westin in 2000 but wisely have changed little, maintaining this as one of the best and most elegant hotels in town. The facilities and décor are excellent and rooms are slowly being upgraded. The deluxe rooms in particular are worth the extra US$20; certainly better value than the cheeky US$18 per person breakfast charge. Look for the fun automatic piano in the lobby. The top-floor restaurant has a buffet blowout and there's also a good Italian restaurant.

XIJIAO STATE GUEST HOUSE Map p256

Xijiáo Bīnguǎn

☎ 6219 8800; fax 6433 6641; 1921 Hongqiao Lu; d US$115

This quiet, sleepy hotel sees relatively few foreign visitors (though Queen Elizabeth II and Japanese Emperor Akihite have both stayed here) but it has some of Shanghai's most spacious gardens and is a great place to escape the concrete jungle. Facilities include a health club with tennis and squash courts.

Cheap Sleeps

INTERNATIONAL EXCHANGE SERVICE CENTRE Map pp242-3

Guójì Jiāoliú Fúwú Zhōngxīn

☎ 6257 9241; fax 6257 1813; 3663 Zhongshan Beilu; d Y150

While it is somewhat out of the way, this foreign-student dormitory (liúxuésheng lóu) at East China Normal University has reasonably priced rooms with bathroom and air-con. The university is a 15-minute walk from the Jinshajiang Lu light railway stop. To find the foreign-student building go through the main gate, cross two bridges then turn left. If the rooms are full you face a long trip back, or try the university's second guesthouse (yíngfūlóu), with doubles for Y380.

XUJIAHUI & SOUTH SHANGHAI

HUATING HOTEL Map p257

Huátíng Bīnguǎn

☎ 6439 1000; fax 6255 0830; 1200 Caoxi Beilu; s/d US$215/235, both discounted to US$110

Formerly known as the Sheraton, this was the first 'modern' hotel to appear in Shanghai, in 1987. It has since been completely handed over to local management but the five-star facilities (indoor pool, tennis court and gym) remain. The Shanghai Stadium metro stop is next door.

The attached **Huating Guest House** (☎ 6439 1818; fax 6439 0322; 2525 Zhongshan Xilu) is a three-star annexe with rooms for Y680, discounted to Y468.

LONGHUA HOTEL Map pp242-3

Lónghuá Yíng Bīnguǎn

☎ 6457 0570; fax 6457 7621; 2787 Longhua Lu; d Y480-580, discounted to Y320-350

It's a shame this modern hotel, attached to and owned by the Longhua Temple, couldn't have incorporated more (or even any!) of the neighbouring temple architecture. Rooms are clean and pleasant but the location is a bit inconvenient. Darker semi-subterranean doubles are gloomy during the day but are also cheaper at Y280, discounted down to Y220.

OLYMPIC HOTEL Map p257

Àolínpīkè Jùlèbù

☎ 6439 1391; olympich@public.shanghai.cnbg.com; 1800 Zhongshan Nanerlu; d Y650-750, discounted to Y500-650

A low-rise hotel near Shanghai Stadium, which gives you access to the outdoor swimming pool and health club. There's a Thai restaurant and a bar which brews its own Canadian beer.

REGAL SHANGHAI EAST ASIA Map p257

Fùháo Dōngyà Jiǔdiàn

☎ 6426 6888; http://regal-eastasia.com/shanghai; 800 Lingling Lu; d from US$160, discounted to US$98

The Regal International's sister hotel has one less star but is cheaper, and if things aren't too busy they may just upgrade you to a deluxe room. The hotel has, shall we say, an interesting location; it's built into the western side of Shanghai Stadium. Some rooms actually face into the stadium so check if there's a rock concert planned during your stay! There's a decent gym, a sports bar and 24-hour restaurant. On-line rates are discounted to US$80.

SPORTS HOTEL Map p257
Yùndòngyuánzhijiā Bīnguǎn
☎ 6438 5200 ext 5128; 1500 Zhongshan Nanerlu; d Y318-338

This is the tall tube next to Shanghai Stadium. It's a bit far from the centre but is close to the metro line and bustling Xujiahui crossroads. Standard two-star rooms on the 8th to 13th floors are sometimes booked by visiting table tennis or football teams.

WEST ASIA HOTEL Map p257
Xīyà Dàjiǔdiàn
☎ 6487 2000; 20 Tianyueqiao Lu; d Y536-605, discounted to Y388-458

The main thing this average hotel has going for it is its convenient location on the bustling Xujiahui crossroads. The main drawback is, well, its noisy location on the bustling Xujiahui crossroads. Rooms are smallish but not bad value.

Excursions

Excursions

When Shanghai's crowds, claustrophobia and concrete begin to grate there are plenty of day and overnight trips to be made outside Shanghai. Hangzhou and Suzhou are two of eastern China's cultural highlights.

The rural areas around Shanghai are traditionally known as Jiangnan (South of the Yangzi) and the 'land of fish and rice', and are today known as Zhejiang Province. The land is crisscrossed by canals and waterways, humpbacked bridges and whitewashed water villages. Recently six of these water villages filed jointly for inclusion on the Unesco World Heritage list: Tongli, Zhouzhuang, Pouzhi, Nanxun, Xitang and Wuzhen. Of these, Zhouzhuang is the most visited; to get off the beaten track try Tongli, Xitang or Wuzhen. Shanghai sightseeing buses run weekend buses to all of these.

AROUND SHANGHAI

Shanghai Municipality covers more than 6340 sq km. This includes the 748 sq km city of Shanghai as well as the surrounding counties of Nanhui, Qingpu, Fengxiang and Chongming Island, plus 29 other islands of the Yangzi. Chongming Island is China's second-largest island (third-largest, if you recognise Taiwan as part of China). The municipality includes the satellite towns of Songjiang, Jiading, Jinshan and Baoshan. Shanghai is bordered by the province of Jiangsu to the northwest and Zhejiang to the southwest.

Transport

City Sightseeing Buses A fleet of green sightseeing buses based at the east end of Shanghai Stadium shuttles tourists to most places of interest outside the city centre. The buses are convenient, comfortable and punctual, and are without a doubt the best way to see the sights around and outside Shanghai. There's no need to book a seat – just turn up. For departure information in Chinese call ☎ 6426 5555. There are similar terminals at Hongkou Stadium (☎ 5696 3248) and Yangpu Stadium (☎ 6580 3210). Current bus routes are as follows:

No 1A To Songjiang's Square Pagoda (Y10); every 30 minutes from 7.30am to 5.30pm.

No 1B To Sheshan (Y10); every 30 minutes from 7.15am to 4.50pm.

No 2 To Nanhui via Shanghai Wild Animal Park (Y14); every 15 minutes from 6.15am to 7.15pm.

No 4 To Qingpu via Shanghai Zoo (Y4), Qushui Park, Zhujiajiao (Y12), Grand View Garden (Y16), and sometimes on to Zhouzhuang; every 30 minutes from 7am to 3pm.

No 5 To Baoyang ferry dock for Chongming's Dongping Forest Park (Y8).

No 6A To Nanxiang's Garden of Ancient Splendour (Y6) and Jiading (Y10); every 40 minutes from 7.30am to 7pm.

No 6B To Anting via Jingdezhen Ceramics Gallery (Y4); every 30 minutes from 6.30am to 5.20pm.

No 8 To Gongqing Forest Park (Y6).

The bus offers return-trip fares *(tàopiào)* that include entry fees. You don't save much money this way, but it may save some hassle.

Jiading Sightseeing bus No 6A goes to Jiading regularly throughout the day, passing through Nanxiang.

Sheshan Sightseeing bus No 1B heads to Sheshan regularly from Shanghai, as do private minibuses (Y6). If you want to combine a visit to Sheshan with Songjiang, head to Sheshan first as it's easier to catch a bus on to Songjiang than vice versa. A taxi to/from Shanghai costs around Y70 one way.

Songjiang If you don't fancy the walk between sights, cycle rickshaws ferry people around town for a few *kuài*. It's possible to combine a visit to Songjiang with Sheshan but you'd need to take a taxi to Sheshan (around Y30), before taking the sightseeing bus back to Shanghai.

The sights listed in this section are in Shanghai Municipality and can be done as day trips. Some sites can even be reached by intrepid bikers, though to really enjoy the trip you may want to transport yourself and your bike part way out of the city in a taxi first.

SONGJIANG

Songjiang County, 30km southwest of Shanghai, was thriving when Shanghai was still a dream in an opium trader's eye, though you get a sense of its antiquity only in the timeless backstreets in the west and southwest of town.

The most famous monument is the **Square Pagoda** (Fāng Tǎ), in the southeast of the town. The 48.5m nine-storey tower was built between 1068 and 1077 as part of the Xingshengjiao Temple, which is long gone. During reconstruction in 1975 a brick vault containing a bronze buddha and other relics was discovered under its foundations.

The screen wall in front of the pagoda shows a legendary *tan,* a monster of such greed that it tried to drink the sea and ended up killing itself. The Buddhist frieze teaches that desire leads to disaster.

Next to the park is the mildly interesting **Songjiang Museum** (Sōngjiāng Bówùguǎn).

Other minor attractions in town include the **Xilin Pagoda**, a 30-minute walk away in the west of town, and the **Toroni Sutra Stela**, built in 859, which is the oldest Buddhist structure in Shanghai. The tower stands rather incongruously in the Zhongshan Primary School, directly opposite the Songjiang Hotel. You are allowed in to look but be prepared to end up shadowed by a trail of nine-year-olds following you like the Pied Piper.

The **Songjiang Mosque** (Sōngjiāng Qīngzhēnsì), in the west of town, is worth a visit. Built between 1341 and 1367, in the Chinese style, it's one of the oldest mosques in China. The minaret, the Bangke Tower, stands to the east and the ornate mihrab points the way to Mecca in the west. There are around 300 Muslims in Songjiang and worshippers converge on the mosque every Friday lunch time. To get to the mosque head south from the junction of Zhongshan Zhonglu and Renmin Nanlu, and follow a signposted alley leading off to the west.

South of the mosque is the **Zuibaichi** (Pool of Drunken Bai). The park is built around the villa of the painter Gu Dashen, who built the pool in 1659 in honour of Li Bai (or Li Bo), the famous Tang poet. Bai drowned when he fell drunk into a pond, trying to grasp a reflection of the moon.

SHESHAN

The only part of Shanghai to have anything that even remotely resembles a hill is **Sheshan National Tourist Vacation Area** (Shēshān Guójiā Lǚyóu Dùjià Qū), 30km southwest of Shanghai.

The main reason to come out here is to see the Catholic **Sheshan Cathedral**, perched magnificently on the top of the hill. The original Holy Mother Cathedral was built here between 1863 and 1866, and the current Basilica of Notre Dame was completed in 1935. The most interesting way to climb the hill is via the south gate, which takes you up along Via Dolorosa, past a smaller church (built 1894), a shop selling crucifixes and statues of the Virgin Mary, and several holy shrines. You can also take a cable car up to the top for Y15 return, or Y8 down.

Sunday is an interesting time to visit, as is May when many local Catholics make pilgrimages here. Note that photography is not allowed in the church.

Just next to the church is the **Jesuit observatory** (Tiānéntái), built in 1900. Its modern counterpart stands to the west. China's latest hi-tech earthquake monitoring system in the East China Sea was named after the observatory. On the east side of the hill is the 20m, seven-storey **Xiudaozhe Pagoda** (976–84).

On the east hill is the **Forest Park** (Sēnlín Gōngyuán), which has a lookout tower on the top of the hill and an impressive aviary *(bǎiniǎoyuàn)* that holds 10,000 birds.

Also in the area are the tacky **Europa World Theme Park** and **Jinjiang Waterworld**; the latter has an excellent collection of water slides.

Intrepid explorers can head 8km southwest of Sheshan to Tianmashan and the **Huzhu Pagoda** (Hùzhū Tǎ), built in 1079 and known as the leaning tower of China. The 19m-high tower started tilting 200 years ago and now has an inclination exceeding the tower at Pisa by 1.5 degrees. There are occasional minibuses from Sheshan to Tianmashan village, which is at the foot of the hill. A better option is to take a taxi (Y20) or a motorcycle taxi (Y10).

JIADING

About 20km northwest of Shanghai this laid-back town, surrounded by a canal, makes for a pleasant day excursion – especially if you pack a picnic for one of the parks. You may have time to visit Nanxiang on the way there or back.

Sightseeing bus No 6A drops passengers at the **Dragon Meeting Pond** (Huìlóng Tán), a peaceful garden built in 1588 and named after the five streams that feed into the central pool.

Exit out of the west gate to get to the **Confucius Temple** (Wén Miào), built in 1219. On the way you'll pass 72 carved lions, representing the 72 outstanding disciples of Confucius. The temple houses the **Jiading County Museum**, which exhibits the history of the county as well as some local bamboo carving.

A five-minute walk north of the temple along Nan Dajie takes you to the seven-storey **Fahua Pagoda**, and the interesting cobbled and canalled heart of the town. There are several enticing shops and places to eat around the pagoda.

Five minutes' walk northeast along the canal on Dong Dajie takes you to the enchanting **Garden of Autumn Clouds** (Qiūxiápǔ), one of the finest gardens around Shanghai. Nearby, across the canal, is a huge produce market.

On the way back to Shanghai, sightseeing bus No 6A passes through the town of Nanxiang, where (if you are not gardened out) you can stop off at the large **Garden of Ancient Splendour** (Gǔyì Yuán), which was built between 1522 and 1566, and then rebuilt in 1746.

Sights & Information

Confucius Temple (🕑 8-11.30am, 1.30-4.30pm)

Dragon Meeting Pond (admission Y5)

Europa World Theme Park (admission Y30)

Forest Park (admission Y18)

Garden of Autumn Clouds (admission Y8)

Jesuit observatory (admission Y6)

Jinjiang Waterworld (admission Y40; 🕑 Jul & Aug)

Sheshan Cathedral (admission hill Y8, church Y2)

Songjiang Mosque (admission Y5)

Songjiang Museum (admission Y2; 🕑 Tue-Sun, closed noon-1pm)

Zuibaichi (Pool of Drunken Bai; admission Y5)

ZHOUZHUANG

Set in the countryside 38km southeast of Suzhou, Zhouzhuang offers a step back in time into what is touted as the first water town of China. Established more than 900 years ago, Zhouzhuang boasts 14 bridges and a large percentage (over 60%) of historic buildings from the Yuan, Ming and Qing dynasties. Unfortunately, Zhouzhuang has been given the dreaded Chinese tourism make-over and from the swarms of rickshaw drivers to the lines of restaurants and souvenir stalls which now dominate the centre of the Old Town, little rings true. The town is extremely popular with Chinese tourists, though surprisingly untouched by those from abroad.

Transport

Distance from Shanghai 52km west

Sightseeing Bus Bus No 4 leaves at 7am, 9am, 12.10pm and 2pm from the west entrance of Shanghai Stadium (p173). Buses return from Zhouzhuang at 9am, 12.50pm, 2.30pm and 4.30pm. An all-inclusive return fare and entry ticket (Y98) is not a bad idea as it saves you money; if you don't have this return ticket you may not be able to just take the bus back to Shanghai. Sightseeing buses depart from and arrive at the Shenjiang Hotel.

Local Bus Slower local buses depart from the Hutai Lu bus station in the north of Shanghai at 9.30am and 1pm. The last bus back from Zhouzhuang bus station leaves around 4pm. Buses returning to Shanghai occasionally arrive at the long-distance bus station at 80 Gongxing Lu, near Shanghai's old train station. Bus No 65 from the Bund passes nearby.

ZHOUZHUANG

0 ___ 100 m
0 ___ 0.1 miles

Approximate Scale

To Bus Station (850m);
Suzhou (38km);
Shanghai (52km)

Quangong Lu

Xianjiang Bridge

Quangong Bridge

Shuang Bridge

Tiyun Bridge

Fu'an Bridge

Longxing Bridge

Zhenfeng Bridge

Puqing Bridge

Bao'en Bridge

Nan Hu (South Lake)

Quanfu Bridge

Excursions – Zhouzhuang

Despite the crowds, a day in Zhouzhuang is worthwhile and can easily be visited on a day trip from Shanghai or as a stopover en route to Suzhou. The cobbled lanes, arched bridges and canals of the **Old Town** are superbly picturesque, a fact confirmed by the many painters seated alongside the canals. The best bet is to avoid weekends and head off the main streets, to where many of the locals continue to go about their day, sitting on their steps, making lace or fishing in the canals with cormorants.

The bus station is 2km northeast of the Old Town. It's an easy 20-minute walk over the bridge into town, or take a rickshaw (Y4). To find the Old Town continue to the Zhouzhuang Travel Service, head east on Quangong Lu and take the first right onto Quanfu Lu. Maps are available everywhere for Y2.5.

Entrance to the Old Town is through the **Ancient Memorial Archway**. South of the archway, Zhouzhuang's narrow cobbled alleys are entirely pedestrianised. Within the Old Town are 10 sights including temples, gardens and the former homes of officers from the Qing and Ming dynasties, many of which are still inhabited by artisans and workers. All of the sights are visited on one ticket, which is available at the main entrance in the northwest or at the entrance to any of the sights. Almost all signs and captions within the sights are in Chinese only.

The **Hall of Shen's Residence** (Shěn Tīng) is considered to be the best of these houses, containing seven courtyards and more than 100 rooms, each connected to a main hall. Inside, wood carvers and weavers are hard at work. North of here, the **Hall of Zhang's Residence** (Zhāng Tīng) dates back more than 500 years and was home to a local officer. This house has six courtyards and more than 70 rooms. Running through the residence is a small waterway that allowed access to the house by boat.

At the southern end of town, **Quanfu Temple** (Quánfú Sì) contains 21 gold buddhas plus a large bronze buddha measuring more than 5m high. The temple is surrounded by pagodas and courtyard buildings, extending into **South Lake Garden** (Nánhú Yuán). This garden was built for Zhang Jiying, a literary man of the Jin dynasty, and consists of bridges crisscrossing over the water.

The **Zhouzhuang Museum** (Zhōuzhuāng Bówùguǎn) is home to nearly 1000 artefacts, including a number from the local fishing and artisan industries. South of the museum is the **Chengxu Temple** (Chéngxū Dàoyuàn), a Taoist temple built during the Song dynasty.

It can be fun to take a **boat tour** of the canals. The ticket office and wharf are just south of Tiyun Bridge. Half-hour trips in an eight-seater cost Y60 per boat. Wooden sailboats tour around South Lake for Y40 (30 minutes). Tickets are sold at the office at the southern end of Nanshi Jie.

Note the imposing **Quanfu Pagoda** (Quánfú Tǎ) just north of the Old Town. The pagoda was built in 1987 to hide the water tower, in preparation for the tourism boom promoted by the provincial government. The campaign seems to have been an enormous success, with Zhouzhuang recently declared an International Heritage Site by the United Nations.

Sights & Information

Old Town (☎ 721 1655; admission including all sights Y60; ☒ 7.30am-6pm)

Zhouzhuang Travel Service (Quanfu Lu)

Eating

In the central area of the Old Town every other building is a restaurant and your best bet is to take your time and look for one with nice ambience and views. Check the prices first as many cater to Chinese tour groups at astronomical prices. For reasonable prices and outdoor seating try the southern end of Nanshi Jie and Nanhu Jie, on either side of the canal between Longxing and Bao'en Bridges. You can also find cheap eats in the small **restaurants** between Zhenfeng and Puqing Bridges, at the western end of town. Zhongshi Jie has some nice **teahouses** along the canal.

Zhouzhuang's speciality is *wànsāntí*, a large, fatty dish of stewed pork knuckle for around Y40.

Pailou Restaurant (Páilóu Càiguǎn; 23 Xianjiang Jie; dishes Y20-50; ☒ 7am-8am) Small courtyard restaurant.

Shopping

A number of local specialities are available in Zhouzhuang, including woven goods, woodcarvings, sweets, lace and Yixing teapots. Of particular note are the locally harvested freshwater pearls. These are available at extremely reasonable prices, in every form, from traditional jewellery to animal and pagoda shapes and even face powder.

Shuixiang Pearl Mill (Shuǐxiāng Zhēnzhūfáng; ☎ 721 2019; Zhongshi Jie; ☒ 8.30am-5.30pm) A reputable shop with fixed prices. Pearl necklaces from Y120 to Y650.

Sleeping

Feng Dan Double Bridge Resort (Fèndān Shuāngqiáo Dùjiàcūn; ☎ 721 1549; Daqiao Lu; d Y220-240, 20% discount Mon-Fri) A fine location with a view of the water compensates for the shabby rooms. Head south on Nanshi Jie and take the first left after the Hall of Shen's Residence.

SUZHOU

Jiangsu's most famous attraction, Suzhou is a famed silk production centre and a celebrated historical retreat brimming with exquisite gardens, humpbacked bridges and waterways. It's important to realise that it's also a modern Chinese city, symbolised by the Singaporean hi-tech business park in the eastern suburbs. Unfortunately, much of the city's charm has been swept away by new developments; the town's main thoroughfare Renmin Lu was a virtual war zone in 2003 during a massive reconstruction project. Nevertheless, a wander through the charming gardens and the tiny remaining pockets of cobbled alleyways makes a visit to Suzhou worthwhile, particularly if you have an interest in silk or Chinese gardens.

History

Dating back some 2500 years, Suzhou is one of the oldest towns in the Yangzi Basin. With the completion of the Grand Canal in the Sui dynasty, Suzhou found itself strategically located on a major trading route, and the city's fortunes and size grew rapidly.

Suzhou flourished as a centre of shipping and grain storage, bustling with merchants and artisans. By the 12th century the town had attained its present dimensions. The city walls, a rectangle enclosed by moats, were pierced by six gates (north, south, two in the east and two in the west). Crisscrossing the city were six canals running north to south and 14 canals running east to west. Although the walls have largely disappeared and a fair proportion of the canals have been plugged, central Suzhou retains some of its 'Renaissance' character.

The story picks up when Marco Polo arrived in 1276, describing the town's flourishing silk trade and 6000 bridges (as ever he was way off base). He added the adjectives 'great' and 'noble', though he reserved his finer epitaphs for Hangzhou.

By the 14th century Suzhou had established itself as China's leading silk producer. Aristocrats, pleasure-seekers, famous scholars, actors and painters were drawn to the city, constructing villas and garden retreats for themselves.

SUString

SUZHOU

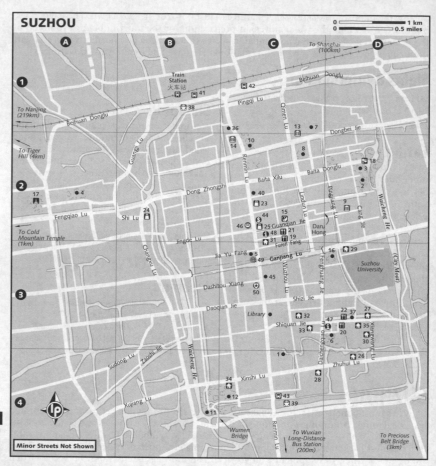

0 ——— 1 km
0 ——— 0.5 miles

Transport

Distance from Shanghai 100km west

Train Suzhou is on the Shanghai–Nanjing railway line so there are many trains; anything headed to Nanjing goes through Suzhou. The double-decker T702 is the best choice for a day trip (Y25, 45 minutes, once a day at 7am). Other trains take up to 1½ hours. There are plenty of trains back, including a fast one at 8pm. Getting a seat isn't a problem. When returning make sure you don't get off at Shanghai Xi (West), the station before Shanghai proper.

Airport Bus Services run from Ganjiang Lu near the PSB office to Shanghai's Hongqiao airport (Y50, two hours) and then Pudong airport (Y80, three hours) from 6.20am to 3pm.

Bus Services to Suzhou (Y26 to Y30, 1½ hours) leave every hour between 7.20am and 5.20pm from the Xujiahui bus station; every 20 minutes or so from Hengfeng bus station, next to Hanzhong Lu metro station; and every hour from the long-distance bus station at Hutai Lu and Zhongshan Beilu, north of Shanghai train station. Weekend sightseeing buses to Suzhou (Y24) depart at 8am from Shanghai Stadium. Suzhou has three long-distance bus stations; most buses arrive and depart from the northern station at the northern end of Renmin Lu, next to the train station. City bus Nos 1 and Y4 run the length of Renmin Lu. No Y2 runs from Tiger Hill to Pan Gate via the eastern side of the city. Bus No Y5 does a loop around the city. All stop near the train station.

Boat Overnight boats travel along the Grand Canal to Hangzhou. Many travellers enjoy the trip but it's worth remembering that the bulk of the trip occurs in darkness. Locals generally prefer to travel by bus or train. Boats to Hangzhou depart daily from the southern boat dock at 5.30pm (a bus takes you from here to the boat) and arrive the next morning at 7am. Berths cost Y78 to Y130 in a twin-bed cabin, or Y60 to Y88 in a four-berth cabin, depending on the boat.

Bicycle This is the best way to get around Suzhou. The bike rental stall (☎ 6753 5890; 672 Renmin Lu) by the North Temple Pagoda Clinic, 100m north of the Suzhou Silk Museum, offers the best rates, at Y5 per day. Stalls opposite the train station charge Y20.

At the height of Suzhou's development in the 16th century, the gardens, large and small, numbered more than 100. The town's tourist formula – 'Garden City, Venice of the East' – is a medieval mix of woodblock guilds and embroidery societies, whitewashed housing, cobbled streets, tree-lined avenues and canals.

Suzhou's reputation was boosted by the reputation of its women as the most beautiful in China, largely thanks to the mellifluous local accent, and was sealed with the famous proverb 'In heaven there is paradise, on earth Suzhou and Hangzhou'.

The wretched workers of the silk sweatshops, protesting against paltry wages and the injustices of the contract hire system, were staging violent strikes even in the 15th century. In 1860, Taiping troops took the town without a blow. In 1896, Suzhou was opened to foreign trade, with Japanese and other international concessions. During WWII it was occupied by the Japanese and then by the Kuomintang. Suzhou escaped relatively unscathed from the ravages of the Cultural Revolution.

In Suzhou today, the **North Temple** (Běisì Tǎ) has the tallest pagoda south of the Yangzi – at nine storeys it dominates the northern end of Renmin Lu. You can climb it for a fine aerial view of the town. The factory chimneys, the new pagodas of Suzhou, loom on the outskirts, as does the haze and smoke they create. The temple complex goes back 1700 years and was originally a residence. The pagoda has been burnt, built and rebuilt. Made

Suzhou, 'Venice of the East' (p177)

of wood, it dates from the 17th century. Off to the side is Nanmu Hall, which was rebuilt during the Ming dynasty, with some of its features imported from elsewhere. There is a teahouse with a small garden out the back.

Found east of the Humble Administrator's Garden (see below), **Suzhou Museum** (Sūzhōu Bówùguǎn) was once the residence of a Taiping leader, Li Xiucheng. The museum offers some interesting old maps, including those of the Grand Canal, Suzhou, and heaven and earth. It also houses Qing dynasty steles forbidding workers' strikes, and relics such as funerary objects, porcelain bowls and bronze swords unearthed or rescued from various sites around the Suzhou district. There are no English captions.

Highly recommended by many, **Suzhou Silk Museum** (Sūzhōu Sīchóu Bówùguǎn) houses a number of fascinating exhibitions that provide a thorough history of Suzhou's silk industry over the past 4000 years. Exhibits include a section on old looms and weaving techniques and a room with live silkworms in various stages of life. A second building displays clothing made of silk from the early 1900s. Many of the captions and explanations are in both Chinese and English.

The heart of what was once Suzhou Bazaar is the Taoist **Temple of Mystery** (Xuánmiào Guàn). It was founded during the Jin dynasty in the 3rd century and laid out between 275 and 279, with additions during Song times. From the Qing dynasty onwards, the bazaar fanned out from the temple, with tradespeople and travelling performers using the grounds. The enormous Sanqing Hall, supported by 60 pillars and capped by a double roof with upturned eaves, dates from 1181. It was burnt and seriously damaged in the 19th century. During the Cultural Revolution, the Red Guards squatted here, and it was later transformed into a library. Today the temple is surrounded by a street market and Suzhou's main commercial district, Guanqian Jie. There are occasional music performances in the temple when there's a group around to warrant it (Y15, plus Y10 for the 'fluttering cymbals' performance). Most people are happy viewing the temple from the outside, before heading off for some shopping or lunch at the nearby Deyuelou or Songhelou restaurants.

In the old city of Suzhou, the small **Museum of Opera & Theatre** (Xìqu Bówùguǎn) is worth visiting for the surrounding area of small cobblestone lanes lined with stalls selling vegetables and inexpensive snacks. The museum houses a moveable stage, old musical instruments, costumes and photos of famous performers. From Linden Lu go east on Daru Hang. At the end of the road go right, then take the first left.

Many consider the **Humble Administrator's Garden** (Zhuózhèng Yuán) to be one of Suzhou's best gardens, second only to the Garden of the Master of the Nets. The garden was built by

Chinese Gardens

Suzhou's gardens rank among China's most exquisite, a fact recognised in 1997 when they were included in Unesco's World Heritage list.

Chinese gardens stand in stark contrast to the manicured lawns and sweeping views of European-style gardens and enjoy more in common stylistically with the Zen gardens of Japan. Central to the gardens' design is the popular Chinese concept of natural beauty, which generally emphasises whimsy over wilderness and harmony over raw nature. The exhibits of unusual stones or contorted roots so common in Chinese gardens reflect these beauty concepts.

Due partly to these cultural ideals, and partly to the physical lack of space, Suzhou's gardens are designed to give the illusion of natural space through artificial means. Everything in a Chinese garden is artfully placed, whether it be framed in a pavilion window or viewed through an arched gateway. The resulting maze of courtyards, screens, miniature hills, grottos, ponds and pavilions are arranged to create a series of miniature views which unfold one after the other.

Water is essential to a Suzhou garden, as are bonsai (*penjing* in Chinese, or potted landscapes). Rocks from neighbouring Tai Lake were especially greatly valued. These ingredients combine to create a microcosm of mountains and valleys that reflect the aesthetics of a Chinese landscape painting, not to replicate a natural wilderness but to create a fusion of architecture and garden, of man and nature, heaven and earth.

Gardens were often created by retired officials or literati and offered a tranquil location in which to read poetry, drink tea and philosophise. Appropriate poetic couplets penned in refined calligraphy reinforce this role, emphasising the fusion of man and nature.

To find out more about the concepts behind Suzhou's gardens read *The Chinese Garden* by Joseph Cho Wang (Oxford University Press) or visit the website www.szgarden.com.

Wang Xianchen, who would probably have been heartbroken to hear his son later sold the garden to pay off gambling debts. Dating back to 1509, this garden's five hectares feature streams, ponds, bridges and islands of bamboo. There's also a teahouse, a bonsai garden and a small museum, housed in the four main north–south halls, that explains Chinese landscape-gardening concepts. In the same area are the Suzhou Museum and several silk mills. Mid-March to mid-May is a good time to visit as the gardens (in particular the azaleas) are in full bloom.

Tip

If you intend to visit several of Suzhou's gardens consider a joint ticket *(taòpiaò)*; it costs Y117 (individual tickets would cost Y150), is valid for three days and covers the Humble Administrator's Garden, Lingering Garden, Lion's Grove Garden, Master of the Nets Garden and Tiger Hill.

Just around the corner from the Humble Administrator's Garden, one-hectare **Lion Grove** (Shīzi Lín) was constructed in 1350 by the monk Tian Ru and other disciples, as a memorial to their master, Zhi Zheng. The garden is famed for its rockeries that evoke the forms of lions. The walls of the labyrinth of tunnels bear calligraphy from famous chisels. There are regular free tours but you may have to wait for an English-language guide.

A small Qing dynasty garden owned by an official called Gu Wenbin, the **Garden of Harmony** (Yí Yuán) is quite young for a Suzhou garden. It has assimilated many of the features of other gardens and blended them into a style of its own. In the east are buildings and courtyards. The western section has pools with coloured pebbles, rockeries, hillocks and pavilions. Entry to the garden is off Renmin Lu.

A bit on the wild side, with winding creeks and luxuriant trees, **Blue Wave Pavilion** (Cānglàng Tíng) is one of the oldest gardens in Suzhou. The buildings date from the 11th century, though they have been rebuilt on numerous occasions since. Originally the home of a prince, the property passed into the hands of the scholar Su Zimei, who gave it its name. The one-hectare garden attempts to create optical illusions with the scenery both outside and inside – you look from the pool immediately outside to the distant hills. **Enlightened Way Hall** (Míngdào Táng), the largest building, is said to have been a site for delivery of lectures during the Ming Dynasty. Close by, on the other side of Renmin Lu, is the former Confucius Temple. The entrance is off Renmin Lu and is signposted as 'Surging Wave' Pavilion.

Garden of the Master of the Nets (Wangshì Yuán) is the smallest garden in Suzhou – half the size of the Blue Wave Pavilion and one-tenth the size of the Humble Administrator's Garden. It's small and hard to find, but well worth the trouble as it's better than all the others combined.

This garden was laid out in the 12th century, abandoned, then restored in the 18th century as part of the residence of a retired official. According to one story, this official announced that he'd had enough of bureaucracy and would rather be a fisherman. Another explanation of the name is that it was simply near Wangshi Lu. The eastern part of the garden is the residential area – originally with side rooms for sedan-chair lackeys, guest reception and living quarters. The central part is the main garden. The western part is an inner garden where a courtyard contains the **Spring-Rear Cottage** (Diànchūn Yí), the master's study. This section and the study, with its Ming-style furniture and palace lanterns, was duplicated and unveiled at the Metropolitan Museum of Art in New York in 1981. A miniature model of the whole garden, using Qingtian jade, Yingde rocks, Anhui paper, Suzhou silk and incorporating the halls, kiosks, ponds, blossoms and rare plants of the original design, was produced especially for a display at the Pompidou Centre in Paris in 1982. The most striking feature of this garden is its use of space. Despite its size, the scale of the buildings is large, but nothing appears cramped. A section of the buildings is used

Sandalwood fan making, Suzhou

Excursions – Suzhou

Useful Websites

Suzhou www.sztravel.gov.cn
Suzhou Garden Society www.szgarden.com
Zhouzhuang www.zhouzhuang.net

by a cooperative of woodblock artists who find the peaceful atmosphere congenial to their work. There are two entrances to the garden. The first is off Shiquan Jie, the second is via a narrow alley just west of the Suzhou Hotel. Going east on Shiquan Lu, turn right onto Daichengqiao Lu, then left down the first alley. Very popular is the nightly performance of dance and song at the Garden of the Master of the Nets. The audience moves from pavilion to pavilion to watch a variety of traditional Chinese performing arts. The show lasts from 7.30pm to 10pm and tickets can be bought from CITS for Y60. Alternatively, turn up shortly before the performance and buy your ticket on the spot.

Extending over an area of three hectares, the **Garden for Lingering In** (Liú Yuán) is one of the largest of Suzhou's gardens, noted for its adroit partitioning with building complexes. It dates from the Ming dynasty and managed to escape destruction during the Taiping Rebellion. A 700m covered walkway connects the major scenic spots, and the windows have carefully selected perspectives. The walkway is inlaid with calligraphy from celebrated masters. The garden has a wealth of potted plants. Outside **Mandarin Duck Hall** (Yuānyáng) is a 6.5m-high Tai Lake piece – it's the final word on rockeries. The garden is about 3km west of the old city walls. Bus No 5 will take you here from Renmin Lu, near the Bank of China, via bridges that look down on the busy water traffic.

Approximately 500m west of the Garden for Lingering In, **West Garden Temple** (Xīyuán Sì) was built on the site of a garden laid out at the same time as the Garden for Lingering In and then donated to the Buddhist community. The temple was destroyed in the 19th century and entirely rebuilt; it contains some expressive Buddhist statues.

One kilometre west of the Garden for Lingering In, **Cold Mountain Temple** (Hánshān Sì) was named after the poet-monk Hanshan, who lived in the 7th century. It was repeatedly burnt down and rebuilt, and was once the site of lively local trading in silk, wood and grain. Not far from its saffron walls lies the Grand Canal. Today, the temple holds little of interest except for a stele by poet Zhang Ji immortalising nearby Maple Bridge and the temple bell (since removed to Japan). However, the fine walls and the humpback bridge are worth seeing.

In the far northwest of town, **Tiger Hill** (Hǔqiū Shān) is extremely popular with Chinese tourists, but less so with those from overseas. The hill itself is artificial, and is the final resting place of He Lu, the King of the state of Wu and founding father of Suzhou. He Lu died in the 6th century BC, and myths have coalesced around him – he is said to have been buried on the hill with a collection of 3000 swords, all guarded by a white tiger. Built in the 10th century, the leaning **Yunyan Pagoda** (Yúnyán Tǎ) stands atop Tiger Hill. The octagonal seven-storey pagoda is built entirely of brick, an innovation in Chinese architecture at the time. The pagoda began tilting more than 400 years ago, and today the highest point is displaced more than 2m from its original position.

In the southwestern corner of the city, straddling the outer moat, this stretch of the city wall known as **Pan Gate** (Pán Mén) contains Suzhou's only remaining original city gate (1351). From the top of the gate there are good views of the moat, surrounding houses and **Ruiguang Pagoda** (Ruìguāng Tǎ), a crumbling pagoda that dates from the 3rd century and is reputedly the oldest pagoda in Jiangsu. This area was once the city docks, where most travellers arrived in the city. Near the southern end of Renmin Lu, cross over the humpbacked Wumen Bridge and follow the ramp down its right side. This will bring you to Nan Men Lu, which you can follow to the gate.

By the canal, south of the train station, you can hire a boat (Y100) to glide you 30 minutes south down the canal to Pan Gate and back. Boats depart from the Foreign Travellers Transportation Company Pier (Waìshī Lǔchē Chuán Gōngsī Mǎtóu).

China's famous **Grand Canal** (Dà Yùnhé), the world's longest artificial waterway, cut out by millions of forced labourers in the early 7th century, cuts to the west and south of Suzhou, within a 10km range of the town. Suburban bus Nos 13, 14, 15 and 16 will get you there. In the northwest, bus No 11 follows the canal for a fair distance, taking you on a tour of the enchanting countryside. Hop off the bus once you find a nice bridge on which you can perch and watch the world of the canal float by.

Straddling the Grand Canal southeast of Suzhou and with 53 arches, **Precious Belt Bridge** (Bǎodài Qiáo) is considered to be one of China's most impressive bridges. The bridge is thought to be a Tang-dynasty construction named after Wang Zhongshu, a local prefect who sold his precious belt to pay for the bridge's construction for the benefit of his people. The three central humpbacks of the bridge are larger to allow boats through. The bridge is no longer used for traffic – a modern one has been built alongside it – but it's a popular spot with fisherfolk. You can get to the bridge by taxi or a 40-minute bike ride. Head south on Renmin Lu, past the south moat, then left at the TV towers.

Sights & Information

Bank of China (490 Renmin Lu)

Blue Wave Pavilion (☎ 6519 4375; admission Y5; ☯ 7.30am-5.30pm)

China Eastern (☎ 6522 6400; 192 Renmin Lu)

Cold Mountain Temple (☎ 6723 2891; 24 Hanshansi Long; admission Y10; ☯ 7.30am-5pm; bus Y3 & Y4 take you nearby from the train station)

Foreign Travellers Transportation Company Pier (☎ 6754 8906)

Garden for Lingering In (☎ 6533 7903; admission Y30; ☯ 7.30am-5.30pm)

Garden of Harmony (admission Y15; ☯ 7.30am-5.30pm)

Garden of the Master of the Nets (☎ 6520 3514; admission Y15; ☯ 8am-5pm)

Humble Administrator's Garden (☎ 6751 0286; 178 Dongbei Jie; adult/child under 1.2m Y45/free, English audio guide Y10, Y200 deposit; ☯ 7.30am-5.30pm)

Jinbo Internet (333 Renmin Lu, next to China Telecom; Y2 per hr; ☯ 8am-midnight)

Lianhe Train Ticket Office (556 Renmin Lu)

Lion Grove (admission Y15; ☯ 7.30am-5pm)

Museum of Opera & Theatre (☎ 6727 3741; 14 Zhongzhangjia Xiang; admission Y3; ☯ 8.30am-4pm)

North Temple Pagoda (☎ 6753 1197; 652 Renmin Lu; adult/child Y15/7.5; ☯ 7.45am-5.30pm)

Pan Gate (☎ 6519 3054; 1 Dong Dajie; admission including boat ride Y40, acoustic guide Y5; ☯ 8am-5pm)

PSB (☎ 6522 5661; 201 Renmin Lu, 200m down Dashitou Xiang alley)

Suzhou Museum (☎ 6754 1534; 204 Dongbei Jie; adult/student/child Y10/5/free; ☯ 8.15am-4.30pm)

Suzhou Silk Museum (☎ 6753 6538; 661 Renmin Lu; adult/student Y7/5; ☯ 9am-5pm)

Temple of Mystery (☎ 6727 6948; Guanqian Jie; admission Y10; ☯ 7.30am-5pm)

Tiger Hill (☎ 6723 2305; Huqiu Lu; admission Y45; ☯ 7.30am-6pm; bus Y1 & Y2)

Tourist Information/Suzhou Overseas Tourist Co (☎ 6518 2820; 115 Shiquan Jie)

Train Station Information (☎ 6753 2831)

West Garden Temple (☎ 6551 7114; Xiyuan Lu; admission Y10; ☯ 7.30am-5.30am)

Eating

Suzhou is a tourist town, and consequently there is no shortage of places dishing up local and tourist cuisine. Shiquan Jie, between Daichengqiao Lu and Xiangwang Lu, is lined with bars, restaurants and bakeries. If you're on a tight budget, try the food courts of the ever-growing number of department stores.

Deyuelou Restaurant (☎ 6523 8940; 43 Taijian Xiang, Guanqian Jie) This has two buildings; the better is the traditional building opposite Songyuelou, which has a decent English menu.

Hexiang Cun (189 Shiquan Jie) Small local restaurant that has cheap draught beer in summer.

Sōnghèlóu Restaurant (☎ 6524 4921; 72 Taijian Xiang, Guanqian Jie) Rated as the most famous restaurant in Suzhou: the Emperor Qianlong is said to have eaten here. Top dishes include squirrel-shaped mandarin fish, pork with pine nuts, and Gusu marinated duck. Prices are relatively high and travellers give the restaurant mixed reviews.

Yang Yang Dumpling House (Yángyáng Jiǎoziguǎn; 44 Shiquan Lu) Popular for *shuijiao*, snails and vegetable dishes. There's a big Lonely Planet sign on the front door — nothing to do with us! Try upstairs for more seating if downstairs is full.

Shopping

Suzhou-style embroidery, calligraphy, paintings, sandalwood fans, writing brushes and silk underclothes are for sale nearly everywhere. For good-quality items at competitive rates, shop along Shiquan Jie, east off Renmin Lu. There are also some interesting shops along Yuanlin Lu, south of the Humble Administrator's Garden.

For silk, try the cloth shops on Guanqian Jie; most cloth shops have tailors on hand who can make simple clothing in about three days. Next to the Temple of Mystery there's a night market that sells very reasonably priced silk.

Dongwu Silk Store (www.dongwu.com; 540 Renmin Lu) Large silk store attached to a silk factory, selling clothes, brocade and bedding.

Shi Lu Night Market (☯ 6.30-9.30pm) Sells food, clothes and all kinds of stuff.

Suzhou Food Centre (Sūzhōu Shí Pǐng Dàshà; 246 Renmin Lu) Sells traditional local specialities and teas in bulk.

Sleeping

Bamboo Grove Hotel (Zhúhuī Fàndiàn; ☎ 6520 5601; www.bg-hotel.com; 168 Zhuhui Lu; d with breakfast Y995-1160, discounted to Y650-750) Four-star facilities include an indoor pool; it's popular with groups.

Dongwu Guesthouse (Dōngwú Fàndiàn; ☎ 6519 4437; s/d Y80/100, s/d/t with bathroom Y180/280/360) Run by Suzhou University International Cultural Exchange Institute, the rooms are spacious, the shared bathrooms are clean and there are single rates for a change.

Friendship Hotel (Yǒuyì Bīnguǎn; ☎ 6529 1601; fax 6520 6221; 243 Zhuhui Lu; east wing r Y240-360, west wing Y380-460) Standard B rooms are the best value in the old east wing. The west wing has new air-conditioned rooms.

Gloria Plaza Hotel (Kǎilái Dàjiùàn; ☎ 6521 8855; www.gphsuzhou.com; 535 Ganjiang Donglu; d Y980, discounted to Y588, plus 15% tax) Upmarket rooms and a good Friday seafood buffet (Y98) make this affordable comfort.

Gusu Hotel (Gūsū Fàndiàn; ☎ 6520 0566; fax 6519 9727; 5 Xiangwang Lu; Y480-560, discounted to Y310-360) Three-stars, clean and comfortable.

Longfeng Hotel (Lóngfēng Bīnguǎn; ☎ 6515 4100; fax 6515 4101; 9 Dajing Xiang; d Y350-420, discounted to Y245-295) Newer, fresher and cheaper than the comparable Leixiang Hotel across the street, this is a good central option.

Nanlin Hotel (Nánlín Fàndiàn; ☎ 6519 4641; fax 6519 1028; 20 Gunxiufang, Shiquan Jie; old-block d Y198-228, new-building d Y538, discounted to Y400) Popular with tour groups, it has pleasant gardens. Old-block rooms are 'lived-in' but good value. Rooms can be smoky. Enter the hotel complex off Shiquan Lu.

Nanyuan Guesthouse (Nányuán Bīnguǎn; ☎ 6519 7661; fax 6519 8806; 249 Shiquan Jie; d Y780-980, discounts of 50%) There are many different buildings in this lovely secluded garden compound, some older than others, so take a look at several rooms. The 'Fragrant Building' has a separate entrance off Daichengqiao Lu.

Sheraton Suzhou (☎ 6510 3388; www.sheraton -suzhou.com; 388 Xinshi Lu; d with breakfast from Y1650, discounted weekends to Y988) Top spot in town, nicely designed, with faux Chinese architecture, a pool and several good bars.

Suzhou Hotel (Sūzhōu Fàndiàn; ☎ 6520 4646; fax 6520 4015; 115 Shiquan Jie; d Y500-850, discounted to Y400-680) A sprawling place which does a brisk trade in tour groups, but there are more charming places for the money.

HANGZHOU

For the Chinese, Hangzhou (along with Guilin) is the country's most famous tourist attraction. The lake gives rise to what must be one of China's oldest tourist blurbs: 'In heaven there is paradise, on earth Suzhou and Hangzhou'. Indeed, you can book your hotel room from on board the train as you ease into Hangzhou train station, while announcements on the platform welcome you to the 'tourist capital of China'. Be warned, droves of tour groups

Transport

Distance from Shanghai 170km southwest

Train Fast trains leave Shanghai train station for Hangzhou every hour or so (the most useful for a day trip leaves at 7.29am), taking around two hours. Trains also run from Shanghai's Meilong train station, in the south of town (a short walk 200m south of the Jinjiang Park metro stop and then over the bridge). Fast train K821 leaves Meilong at 8.18am, arriving at 10.06am. Trains return at 5pm (K972) and 6.21pm (K828). Fares are Y25/40 for hard/soft seat from Meilong and Y33/57 from the main station.

Hangzhou's new train station is state of the art. Same day tickets are sold on the ground floor. For tickets up to five days in advance head upstairs and to the far right hall (counter No 3). Train No K256 departs Hangzhou at 9.39am for Suzhou (1¾ hours) via Shanghai west station.

Airport Bus Services run every 30 minutes to Hangzhou airport (Y15), 15km away, or take a taxi (Y100). Buses also shuttle seven times daily (6am to 3pm) between Hangzhou CAAC office and Hongqiao airport's No 2 terminal (Y85).

Bus Deluxe buses leave frequently for Hangzhou's east bus station (Y55, 2½ hours) from Shanghai's Hengfeng Lu bus station, Xujiahui bus station and the long-distance bus station at Hutai Lu and Zhongshan Beilu. A sightseeing bus leaves at 7.35am (Y50) from Shanghai Stadium on the weekend. City Bus No 7 connects the train station with the eastern side of the lake. Bus No 15 connects the north and west bus stations to the northwest area of West Lake. Bus No 27 is useful for getting between the eastern and western sides of the lake.

Boat There's one boat daily for Suzhou, leaving at 5.30pm (14 hours). See the Suzhou Transport box (p179) for details. Buy tickets at the wharf just north off Huancheng Beilu.

Bicycle Cycling is the best way to get around but there's not much choice for rentals. The stall outside the Overseas Chinese Hotel is extortionate at Y6 per hour. The Radisson Plaza has quality mountain bikes for Y20 per hour or Y100 for the day.

Electric carts run around the lake, including the Sudi Causeway, for around Y10 per trip or Y30 all around the lake.

descend on the city during all seasons, peaking on holidays and weekends and resulting in a blight of tacky tourist amenities and costly hotels. But don't despair – even this tourist excess has not diminished the subtle beauty of Hangzhou's West Lake area.

West Lake is a large freshwater lake, bordered on three sides by hills. Its banks and islands are blanketed with small gardens and temples, all of which have their classically prescribed sights and activities. Hangzhou is bounded to the south by the Qiantang River, which once flowed into the lake. The eastern shore of the lake is the modern developed business district; the western shore is quieter.

History

Hangzhou has been in existence from at least the start of the Qin dynasty (221 BC). When Marco Polo passed through Hangzhou in the 13th century he described it as one of the finest and most splendid cities in the world.

Other travellers such as Odoric of Pordenone also visited the city (he referred to it as Camsay), returning with tales of the majesty of the place. Although Hangzhou prospered greatly after it was linked with the Grand Canal in 610 (the canal ferried the region's grain and silk tribute up to Beijing), it really came into its own after the Song dynasty (based at Kaifeng) was overthrown by the invading Jurchen in 1126. The Song court fled south and finally settled in Hangzhou, establishing it as the capital of the Southern Song dynasty.

China had gone through an economic revolution in the preceding years, producing huge and prosperous cities, an advanced economy and a flourishing inter-regional trade. With the Jurchen invasion, the centre of this revolution was pushed south from the Yellow River valley to the lower Yangzi valley and to the coast between the Yangzi River and Guangzhou.

While the north remained in the hands of the invaders (who rapidly became Sinicised), in the south Hangzhou became the hub of the Chinese state. The court, the military, the civil officials and the merchants all congregated in Hangzhou, whose population rose from half a million to 1.75 million by 1275. The city's large population and its proximity to the ocean promoted the growth of river and sea trade, and of ship building and other naval industries.

Though the city lost its status as China's capital when the Mongols established the Yuan dynasty court at Beijing, Hangzhou retained its standing as a prosperous commercial city. It did take a beating in the Taiping Rebellion: in 1861 the Taipings laid siege to the city and captured it, but two years later the imperial armies took it back. These campaigns reduced almost the entire city to ashes, led to the deaths of more than half a million of its residents through disease, starvation and warfare, and finally ended Hangzhou's significance as a commercial and trading centre.

Few monuments survived the devastation, and most of those that did became victims of the Red Guards 100 years later during the Cultural Revolution. Much of what may be seen in Hangzhou today is of fairly recent construction.

West Lake

There are 36 lakes in China called **West Lake** (Xī Hú), but this one is by far the most famous. Indeed it is the West Lake on which all other west lakes are modelled. Most of the sights are connected with famous people who once lived there – poets, emperors who visited (Hangzhou was very popular with the ruling elite), and Chinese patriots. The lake is lined with famous viewpoints and dense with literary associations which are lost on most foreigners. The sights – a collection of gardens, bridges and pavilions – are scattered around the lake. There's no need to visit all of them, just pick a couple to get a feel for the architecture and views.

West Lake was originally a lagoon adjoining the Qiantang River. In the 8th century the governor of Hangzhou had it dredged; later a dyke was built that cut it off from the river completely. The resulting lake is about 3km long and a bit under 3km wide. Two causeways, the Baidi and the Sudi, split the lake into sections and you can walk or bicycle along these.

The lake makes for a pleasant outing, particularly on a bike, though some of its charm has fallen victim to the plundering of tour groups and tacky facilities. Dawn, twilight and evening are the best times to view the lake, especially when it is layered with mist.

The eastern shore is the most developed and the northeastern corner is currently undergoing a major redevelopment. The southeastern shore is lined with new parks and a branch of Shanghai's **Xintiandi** complex, which will attract a similarly high-end collection of

HANGZHOU

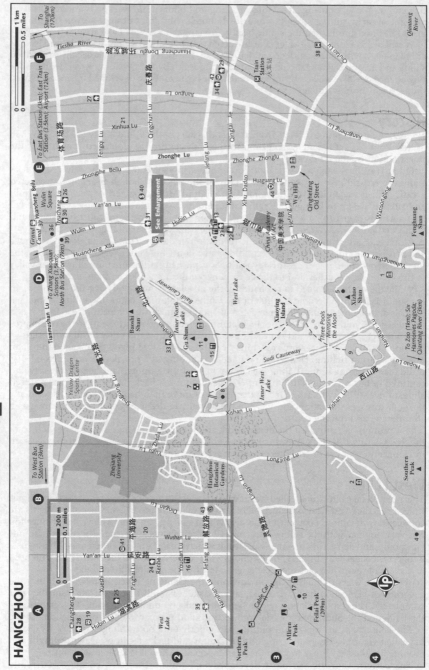

To Shanghai (170km)

Tiesha River

To East Station (3km); East Train Station (3.5km); Airport (12km)

庆春东路 Huancheng Donglu

Qiantang River

To East Bus Station (3.5km) North Bus Station

27

Qingchun Lu

Xinhua Lu

Jianguo Lu

Train Station 火车站

38

Qikai Lu

Fengqi Lu

庆春路 Qingchun Lu

42

34 29

Jianghang Lu

Zhonghe Lu

Zhonghe Beilu

Zhonghe Zhonglu

Liefang Lu

Qingtai Jie

Zhongshan Lu

体育场路 Tiyuchang Lu

Yan'an Lu

Huancheng Beilu Wulin Square

30 26

40

Kaiyuan Lu

Xihu Dadao

Huaguang Lu

3

Wu Hill

Wansongling Lu

Grand Canal 37

36

Wulin Lu

39

31

Hubin Lu

44

Qinghefang Old Street

Huancheng Xilu

18

14 13

23 22

China Academy of Art 中国美术院

Hefang Jie

Fenghuang Shan 凤凰山

Tianmushan Lu

To Zhang Xiaoquan Scissors (3.5km); North Bus Station (7km)

Yellow Dragon Sports Centre

Baidi (Causeway)

Baoshi Shan 宝石山

Inner North Lake

12

West Lake

Xiaoying Island

Yuhangshan Lu

Nanshan Lu

1

Shuguang Lu

保俶路 Baochu Lu

33

Gu Shan 孤山

11

15

Three Pools Mirroring the Moon

Xizhao Shan

5

To Zoo (1km); Six Harmonies Pagoda; Qiantang River (3km)

Zhejiang University

曙光路

7 32

8

Sudi Causeway

9

Nanshan Lu

西山路

Hupao Lu

Zheda Lu

Inner West Lake

Xishan Lu

Xishan Lu

To West Bus Station (3km)

Hangzhou Botanical Gardens

灵隐路 Lingyin Lu

Xishan Lu

Longjing Lu

Southern Peak

Dingan Lu

2

Northern Peak

平海路 Pinghai Lu

41

Wushan Lu

20

43

Southern Peak

Xueshi Lu

Yan'an Lu

延安路

24 Renhe Lu

Youdian Lu

16

Liefang Lu

Nanshan Lu

Changcheng Lu

28

25

Hubin Lu 湖滨路

West Lake

35

19

Cable Car

17

10

Feilai Peak (209m)

Mifen Peak

6

Northern Peak

4

0   1 km
0   0.5 miles

0   200 m
0   0.1 miles

restaurants, cafés and upmarket shops. The complex will be larger than Shanghai's when finished in 2005. Also on the eastern shore is the impressive new Chinese Academy of Art building, with several galleries nearby.

The largest island in the lake is **Gushan (Solitary Hill) Island**, once the haunt of classical Chinese scholars, poet-magistrates and even emperors, and still a major cultural focal point. The Zhejiang Provincial Museum, the Louwailou Restaurant, the provincial Seal Engravers Society and Sun Yatsen Park (Zhōngshān Gōngyuán) are here, the latter part of an old imperial garden. The Baidi causeway links the island to the mainland.

In the northwestern corner, just south of the Yue Fei Mausoleum is the **Quyuan Garden** (Qūyuàn Fēnghé), a famous place to see and smell the lotus blossoms in spring. At the other end of the 3km-long Sudi causeway is **Red Carp Pond** (Huāgǎng Guānyú), another of the prescribed 10 sights, home to a few thousand red carp and studded with earthen islets.

It's possible to climb to the top of the eye-catching **Leifeng (Thunder Peak) Pagoda** (Léifēng Tǎ), further east along the southern shore, for fine views of the lake. The original pagoda

Sunset over West Lake (p185), Hangzhou

The laughing Buddha of Lingyin Temple (below), Hangzhou

was for centuries a popular spot to watch the sun set over the lake, but it collapsed in 1924. Across the road is the **Jingci (Pure Compassion) Monastery**, which was once famed for the sound of its ancient bell.

Boating trips on the lake are very popular and there's a range of choices. Cruise boats shuttle frequently from four points around the lake to the Mid-Lake Pavilion and **Xiaoying Island** (Xiǎoyíng Zhōu), which has a fine central pavilion and 'nine-turn' causeway. From the island you can look over at the **Three Pools Mirroring the Moon** (Sāntán Yìnyuè), a string of three small towers in the water, each of which has five holes that release shafts of candlelight on the night of the moon cake festival in mid-autumn, when the moon is full. You can take a cruise boat back to any of the four docks.

If you want to contemplate the moon at a slower pace there are places around the lake, particularly on the eastern shore, where you can hire paddle boats, either self-propelled (Y10 per hour) or rowed by a boatman (Y80 per hour for up to four people).

Lingyin Temple (Língyīn Sì), roughly translated as either 'Temple of Inspired Seclusion' or 'Temple of the Soul's Retreat', is really Hangzhou's main sight. It was built in 326 and, due to war and calamity, has been destroyed and restored no fewer than 16 times.

The walk up to the temple flanks the Peak Flying from Afar (Fēilái Fēng), which is supposed to have been magically transported here from India. The real highlight here are the **Buddhist carvings** lining the riverside and hillsides, 470 in all, dating from the 10th to 14th centuries. To get a close-up view of the best carvings, including the famous 'laughing' Maitreya Buddha image, follow the paths along the far (east) side of the stream. The place is normally crawling with tourists but with some leg work you can find some peace. Nearby is the Li Gong pagoda, named after the monastery's Indian founder.

The main **temple buildings** are restorations of Qing dynasty structures. The Hall of the Four Heavenly Guardians at the front of the temple is inscribed with the couplet, 'cloud forest Buddhist temple', penned by the Qing emperor Kangxi, who was a frequent visitor to Hangzhou and was inspired on one occasion by the sight of the temple in the mist and trees. On either side of the entrance are two 1000-year-old stelae.

Behind this hall is the Great Hall, where you'll find the magnificent 20m-high statue of Siddhartha Gautama. This was sculpted from 24 blocks of camphor wood in 1956 and was based on a Tang dynasty original. Behind the giant statue is a startling montage of 150 small figures, which charts the journey of 53 children on the road to buddhahood. During the time of the Five Dynasties (907–60) about 3000 monks lived in the temple.

Behind the Lingyin Temple is **Northern Peak** (Běi Gāofēng), which can be scaled via a cable car (Y24 up, Y16 down or Y34 return, children half-price). From the summit there are sweeping views across the lake and city.

The **Mausoleum of General Yue Fei** (Yuè Fēi Mù) is bounded by a red-brick wall a few minutes' walk west of the Hangzhou Shangri-La Hotel. During the 12th century, when China was attacked by Jurchen invaders from the north, General Yue Fei (1103–41) was commander of the Song armies. Despite his initial successes against the invaders, he was recalled to the Song court, where he was executed after being deceived by Qin Hui, a treacherous court official. More than 20 years later, in 1163, Song emperor Gao Zong exonerated Yue Fei and had his corpse reburied at the present site. Iron statues of Qin Hui and his wife, Wang Shi, were traditionally cursed at and spat upon by local tourists.

The mausoleum was ransacked during the Cultural Revolution, but has since been restored. Inside is a large statue of the general and the words, 'return the mountains and rivers to us', a reference to his patriotism and resistance to the Jurchen.

To the southwest of the city stands an enormous rail-and-road bridge, which spans the Qiantang River. Close by is the 60m-high octagonal **Six Harmonies Pagoda** (Liùhé Tǎ), first built in 960 and named after the six codes of Buddhism. The pagoda also served as a lighthouse, and was supposed to have magical power to halt the 20ft-high tidal bore, which thundered up the Qiantang River in mid-September every year. Behind the pagoda is a charming walk through terraces dotted with sculptures, bells, shrines and inscriptions.

Travellers have recommended the **China Silk Museum** (Zhōngguó Sīchóu Bówùguǎn), just south of the lake on Yuhuangshan Lu. It has good displays of silk samples, and also on the history and processes of silk production. English-speaking tour guides are available.

The interesting **Zhejiang Provincial Museum** (Zhèjiāng Shěng Bówùguǎn) is on Gushan Island, a short walk from the Hangzhou Shangri-La Hotel. Its buildings were part of the holiday palace of Emperor Qianlong in the 18th century. Most of the museum is concerned with natural history, with a large whale skeleton and a dinosaur skeleton.

For all you ever needed to know about green tea try the **China Tea Museum** (Zhōngguó Cháyè Bówùguǎn), southwest of the lake. The surrounding region produces some of China's most famous tea and you'll find plenty of places selling the stuff at nearby Longjing (Dragon Well) village.

Sights & Information

Bank of China (140 Yan'an Lu, near Qingchun Lu; 9am-5pm)

CAAC (8510 7160; 390 Tiyuchang Lu; 7.30am-8pm)

China Silk Museum (8706 2079; 73-1 Yuhuangshan Lu; adult/student Y10/5; 8.30am-4.30pm; bus 31)

China Tea Museum (8796 4221; Longjing Lu; admission Y10; 8.30am-4.30pm; bus 3 or 27 from Beishan Lu)

Dragonair (8506 8388; 5th fl Radisson Plaza Hotel, 333 Tiyuchang Lu) Twice daily flights to Hong Kong Y1860 one way.

Ferry Ticket Office (8515 3185; 138 Huancheng Beilu; 6.45am-6pm)

Hangzhou Botanical Gardens (Hángzhōu Zhíwùyuán; 8702 5793; Lingyin Lu; admission Y10; 8am-6pm)

Leifeng Pagoda (adult/child Y30/15)

Lingyin Temple (8796 7426; Lingyin Lu; adult/child Y15/7.5, to the valley extra Y20/10; 7am-5pm; bus K7 from the train station & Beishan Lu, or bus Y1, Y2 & Y4)

Mausoleum of General Yue Fei (8799 6663; Beishan Lu; adult/child/child under 1m Y20/10/free; 7.30am-5.30pm)

OTC Travel Service (8707 4401; fax 8706 5149; 37 Hubin Lu, beside the Overseas Chinese Hotel) Will get you train tickets for Y40 commission.

Pacific Internet Café (Tàipíngyáng Wǎngba; 2nd fl, 243 Jiefang Lu; 8am-midnight; Y3 per hr)

PSB (8706 8080; 35 Huaguang Lu)

Quyuan Garden (admission Y5; 6.30am-5.30pm)

Red Carp Pond (adult/child Y10/5; 6.30am-5.30pm)

Six Harmonies Pagoda (8659 1401; 16 Zhijiang Lu; admission Y15; bus 308 from Yan'an Lu)

Train Ticket Booking Office (199 Wulin Lu; 8am-5pm)

West Lake Boat Cruise (adult/child 1 1.3m/child under 1m Y35/17.50/free, includes entry to the Three Pools)

Zhejiang Provincial Museum (8797 1177; 25 Gushan Lu; adult/student Y10/5; 8.45am-4.30pm; bus 850)

Eating

Xintiandi should attract several top-end restaurants by 2005, including a branch of Shanghai's Va Bene.

For a rundown on Hangzhou cuisine see the Food & Drink chapter (p33).

La Luna Smart lakeside bar and café.

L'Opera Coffee, smoothies, cakes and sandwiches in a pleasant coffee-house environment.

Louwailou Restaurant (Lóuwàilóu Càiguǎn; ☎ 8796 9023; 30 Gushan Lu) On Solitary Hill Island, right on West Lake, this is Hangzhou's most famous restaurant, founded in 1838 but since rebuilt. Lu Xun and Zhou Enlai both ate here (but not together). Apart from excellent views of the lake, however, its fame has made the chefs complacent.

Roast Duck Restaurant (Kǎoyā Diàn; ☎ 8708 7122; 49 Youdian Lu) Half a Beijing duck costs Y30 (enough for two), or there are lots of decent-priced Hangzhou specialities like water shield soup (Y25), beggar's chicken (Y60), Dongpo pork (Y7), longjing tea shrimp (Y68 for 250g) and West Lake fish (Y20 for 650g), with an English menu.

Tianwaitian Restaurant (Tiānwàitiān Càiguǎn; ☎ 8796 5450; 2 Lingying Tianzhu Lu) Branch of Louwailou beside the entrance to Lingyin Temple, offering Hangzhou specialities like beggar's chicken (Y85 for 1kg).

Entertainment

Casablanca Country Pub (⊗ 6pm) A rustic place on the lake shore.

Paradise Rock Pub and restaurant next to the Overseas Chinese Hotel.

Shopping

Hangzhou is well known for its tea, in particular Longjing green tea (grown in the Longjing District, southwest of West Lake), silk, fans and, of all things, scissors.

Wushan Lu Night Market One of the best places to look for souvenirs is this evening street market. Stalls go up in the early evening and are piled high with a fascinating confusion of collectables. Fake ceramics jostle with Chairman Mao memorabilia, ancient pewter tobacco pipes, silk shirts and pirated CDs. Bargain hard if anything catches your eye.

Xinhua Lu Silk Market Probably the best place for silk, a couple of blocks east of Zhongshan Lu. Make sure you check that the silk is genuine and not a polyester clone – it should feel smooth and soft between your thumb and finger.

Sleeping

Hangzhou's hotels are divided into two groups; tourist hotels near the lakeshore, which offer partial lake-view rooms for a premium, and business hotels to the northeast of the lake in the urban centre.

Dahua Hotel (Dàhuá Fàndiàn; ☎ 8701 1901; 171 Nanshan Lu; d Y688-888, discounted to Y480-620) Fine location next to the lake and Xintiandi. Mao once stayed here.

Dongpo Hotel (Dōngpō Bīnguǎn; ☎ 8706 9769; 52 Renhe Lu; s Y280, d Y280-360, discounts of 35%) The cheaper doubles face inwards, which makes them darker, but quieter.

Grand Hyatt Regency (Hángzhōu Kǎiyuè Jiǔdiàn; ☎ 8779 1234; www.hangzhou.regency.hyatt.com; 28 Hubin Lu) Massive horseshoe-shaped complex which includes a pool, outdoor café, teahouse and spa. Opened in late 2003.

Hangzhou Hotel (Hángzhōu Dàjiǔdiàn; ☎ 8516 6888; 546 Yan'an Lu; d Y380-560, discounted to Y305-371) Currently the tallest building in Hangzhou, with a revolving restaurant on the 32nd floor. Rooms are good value.

Holiday Inn (Guóji Jiǎrì Jiǔdiàn; ☎ 8527 1199; 289 Jianguo Beilu; d Y1100, discounted to Y568)

Overseas Chinese Hotel (Huáqiáo Fàndiàn; ☎ 8707 4401; fax 8707 4978; 15 Hubin Lu; d Y544-603, discounted to Y380-450) On the eastern side of the lake, this has a convenient location, though the views are nothing special.

Post Office Hotel (Yóuzhèng Bīnguǎn; ☎ 8780 0568; 18 Huancheng Donglu; s/d/t Y300/330/360, discounted to Y180/200/240) Clean and pleasant two-star budget choice, but out near the train station.

Radisson Plaza (Guódá Léidílín Guǎngchǎng Jiǔdiàn; ☎ 8515 8888; www.radisson.com/hangzhoucn; 333 Tiyuchang Lu; d US$190, discounted to US$107) Business-oriented five-star luxury, with Hangzhou, Italian and Japanese restaurants, indoor pool, sky lounge and club floor rooms.

Ramada Plaza (Huáměidá Guǎngchǎng Hángzhōu Hǎihuá Dàjiǔdiàn; ☎ 8721 5888; haihua@ramada.hzcnc.net; 298 Qingchun Lu; city-view s/d US$67/110, lake-view s/d US$83/126, d discounted by 40%) Comfortable and efficient four-star chain with a small indoor pool, nonsmoking floor and Cantonese and French restaurants. Discounted doubles are good value.

Shangri-La (Hángzhōu Xiānggé Lǐlā Fàndiàn; ☎ 8707 7951; slh@shangri-la.com; 78 Beishan Lu; s/d from US$180/210, discounts of 40%) The most elegant and romantic place in the city, surrounded by spacious forested grounds on the northern lakeshore. An extra US$10 gets you a garden view; another US$50 gets you a lake view. If you can't stay there, at least go for a drink or a wander around. There's a Saturday seafood buffet for Y188.

Xinxin Hotel (Xīnxīn Fàndiàn; ☎ 8798 7101; fax 8705 3263; 58 Beishan Lu; d Y248-528, discounted to Y248-320, lake-view d Y600, discounted to Y530) A pleasant but roadside location on the north edge of West Lake with old and new wings.

Zhehua Hotel (Zhèhuá Fàndiàn; ☎ 8780 2366; fax 8780 7440; 5 Jiefang Lu; s/d/t Y360/360/480, discounted to Y120/160/200) Inconvenient location 10 minutes' walk from the train station, but cheap rooms. Singles are small and road noise can be a problem.

Directory

Directory

TRANSPORT

Shanghai is easy to get to. It is China's second-largest international air hub (third-largest if you count Hong Kong) and if you can't fly direct, you can go via Beijing or Hong Kong. With rail and air connections to places all over China, ferries travelling up the Yangzi River, many boats along the coast, and buses to destinations in adjoining provinces, you'll be hard pushed to find somewhere you can't get to.

Once there, the city isn't exactly a walker's paradise. There are some fascinating areas to stroll around, but new road developments, building sites and shocking traffic conditions conspire to make walking an exhausting, stressful and sometimes dangerous experience.

Travelling on buses can also be hard work; the routes, and particularly the stops, are not easy to figure out and buses are packed at rush hour. The metro and light railway system, on the other hand, work like a dream. Taxis are cheap and hassle-free as long as you avoid the rush hours. As private cars become increasingly affordable to the new middle class, traffic is becoming noticeably heavier, a trend that will only worsen.

The city took a big swipe at traffic congestion in 1999, investing more than a billion dollars in transport – building overpasses, a second metro line and a light railway within a year. Unfortunately there is still not enough space for everyone at rush hour and from around 7am to 9.30am and 4pm to 6.30pm it's every frail old man for himself. Cool aggression and elusive speed, along with a friendly smile, keep things from getting ugly.

AIR

China Eastern Airlines operates out of Shanghai and is China's third-largest carrier in terms of fleet. Shanghai Airlines is a much smaller airline, with limited international routes.

For domestic and international flights on Chinese airlines the baggage allowance for an adult passenger is 20kg in economy class and 30kg in 1st class. You are also allowed 5kg of hand luggage, though this is rarely weighed.

The charge for excess baggage is 1% of the full fare for each kilogram over the allowance.

Airline information in Chinese is available at ☎ 6247 5953 (domestic) and ☎ 6247 2255 (international).

By 2004 it should be possible to check in at the **new airport city terminal** (Map pp250-2; Nanjing Xilu) and then proceed to the airport by bus (from the terminal basement) or metro without hauling your luggage with you.

Airlines

China Eastern has many sales offices, as well as ticket sales counters at most major hotels and at China International Travel Service (CITS; see p200) on Jingling Donglu near the Bund.

Air China (Map pp246-9; ☎ 6269 2999; www.airchina .com.cn; 600 Huashan Lu)

China Eastern (Map pp246-9; ☎ 6247 5953 domestic, ☎ 6247 2255 international; www.ce-air.com; 200 Yan'an Xilu) This main office is open 24 hours a day.

China Northwest Airlines (Map pp250-1; ☎ 6267 4475; www.cnwa.com; 258 Weihai Lu) Flights daily to Nagoya and three or four times weekly to Hiroshima and Niigata.

Shanghai Airlines (Map pp250-2; ☎ 6255 0550, toll free 800-620 8888; www.shanghai-air.com, Chinese language only; 212 Jiangning Lu)

International airlines in Shanghai include:

Aeroflot Russian Airlines (Map pp250-2; ☎ 6279 8033; aeroflot@online.sh.cn; Suite 203A Shanghai Centre, 1376 Nanjing Xilu) Flights to/from Moscow three times a week.

Air Canada (Map pp244-5; ☎ 6375 8899; www.air canada.ca; Suite 702, Central Plaza, 227 Huangpi Beilu) Daily flights to Vancouver, Toronto, Montreal and Ontario via Beijing or Tokyo, though all flights from Shanghai are with other airlines, such as China Eastern or JAL.

Air France (Map pp244-5; ☎ 6360 6688; www.airfrance .com.cn; Room 1301, Novel Plaza, 128 Nanjing Xilu) Flights to/from Paris three times a week.

Air Macau (Map pp246-9; ☎ 6248 1110; www.airmacau .com.mo; Room 104, Hotel Equatorial, 65 Yan'an Xilu) Flights to/from Macau twice daily.

All Nippon Airways (ANA; Map pp250-2; ☎ 6279 7000; www.ana.com.cn/shanghai; Room 208, Shanghai Centre, 1376 Nanjing Xilu) Flights twice weekly to Tokyo, twice daily to Osaka.

Asiana (Map p256; ☎ 6219 4000; us.flyasiana.com; 2nd fl, Rainbow Hotel, 2000 Yan'an Xilu) Flights twice daily to/from Seoul.

Austrian Airlines (Map pp244-5; ☎ 6375 9051; www.aua.com; Suite 1103, Central Plaza, 227 Huangpi Beilu) Flights twice weekly to/from Vienna.

Dragonair (Map pp254-5; ☎ 6375 6375; www.dragonair.com; Suite 2103-4, Shanghai Sq, 138 Huaihai Zhonglu) Nine flights daily to/from Hong Kong.

JAL (Map pp250-2; ☎ 6288 3000; www.jal.com; Room 435, Plaza 66, 1266 Nanjing Xilu) Flights daily to/from Tokyo and Osaka.

KLM (Map pp250-2; ☎ 6884 6884; www.klm.com; Room 2810, Plaza 66, 1266 Nanjing Xilu) Flights twice weekly to/from Amsterdam.

Korean Air (Map p256; ☎ 6275 6000; www.koreanair.com; 1st fl, Office Tower, Yangtze New World, 2099 Yan'an Xilu) Five flights weekly to Pusan.

Lufthansa (☎ 5830 4400; cms.lufthansa.com; 24th fl, Puxiang Plaza, 1600 Shiji Dadao) Five flights weekly to/from Frankfurt.

Malaysia Airlines (Map pp250-2; ☎ 6279 8579; www.malaysiaairlines.com; Suite 209, Shanghai Centre, 1376 Nanjing Xilu) Twice-daily flights to/from Kuala Lumpur.

Northwest Airlines (Map pp250-2; ☎ 6884 6884; www.nwa.com; Suite 207, Shanghai Centre, 1376 Nanjing Xilu) Flights four times weekly to/from Los Angeles, San Francisco, Detroit and New York – all via Tokyo.

Qantas (Map pp250-2; ☎ 6279 8660; www.qantas.com.au; Suite 208, Shanghai Centre, 1376 Nanjing Xilu) Flights three times weekly to/from Sydney.

Royal Nepal Airlines (Map pp250-2; ☎ 3214 0717; www.royalnepal.com; Room 405, Block B, Universal Bldg, 1 Wanhangdu Lu) Flights twice weekly to Kathmandu.

Singapore Airlines (Map pp250-2; ☎ 6289 1000; www.singaporeair.com; Suite 606-608, Kerry Centre, 1515 Nanjing Xilu) Daily flights to/from Singapore.

Swiss International Air Lines (Map pp250-2; ☎ 6218 6810; www.swiss.com; Room 2602, Westgate Tower, 1038 Nanjing Xilu) Flights four times weekly to/from Zurich.

Thai Airways International (Map pp250-2; ☎ 5298 5555, fax 5298 6166; www.thaiairways.com; No 105 Kerry Centre, 1515 Nanjing Xilu) Daily flights to/from Bangkok.

Turkish Airlines (Map pp250-2; ☎ 3222 0022; www.thy.com; Room 211, Shanghai Centre, 1376 Nanjing Xilu) Flights twice weekly to/from Istanbul via Beijing.

United Airlines (Map pp250-2; ☎ 6279 8009; www.united.com; Suite 204, Shanghai Centre, 1376 Nanjing Xilu) Flights five times weekly direct to San Francisco and daily to New York via Tokyo.

Virgin Atlantic (Map pp244-5; ☎ 5353 4600; www.virgin-atlantic.com; Room 221, 12 Zhongshan Dong Yilu – the Bund) Flights four times weekly to/from London.

Airports

Shanghai is the only city in China to have two international airports.

Almost all international flights (and a few domestic flights) operate out of Pudong international airport, with most (but not all) domestic flights operating out of Hongqiao airport on Shanghai's western outskirts. If you are making an onward domestic connection from Pudong it is essential that you find out whether the domestic flight leaves from Pudong or Hongqiao, as the latter will require *at least* an hour to cross the city. Your ticket should indicate which airport you are flying to/from; Pudong's airport code is PVG, Hongqiao's is SHA. If you do have to transfer, airport buses and taxis connect the two airports.

HONGQIAO AIRPORT

Shanghai's **Hongqiao airport** (☎ 6268 8899, 6268 8918) is shaped like a horseshoe, with arrivals on the ground floor and departures above. Minibuses to surrounding cities are across the street.

The Bank of China branch, located near the baggage claim in the international arrivals hall (inside the customs gate), changes cash and travellers cheques at the standard rate. Otherwise a full-service Bank of China is about 15 minutes' walk away, next to the International Airport Hotel (see p194). Note that currently you can't change Renminbi back into US dollars at this airport.

The tourist information office is very helpful and can book discounted accommodation, as well as offer advice on transportation into town, and write the Chinese script for a taxi. Avoid the hotel touts. A post office is located in the international departures hall. Public telephones take coins or phonecards, for sale at the tourist information office.

Luggage storage is available in the international departures hall and also to the left of the domestic arrivals hall as you exit. Bags must be locked, a passport or ID is required and the maximum storage period is 30 days.

If you've missed your flight or need to kill some time the **Huamao Hotel** (Huámào Bīnguǎn; Map pp242-3; ☎ 6268 2266) is about two minutes' walk to the right of the international hall as you exit. It offers half-day rooms (a block of six hours) for Y150, a coffee shop, good souvenir shops, a gymnasium and a billiards room.

A pricier option is the **International Airport Hotel** (Shànghǎi Guójì Jīchǎng Bīnguǎn; Map pp242-3; ☎ 6268 8866), a 10-minute walk from the terminal; rooms cost Y880.

PUDONG AIRPORT

Formally opened on 1 October 1999, the new **Pudong airport** (☎ 6834 1000, flight information in English & Chinese ☎ 3848 4500) is expected eventually to handle 20 million passengers per year. The airport is inconveniently located 30km southeast of Shanghai, near the East China Sea, making it considerably more difficult to get to than Hongqiao airport.

The airport is easy to navigate. Departures are on the upper level and arrivals are on the lower level. The middle level is dedicated to restaurants and parking. Departure tax is paid (in Renminbi only) after check-in on the upper level. Trolleys are available for free and porters cost a modest Y10; tipping is forbidden.

There is a tourist information counter on the lower level near Door 10. There are also branches of CITS and China Youth Travel Service (CYTS) in the arrivals hall.

It's possible to change Renminbi back into US dollars at a **Bank of China branch** (🕒 8.30–11.30am & 2.30–10.30pm) at the international end of the upper level, if you have your original exchange receipts. The Shanghai Pudong Development Bank, at the international end of the lower level, will cash travellers cheques and give Visa credit card cash advances. There are ATMs in front of the departure tax desks on the upper level and outside the arrivals hall (Door 12).

Baggage storage is available in both arrivals halls (7am to 9.30pm, Y5 to Y20). Bags must be locked, a passport or ID is required, and the maximum storage period is 30 days.

There are post offices in both departures halls and in the domestic arrivals hall. Most restaurants are located on the 2nd floor, though a few nice cafés are on the upper level.

The souvenir shops in the departures halls have several interesting items to drain your last few *kuài*, like Bund stationery, cigarette girl sweatshirts, calligraphy pillows, and Chinese wine in elaborate jugs.

A short-stay hotel on the middle level charges Y60 per hour for passengers in transit. It is accessible only after preflight check-in or before customs clearance on arrival. If you have to stay the night, the two-star **Jinjiang Inn** (Jǐnjiāng Zhīxīng; ☎ 6835 3568) is a Y10 taxi ride away.

To/From the Airports

Most top-end hotels operate a shuttle bus to/from their hotels at fixed times (Y30 to Pudong, free to Hongqiao). Ask at hotel desks at the airports.

HONGQIAO AIRPORT

Hongqiao airport is 18km from the Bund and getting there takes about 30 minutes if you're lucky, and more than an hour if you're not.

Bus Nos 925 and 505 run between the domestic hall and Renmin Square (Y4, one hour). Bus No 831 also runs between the airport and Jinling Lu, just off the Bund. Alternatively, you can take No 938 to the **Huating Hotel** (Map p257; Y3) and catch the metro to anywhere else in the city. A white-and-blue airport shuttle bus runs directly to the **airport city terminal** (Map pp250-2; Nanjing Xilu; Y4); the bus is unmarked, so you might have to ask around. Minibus No 806 runs from the airport to Xujiahui.

A taxi to the Bund will cost from Y50 to Y60, plus Y15 in toll fees; tipping is not expected. There is a queuing system just outside and to the left of the arrivals hall; don't go with the taxi sharks who solicit you on arrival. A taxi fare to the airport should not include the Y15 toll.

Airport shuttle bus No 1 leaves every half-hour for Pudong airport (60 to 90 minutes). A taxi to Pudong airport costs about Y180 with tolls.

Buses leave for Suzhou (Y50, one hour, eight daily) from opposite the arrivals hall, arriving near the **Public Security Bureau** (PSB; Map p178) office on Renmin Lu, and for Hangzhou (Y70, two hours, three daily), arriving at the office of the **Civil Aviation Administration of China** (CAAC; Map p186).

MagLev

The Shanghai government is proud of its MagLev (Magnetic Levitation; Cífú Lièchē) line. First, the technology is revolutionary, which always goes down well in communist China. Magnets in both vehicle and track mean that the train has no contact with the track; propulsion comes from the track rather than the train. This means low noise, low energy and high speeds, the 30km run to Pudong airport taking eight minutes at 285km/h. It's also the first of its kind in the world (the German inventors have yet to persuade anyone else of the line's cost-effectiveness). There's a small exhibition hall by the terminal at Longyang Station.

The MagLev is currently running on national holidays only, for Y150 return, but this is expected to drop to Y50 one way when a regular service starts in 2004.

PUDONG AIRPORT

Pudong airport operates five airport bus routes. They drop off at both the domestic and international departures halls and pick up outside arrivals between Doors 7 to 15. A private **airport bus** (☎ 6834 6912) runs from the **Regal Shanghai East Asia Hotel** (Map p257) next to Shanghai Stadium to Pudong airport (Y30, 1½ hours), picking up passengers at the **Huating and Jianguo Hotels** (Map p257) en route, between 6am and 8pm.

The journey into Puxi takes between 60 and 90 minutes. Only bus No 5 stops in Pudong. The first bus to Pudong airport leaves at around 6am, and then runs every 30 minutes or so until around 8pm. The last bus back from the airport is around 9pm.

The bus routes are as follows:

No 1 Pudong to/from Hongqiao airport (Y22)

No 2 Pudong to/from Airport City Terminal on Nanjing Xilu (Y19)

No 3 Pudong to/from Xujiahui and Galaxy Hotel and Renaissance Yangtze Hotel in Hongqiao (Y18 to Y20)

No 4 Pudong to/from Wujiaochang, Da Baishu and Jiangwan Donglu in northeast Shanghai (Y16 to Y18)

No 5 Pudong to/from Pudong's Dongfang (East) Hospital, Renmin Square and Shanghai train station (Y15 to Y18)

A taxi ride into central Shanghai will cost around Y140 and will take about an hour. A taxi to Hongqiao airport costs around Y180. Most taxi drivers in Shanghai are honest, though make sure you use the meter unless you know the approximate cost and can bargain the fare down.

The MagLev train may be a modern wonder of the modern world but it's of limited use in getting into central Shanghai. Regular passenger services haven't yet started and even when they do they'll only take you as far as the terminus at **Longyang Station** (Map pp242-3) in Pudong, from where you'll have to lug your luggage a few hundred metres to the **metro station** (Map pp242-3) of the same name to continue your journey.

Eventually the No 2 metro line will link Hongqiao and Pudong airports but this is still a few years away.

To the Rest of China

Daily (usually several times daily) domestic flights connect Shanghai to every major city in China. Minor cities are less likely to have daily flights, but chances are there will be at least one flight a week, probably more, to Shanghai. You can buy tickets from hundreds of airline offices and travel agencies around town, though only a few take credit cards.

Business-class tickets cost 25% over economy class, and 1st-class tickets cost an extra 60%. Babies are charged 10% of the adult fare; children aged two to 12 are charged 50% of the adult fare; those over 12 are charged adult fare.

Cancellation fees depend on how long before departure you cancel. On domestic flights, if you cancel 24 to 48 hours before departure you lose 10% of the fare; if you cancel between two and 24 hours before the flight you lose 20%; and if you cancel less than two hours before the flight you lose 30%. If you don't show up for a domestic flight, you are entitled to a refund of 50%.

Domestic air fares from Shanghai

Destination	One-way fare
Beijing	Y1150
Chengdu	Y1610
Chongqing	Y1720
Fuzhou	Y730
Guangzhou	Y1620
Guilin	Y1310
Haikou	Y1590
Huangshan	Y500
Kunming	Y1790
Ningbo	Y300
Shenzhen	Y1270
Tianjin	Y1110
Xiamen	Y910
Xi'an	Y1280

Prices are approximate only; you're advised to check current fares with the relevant airlines.

BICYCLE

Most Shanghainese commute by bicycle; there are some 6.5 million bikes in Shanghai. It's not a bad way to get around if you pack in with the masses, though the traffic is madness and there's always a chance that you'll get wiped out by a novice taxi driver. Officially, foreigners need to register their bikes in order to pedal around the city, but in practice no-one will question you. The problem is a lack of places to hire bikes. The best area for a casual bike ride is without doubt the French Concession.

Around 130 bikes are stolen every day in Shanghai so make sure that you have your own bicycle cable lock. Bike parks are available at most shopping areas for a few *máo*.

Bikes are cheap to buy in Shanghai so there's not much point in bringing one from home. You can get a decent mountain bike for around Y400. See p136 for bike stores and more information on cycling in Shanghai.

BOAT
To the Rest of China

Boat travel is definitely one of the best ways to leave Shanghai and is also often the cheapest, though there are some safety concerns. In 1999 more than 200 passengers drowned after a Yantai–Dalian ferry sank in heavy seas.

Boat tickets can be bought from CITS (which charges a commission), the **ferry booking office** (Map pp244-5; 1 Jinling Donglu) or at **Shiliupu wharf** (Map pp253-4; ☎ 6326 1261; 111 Zhongshan Dongerlu), from where all domestic sailings depart. The departure point for both domestic and international ferries is eventually to be moved out to the Yangzi near Wusongkou, though no timetable has been set for this yet.

Overnight boats to Putuoshan depart Shanghai daily at 6pm and take 12 hours. Tickets cost Y47 to Y53 for a seat, Y81 to Y102 in a 4th-class dorm, Y96 to Y118 in a six- to eight-bed cabin, Y172 to Y262 in a four-bed cabin, or you can have your own twin berth for Y292 to Y322. There is often a second departure on Friday night to cater for the weekend crowd. It's easy to upgrade once you are on board. If there's a rough sea, keep in mind that this can be a difficult trip for those prone to seasickness.

A high-speed ferry service departs daily and costs Y185/255 on the lower/upper deck. Buses depart daily at 8am and 1.30pm from Shiliupu wharf to take you, in two hours, to either the port of Luchao or Dinghai. The ferry then takes an additional 2½ hours. Boats leave Putuoshan daily at noon and 12.45pm for the return trip to Shanghai.

The main destinations of ferries up the Yangzi River are Nantong, Nanjing, Wuhu, Guichi, Jiujiang and Wuhan. If you're going only as far west as Nanjing, take the train, which is much faster than the boat. There are daily departures to all destinations. Boats leave every four days for Dalian (Y180 to Y380, 36 hours) but boats to Qingdao and Ningbo had been axed at the time of writing.

Many people travelling to Shanghai set their sights on a Three Gorges river trip, though the gorges themselves are shrinking fast under dam waters. Looking at the map you might consider continuing the boat trip all the way to Shanghai. The snag is that the most interesting part of the trip is from Chongqing to Yichang or Wuhan; the trip downstream from Wuhan to Shanghai is actually quite dull as the Yangzi spreads to a width of more than 1km. You're generally better off flying the Wuhan–Shanghai leg.

If you decide to take a return trip from Shanghai the best bet is to fly to Chongqing, take the boat trip to Yichang and then fly back to Shanghai. Most travel agencies listed in this chapter (p200) offer this kind of package. Note that the trip is considerably slower (but cheaper) upstream compared with downstream. For more information on the Three Gorges trip see Lonely Planet's *China* guide.

BUS

The closest thing to revolutionary fervour in Shanghai today is the rush-hour bus ambush. During rush hour and on the weekend, buses are often packed to the hilt, and at times impossible even to board. As you squeeze yourself on and off, and while you are on board, keep your valuables tucked away since it is easy for pickpockets to operate under such conditions.

The main problem with taking the bus (once you've found the right number and right route and managed to get on the bus) is that you can never be quite sure where it is going to stop. The bus route may run straight past your destination but you may find the nearest stop up to a kilometre away. Only readers of Chinese will be able to read the bus-stop route plans. In general try to get on at the terminus, thus guaranteeing you a seat, avoid rush hours, and stick to a few tried-and-tested routes. Most buses now have recorded messages announcing the next stop in English.

Older buses have wooden seats and no air-con and cost Y1. New buses with air-con cost Y2 and are a godsend in summer. Private minibuses (Y2) serve some routes on the edges of town.

Suburban and long-distance buses don't carry numbers – the destination is in characters. Buses generally operate from 5am to 11pm, except for 300-series buses, which operate all night.

To the Rest of China

Travelling by bus is not a very useful way to leave or enter Shanghai, though the

Shanghai–Nanjing Hwy has cut road travel time to less than three hours to Nanjing. The Beijing–Shanghai Expressway will speed up journeys to the north (currently 14 hours). For information on getting to/from Suzhou, Hangzhou and Zhouzhuang see the Excursions chapter (p171).

The most useful long-distance bus station is probably the **Hengfeng Lu Bus Station** (Map pp250-2; ☎ 5663 0230), next to the Hanzhong Lu metro station. Deluxe buses leave every hour for Nanjing (Y88, four hours), Ningbo (Y97, four hours) and Wuxi (Y37 to Y43, two hours). The main **long-distance bus station** (Map pp242-3; ☎ 5661 8801) at the junction of Hutai Lu and Zhongshan Beilu, has buses for the above destinations and also to Shaoxing (Y70, three hours).

The new **Xujiahui bus station** (Map p257; ☎ 6469 7325; 211 Hongqiao Lu) has departures to Nanjing (Y76 to Y85) at 8am, 9am and 2pm, and to Yangzhou at 7am, 9am, 1pm and 3pm (Y83). There are eight departures daily along the high-speed highway to Ningbo (Y91 to Y97), as well as long-distance buses to Wuhan and Hefei.

Buses to Nanjing's Jinling Hotel (Y88) depart daily at around 7.20am and 8.20am, and 1.30pm and 3.30pm from the Shanghai Stadium, calling at the Renaissance Yangtze Hotel in Hongqiao half an hour later. There are also eight buses daily from the stadium to Wuxi train station (Y43, two hours) and Lingshan (Y53), as well as weekend-only buses to Yangzhou (Y70, three hours) leaving at 7.30am.

CAR

It's possible to hire a car in Shanghai by the day or longer, though there are so many taxis that it doesn't make much sense unless your boss is coming into town and demands a BMW. With Shanghai's anarchic traffic in mind it is strongly recommended that you hire a driver as well.

Hertz (☎ 800-810 8883 countrywide) is a recent entry to Shanghai, with offices in the Hotel Equatorial (☎ 6249 7988), Huamao Hotel (☎ 6269 0010; Hongqiao airport), at the China Development Bank Tower (☎ 6888 3636; 500 Pudong Nanlu) and doubtless soon at Pudong airport. A Volkswagen Santana with driver and petrol costs Y570 per day for up to 120km. Self-drive costs Y380 per day if you have a Chinese driver's licence.

Avis operates through **Angel Car Rental** (☎ 6229 1119; 1387 Changning Lu). Other car rental agencies include **Dazhong** (☎ 6318 5666; 98 Guohuo Lu), and most of the taxi companies listed in the Taxi section (p198). Prices start at Y320 a day for a Santana and Y540 for an Audi, without a driver.

To drive in Shanghai, resident expats must fill in two forms from the **Shanghai Transport Bureau** (☎ 6516 8168; 1101 Zhongshan Beiyilu), get a health certificate, translate their original driving licence into Chinese and pass an examination at the Transport Bureau, even if they have an international driver's licence. Foreigners are technically allowed to drive in Shanghai municipality only, though expats report few problems driving into neighbouring Jiangsu and Zhejiang. If you have your own car and need some spare parts, Weihai Lu (Map pp250-2) is lined with car accessory shops.

FERRY

Several ferries cross the Huangpu between Puxi and Pudong. The most useful one operates between the southern end of the Bund and Pudong. The trip costs eight *máo* eastbound (free west-bound) and departs every 15 minutes all day.

METRO & LIGHT RAILWAY

The city's metro trains are easily the best way to get around Shanghai. They are fast, cheap, clean and easy, though it's hard to get a seat at the best of times.

There are currently two metro lines and a light rail line that acts as a third line. Several more lines are under construction. The No 1 line runs from the train station in the north through Renmin Square along Huaihai Zhonglu, through Xujiahui and down to Xinzhuang in the southern suburbs.

The No 2 line runs from Zhongshan Park in the east to Longyang Lu in distant Pudong, site of the MagLev terminus, passing through Nanjing Lu at several places in the centre of town. The line will eventually connect Hongqiao and Pudong airports, though it will be a few years before this happens. The two lines connect at Renmin Park/Renmin Square interchange, the busiest of all the stations.

Line No 3 is also known as the Pearl Mass Transit light railway, and runs mostly above ground. The line follows the route of the old Shanghai–Hangzhou railway and currently runs 25km from Caohejing in the southern suburbs to Jiangwan in the north, passing through much of western and northern Shanghai en route. The elevated line connects with the No 1 metro line at Shanghai train station and Zhongshan Park. The second phase of the light rail project is proposed to run from Baoshan Lu in the north to Hongqiao in the southwest, making a giant loop through Pudong; it's tentatively due to open in 2004.

Tickets cost Y2 to Y6 depending on the distance you travel. Keep your ticket until you exit. At the moment there are no bulk-buy savings or travel cards. You can buy a carnet of prepaid tickets for Y50, though you'll save nothing except the time it takes to queue for tickets. Eventually an integrated bus, metro and light railway smart card will be available.

Trains run frequently from around 5am to 11pm. Stations can provide a bilingual time-table of first and last trains from the various stations. Stops are announced in English as well as Chinese but it can be hard to see the station name when you pull into a station, thanks to the clumsy arrangements of pillars. The metro is nonsmoking and there are no toilets at any of the stations.

The metro station exits can be very complicated (Xujiahui stop alone has 14 exits!) and it's sometimes important that you get the right exit number. To find a metro station look for the red symbol that looks like an 'M'.

TAXI

Shanghai has around 80,000 taxi drivers and 41,000 taxis. Most are Volkswagen Santanas, though these are due to be upgraded to Volkswagen Passats (Volkswagen has a factory in Shanghai).

Shanghai's taxis are reasonably cheap, hassle-free and easy to flag down outside rush hour. Flag fall is Y10 for the first 3km, and Y2 per km thereafter; tipping is not common. Most rides around town cost from Y14 to Y20. Most taxi drivers are surprisingly honest, though you should always go by the meter. A few taxis now even take credit cards. At night you can tell if a taxi is empty by the red 'for hire' sign on the dashboard of the passenger side. The driver should push this down to start the meter when you get in the cab.

A night rate operates from 11pm to 5am, when the flag fall is Y13, then Y2.6 per km. It's always worth asking for a printed receipt, as this gives not only the fare but also the driver and car number, the distance driven,

waiting time and the number to call if there are any problems.

Note that taxis can't take the tunnel to Liujiazui in Pudong from 8am to 9.30am and 5pm to 6.30pm.

In general, taxi drivers are surprisingly bad at finding their way around. If you don't speak Chinese, take a Chinese character map or have your destination written down in characters. It also helps if you have your own directions and sit in the front with a map. If you look particularly clueless you may literally be taken for a ride. Drivers must earn a quota of about Y4000 a month but pocket most of the money after that.

Shanghai's main taxi companies include **Dazhong Taxi** (☎ 6258 1688), **Qiangsheng** (☎ 6258 0000) and **Bashi** (☎ 6431 2788). A few Red Flag limousines, once reserved for top Communist Party officials, now operate as cabs in Shanghai and cost the same as normal cabs. **Jinjiang Taxis** (☎ 6275 8800) have 10-seater minibuses that are very useful for groups and cheap at Y15 for the first 3km.

Motorcycle taxis wait at most intersections and metro stations to whisk travellers off to nearby destinations. The advantages of these are that you save money if you are alone, and the motorcycles can take many roads that are off-limits to normal taxis. The disadvantages are that you have to cling on to the motorcycle for dear life (helmets are provided and strongly recommended!), and your travel insurance probably won't cover you if you fall off. Most trips cost less than Y10.

TRAIN

China's rail service is gargantuan, excellent and more than a little mind-boggling. At any given time it is estimated that over 10 million Chinese are travelling on a train in China and over a billion train tickets are sold every year. Chinese train travel is a subculture unto itself and if you have time to travel around China after a visit to Shanghai you should try to incorporate at least one train journey into your itinerary.

Buying Tickets

There are many options for buying train tickets in Shanghai. At Shanghai train station, the easiest place is the ground floor of the **Longmen Hotel** (Map pp250-2; ☺ 8am–5pm), a short walk west of the train station. You can book sleepers up to four days in advance, for which there's a Y3 to Y5 service charge. It's definitely the easiest place for Hong Kong tickets. The main (24-hour) ticket office is on the other (east) side of the station; ticket office No 10 claims its staff are English-speakers.

In town, CITS on Jinling Donglu will book tickets for a Y10 service charge. You can also book train tickets across the street at the ferry ticket office (Y5 service charge). CYTS on Hengshan Lu also sells advance train tickets. Other train ticket outlets are at 230 Beijing Donglu and 121 Xizang Nanlu (8am to 5pm daily). Train information is available over the phone in Chinese (☎ 6317 1880, 6317 9090).

Buying train tickets is very difficult the week before and after Chinese New Year, as Shanghai's migrant workers desert the city en masse. Try not to make any travel plans at this time. Long-distance tickets should always be bought at least 24 hours, preferably several days, in advance.

Classes

In socialist China there are no classes; instead you have hard seat, hard sleeper, soft seat and soft sleeper.

The most comfortable way to get to destinations around Shanghai is on a soft seat (ruǎnzuò). Seats are numbered and smoking is prohibited; if you must light up, you'll have to stand in the corridor between the cars. Coffee, tea and snacks are sold. Hard seat (yìngzuò) is more crowded and smokier and can be packed to the gills on longer trips.

For overnight trips, hard sleepers (yìngwò) are relatively comfortable and only a fixed number of people are allowed in the sleeper carriage. The carriage is made up of doorless compartments with half-a-dozen bunks in three tiers and little foldaway seats by the windows. Newer services such as the train to Hong Kong are nonsmoking (though some passengers need reminding). Sheets, pillows and blankets are provided. Competition for hard sleepers has become keen in recent years, and you'll be lucky to get one at short notice (one or two days before you travel). Prices vary according to which berth you get: upper, middle or lower. Lower berth (xiàpù) is pricier as you get to sit and have more space but it is often invaded by all and sundry who use it as a seat during the day. The top berths (shàngpù) are cheapest as you get the least space and nowhere to sit if lower-berth passengers are asleep.

Soft sleepers (ruǎnwò) get the works, with four comfortable bunks in a closed, carpeted compartment – complete with straps to keep the top-bunk incumbent from falling off in the middle of the night. Soft sleepers cost about twice as much as hard sleepers. Deluxe two-person soft-sleeper cabins are available on the Beijing and Hong Kong lines only; they are only marginally cheaper than flying.

Services

Most trains depart and arrive at the main **Shanghai train station** (Map pp250-2), but some depart and arrive at the **Shanghai west train station** (Map pp242-3). Be sure to find out which one you should leave from. Some trains to Hangzhou also leave from Meilong train station, a short walk from the Jinjiang Amusement Park metro station in the southwestern suburbs.

Special double-decker 'tourist trains' operate between Shanghai and Hangzhou, and Shanghai and Nanjing (with stops at Wuxi, Suzhou, Changzhou and Zhenjiang). A seat to Nanjing costs Y41 to Y72, depending on the train, and takes three hours. For details on trains to Hangzhou and Suzhou see the Excursions chapter (p171).

To Beijing there are overnight express trains at 6pm (train No T14), 6.08pm (T22), 7pm (T104) and 8pm (T110). All trains take 14 hours. Train No T22 offers deluxe soft sleepers with luxuries such as personal TV screens, mobile phone chargers, modem connections and a bar. Express trains cost around Y306 to Y327 hard sleeper, Y487 to Y499 soft sleeper and Y871 to Y911 deluxe soft sleeper. (For an explanation of train classes see Classes, above). Slower trains are 40% cheaper but take an additional seven hours or so. Berths go quickly on this popular line so book at least a couple of days in advance.

Travel times to other destinations include Fuzhou (21 hours), Guangzhou (27 hours), Guilin (27 hours), Huangshan (12 hours), Kunming (56 hours) and Xi'an (24 hours).

TO/FROM HONG KONG

Direct trains run between Shanghai and Kowloon in Hong Kong on alternate days and take 24 hours. Train No K99 departs Shanghai at 12.25pm and tickets cost Y559/571/583 for an upper/middle/lower berth in hard sleeper, Y908 in soft sleeper, or Y1143 in deluxe soft sleeper (a two-berth cabin). The train stops in Hangzhou East, for an hour in Guangzhou East, and at Dongguan, 1¼ hours from Hong Kong, where Chinese immigration formalities take place. Note that trains and timetables list the destination as Jiulong, the official Mandarin Pinyin spelling for Kowloon.

Many of Shanghai's train ticket offices won't sell tickets for this service so you are better off heading to the Longmen Hotel ticket office (see Buying Tickets, p198), which will accept phone reservations up to two months in advance and issue tickets on the spot for travel within eight days.

From Hong Kong to Shanghai, berths cost HK$508/519/530 in hard sleeper, HK$825 in soft sleeper and HK$1039 in deluxe soft sleeper. Trains leave Hong Kong's Hung Hom KCR station in Kowloon's east Tsim Sha Tsui at 3pm and arrive in Shanghai at 6.45pm the next day. You should arrive at the station at least 45 minutes before departure to go through Hong Kong immigration. Tickets (including the return leg) can be bought at Hung Hom up to 30 days before departure, as well as at other KCR stations and agents such as China Travel Service (CTS). Facilities at Hung Hom station include ATMs of most banks and luggage storage. For more information call the **inquiry hotline** (☎ 852-2947 7888).

Changes to the date of travel of Shanghai–Hong Kong tickets can be made up to a day before departure. Full refunds are given 15 days before departure, 70% is refunded up to three days in advance and 50% of the ticket is refunded up to the day before departure.

It's also possible to travel by train to Guangzhou (Y400/600 for a hard/soft sleeper) and then catch either the express train to Hong Kong or a combination of the local train to Shenzhen and then the MCR metro to Hong Kong but this won't save all that much money and it's much more inconvenient.

TRAVEL AGENCIES

The big government travel agencies are CITS, CTS and CYTS. Their Shanghai branches can arrange almost everything, from train tickets to city tours, though they often have separate offices for separate divisions. CITS and CTS are represented overseas.

Shanghai CYTS (Map pp246-9; ☎ 6445 5396; www.statravel.com.cn; 2 Hengshan Lu) recently teamed up with STA Travel to become their representative in Shanghai. ISIC cards are available for Y70. CYTS can book train tickets for a Y3 to Y10 commission.

Private agencies can book discounted international air tickets and put together discounted hotel packages, but they aren't really all that switched on yet. You'll do best if you know exactly what you are asking for rather than relying on them to find the best deal. Most agencies in Shanghai accept international credit cards.

The **CITS office** (Map pp244-5; ☎ 6323 8749; 2 Jinling Donglu) on the ground floor of the Guangming building is the most useful for tourists though people have complained of some unhelpful staff. There's another CITS office near the Peace Hotel, on Nanjing Donglu by Gino Café, but it's mostly for booking air tickets.

CTrip (☎ 3406 4880, 800-820 6666; http://english.ctrip.com) is an online agency that is good for hotel bookings.

With middle-class Shanghainese starting to travel the world, a rash of local travel agents has sprung up, offering domestic tours and overseas trips to Australia, Hong Kong, Thailand etc. These are mostly for local Chinese clients and will probably have little to offer foreign travellers.

In Shanghai, the following agencies are reputable:

FASCO (Map pp246-9; ☎ 6472 3131; 59 Maoming Nanlu, gateway of the Jinjiang Hotel)

Nonggongshang Air Travel Service (Map p256; ☎ /fax 6275 4477; guolong8@shtel.net.cn; Shartex Plaza, 88 Zunyi Lu, Hongqiao) IATA bonded.

Shanghai China International Travel Service (CITS; Map pp250-2; ☎ 6289 8899; fax 6289 4928; 1277 Beijing Xilu)

CITS (Map pp246-9; ☎ 6387 4988; 146 Huangpi Nanlu, cnr Huaihai Zhonglu)

CITS (Map pp244-5; ☎ 6323 4067; 2nd fl, 66 Nanjing Donglu) For air tickets.

CITS (Map pp244-5; ☎ 6323 8770; 2 Jinling Donglu) For train and boat tickets and China Eastern air tickets.

Shanghai China Travel Service (SCTS; Map pp246-9; ☎ 6247 5665; fax 6247 5878; webmaster@scts.com; 881 Yan'an Zhonglu)

Shanghai Jinjiang Tours (Map pp246-9; ☎ 6466 2828; www.jjtravel.com/en; 191 Changle Lu, near the Garden Hotel)

Shanghai Spring International Travel Service (Map pp244-5; ☎ 6351 6666; spring@china-sss.com; 347 Xizang Zhonglu)

PRACTICALITIES
BUSINESS

Many a business deal has been lost due to social disgraces. If you are doing business in China, it is important to refer to p11, have patience, a sense of humour, cultural adaptability and a tolerance for smoky rooms.

In bureaucratic China, even simple things can be made difficult. Renting property, getting a telephone installed, hiring employees, paying taxes and so on can generate mind-boggling quantities of red tape. Many foreign businesspeople working in Shanghai and elsewhere say that success is usually the result of dogged persistence and finding cooperative officials. One thing to make sure of is that you are meeting with the right people – those who have the power to give you the permission you seek. Knowing who holds the reins of power in Shanghai is essential.

Buying is simple, selling is more difficult, but setting up a business in Shanghai is a whole different can of worms. If yours is a hi-tech company, you can go into certain economic zones and register as a wholly foreign-owned enterprise. In that case you can hire people without going through the government, enjoy a three-year tax holiday, obtain long term income tax advantages and import duty-free personal items for corporate and expat use (including a car!). The alternative is listing your company as a representative office, which doesn't allow you to sign any contracts in China – these must be signed by the parent company.

It's easier to register as a representative office. First find out where you want to set up (the city or a special economic zone), then go through local authorities (there are no national authorities for this). Go to the local Commerce Office, Economic Ministry, Foreign Ministry, or any ministry that deals with foreign economic trade promotion. Contact your embassy and national trade organisation first – they can advise you.

The most important thing to remember when you go to register a company is not to turn away when you run into a bureaucratic barrier. Bureaucrats will tell you that everything is 'impossible'. In fact, anything is possible – it all depends on your *guānxì* (relationships). Whatever you have in mind is negotiable, and the rules may not necessarily be rules at all. The flip side of this is that without a legal framework in China, companies often find themselves with no legal recourse in the event of a dispute, such as when your staff leaves en masse to set up an identical enterprise across the road.

Taxation rates vary from zone to zone, authority to authority. They seem to be negotiable but 15% is fairly standard in economic zones. Every economic zone has a reasonably

comprehensive investment guide, which is available in English and Chinese – ask at the economic or trade section of your embassy, which might have copies of these.

Finally, don't expect to make a quick buck in Shanghai. Of the 18,000 foreign enterprises operating in Shanghai, over half of them are losing money and most don't expect investments to pay off for another decade.

Exhibitions & Conventions

Apart from the monster venues listed in this section, all the top-end hotels provide conference facilities (see individual entries in the Sleeping chapter, p155). A new conference centre is currently being built in Pudong's Central Park.

Intex Shanghai (Shànghǎi Guójì Zhǎnlǎn Zhōngxīn; Map p256; ☎ 6275 5800; intex@public.sta.net.cn; 88 Loushanguan Lu)

Shanghai Everbright Convention & Exhibition Centre (Shànghǎi Guāngdà Huìzhǎn Zhōngxīn; Map p257; ☎ 6451 6345; fax 6436 0000; 40-80 Caobao Lu) Has an attached four-star hotel.

Shanghai Exhibition Centre (Shànghǎi Zhǎnlǎn Zhōngxīn; Map pp250-2; ☎ 6270 0279; fax 6247 4598; 1000 Yan'an Zhonglu) This centre houses 42 exhibition halls covering 15,000 sq m, plus a theatre, restaurants and cafés.

Shanghai International Convention Centre (Shànghǎi Guójì Huìyì Zhōngxīn; Map pp253-4; ☎ 5879 2727; www.shicc.net; 2727 Binjiang Dadao, Pudong) Opened in 1999 for the Fortune 500 forum, this centre offers a 3000-seat ballroom, an 800-seat conference room and a hotel.

Shanghai New International Expo Centre (Shànghǎi Xīn Guójì Bózhǎn Zhōngxīn; Map pp242-3; ☎ 2890 6666; www.sniec.net; 2345 Longyang Lu, Pudong)

Shanghaimart (Shànghǎi Shìmào Shāngchéng; Map p256; ☎ 6236 6888; smtexc@shangmart.com.cn; 2299 Yan'an Xilu)

Shanghai Worldfield Convention Centre & Hotel (Shànghǎi Shìbó Huìyì Dàjiǔdiàn; Map pp242-3; ☎ 6270 3388; www.conventhotel.com; 2106 Hongqiao Lu)

Office Space

There is heaps of available office space and buildings keep going up, despite current occupancy rates of about 60% (40% in Pudong). If you are looking for a temporary office the following companies offer 'instant offices' equipped with bilingual secretaries and computer services.

Bellsouth (Map pp250-2; ☎ 6729 8900; 4th fl, Shanghai Centre, 1376 Nanjing Xilu)

The Executive Centre (Map pp250-2; ☎ 5252 4618; www.executivecentre.com; 35th fl, CITIC Sq, 1168 Nanjing Xilu)

Office General (Map pp250-2; ☎ 6288 388; www.office general.com; 39th fl, Plaza 66, 1266 Nanjing Xilu)

Regus (Map pp253-4; ☎ 6465 1308, 5047 8837; www .regus.com; 31st fl, Jinmao Bldg, Pudong)

Servcorp (Map pp253-4; ☎ 2890 3000; www.servcorp .net; HSBC Tower, Pudong)

For couriers see p214.

Printing

The following companies offer copying, design, printing, laminating, binding, and IBM and Macintosh computer hire.

Copy General (Map pp250-2; ☎ 6279 1694; www.copy general.com; 88 Tongren Lu) There is another branch in Pudong (Map pp253-4; ☎ 5879 8238; Room 2113, China Merchants Tower, 161 Liujiazui Donglu)

Snap Printing (Map p256; ☎ 6209 9392; www.snap printing.com; 835 Zhongshan Xilu)

Translation Services

Businesspeople should always hire their own translator, who should speak both Mandarin and Shanghainese dialect.

International Communication Concepts (☎ 5830 4990) Offers simultaneous translation over the phone, 24 hours a day.

President Translation Services (☎ 5490 1919; www .ptsgi.com; 7th fl, Hujia Mansion, 41 Caoxi Beilu)

Useful Organisations

The Shanghai Foreign Investment Development Board, under the auspices of the Foreign Economic Relations and Trade Commission, has been set up to keep foreigners informed of the government's latest economic regulations.

Access Asia Has a useful website on business in China at www.accessasia.com.

American Chamber of Commerce (AmCham; Map pp250-2; ☎ 6279 7119; 4th fl, Shanghai Centre, 1376 Nanjing Xilu) This office helps members only.

British Chamber of Commerce (BritCham; Map pp250-2; ☎ 6218 5022; british@uninet.com.cn; Room 1701-1702, Westgate Tower, 1038 Nanjing Xilu) The China Britain Business Council (☎ 6218 5183) is also here.

China Australia Chamber of Commerce (☎ 6248 8301; Room 531, 1440 Yanan Zhonglu, near Huashan Lu)

US Commercial Center (Map pp250-2; ☎ 6279 7640; Room 631, Shanghai Centre, 1376 Nanjing Xilu) This is the

overseas office of the US Department of Commerce and can assist US businesses to find Chinese business partners.

BUSINESS HOURS

Banks, offices and government departments are normally open Monday to Friday from 9am to noon and about 2pm to 4.30pm. Most major post offices open daily 8.30am to 6pm, sometimes until 10pm. Central telecom offices are open 24 hours. Local post offices are closed on the weekend. Bank of China branches are normally open weekdays from 9.30am to 11.30am and 1.30pm to 4.30pm, and most now have 24-hour ATMs.

Most museums are open on the weekend; a few close on Monday. They usually stop selling tickets 30 minutes before they close. The majority of shops and department stores stay open daily to around 10pm, especially on the weekend.

Note that businesses in China close for three week-long annual holidays – see p208 for details.

Shanghai's entertainment pulses round the clock. Several Shanghainese restaurants and many hotel coffee shops are open 24 hours and bars on Julu Lu stay open until dawn.

CHILDREN

China's one-child policy has created a generation of spoiled, demanding and, more often than not, overweight 'Little Emperors'. Fortunately for visitors with children, Shanghai's entrepreneurs have devised plenty of ways of keeping kids occupied.

Amusement and water parks like **Dino Beach** (p82), **Aquaria 21** (p81) and **Jinjiang Amusement Park** (p82) are favourites and a blessing in summer when temperatures can be uncomfortably high.

Shanghai's parks can be a bit tame for kids, though **Fundazzle** (p81) in Zhongshan Park is a favourite, especially as McDonald's, Pizza Hut and KFC are all nearby. Several McDonald's restaurants offer play areas for young children. The **Shanghai Botanical Gardens** (p83) have a nice children's park. The zoo and circus are other favourite standbys, and children often enjoy activities like **paintball** (p138) and **karting** (p138). There are several kids' stores around town, particularly along Nanjing Donglu.

In general 1.4m is the cut-off height for children's cheaper fares or entry tickets. Children under 0.8m normally get in free.

For advice on travelling with children pick up *Travel with Children*, published by Lonely Planet.

Active Kidz Shanghai (☎ 6406 6757; www.activekidz.org; Nice Year Villas, Clubhouse, Level 2, 3333 Hong Mei Lu, Hongqiao) is a nonprofit initiative aimed at prising expat kids away from the TV screen by providing sports and recreational activities, including after-school sports and summer camps, Saturday baseball and Sunday football.

CLIMATE

Shanghai starts the year shivering in mid-winter, when temperatures can drop below freezing and the vistas are grey and misty. All hell breaks loose in late January/early February when Chinese New Year grinds the city to a halt and swamps local transport with domestic travellers. This is a time to avoid or lie low. The rest of winter offers good hotel discounts and few tourists.

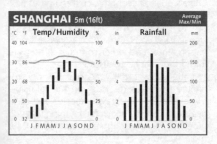

Spring brings warming days and lovely blossoms in the **Yuyuan Gardens** (p67). April to mid-May is probably one of the best times to visit weather-wise, along with autumn (late September to mid-November). Summer is the peak travel season but the hot and humid weather makes conditions outside uncomfortable, with temperatures sometimes as high as 40°C (104°F) in July and August. September and November host several interesting arts festivals. This is the most popular time for trade fairs and exhibitions so there are fewer discounts. By December the thermal underwear is being unpacked again for another cold winter.

In short, you'll need silk long johns and down jackets for winter, an ice block for each armpit in summer and an umbrella wouldn't go astray in either of these seasons.

COURSES
Language

Several parks have English corners where locals come to practise English for which they are more than happy to swap some Chinese tuition. Try **Fuxing Park** (Map pp246-9) or **Renmin Park** (Map pp244-5) on Sunday at 1pm. It's also possible to find a private tutor from any university who is willing to moonlight; try the noticeboard of **City Supermarket** (Map pp250-2) in the Shanghai Centre.

The following language schools are reputable and offer group or private tuition.

I Mandarin (Map pp250-2; ☎ 3222 1028; www.imandarin.net; Suite 721, Shanghai Centre, 1376 Nanjing Xilu)

Mandarin Centre (Map pp242-3; ☎ 6270 7665; www.mandarin-center.com; 16 Songyuan Lu, cnr Hongqiao Lu) Part-run by the humanities department of Fudan University, with evening and weekend Mandarin classes, as well as instruction in Shanghainese dialect.

Web International Mandarin (☎ 6447 7909; www.webmandarin.com; 33rd fl, Jianhui Bldg, 922 Hengshan Lu) Run by Jiaotong University.

Other Courses

There are plenty of other courses in Shanghai but you may have to dig them out. Once again, the local listings magazines are the best places to look.

Occasional courses in Chinese medicine are held at **Shanghai University of Traditional Chinese Medicine** (☎ 6417 4600). Music courses are held at **Shanghai Music Conservatory** (Map pp246-9).

The informal expat association Big World runs courses in various aspects of Chinese culture, including cooking, t'ai chi and calligraphy. Details are listed in local magazines.

The Mandarin Centre and I Mandarin (see Language above) also run occasional Chinese cultural appreciation classes.

See the Food & Drink chapter (p33) for details of cookery courses.

The popular Beijing-based **Chinese Culture Club** (☎ 6445 9797; www.chineseculture club.org) is setting up a Shanghai branch, which will bring a wide range of cultural classes and lectures by experts in their fields, aimed at expats.

There are several places that offer classes in art and pottery.

Ambiance (Map p256; ☎ 6219 3474; 1438 Hongqiao Lu) Runs a series of classes, from Chinese painting to floral arrangement, for international expats, with kids' courses at 4pm. Contact Maureen Pickering. Costs are Y1700 to Y2500 for a 12- to 20-hour course or Y150 for a day attendance.

Pottery Workshop (Map pp246-9; ☎ 6445 0902; www.ceramics.com.hk; 220 Taikang Lu) Runs children's (One hour, weekends; Y400 per month) and adults' courses (three hours, weekly; Y600 per month).

Shanghai Harvest Studio (Map pp246-9; ☎ 6473 4566; harveststudio108@sina.com; Room 118, No 3 Bldg, 210 Lane, Taikang Lu) Runs Miao embroidery classes from its studio and shop in the Taikang Lu arts development area (p150). Small class tuition costs Y500 per person for four lessons (plus Y150 for materials) or arrange personal tuition (see also p150).

CULTURAL CENTRES & LIBRARIES

The following are useful places to keep you culturally connected to your home country and are also a good place to meet internationally minded Shanghainese.

Alliance Française (Map pp244-5; ☎ 6357 5388; www.alliancefrancaise.org.cn; 5th fl, 297 Wusong Lu) Excellent French films are shown every Friday at 6.30pm and there's unedited TV5 (France's version of CNN), plus a large French library with magazines, newspapers, videos and the occasional exhibition. The centre also offers French language classes and Internet access. Membership is Y120 per year but short-term visitors can just pop in.

British Council (Map pp244-5; ☎ 6391 2626; www.britishcouncil.org.cn; Pidemco Tower, 318 Fuzhou Lu) Of interest mainly to Chinese wishing to study in the UK, but it does have recent British newspapers and music magazines like *Q* and *NME*.

German Centre (Map pp242-3; ☎ 6501 5100; www.germancentreshanghai.com; 1233 Siping Lu) In the middle of nowhere at Tongji University in Shanghai's northeastern suburbs, the centre holds regular consular events and shows German films every Friday night; will be moving to the Zhangjiang district of Pudong.

Goethe Institute (Map pp244-5; ☎ 6391 2068; www.goethe.de/china; Pidemco Tower, 318 Fuzhou Lu)

Shanghai Library (Map pp246-9; ☎ 6445 5555; 1555 Huaihai Zhonglu) This is the biggest library in Asia. For Y25 you can get a reading card valid for up to six months, which allows you to read but not borrow publications. The 3rd floor has a wealth of foreign magazines and newspapers such as *Newsweek* and *National Geographic*. For English books published within the last four years head for the 3rd floor, otherwise you have to track books down on the computer system then order them through the stacks.

US Consulate Bureau of Public Affairs (Map pp250-2; ☎ 6279 7662; Room 532, Shanghai Centre, 1376 Nanjing Xilu) This has a reading room with American newspapers and periodicals.

CUSTOMS

Customs formalities are so streamlined in Shanghai that you won't need to fill in a customs form, even if you are carrying a laptop computer, video camera etc. There are clearly marked 'green channels' and 'red channels'.

Duty-free, you're allowed to import up to: 400 cigarettes or the equivalent in tobacco products; two litres of alcoholic drink; 72 rolls of still film; and 50g of gold or silver. Importation of fresh fruit is prohibited. You can legally bring in or take out only Y6000 in Chinese currency. There are no restrictions on foreign currency; however, you should declare any cash that exceeds US$5000 (or its equivalent in another currency).

It's illegal to import into China printed material, film, tapes etc that are 'detrimental to China's politics, economy, culture and ethics'. But don't be too concerned about what you take to read. Pirated VCDs (video CDs) and CDs are illegal exports from China as well as illegal imports into most other countries. If they are found they will be confiscated.

Antiques over 200 years old may be prohibited from export. To be on the safe side, make sure that you have a receipt and business card from the dealer for anything that you purchase. See the Shopping chapter (p141) for more details.

Our favourite Chinese customs regulation is the one that strictly forbids anyone bringing more than 20 pieces of underwear into the People's Republic of China (PRC).

DEPARTURE TAX

International departure tax (known as an 'airport construction fee') is Y90. The domestic departure tax is Y50. Both taxes are paid at the airport, after check-in. Children under 12 years are exempt.

DISABLED TRAVELLERS

Shanghai's traffic and the city's many over- and underpasses pose the greatest challenges to disabled travellers. The metro system currently isn't wheelchair friendly, though elevator access is increasing.

That said, Shanghai is placing increasing emphasis on accessibility, especially as the city is due to host the 2007 Paralympics. Deng Pufang, eldest son of Deng Xiaoping (and himself a paraplegic), is director of the Chinese Federation for the Disabled and has used his influence to push through many proposals. An increasing number of modern buildings, museums, stadiums and most new hotels display the white symbol of a wheelchair, showing that they are wheelchair accessible. Bashi Taxi has a number of minivan taxis that are wheelchair accessible. All the top-end hotels have wheelchair-accessible rooms. Disabled travellers are advised to travel with at least one able-bodied companion; it's best not to rely on the kindness of the Shanghainese.

China's sign language has regional variations, as well as some elements of American Sign Language (ASL), so foreign signers may have some problems communicating in sign language.

DOCUMENTS

Business name cards are essential, even if you don't do business – exchanging name cards with someone you've just met goes down well. It's particularly good if you can get your name translated into Chinese and have that printed just next to your English name. You can get name cards made cheaply in Shanghai at local printers, but it's better to have some in advance of your arrival.

Student cards can get you cheaper entrance to sites like the Shanghai Museum, and free entry and cheap beers at several clubs in Shanghai.

It might be useful to have a photocopy of your passport and air ticket in the unfortunate event that your originals get lost or stolen.

ELECTRICITY

Electricity is 220v, 50 cycles AC. Plugs come in at least four designs: three-pronged angled pins (as in Australia), three-pronged round pins (as in Hong Kong), two flat pins (US-style but without the ground wire), and two narrow round pins (European-style).

Conversion plugs and voltage converters are easily found if you need to convert from a Chinese to foreign system but are a pain to track down the other way round. Bring all your converters with you.

EMBASSIES & CONSULATES
Chinese Embassies & Consulates

For a full list of diplomatic representation abroad go to the Ministry of Foreign Affairs website at www.fmprc.gov.cn/eng/.

Australia (☎ 02-6273 4780, 6273 4781; www.china embassy.org.au; 15 Coronation Dr, Yarralumla, ACT 2600) Consulates in Sydney (☎ 02-9699 2216; www.chinacon sulatesyd.org), Melbourne (☎ 03-9822 0604) and Perth (08-9321 8193).

Canada (☎ 613-789 3509; www.chinaembassycanada.or g; 515 St Patrick St, Ottawa, Ontario K1N 5H3) Consulates-general in Toronto (☎ 416-964 7260), Vancouver (☎ 604-736 3910) and Calgary (☎ 403-264 3322).

Denmark (☎ 039-625 806; fax 039-625 484; Oregards Alle 25, 2900 Hellerup, Copenhagen)

France (☎ 01 47 36 02 58; fax 01 47 36 34 46; www.amb -chine.fr; 9 Ave Victor Cresson, 92130 Issy-les-Moulineaux, Paris)

Germany (☎ 0228-955 9716; www.china-botschaft.de, German & Chinese only; Kurfürstenallee 12, 53177 Bonn) Consulates in Berlin, Hamburg and Munich.

Ireland (☎ 1269 1707; fax 283 9938; 40 Ailesbury Rd, Ballsbridge, Dublin 4)

Japan (☎ 03-3403 3380, 3403 3065; 3-4-33 Moto-Azabu, Minato-ku, Tokyo 106) Consulates in Fukuoka, Osaka and Sapporo.

Malaysia (☎ 03-242 8495; 229 Jalan Ampang, Kuala Lumpur) Consulate in Kuching.

Netherlands (☎ 070-355 1515; Adriaan Goekooplaan 7, 2517 JX, The Hague)

New Zealand (☎ 04-587 0407; 104A Korokoro Rd, Petone, Wellington) Consulate in Auckland.

Singapore (☎ 734 3361; 70 Dalvey Rd)

South Korea (☎ 743 1491; fax 743 1494; 1 10 Ka Hye Dong, Joungro ku, Seoul)

Thailand (☎ 02-245 7032/49; 57 Th Ratchadaphisek, Bangkok)

UK (☎ 020-7636 8845, 7631 1430, 24 hr premium-rate visa information ☎ 0891-880 808; www.chinese -embassy.org.uk; 31 Portland Place, London W1N 5AG) Consulates-general in Manchester (☎ 0161-224 7480) and Edinburgh (☎ 0131-316 4789). Visas cost £25 and are issued in three days.

USA (☎ 202-338 6688; fax 588 9760; www.china -embassy.org; Room 110, 2201 Wisconsin Ave, NW Washington DC, 20007) Consulates in Chicago (☎ 312-803 0098), Houston (☎ 713-524 4311), Los Angeles

(☎ 213-380 2508), New York (☎ 212-330 7410) and San Francisco (☎ 415-563 9232). Single-/double-entry visas cost US$30/40.

Consulates in Shanghai

There is a growing band of consular missions in Shanghai, some located in the choicest 1930s-style real estate in the city. Your own country's consulate is worth a visit – not just if you've lost your passport, but also for up-to-date newspapers from home and to register if you are staying for a while (some offer this service online). Most consulates defer to their embassies in Beijing; the offices listed below are consulates-general.

Consulates often have useful information packs for long-term residents, covering things like estate agents, lawyers and hospitals. The US Embassy produces a brochure entitled *Tips for Travellers to the People's Republic of China*, which you can get before you travel.

If you are planning a trip to Southeast Asia you'll have to go to Beijing or Hong Kong for a visa for Vietnam, Laos or Myanmar. There is a Vietnamese consulate in Guangzhou, and Thai, Lao and Myanmar embassies in Kunming.

Australia (Map pp250-2; ☎ 5292 5500; www.aus-in -shanghai.com.cn; 22nd fl, CITIC Sq, 1168 Nanjing Xilu) A visa office is located in the Shanghai Centre (☉ 8.30am-noon Mon-Fri).

Canada (Map pp250-2; ☎ 6279 8400; www.shanghai .gc.ca; Suite 604, Shanghai Centre, 1376 Nanjing Xilu)

France (Map pp250-2; ☎ 6289 7414; www.consulfrance -shanghai.org; 1204, United Plaza, 1468 Nanjing Xilu)

Germany (Map pp250-2; ☎ 6217 2884; fax 6271 4650; 18th fl, Jing'an New Century Plaza, 188 Wujiang Lu)

Ireland (Map pp250-2; ☎ 6279 8729; ireland@sh163.net; Room 700A, Shanghai Centre)

Japan (Map p256; ☎ 6278 0788; fax 6278 8988; 8 Wanshan Lu, Hongqiao)

Netherlands (Map p256; ☎ 6209 9076; www.cgshanghai .org; 4th fl, East Tower, Sun Plaza, 88 Xianxia Lu)

New Zealand (Map pp246-9; ☎ 6471 1108; www.nzembassy.com; 15th fl, Qihua Tower, 1375 Huaihai Zhonglu) Visa office in Shanghai Centre (Map pp250-2).

Russia (Map pp244-5; ☎ 6324 8383; fax 6306 9982; 20 Huangpu Lu; ☉ 9.30am-noon Mon, Wed & Fri)

Singapore (Map p256; ☎ 6278 5566; www.mfa.gov.sh /shanghai; 89 Wanshan Lu)

South Korea (Map p256; ☎ 6219 6417; fax 6219 6918;

4th fl, Shanghai International Trade Centre, 2200 Yan'an Xilu)

Thailand (Map pp244-5; ☎ 6323 4095; www.thai shanghai.com; 3rd fl, 7 Zhongshan Dong Yilu, Bund; visa section ☉ 9.30-11.30am, Mon-Fri)

UK (Map pp250-2; ☎ 6279 7650; www.britishconsulate .sh.cn; Room 301, Shanghai Centre, 1376 Nanjing Xilu)

USA (Map pp246-9; ☎ 6433 6880; www.usembassy -china.org.cn/shanghai; 1469 Huaihai Zhonglu, entrance on Wulumuqi Lu) Consular section (US Citizen Services & Visas; Map pp250-2; ☎ 3217 4650, after-hours emergency number for US citizens 6433 3936; 8th fl, Westgate Tower, 1038 Nanjing Xilu).

GAY & LESBIAN TRAVELLERS

Local law is ambiguous on this issue, but generally the authorities take a dim view of gays and lesbians. Certainly a scene exists in Shanghai and has done for a while (WH Auden and Christopher Isherwood investigated gay Shanghai together in 1938) but few dare say so too loudly. While the police tend not to care what foreigners do, things can get heavy when Chinese nationals are involved. Chinese men sometimes hold hands; this carries no sexual overtones in China.

For excellent and up-to-date information on the latest gay and lesbian hot spots in Shanghai and elsewhere throughout China try the **Utopia website** (www.utopia-asia.com /chinshan.htm).

HEALTH

Health concerns for Shanghai include pollution, traveller's diarrhoea and winter influenza. Health facilities have improved enormously over the last 10 years and you can expect to find a more than adequate standard of medical care (see Medical Services, p210) providing you have good travel insurance.

If you have arrived from South America or Central Africa you are required to show proof of a yellow fever vaccination within the last 10 years.

It's a good idea to consult your government's travel health website before departure, if one is available.

Australia (www.dfat.gov.au/travel)

Canada (www.hc-sc.gc.ca/pphb-dgspsp/tmp-pmv/pub _e.html)

New Zealand (www.mfat.govt.nz/travel)

United Kingdom (www.doh.gov.uk/traveladvice)

United States (www.cdc.gov/travel)

Recommended Vaccinations

You should see your doctor at least three months before your trip in order to get your vaccinations in time. The following immunisations are recommended for Shanghai.

Diphtheria and tetanus (DT) 0.5ml every 10 years. It will cause a sore arm and redness at the injection site.

Polio 0.5ml of syrup orally every 10 years. There are no side effects.

Hepatitis A and B (combined in Twinrix) 1ml at Day 1, Day 30 and six months. Minimal soreness at injection site. You are not immune until after the final shot. If you don't have time for the six-month booster you will be fully immune for one year for hepatitis A after the second shot and have some immunity for hepatitis B. You may be able to get the third shot at an international medical clinic while travelling.

Typhoid 0.5ml every three years. Minimal soreness at injection site.

Influenza 0.5ml is recommended if you are travelling in the winter months and especially if you are over 60 years of age or have a chronic illness. It should not be given if you are allergic to eggs. Immunity lasts for one year.

Japanese encephalitis A series of three shots over one month only if you plan on being in rural areas for longer than a month. Immunity will last for three years. As there is a risk of an allergic reaction to the second and third shots you must remain close to medical care after you receive these.

Do not have any of these immunisations if you are pregnant or breastfeeding. It is possible to have a shot of gammaglobulin in pregnancy, which gives short term (four to five months) protection against hepatitis and other viral infections. It is not a common thing to do because it is derived from blood products.

Diseases
AIDS & SEXUALLY TRANSMITTED DISEASES

AIDS is increasing in China and the exact figures are unknown. Always wear a condom if you have sex with a stranger and never share needles.

CHOLERA

This bacterial infection comes in epidemics and is spread from sewage contamination in poverty-stricken areas. It causes profound vomiting and diarrhoea. The World Health Organization stopped recommending the cholera vaccine because it is ineffective. The best way to prevent cholera is to avoid local seafood restaurants, local water and street stall food where hygiene is substandard.

GIARDIASIS

This parasite often jumps on board when you have diarrhoea. It then causes a more prolonged illness with intermittent diarrhoea or looseness, bloating, fatigue and some nausea. There may be a metallic taste in the mouth. You can prevent giardiasis by avoiding potentially contaminated foods and always washing hands before eating. Treatment is with Fasigyn or Flagyl.

HEPATITIS A

This virus is common in Shanghai and is transmitted through contaminated water and shellfish. It is most commonly caught at local seafood restaurants. Immunisation and avoiding suspicious restaurants will avoid it. If you do get hepatitis A it means six to eight weeks of illness and future intolerance to alcohol.

HEPATITIS B

Whilst this is common in the area, it is transmitted only by unprotected sex, sharing needles, treading on a discarded needle, or receiving contaminated blood. You should always use a condom, never share needles, and protect your feet on commonly used beaches. Vaccination against hepatitis B before you travel is a wise option as it can be a chronic, debilitating illness.

INFLUENZA

Shanghai has a bad flu season over the cold winter months from December to March. The flu is a cold but with a high fever and aches and pains. You should wash your hands frequently, avoid anybody you know who has the flu, and think about having a flu shot before you travel. Secondary bronchitis is the most common complication of the flu and may require antibiotics.

JAPANESE ENCEPHALITIS

Mosquitoes that feed on birds carry this potentially fatal virus, hence it is limited to rural areas of China, particularly near rice fields. It is most common in summer and autumn. If you avoid mosquito bites you will not get this! Vaccination is recommended if you are travelling in rural areas for longer than one month.

MALARIA

Prophylactic tablets are required only if you are travelling to remote rural communities below 1500m: from July to November north of latitude 33°N, from May to December between 33°N and 25°N, and throughout the year south of 25°N. For day trips out of Shanghai you do not need tablets, though you should take precautions against bites. Mosquitoes that bite between dusk and dawn transmit malaria, so use your DEET insect repellent often.

TRAVELLER'S DIARRHOEA

This is the most common disease that a traveller will encounter throughout Asia. Many different types of organisms, usually bacteria (eg *E. coli*, salmonella) are responsible and the result is sudden diarrhoea and/or vomiting, with or without fever. It is caught from contaminated food or water. Most locals become immune to the bugs after living in an area for a while so travellers are more at risk, and it usually occurs within the first week of exposure.

TUBERCULOSIS (TB)

The risk of this bacterial infection for travellers is low as it requires prolonged exposure to a weakened immune system to catch it. However, children should have the BCG inoculation if you are going to live in China for longer than six months. Adults should never receive the BCG as it is ineffective against the strains of TB that they are more susceptible to, and can cause a nasty reaction at the injection site.

TYPHOID FEVER

Otherwise known as salmonella, typhoid fever is common throughout China and is caught from faecally contaminated food, milk and water. It manifests as fever, headache, cough, malaise and constipation or diarrhoea. Treatment is with quinolone antibiotics and the vaccine is recommended before you travel.

Environmental Hazards
POLLUTION

The air quality in Shanghai is fair, but getting worse. If you suffer from asthma or other allergies you may anticipate a worsening of your symptoms here and you may need to increase your medication. Eye drops may be a useful addition to your travel kit, and contact lens wearers may have more discomfort here.

WATER

Don't drink tap water or eat ice. Bottled water is readily available. Boiled water is OK.

Online Resources

There is a wealth of travel health advice on the Internet. For further information, the **Lonely Planet website** (www.lonelyplanet.com) is a good place to start. The World Health Organization publishes a superb book, called *International Travel and Health*, which is revised annually and is available online at no cost at www.who.int/ith/.

SARS

The outbreak of SARS (Severe Acute Respiratory Syndrome) in March 2003 was devastating for China; however, it remains a mystery as to how Shanghai avoided the catastrophe. As of June 2003 there were only eight recorded cases in Shanghai compared to thousands in Beijing and Hong Kong.

The diagnostic criteria for SARS are:

- Cough or breathing difficulty
- Fever greater than 38°C
- General malaise or muscle aches
- History of chills in the past two days
- Known history of exposure
- X-ray evidence of pneumonia

Travellers should keep track of the SARS situation in Asia through www.who.int/en/. If you suspect you have SARS based on the above criteria, you should call your nearest public hospital to find out which of the hospitals are accepting possible SARS patients. Many hospitals and doctors' offices will not let you enter if you suspect you have SARS.

HOLIDAYS

New Year's Day (Yuándàn) 1 January

Spring Festival (Chūn Jié) 22 January 2004; 9 February 2005; 29 January 2006. A week-long break, also known as Chinese New Year.

International Women's Day (Fùnǚ Jié) 8 March

International Labour Day (Láodòng Jié) 1 May. A week-long break – the closest thing communists have to a worldwide religious holiday.

Youth Day (Qīngnián Jié) 4 May

Children's Day (Ertóng Jié) 1 June

Anniversary of the Founding of the Chinese Communist Party (Zhōngguó Gòngchǎndǎng Qìng) 1 July

Anniversary of the Founding of the People's Liberation Army (Jiěfàng Jūn Jié) 1 August

National Day (Guóqìng Jié) 1 October. Celebrates the founding of the PRC in 1949, with fireworks over the Bund and a week-long break. Streets in the city centre are often closed.

INSURANCE

It's very likely that a health insurance policy you contribute to in your home country will *not* cover you in China – if unsure, ask your insurance company. If you're not covered, it would be prudent to purchase travel insurance.

The best policies will reimburse you for a variety of mishaps such as accidents, illness, theft and even the purchase of an emergency ticket home. Paying for your air ticket with a credit card often provides limited travel-accident insurance. Ask your credit card company exactly what it covers.

Some backpacker policies offer a cheaper option, which covers only medical cover and not baggage loss, which might be worthwhile if you are not carrying any valuables in your grotty, 10-year-old suitcase. Many policies require you to pay the first US$100 or so anyway and only cover valuables up to a set limit, so if you lose a US$1000 camera you might find yourself only covered for US$350 and having to pay the first US$100!

To make a claim for compensation, you will need proper documentation (hopefully in English). This can include medical reports, police reports and baggage receipts from airlines. You may prefer a policy that pays hospitals directly rather than you having to pay on the spot (often before you receive treatment) and claiming later. Check that the policy covers repatriation and an emergency flight home.

Insurance policies can normally be extended once you are in Shanghai by a phone call or fax (and a credit card). Make sure you do this *before* the policy expires or you may have to pay a more expensive premium.

INTERNET ACCESS

Shanghai is easily the most wired city in China and many businesses and individuals have an address. A major stumbling block is that the government monopolises telecommunications, so only state-run companies offer services.

Foreign companies such as CompuServe have tried to set up local nodes in Shanghai, but the government gives them so little bandwidth that their systems soon overload. As a result, you'll have much difficulty getting on line in Shanghai if you want to use a foreign-based Internet service provider (ISP). If you're travelling with a portable computer and want to access your email, your only alternative may be to make an expensive call to Hong Kong or abroad.

Probably the cheapest way to keep in touch while on the road is to sign up for a free account with **Hotmail** (www.hotmail .com) or **Yahoo** (www.yahoo.com) and access your account from an Internet café.

Email Centres & Internet Cafés

Internet cafés in Shanghai are not as prevalent as they once were due to a government crackdown on unregistered cafés following a fire in an unlicensed Beijing Internet café in July 2002 that left 25 people dead. You now need some form of ID to register. Connections range from lightning fast to maddeningly slow.

Shanghai Library (Map pp246-9) has terminals in the basement and is the cheapest and most pleasant place in the city for Internet use at Y4 per hour (minimum one hour). It's open from 9am to 6pm daily. Bring your passport or ID if you have no library card. Connections are generally pretty fast.

China Telecom (Map pp244-5) on Nanjing Donglu offers Internet access for Y10 per hour from 7am to 10pm daily.

Digital Legend Internet (6th fl, Grand Gateway, Xujiahui) has Internet access inside for Y5 per hour, or on the balcony overlooking the mall for Y7 to Y8.

There are several **Public Internet Clubs** (PIC; Gōngzhòng Diànnǎo Shì) recognisable by their signs. They are mostly dingy places full of kids playing ultraviolent computer games through a thick haze of cigarette smoke, but you can get Web access for around Y3 per hour, though connections can be slow. Internet cafés are constantly in flux.

The huge **Internet Centre** (Zhìgāo Diànwǎng Luòxiūxián Zhōngxīn; Guangyan Lu) near Jiaotong University has access at Y5 to Y8 per hour.

LEGAL MATTERS

China does not officially recognise dual nationality or the foreign citizenship of children born in China if one of the parents is a PRC national. If you have Chinese and another nationality you may in theory not be allowed to visit China on your foreign passport. In practice, Chinese authorities are not switched on enough to know if you own two passports, and will accept you on a foreign passport. Dual-nationality citizens who enter China on a Chinese passport are subject to Chinese laws and are legally not allowed consular help.

China takes a particularly dim view of opium and all its derivatives. Shanghai's foreign concessions owe their entire existence to the 1842 Opium War and many a foreign fortune (including some of Hong Kong's largest companies) was made through the opium trade. Today Shanghai has a growing drug problem, this time in heroin. The city's Uyghur population is largely blamed for heroin trafficking.

Foreign-passport holders have been executed in China for drug offences and one US citizen convicted on drug-related charges received a 15-year prison sentence. Trafficking in more than 50g of heroin can lead to the death penalty. In 1998 another US citizen was sentenced to death, with a two-year reprieve, on a conviction of drug dealing.

Many Uyghurs deal quite openly in marijuana (hashish). It's uncertain what attitude the police would take towards a foreigner caught using marijuana – they often don't care what foreigners do behind closed doors if no Chinese are involved. Then again, Chinese authorities like to make examples of wrongdoers – 'killing the rooster to frighten the monkey' – so steer clear of all drugs if you don't want to become a surrogate rooster.

In the unlikely case that you are arrested, most foreign citizens have the right to phone their embassy. Consuls shall be notified within two days of your arrest and consular officials have the right to visit any detainee within two days of requesting to do so.

MAPS

The best maps of Shanghai are published abroad, though you can normally get them in Shanghai at the **Foreign Languages Bookstore** (p145) and most top-end hotels.

Geocenter's *Shanghai* has a detailed map of central Shanghai, with a street index on the back; the index is particularly useful if you are searching for an address. Periplus is another good choice, with a clear, bilingual 1:15,000 map of Shanghai, an additional 1:85,000 map

of Pudong and inserts of Suzhou, Hangzhou and the surrounding provinces.

Locally made English maps of Shanghai are available from most bookshops. The best two are the *Shanghai Tourist Map*, and the *Shanghai Official Tourist Map* (which has details of Shanghai's main shopping streets). Both are produced by the Shanghai Municipal Tourism Administration. The 'English maps' offered by hawkers on the Bund are usually just a maze of characters.

There is an infinite variety of Chinese-language maps covering every district of Shanghai municipality. You can track these down at any Chinese bookstore.

MEDICAL SERVICES

Shanghai is credited with the best medical facilities and most advanced medical knowledge in China. The main foreign embassies keep lists of the English-speaking doctors, dentists and hospitals that accept foreigners.

Pregnant women travelling to Shanghai should have no specific problems. However it is worth noting that many Westerners living here choose to travel to Hong Kong to have their babies delivered in the private system.

Huashan Hospital (Huáshān Yīyuàn; Map pp246–9; ☎ 6248 9999, ext 1921; 12 Wulumuqi Zhonglu) Hospital treatment and out-patient consultations are available at the 19th-floor foreigners' clinic, which has a Hong Kong joint-venture section.

International Medical Care Centre (IMCC)/Shanghai First People's Hospital (Dìyī Rénmín Yīyuàn; Map pp244–5; ☎ 6306 9480, 6324 0090 ext 2101; 585 Jiulong Lu, northeast Shanghai)

New Pioneer International Medical Centre (NPIMC; Xīnfēng Yīliáo Zhōngxīn; Map p257; ☎ 6469 3898; fax 6469 3897; 2nd fl, Geru Bldg, 910 Hengshan Lu, just north of Xujiahui) Provides comprehensive private medical care by expat doctors as well as dentists and specialists and is affiliated with BUPA International (Britain's largest private medical plan). It can provide individual and corporate health-care plans, home visits, ambulances and evacuation services; the centre is open 24 hours. For nonmembers, expect a doctor's consultation fee of US$70 and an ambulance charge of US$100.

World Link (Ruìxīn Guójì Yīliáo Zhōngxīn; Map pp250–2; ☎ 6279 7688; www.worldlink-shanghai.com; Suite 203, Shanghai Centre, 1376 Nanjing Xilu; ⏱ 9am-7pm Mon-Fri, 9am-4pm Sat, 9am-3pm Sun) Offers similar medical services to NPIMC and also provides family and corporate health plans, Chinese traditional medicine and health-education classes. The consultation fee is US$70. After-hours services and an emergency hotline are provided for members. The Hongqiao clinic (Map p256; ☎ 6405 5788; fax 6405 3587; Unit 30, Mandarine City, 788 Hongxu Lu; ☺ 9am-5pm Mon-Fri) also offers dental work.

Other contacts for medical assistance include:

Australian Clinic (☎ 6433 4604; 17 Fuxing Xilu; ☺ 9am-4.30pm Mon, 9am-1pm Thu & Fri) For Australian-passport holders, though other passport holders can phone for advice on other facilities.

Dr Anderson & Partners (Map p256; ☎ 6270 3263; fax 6209 6099; Room 1001, New Century Plaza, 48 Xingyi Lu, Hongqiao) This private clinic welcomes walk-in patients.

Huadong Hospital (Map pp246-9; ☎ 6248 3180, ext 3106; 221 Yan'an Xilu, 2nd fl, Foreigners Clinic)

International Peace Maternity Hospital (Map p257; ☎ 6438 2434; 910 Hengshan Lu)

Ruijin Hospital (Map pp246-9; ☎ 6437 0045; fax 6431 2610; 197 Ruijin Erlu)

Shanghai Chiropractic & Osteopathic Clinic (Map pp250-2; ☎ 5213 0008; www.scaoc.com; Guobin Medical Centre, Suite 2104, 511 Weihai Lu)

Shanghai Medical University Children's Hospital (Map pp246-9; ☎ 6403 7371; 183 Fenglin Lu) Staff will make house calls.

Dental Services

Shanghai Dental Medical Centre (Map pp254-5; ☎ 6313 3174; fax 6313 9156; 7th fl, 9th People's Hospital, 639 Zhizaoju Lu)

Shanghai Ko Sei Dental Clinic (Map pp246-9; ☎ 6247 6748; 666 Changle Lu) This clinic is a Sino-Japanese joint venture.

Shenda Dental Clinic (☎ 6437 7987; fax 6466 1798; 1, Lane 83, Taiyuan Lu)

World Link (Map p256; ☎ 6405 5788; fax 6405 3587; 788 Hongxu Lu, Hongqiao)

Medical Testing

Foreigners planning to live in Shanghai for a period of six months or more are required to undergo an AIDS test. You can do the test outside China and present the results (on an official Chinese form, stamped by your doctor or hospital) to obtain the required certificate but there is a chance that you may still have to take a local test.

For inquiries and medical tests contact the **Shanghai Health & Quarantine Bureau** (☎ 6286 8851; 1701 Hami Lu).

Traditional Chinese Medicine

Traditional Chinese medicine is extremely popular in Shanghai, both for prevention and cure. There are many Chinese medicine shops, but English is not widely spoken and ingredients are often unknown and from endangered species. Chiropractic care, reflexology and acupuncture are popular, but be sure to check that disposable needles are used.

Dr Li Jie's Chinese Medical Clinic (☎ 3424 1989; 5C Shiye Apts, 28 Caoxi Beilu, Xujiahui)

Longhua Hospital (Map pp242-3; ☎ 6438 5700; 132 Lingling Lu, 1km east of Shanghai Stadium)

Shuguang Hospital (Map pp254-5; ☎ 6326 1650; 185 Pu'an Lu, next to Huaihai Park)

One of Shanghai's most famous Chinese herbal medicine stores is **Cai Tong De** (Map pp244-5), at 450 Nanjing Donglu, with a branch at 396 Jinling Donglu.

MONEY

For information regarding exchange rates see Quick Reference on the inside front cover. The City Life chapter (p7), gives you some idea of costs you are likely to incur during your stay in Shanghai.

ATMs

Most of Shanghai's ATMs now accept foreign credit and debit cards, but the system is not foolproof; save receipts and compare them later with your bank statements. There's a useful 24-hour Citibank ATM next door to the Peace Hotel on the Bund. You can get up to Y2000 with a single transaction. The Shanghai Centre has Hongkong and Shanghai Banking Corporation (HSBC), Bank of China and Industrial and Commercial Bank of China (ICBC) ATMs.

Other Bank of China branches with 24-hour ATMs include: Nanjing Donglu, next to the Peace Hotel (Map pp244-5); Huaihai Lu, at the corner of Huangpi Nanlu (Map pp246-9); 698 Huaihai Zhonglu (Map pp246-9); 1207 Huaihai Zhonglu, near Huating Market (Map pp246-9); Fuzhou Lu, next to the Wugong Hotel (Map pp244-5); and the southwest corner of the Grand Gateway, Xujiahui (Map p257).

The ICBC and the China Construction Bank also have ATMs that take MasterCard and Cirrus, and often other cards. Many of the large department stores have ATMs inside. Look on the back of your card to see which systems are compatible. ATM screens show messages in English and Chinese. Only yuan are dispensed.

Bank Accounts

Foreigners can open both RMB and US dollars bank accounts in China. You do not need to have resident status – a tourist visa is sufficient. Take your passport to a branch of the Bank of China or CITIC to open the account. You can then access the account at any Bank of China branch in Shanghai (but not branches outside Shanghai).

Changing Money

You can change foreign currency and travellers cheques at moneychanging counters at almost every hotel, even cheapies like the Pujiang, and at many shops and department stores, as long as you have your passport. Some top-end hotels will change money only for their guests. Exchange rates in China are uniform, wherever you change money, so there's little need to shop around. The Bank of China charges a 0.75% commission to change cash and travellers cheques.

Hong Kong dollars, Japanese yen, Australian dollars and most Western European currencies can be changed at major banks, but US dollars are still the easiest to change.

Whenever you change foreign currency into Chinese currency you will be given a money-exchange voucher recording the transaction. You need to show this to change yuan back into foreign currency. Changing Chinese currency outside China is a problem, though it's easily done in Hong Kong.

The enormous main branch of the **Bank of China** (Map pp244-5), right next to the Peace Hotel, tends to get crowded, but is the best place for tricky things like transfers (and it's worth a peek for its grand interior). Most Bank of China branches are open on weekdays from 9.30am to 11.30am, and 1pm to 4pm.

American Express (Map pp250-2; ☎ 6279 8082; Room 206, Shanghai Centre, 1376 Nanjing Xilu) is open from 9am to 5.30pm on weekdays and between 9am and noon on Saturday. Amex cardholders can cash personal cheques with their card at branches of the Bank of China, China International Trust & Investment Corporation (CITIC), Industrial Bank or the Bank of Communications.

Credit Cards

Credit cards are more readily accepted in Shanghai than in other parts of China. Most tourist hotels will accept major credit cards such as Visa, Amex, MasterCard, Diners and JCB, as will banks, upper-end restaurants, friendship stores and tourist-related shops, airlines and most travel agencies. Credit hasn't caught on among most Chinese and most local credit cards are in fact debit cards.

Credit-card cash advances are commonplace at Bank of China branches. A 3% commission is deducted and you can get the money within minutes in US dollars or Chinese yuan.

The following are emergency contact numbers in case you lose your card.

American Express (☎ 6279 8082; ⊙ 9am-5.30pm) Out of business hours call the 24-hour refund line in Hong Kong (☎ 852-2811 6122).

MasterCard (☎ 108-00-110 7309)

Visa (☎ 108-00-110 2911)

Currency

The Chinese currency is known as Renminbi (RMB), or 'people's money'. Formally the basic unit of RMB is the *yuán* (Y), which is divided into 10 *jiǎo*, which again is divided into 10 *fēn*. In spoken Chinese the yuan is referred to as *kuài* and jiao as *máo*. The fen has so little value these days that it is rarely used.

The Bank of China issues RMB bills in denominations of two, five, 10, 50 and 100 yuan. Coins are in denominations of one yuan, five jiao and one, two and five fen. There are still a lot of paper versions of the coins floating around, but these will gradually disappear in favour of the coins. New-style bills were introduced in 2000; both old and new bills are legal tender.

International Transfers

You can have money wired to and from a Bank of China account (see Bank Accounts above) but the process is still vulnerable to hitches. You may need to find out the details of the clearing bank used by your bank to send money to China. If US dollars are wired you can withdraw US currency.

Western Union (☎ 800-820 8668, 021-6864 4548) operates through its Chinese partner China Courier Service Corp (CCSC). There is a service fee of 0.5% and you can pick up the money (in US dollars or RMB only) on presentation of your passport at any of their offices, including the international post office on Sichuan Beilu or the Agricultural Bank.

Security

A money belt or pockets sewn inside your clothes are the safest ways to carry money. Waist bags are popular but just advertise all your goodies. Be particularly careful of pickpockets in crowded markets, buses and the train station.

It pays to not keep all your money in one place. Keep an emergency stash of money (say US$100) buried deep in your luggage or in your hotel safe with a record of the serial numbers of your travellers cheques, and your passport number.

Travellers Cheques

Besides the advantage of security, travellers cheques are useful to carry in China because the exchange rate is actually more favourable than what you get for cash. You can even cash US dollars travellers cheques into US dollars cash for the standard 0.75% commission.

Cheques from most of the world's leading banks and issuing agencies are now acceptable in China – stick to the major companies such as Thomas Cook, American Express and Citibank and you'll be OK. You can buy US dollars or RMB travellers cheques from the Bank of China at a commission of 1.5% (cash) or 4% (credit card).

NEWSPAPERS & MAGAZINES

In the late 1990s, life for foreigners in Shanghai improved considerably with the appearance of entertainment publications edited and compiled by native speakers of English. If you want to know what's going on in Shanghai, these are your best sources of information. They're free and available in most of the Western-style bars and restaurants and some hotels. The classified sections are a good place to find a flat, a VCD for sale, language teachers and even a job.

The most comprehensive is the glossy monthly magazine *That's Shanghai* (www.thats shanghai.com), the Shanghai equivalent of London's *Time Out*, packed with cultural info and entertainment listings. *City Weekend* is another excellent listings magazine.

The monthly *Shanghai Talk*, put out by Ismay Publications, is another excellent insight

into Shanghai's cultural life and entertainment scene. *Quo* is an artsier magazine but also with Shanghai listings, as is *Metro*. *Shanghai Scene* has a more expat focus.

Shanghai's other English-language papers and periodicals appear anaemic by comparison. Apart from the national *China Daily*, there is the more locally focused but equally insipid *Shanghai Daily* (www.shanghaidaily.com). The *Shanghai Star* (www.shanghai-star.com.cn), owned by *China Daily*, comes out weekly and is the best of the bunch, with listings of events, hotel buffets and airline schedules.

Several foreign newspapers and magazines are available from the larger tourist hotels (eg Park, Jinjiang, Hilton) and some shops. They are relatively expensive, however, with *Newsweek* and *Time* usually costing about Y35, and the *Far Eastern Economic Review* double this. The bookshop at the Hilton stocks German newspapers.

The **China National Publications Import & Export Co** (Map pp250-2; ☎ 6255 4199; 555 Wuding Lu) can arrange subscriptions to more than 400 periodicals from around the world.

PHARMACIES

The Hong Kong store **Watson's** (Qūchénshì; Map pp246-9, 787 Huaihai Zhonglu; Map pp244-5, Nanjing Donglu near the Ramada Plaza Hotel; Map pp250-2, Westgate Mall) sells imported toiletries and over-the-counter pharmaceuticals. For contact lens solution and the like try one of the many branches of **America's Eyes** (p143) .

For harder-to-find foreign medicines try the **Shanghai No 1 Dispensary** (Map pp244-5; 616 Nanjing Donglu) or the 24-hour **Huashan Pharmacy** (Huáshān Yàofáng; Map pp246-9) outside the Huashan Hospital on Wulumuqi Zhonglu.

PHOTOGRAPHY

Big-name colour print film (Kodak, Fuji etc) is available almost everywhere, but is mostly 100 ISO. Black-and-white film can be found at a few select photo shops, but it's expensive to process in Shanghai. Costs are around Y20 for 36-exposure 100 ISO Kodak print film. Slide film *(fanzhuanpiàn)* is relatively easy to get in Shanghai. A roll of 36 exposures costs from Y45 for 100 ISO Elite Chrome to Y59 for 100 ISO Sensia. Grey weather can last for weeks, especially in winter, so it's worth having a range of film speeds.

Film processing is available everywhere, courtesy of the Kodak franchising empire, but it's not especially cheap. It costs around Y34 for 36 prints (10cm by 15cm). Slide processing costs around Y65 to Y87 for 36 exposures for a standard next-day service. For where to buy and process film see p146.

Lithium batteries can be found at photo shops, but you should always carry a spare. There are instant passport photos booths at most metro stations.

POST

The larger tourist hotels and foreign business towers have post offices from where you can mail letters and small packages, and this is by far the most convenient option.

Shanghai's **international post office** (Map pp244-5) is a fine old British building (built 1924) at the corner of Sichuan Beilu and Bei Suzhou Lu. The section for stamps and poste restante is on the upper floor. Parcels and customs are located downstairs at counter No 11, packing

materials are at counter No 17. Express Mail Service (EMS) is at No 5. The international mail counters are open daily from 7am to 7pm, until 10pm in the upstairs room.

Letters take about a week to reach most overseas destinations; EMS cuts this down to three or four days. Courier companies can take as little as two days.

The international post office is the easiest place from which to send parcels. Bear in mind that most countries impose a maximum weight limitation (10kg is typical) on packages received. If you have a receipt for the goods, then put it in the box when you're mailing it, since it may be opened again by customs further down the line.

Courier Companies

Several foreign courier companies operate in China, in joint ventures. Prices seem fairly standard. An express document of 500g costs Y210/220 to the USA/UK, plus Y80 per additional 500g. Australia is slightly cheaper at Y189, plus Y55 per additional 500g. Packages are a little pricier at Y300/320 to the USA/Europe, plus Y80 per additional 500g. Australia is Y260, plus Y55. Express documents can take as little as two days to arrive.

The following companies offer door-to-door pick-up and delivery.

DHL (☎ 6536 2900, 800-810 8000; www.dhl.com)

Shanghai Central Plaza (Map pp246-9; 381 Huaihai Zhonglu) **Shanghai Centre** (Map pp250-2; 1376 Nanjing Xilu) **Shanghai International Trade Centre** (Map p256; 2200 Yan'an Xilu, Hongqiao) Offices also in Hangzhou and Suzhou.

UPS (Map pp246-9; ☎ 6391 5599; Room 1318-38, Shanghai Central Plaza, 381 Huaihai Zhonglu)

Postal Rates

Like elsewhere, registered mail costs extra in China, but cheaper postal rates are available for printed matter, small packets, parcels, bulk mailings and so on.

An airmail letter costs Y5.40 to Y6.40 for around 20g to all countries except Hong Kong, Macau and Taiwan (Y2.50). A postcard costs Y4.20 (Y1.5 to Hong Kong). A domestic letter/postcard costs Y0.80/Y0.30.

EXPRESS MAIL SERVICE

Domestic EMS parcels up to 200g cost Y15; each additional 200g costs Y5. Sample mini-

MOVING TO SHANGHAI

These companies can box it up, ship it over, deal with customs officers, and deliver to your new home, though officially only if you have local residency. Prices vary from around US$275 to US$500 per cubic metre, depending on the destination and how much you have to ship.

Asia-Pacific Worldwide Movers (☎ 6209 6690; aspac@mail.online.sh.cn; Room 1808, Block 1, 1024 Hongqiao Lu)

Asian Express International Movers (☎ 6258 2244; www.aemovers.com.hk; Room 1403-A, Xincheng Bldg, 167 Jiangning Lu)

Crown Relocations (☎ 6472 0254; www.crown relo.com; 6303-5 Ruijin Business Centre, 118 Ruijin Erlu)

Schenker (☎ 5292 5088; www.schenker.com; 13th fl, CITIC Sq, 1168 Nanjing Xilu)

Sino Santa Fe (☎ 6233 9700; www.santaferelo .com; 5th fl, Tianhong Bldg, 80 Xianxia Lu, Hong-qiao)

For moves within Shanghai or elsewhere in China try **Linmin Home Moving Service** (☎ 6377 1260; 1470 Zhongshan Nanlu)

mal rates (up to 500g parcels) overseas include Australia (Y164), Hong Kong and Macau (Y94), USA (Y184) and UK (Y224), with each additional 500g Y75 to the US/UK or Y55 to Australia to a maximum of 30kg.

PARCELS

Albert Einstein may have developed the theory of relativity but he would not have stood a chance against China Post's system of pricing international parcels. All we can say is that the system works well and that it's not all that cheap. Prices vary from Y148 to Y167 to send a 1kg parcel airmail to Australia, the UK or USA. After this, for every extra 500g add on Y54 to Australia, Y84 to the US and Y90 to the UK, and then expect the final amount due to be completely different! Airmail carries a maximum of 20kg.

RADIO

The BBC World Service can be picked up on 17760, 15278, 21660, 12010 and 9740 kHz. Voice of America (VOA) is often a little clearer at 17820, 15425, 21840, 15250, 9760, 5880 and 6125 kHz. You can find tuning information for the BBC on the Web at www.bbc.co.uk /worldservice/tuning/, for Radio Australia at www.abc.net.au/ra/, and for VOA at www .voa.gov/.

SAFETY

The crime rate is really quite low in Shanghai; even the taxi drivers don't try to rip you off. One of the most unsavoury parts of town lies around the train station, where many migrant workers end up scraping a living until they get proper jobs.

If you do get something stolen you need to report the crime at the district PSB office and get a police report. If you have something stolen on the metro, the Renmin Square metro station has its own PSB office.

Traffic is a major danger in Shanghai; it is essential to look in five directions at once (including above you, in case of falling construction debris) whenever you cross the street. Don't ever expect any vehicle to stop for you. Shanghai's most annoying traffic problem is the swarm of mopeds and bikes that weave up and down the pavements dodging pedestrians (because certain sections of Shanghai's roads are off-limits to bikes).

TAXES

All four- and five-star hotels and some top-end restaurants add a tax or 'service charge' of 10% or 15%, which extends to the room and food; all other consumer taxes are included in the price tag.

TELEPHONE

China's phone system is generally excellent and in Shanghai you are never far from an international-dialling phone of some description. Shanghai's **main telecommunications building** (Map pp244-5) is at the corner of Yan'an Zhonglu and Huangpi Lu.

Long-distance phone calls can be placed from hotel rooms and don't take long to get through, though you pay for this with a surcharge of up to 30% and sometimes a three-minute minimum. You may have to ask the hotel staff for the dial-out code for a direct line. The usual procedure is that you make the call and someone comes to your room five or 10 minutes later to collect the cash. Local calls are normally free.

If you are expecting a call to your hotel room, try to advise the caller beforehand of your room number as operators frequently have trouble with Western names. Otherwise, inform the receptionist that you are expecting a call and write down your name and room number.

Apart from card phones (see Phonecards p216) the other major form of public phone is just a phone attached to a magazine booth or small shop. Just pick up the phone, make your call, and then pay the attendant (usually five máo for a local call).

A variant of this, found in many bars and hotels, is an oversized white phone with a slot for coins on top. Local calls from these phones cost Y1 per minute, Y0.5 with a phone (IC) card.

Long-distance calls and faxes can also be made from any telecom office. A useful 24-hour telecom office is conveniently located next to the Peace Hotel at 30 Nanjing Donglu.

Most international calls cost Y8.2 per minute or Y2.2 to Hong Kong. You are generally required to leave a Y200 deposit for international calls.

It's relatively easy to buy a mobile phone from China Telecom and then use pay-as-you-go cards that slot into the phone. Many hotels have mobile phone chargers in the lobby.

A one-page fax sent from the post office costs Y2 plus the cost of the phone call. Expect a one-page fax transmission to take up to three minutes. Hotel business centres cost much more and add on a service charge.

The English-language Shanghai Yellow Pages is available at most business centres or online at www.yellowpage.com.cn.

Home Country Direct

Another option is to dial the home country direct dial number (☎ 108), and then your country code, which puts you straight through to a local operator in that country. You can then make a reverse-charge (collect) call or a credit-card call with a telephone credit card valid in the destination country. Several top-end hotels like the Westin Taipingyang and the Garden Hotel have home country direct phones in the lobby that put you through to an operator in Canada, the UK, Japan, Hong Kong or the USA at the touch of a button.

Dialling codes include:

Country	Direct dial	Home country direct
Australia	☎ 00-61	☎ 108-610
Canada	☎ 00-1	☎ 108-1
France	☎ 00-33	☎ 108-330
Hong Kong	☎ 00-852	☎ 108-852
Japan	☎ 00-81	☎ 108-810
Netherlands	☎ 00-31	☎ 108-310
New Zealand	☎ 00-64	☎ 108-640
UK	☎ 00-44	☎ 108-440
USA	☎ 00-1	☎ 108-1*

* For the USA you can dial ☎ 108-11 (AT&T), ☎ 108-12 (MCI) or ☎ 108-13 (Sprint).

Phonecards

Telephone (IC) cards, available from any China Telecom office, can be used in public phones along the main streets, in telecom offices and in most hotels. Cards come in denominations of Y20, Y50, Y100 and Y200, and there are two kinds: one for use only in Shanghai, the other nation-wide.

A recent innovation is the Internet phonecard (IP), which works in the same way as a prepaid phonecard but connects via the Internet. You can use any home phone and some public phones (but not card phones) to dial a special telephone number and then a password (there are English and Chinese instructions). The main advantage here is the cost, currently Y2.4 per minute to North America and Y3.2 to most other countries, about a third of the price of a traditional phone call. There is

an additional charge of Y0.1 per minute to be paid to the local phone. Cards can be bought in a growing number of shops around Shanghai as well as the main telecommunications building on Yan'an Zhonglu. Cards come in denominations of Y50, Y100, Y200 and Y500. Again, some cards are valid for most major cities in China, while others can only be used in Shanghai, so make sure you buy the right one (and check the expiry date).

TV

Expats and travellers staying in mid-range and top-end hotels can get their fix of CNN, ESPN and Star TV. For the rest of us it's slim pickings.

Record-breaking grain harvests and other encouraging news about Shanghai's development is broadcast in English on Shanghai Broadcasting Network (SBN) on weekdays at 10pm. CCTV4 has a slightly better English-language news programme on weekdays at 7pm and 11pm, and at noon on the weekend. CCTV9 is an English-language cable channel.

TIME

Time throughout China is set to Beijing local time, which is eight hours ahead of GMT/UTC. There is no daylight-saving time. When it's noon in Shanghai, it's 8pm (the day before) in Los Angeles, 11pm (the day before) in Montreal and New York, 4am (the same day) in London, 5am in Frankfurt, Paris and Rome, noon in Hong Kong, 2pm in Melbourne, and 4pm in Wellington.

TIPPING

China is one of those wonderful countries where tipping is generally unexpected and is even discouraged by the authorities. However, Shanghai has always been open to Western ideas and keen to make a buck, so staff are becoming used to it in fancy restaurants, where most people round up the bill. In general there is no need to tip if a service charge has already been added.

TOILETS

Shanghai has plenty of public toilets, normally marked by English signs; they run the gamut from a communal ditch costing three *máo* to a flash computer-controlled portaloo for Y1. The best bet is to head for a top-end hotel, where someone will hand you a towel, pour you some aftershave or exotic hand lotion and wish you a nice day.

The golden rule is: always carry an emergency stash of toilet paper – you never know when you'll need it. You can often buy a piece of industrial-strength cardboard at a public toilet but this is a worst-case scenario.

Toilets are generally sitters not squatters, especially in hotels, museums etc. In all but the cheapest hotels it's safe to flush toilet paper down the toilet. If you see a small wastepaper basket in the corner of the toilet, that is where you should throw the toilet paper. Tampons always go in the basket.

Remember, the Chinese characters for men and women are:

men: 男   women: 女

TOURIST OFFICES

Shanghai operates **Tourist Information Centres** (☎ 6439 8947, 6439 9806) in the metro stations at the Shanghai train station and **Renmin Square** (☎ 6438 1693), with a third in the international arrivals hall of **Hongqiao airport** (☎ 6268 8899). The staff at these centres are professional and polite, and sell maps of Shanghai published in many languages.

In addition to this, there are a further dozen or so Tourist Information and Service Centres (Lǚyóu Zīxún Fúwù Zhōngxīn) around Shanghai. The level of information and standard of English varies from good to nonexistent. All are due to have touch-screen computerised information. Locations include:

Huangpu (Map pp244-5; ☎ 5353 1117; Century Sq, 561 Nanjing Donglu; ◔ 9.30am-8pm)

Jing'an (Map pp250-2; ☎ 6253 4058; 1612 Nanjing Xilu)

Luwan (Map pp246-9; ☎ 6372 8330, 6318 1882; 127 Chengdu Nanlu, just off Huaihai Zhonglu)

Pudong (Map pp242-3; ☎ 6475 0593; 541 Dongfang Lu)

Shanghai train station (Map pp250-2; ☎ 5623 4880)

Yuyuan Gardens (Map pp254-5; ☎ 6355 5032; 149 Jiujiaochang Lu southwest of Yuyuan Gardens)

The **Tourist Hotline** (☎ 6253 4058; ◔ 10am-9pm) has a useful English-language service.

UNIVERSITIES

Shanghai has some of China's finest universities and with its international outlook, good entertainment scene and general modernity, it's a fairly popular place for foreigners looking to study Chinese.

Two of the most famous universities in Shanghai are **Fudan University** (Fùdàn Dàxué; ☎ 6549 2222; 220 Handan Lu), the biggest and best of Shanghai's universities, and **Tongji University** (Tóngjì Dàxué, ☎ 6598 1057; 1239 Siping Lu). Both are way out in Shanghai's northeastern suburbs (Map pp242-3). Around here you'll find the majority of Shanghai's foreign students, as well as a collection of local student bars and restaurants.

VISAS

Visas are easily obtainable from Chinese embassies and consulates in most Western countries. Most tourists are issued with a single-entry visa, valid for entry within three months of the date of issue, for a 30-day stay.

Directory – Practicalities

Top Travel Websites

- **That's Shanghai** (www.thatsshanghai.com) An excellent guide to what's happening in Shanghai entertainment.
- **City Weekend** (www.cityweekend.com.cn) Excellent listings website with searchable database of articles.
- **Shanghai-Ed** (www.shanghai-ed.com) Everything from what's on to historical essays, though parts are a bit outdated.
- **Tales of Old China** (www.talesofoldchina.com) Lots of reading on Old Shanghai, with the text of hard to find books on line.
- **Expat Shanghai** (www.expatsh.com) A must-see if you are thinking of relocating to Shanghai, though some links don't work.
- **Asia Expat Shanghai** (http://shanghai.asiaxpat.com) Another site aimed at expats; you can ask an expert if you have a specific query.
- **Shanghai Hotels** (www.shanghaihotels.com) Hotel bookings and restaurant reviews.
- **Shanghai Guide** (www.shanghaiguide.com) Good collection of links, though info is patchy, with some very dated news articles.

The easiest place to get a visa is probably Hong Kong (see below).

Processing times and fees depend on where you're applying, but normally visas take three working days. Express services cost twice the normal fee. Fees are normally paid in cash at the time of application and you'll need two passport photos.

On the visa application you must identify an itinerary and entry/exit dates and points, though nobody will hold you to them once you're in the country. To avoid snags, don't mention Tibet or give your occupation as journalist or writer. The visa you end up with is the same regardless.

Chinese embassies abroad have been known to stop issuing visas to independent travellers during the height of summer or in the run-up to sensitive political events or conferences, in an attempt to control the numbers of tourists entering China at peak times.

Visas valid for longer than 30 days are often difficult to obtain anywhere other than in Hong Kong, though some embassies abroad (for example, in the UK) may give you a 60-day visa outside the high tourist season if you ask nicely.

If you request it, you can also receive a double-entry or multiple-entry travel visa (each entry valid for 30 days) or sometimes a single-entry three-month visa. These visas cost more than the standard 30-day visa, but may be worth it, depending on your itinerary. Note that if your itinerary takes you to China, Hong Kong and then back to Shanghai you will need a double-entry visa to get 'back' into China, even though Hong Kong returned to Chinese rule in 1997. If you have trouble getting more than 30 days or a multiple-entry visa, head to a visa or travel agency in Hong Kong.

Note that a 30-day visa is activated on the date you enter China, and must be used within three months of the date of issue. Longer-stay visas often start from the day they are issued, not the day you enter the country, so you should double-check this.

Officials in China are sometimes confused over the validity of the visa and look at the 'valid until' date. On most 30-day visas, however, this is actually the date by which you must have *entered* the country, not left.

A business visa is multiple-entry and valid for three to six months from the date of issue, depending on how much you paid for it. Until recently these visas allowed stays of only 30 days each visit but now they allow you to stay

for the full six months. These visas are easy to get – you do not need to prove that you will be doing business – but are hard to extend. Even so, you'd be surprised how many businesspeople are in Shanghai on a tourist visa!

When you check into a hotel, there is usually a question on the registration form asking what type of visa you have. The letter specifying your visa category is usually stamped on the visa itself. There are seven categories of visas, as follows:

Type	Description	Chinese name
L	Travel	lǚxíng
F	Business or student	fǎngwèn (less than 6 months)
D	Resident	dìngjū
G	Transit	guòjìng
X	Long-term student	liúxué
Z	Working	rènzhí
C	Flight attendant	chéngwù

Getting a Visa in Hong Kong

Hong Kong is a favourite place for Shanghai residents and businesspeople to renew a visa and pick up some imported goodies like coffee and books at the same time.

Chinese visas are most cheaply processed at the **Visa Office** (☎ 2585 1794, 2585 1700; Ministry of Foreign Affairs of the People's Republic of China; 5th floor, Low Block, China Resources Bldg, 26 Harbour Rd, Wanchai). Fees are HK$100 (single entry), HK$150 (double entry) or HK$200 (multiple entry). US-passport holders face an additional surcharge. Visas are issued within two or three working days. Same-day and 24-hour service are more than double the price. The office is open Monday to Friday 9am to 12.30pm and 2pm to 5pm, and on Saturday from 9am to 12.30pm.

The easiest place to get a visa is through **CITS** (☎ 2315 7188; 27-33 Nathan Rd, Tsim Sha Tsui). There's a branch office at the Hung Hom train station and the head office (☎ 2853 3533) is on the 4th floor of CTS House, 78-83 Connaught Rd, Central. Single-entry 90-day tourist visas cost HK$160 for processing within three working days, or HK$210 for two working days (which means next-day pick-up if you hand in your application before 3pm). The office can get you six-month multiple-entry business visas for HK$850/1050 in three/two working days, though you need to supply the business card of someone in China and have a stamp in your passport proving that you have been to China before. US-passport holders face an additional HK$160 surcharge.

Residence Permit

The 'green card' is a residence permit issued to English teachers, businesspeople, students and other foreigners who are authorised to live in the PRC. Green cards are issued for a period of six months to one year, depending on the status of your employer.

To get a residence permit you first need to arrange a work permit (normally obtained by your employer), health certificate (see p211) and temporary 'Z' visa. If your employer is switched on you can arrange all of this before you arrive in Shanghai.

You then need to go to the PSB office with your passport, health certificate, work permit, your employer's business registration licence or representative office permit, your employment certificate (from the Shanghai Labour Bureau), the temporary residence permit of the hotel or local PSB where you are registered, a handful of passport photos and a letter of application from your employer. You must pay a fee of around Y400 in RMB.

In all, the process usually takes from two to four weeks. Expect to make several visits and always carry multiple copies of every document you can think of. Each member of your family needs a residence permit and visa. In most cases your employer will take care of much of the process for you.

Visa Extensions

Extensions of 30 days are given for any tourist visa, though you may have to present proof of registration, either at a hotel, or if you are staying in a flat, with your local PSB office. You may be able to wangle more, especially with cogent reasons such as illness or transport delays, but second extensions are usually only granted for one week, on the understanding that you are on your way out of China. Visa extensions take three days to be issued and cost Y100 for Australians, Y160 for British and French, and Y125 for Americans. The penalty for overstaying your visa is a fine of up to Y300 per day.

To extend a business visa, you need a letter from a Chinese work unit willing to sponsor you. If you're studying in China, your school can of course sponsor you for a visa extension.

Visa extensions are available from the **PSB office** (Gōngānjú; Map pp244-5; ☎ 6357 7925;

333 Wusong Lu, near the intersection with Kunshan Lu; ⊗ 9-11.30am & 1.30-4.30pm Mon-Sat; bus 61 from the intersection of Wusong Lu & Tiantong Lu, 55 from the Bund).

Visa-Free Transit

In January 2000 Shanghai announced that all overseas travellers who are connecting to an onward flight are allowed 24 hours visa-free transit through Shanghai. The regulation is primarily aimed at travellers transferring between Hongqiao and Pudong airports, but it applies to anyone. Travellers from the US, Canada, Australia, New Zealand, Japan, Korea and most European countries (but not the UK) are allowed a longer transit of 48 hours, and other countries may follow. There is no charge for transit. You should double-check this with the Chinese embassy and airlines as not many people seem to know about this loophole.

WEIGHTS & MEASURES

The metric system is widely used in China. However, traditional Chinese weights and measures persist, especially in local markets. Fruit and vegetables are weighed by the *jīn* (500g). Smaller weights (for dumplings, tea, herbal medicine etc) are measured in *liǎng* (50g).

Metric	Chinese	Imperial
1m *(mǐ)*	3 *chǐ*	3.28 feet
1km *(gōnglǐ)*	2 *lǐ*	0.62 miles
1L *(gōngshēng)*	1 *shēng*	0.22 gallons
1kg *(gōngjīn)*	2 *jīn*	2.2 pounds

WORK

It's not too difficult to find work in Shanghai, though technically you cannot work without a work visa. You may have to line up a job and then take a trip to Hong Kong to catch up on the paperwork. You should arrive in Shanghai with enough funds to keep you going for at least a few weeks until a job opens up. Bear in mind that most big companies tend to recruit from home, offering comfortable expat packages.

Volunteering

Several foreign-run charities exist in Shanghai, for those who wish to contribute something back to the city.

China Volunteers United (☎ 6464 0180; www.cvu.org.cn) Coordinates several volunteer opportunities in the Shanghai community.

Friends of Hope (☎ 6384 0609; www.projecthopehk.org /foh) Supports and raises money for Project Hope, a US programme aimed at raising levels of health care in China.

Projects in Shanghai include a children's medical centre. Volunteers also teach English to hospital staff.

Shanghai Sunrise (www.shanghaisunrise.com) Arranges for expats to sponsor the education of a local underprivileged child for about Y2500 per year, and also provides education and library materials. Volunteers are needed to help find sponsors, organise libraries and visit children's homes.

Language

Language

It's true – anyone can speak another language. Don't worry if you haven't studied languages before or that you studied a language at school for years and can't remember any of it. It doesn't even matter if you failed English grammar. After all, that's never affected your ability to speak English! And this is the key to picking up a language in another country. You just need to start speaking.

Learn a few key phrases before you go. Write them on pieces of paper and stick them on the fridge, by the bed or even on the computer – anywhere that you'll see them often.

You'll find that locals appreciate travellers trying their language, no matter how muddled you may think you sound. So don't just stand there, say something! If you want to learn more Mandarin than we've included here, pick up a copy of Lonely Planet's comprehensive but user-friendly *Mandarin phrasebook*.

PRONUNCIATION
Pinyin
In 1958 the Chinese adopted a system of writing their language using the Roman alphabet, known as *pīnyīn*. Pinyin is often used on shop fronts, street signs and advertising billboards, but very few Chinese are able to read or write it.

A few consonants in pinyin may cause confusion when compared to their counterparts in English:

c	as the 'ts' in 'bits'
ch	as in 'chop', but with the tongue curled back
q	as the 'ch' in 'cheese'
r	as the 's' in 'pleasure'
sh	as in 'ship', but with the tongue curled back
x	as the 'sh' in 'ship'
z	as the 'dz' sound in 'suds'
zh	as the 'j' in 'judge', but with the tongue curled back

Tones
Chinese is a language with a large number of words with the same pronunciation but a different meaning; what distinguishes them are 'tones' – rises and falls in the pitch of the voice on certain syllables. The word *ma*, for example, has four different meanings depending on tone:

high tone	mā	(mother)
rising tone	má	(hemp, numb)
falling-rising tone	mǎ	(horse)
falling tone	mà	(to scold, to swear)

Mastering tones is tricky for newcomers to Mandarin, but with a little practice it gets a lot easier.

SOCIAL
Meeting People
Hello.
nǐ hǎo — 你好
Goodbye.
zàijiàn — 再见
Please.
qǐng — 请
Thank you.
xièxie — 谢谢
Thank you very much.
tài xièxie le — 太谢谢了
Yes.
shìde — 是的
No. (don't have)
méi yǒu — 没有
No. (not so)
búshì — 不是
Do you speak English?
nǐ huì shuō yīngyǔ ma? — 你会说英语吗？
Do you understand?
dǒng ma? — 懂吗？
I understand.
wǒ tīngdedǒng — 我听得懂
I don't understand.
wǒ tīngbudǒng — 我听不懂

Could you please ...?
nǐ néng bunéng ...
你能不能 ...？

repeat that		6	liù 六
chóngfù 重复		7	qī 七
speak more slowly		8	bā 八
màn diǎnr shuō 慢点儿说		9	jiǔ 九
write it down		10	shí 十
xiě xiàlái 写下来		11	shíyī 十一
		12	shí'èr 十二

Going Out

What's on ...?
... yǒu shénme yúlè huódòng?
... 有什么娱乐活动?
  locally
  běndì 本地
  this weekend
  zhège zhōumò 这个周末
  today
  jīntiān 今天
  tonight
  jīntiān wǎnshang 今天晚上

Where are the ...?
... zài nǎr?
... 在哪儿?
  clubs
  jùlèbù 俱乐部
  gay venues
  tóngxìngliàn chángsuǒ 同性恋场所
  places to eat
  chīfàn de dìfang 吃饭的地方
  pubs
  jiǔbā 酒吧

Is there a local entertainment guide?
yǒu dāngdì yúlè zhǐnán ma?
有当地娱乐指南吗?

PRACTICAL
Question Words

Who?
shuí 谁
What?
shénme 什么
When?
shénme shíhou 什么时候
Where?
nǎr 哪儿
How?
zěnme 怎么

Numbers & Amounts

1	yī/yāo	一/幺
2	èr/liǎng	二/两
3	sān	三
4	sì	四
5	wǔ	五

13	shísān 十三
14	shísì 十四
15	shíwǔ 十五
16	shíliù 十六
17	shíqī 十七
18	shíbā 十八
19	shíjiǔ 十九
20	èrshí 二十
21	èrshíyī 二十一
22	èrshíèr 二十二
30	sānshí 三十
31	sānshíyī 三十一
40	sìshí 四十
50	wǔshí 五十
60	liùshí 六十
70	qīshí 七十
80	bāshí 八十
90	jiǔshí 九十
100	yìbǎi 一百
200	liǎngbǎi 两百
1000	yìqiān 一千
2000	liǎngqiān 两千
10,000	yíwàn 一万
20,000	liǎngwàn 两万
100,000	shíwàn 十万
200,000	èrshíwàn 二十万

Days

Monday
xīngqīyī 星期一
Tuesday
xīngqīèr 星期二
Wednesday
xīngqīsān 星期三
Thursday
xīngqīsì 星期四
Friday
xīngqīwǔ 星期五
Saturday
xīngqīliù 星期六
Sunday
xīngqītiān 星期天

Banking

I'd like to ...
wǒ xiǎng ... 我想 ...
  change money
  huàn qián 换钱

change travellers cheques
huàn lǚxíng zhīpiào　　换旅行支票
cash a cheque
zhīpiào　　支票

Excuse me, where's the nearest ...?
qǐng wèn, zuìjìnde ... zài nǎr?
请问，最近的 ... 在哪儿?
　automatic teller machine
　zìdòng guìyuánjī
　自动柜员机
　foreign exchange office
　wàihuì duìhuànchù
　外汇兑换处

Post

Where is the post office?
yóujú zài nǎlǐ?
邮局在哪里?

I'd like to send a ...
wǒ xiǎng jì ...
我想寄 ...
　letter
　xìn　　信
　fax
　chuánzhēn　　传真
　package
　bāoguǒ　　包裹
　postcard
　míngxìnpiàn　　明信片

I'd like to buy (a/an) ...
wǒ xiǎng mǎi ...
我想买 ...
　aerogram
　hángkōngyóujiǎn　　航空邮简
　envelope
　xìnfēng　　信封
　stamps
　yóupiào　　邮票

Phone & Mobile Phones

I want to buy a phone card.
wǒ xiǎng mǎi diànhuà kǎ　我想买电话卡

I want to make ...
wǒ xiǎng dǎ ...
我想打 ...
　a call (to ...)
　diànhuà (dào ...)
　打电话 (到 ...)
　a reverse-charge/collect call
　duìfāng fùfèi diànhuà
　对方付费电话

Where can I find a/an ...?
nǎr yǒu ...
哪儿有 ...?
I'd like a/an ...
wǒ xiǎng yào ...
我想要 ...
　adaptor plug
　zhuǎnjiēqì chātóu
　转接器插头
　charger for my phone
　diànhuà chōngdiànqì
　电话充电器
　mobile/cell phone for hire
　zūyòng yídòng diànhuà
　租用移动电话 or
　zūyòng shǒujī
　租用手机
　prepaid mobile/cell phone
　yùfù yídòng diànhuà
　预付移动电话 or
　yùfù shǒujī
　预付手机
　SIM card for your network
　nǐmen wǎngluò de SIM kǎ
　你们网络的SIM卡

Internet

Is there a local Internet café?
běndì yǒu wǎngbā ma?
本地有网吧吗?
Where can I get online?
wǒ zài nǎr kěyǐ shàng wǎng?
我在哪儿可以上网?
Can I check my email account?
wǒ chá yīxià zìjǐ de email hù, hǎo ma?
我查一下自己的email户, 好吗?

computer
diànnǎo　　电脑
email
diànzǐyóujiàn　　电子邮件 (often
　　　　　　　　　　called 'email')
Internet
yīntè wǎng/hùlián wǎng　因特网/互联网
　　　　　　　　　　(formal name)

Transport

What time does ... leave/arrive?
... jǐdiǎn kāi/dào?
... 几点开/到?
　the bus
　qìchē　　汽车
　the train
　huǒchē　　火车

Language

the plane
fēijī 飞机
the boat
chuán 船

When is the ... bus?
... qìchē jǐdiǎn kāi?
... 汽车几点开?
  first
  tóubān 头班
  next
  xià yìbān 下一班
  last
  mòbān 末班

Is this taxi available?
zhèi chē lā rén ma?
这车拉人吗?
Please use the meter.
dǎ biǎo
打表

How much (is it) to ...?
qù ... dūoshǎo qián?
去 ... 多少钱?
I want to go to ...
wǒ yào qù ...
我要去 ...
  this address
  zhège dìzhǐ
  这个地址

FOOD
breakfast
zǎofàn 早饭
lunch
wǔfàn 午饭
dinner
wǎnfàn 晚饭
snack
xiǎochī 小吃
eat
chī 吃
drink
hē 喝

Can you recommend a ...
nǐ néng bunéng tūijiàn yíge ...
你能不能推荐一个 ...
  bar/pub
  jiǔbā/jiǔguǎn 酒吧/酒馆
  café
  kāfēiguǎn 咖啡馆
  restaurant
  cānguǎn 餐馆

Is service/cover charge included in the bill?
zhàngdān zhōng bāokuò fúwùfèi ma?
帐单中包括服务费吗?

*For more detailed information on food and
dining out, see the Food & Drink chapter,
pp33-44 and the Eating chapter, pp97-114.*

EMERGENCIES
It's an emergency!
zhèshì jǐnjí qíngkuàng!
这是紧急情况!
Could you help me please?
nǐ néng bunéng bāng wǒ ge máng?
你能不能帮我个忙?
Call the police/a doctor/an ambulance!
qǐng jiào jǐngchá/yīshēng/jiùhùchē!
请叫警察/医生/救护车!
Where's the police station?
jǐngchájú zài nǎr?
警察局在哪儿?

HEALTH
Excuse me, where's the nearest ...?
qǐng wèn, zuìjìnde ... zài nǎr?
请问,最近的 ... 在哪儿?
  chemist
  yàodiàn 药店
  chemist (night)
  yàodiàn (yèjiān) 药店 (夜间)
  dentist
  yáyī 牙医
  doctor
  yīshēng 医生
  hospital
  yīyuàn 医院

Is there a doctor here who speaks English?
zhèr yǒu huì jiǎng yīngyǔ de dàifu ma?
这儿有会讲英语的大夫吗?

Symptoms
I have (a/an) ...
wǒ ...
我 ...
  diarrhoea
  lādùzi 拉肚子
  fever
  fāshāo 发烧
  headache
  tóuténg 头疼

GLOSSARY

Refer to the Food & Drink chapter for a detailed glossary of food items you're likely to encounter on menus.

arhat – Buddhist, especially a monk who has achieved enlightenment and passes to nirvana at death

báijiǔ – literally 'white alcohol', a type of face-numbing rice wine served at banquets and get-togethers
Ba Jin – a popular and prolific anarchist writer of the 1930s and 1940s. Li Feigan (his real name) is probably best known for his 1931 novel *Jiā* (*The Family*).
bāozi – steamed savoury buns with tasty meat filling
běi – north
biéshù – villa
bīnguǎn – tourist hotel
Bodhisattva – one worthy of nirvana but who remains on earth to help others attain enlightenment
bówùguǎn – museum

CAAC – the Civil Aviation Administration of China
cadre – Chinese government bureaucrat
cāntīng – restaurant
CCP – Chinese Communist Party, founded in Shanghai in 1921
cheongsam – (Cantonese) originating in Shanghai, a fashionable tight-fitting Chinese dress with a slit up the side
Chiang Kaishek – (1887–1975) leader of the Kuomintang, anticommunist and head of the nationalist government from 1928 to 1949
chop – a carved name seal that acts as a signature
CITS – China International Travel Service; deals with China's foreign tourists
Confucius – (551–479 BC) legendary scholar who developed the philosophy of Confucianism, which defines codes of conduct and patterns of obedience in society
CTS – China Travel Service; originally set up to handle tourists from Hong Kong, Macau, Taiwan and overseas Chinese
Cultural Revolution – a brutal and devastating purge of the arts, religion and the intelligentsia by Mao's Red Guards and later the PLA from 1966 to 70
cūn – village
CYTS – China Youth Travel Service

dàdào – boulevard
dàfàndiàn – large hotel
dàjiē – avenue
dàjiǔdiàn – large hotel
dàshà – hotel, building
dàxué – university
Deng Xiaoping – (1904–97) considered to be the most powerful political figure in China from the late 1970s until his death. Deng's reforms resulted in economic growth, but he also instituted harsh social policies and authorised the military force that resulted in the Tiananmen Incident in Beijing in 1989.

dōng – east
dòng – cave
dòngwùyuán – zoo

fàndiàn – a hotel or restaurant
fēn – one-tenth of a *jiǎo*
fēng – peak
fēngshui – geomancy, literally 'wind and water'. The art of using ancient principles to maximise the flow of *qi* (universal energy).
fó – buddha

Gang of Four – members of a clique, headed by Mao's wife, Jiang Qing, who were blamed for the disastrous Cultural Revolution
gé – pavilion, temple
gōng – palace
gōngyuán – park
Great Leap Forward – failed socioeconomic programme that resulted in a devastating famine in the early 1960s
guānxì – advantageous social or business connections
gùjū – house, home, residence

hé – river
hong – (from Cantonese) a company, usually engaged in trade. Often used to refer to Hong Kong's original trading houses, such as Jardine Matheson.
hú – lake
hútòng – a narrow alleyway in Beijing

jiāng – river
jiǎo – unit of currency, one-tenth of a *yuán*
jīn – unit of measurement (500g)
jiē – street
jié – festival
jìniànguǎn – memorial hall
jiǔdiàn – hotel
jū – residence, home
junk – originally referred to Chinese fishing and war vessels with square sails. Now applies to various types of boating craft.

kuài – in spoken Chinese, colloquial term for the currency, *yuán*
Kuomintang – Chiang Kaishek's Nationalist Party. The dominant political force after the fall of the Qing dynasty.

liǎng – unit of measurement (50g)
Lin Biao – (1907–71) military commander and CCP leader whose roles included Minister of Defence. Lin's death, which came shortly after he plotted to kill Mao Zedong, remains a mystery.
lòngtáng – a narrow alleyway in Shanghai
lóu – tower
lù – road
Lu Xun – (1881–1936) acclaimed writer whose works tackled Confucian culture

máo – in spoken Chinese, colloquial term for the *jiǎo*, 10 of which equal one *kuài*

Mao Zedong – (1893–1976) leader of the early communist forces, he founded the PRC and was party chairman until his death

mătóu – dock

mén – gate

Mencius – (372–289 BC) a scholar who raised Confucian ideals into the national consciousness

miào – temple

mù – tomb

nán – south

overseas Chinese – Chinese people who have left China to settle overseas

PLA – People's Liberation Army

Polo, Marco – Italian merchant who (supposedly) visited China and the Far East in the 13th century

PRC – People's Republic of China

PSB – Public Security Bureau; the arm of the police force set up to deal with foreigners

qiáo – bridge

qīngzhēnsì – mosque

qipao – the figure-hugging dress worn by Chinese women (also called a *cheongsam*)

Red Guards – a pro-Mao faction who persecuted rightists during the Cultural Revolution

rénmín – people, people's

Rénmínbi – literally 'people's money', the formal name for the currency of China. Shortened to RMB.

shān – mountain

shěng – province, provincial

shì – city

shìchang – market

shìjiè – world

shíkùmén – stone gatehouse

sì – temple, monastery

Sun Yatsen – (1866–1925) first president of the Republic of China. A revolutionary loved by republicans and communists alike.

tă – pagoda

t'ai chi (tai'chi ch'uan or tàijíquán) – slow motion shadow boxing. The graceful, flowing exercise that has its roots in China's martial arts.

Taiping Rebellion – a 1.1 million-strong rebellion that attempted to overthrow the Qing dynasty from 1850–64

tíng – pavilion

triads – secret societies. Originally founded to protect Chinese culture from the influence of usurping Manchurians, their modern-day members are little more than gangsters, involved mainly in drug running, gun running, prostitution and protection rackets.

xī – west

xiàn – county

yuán – the Chinese unit of currency, the basic unit of RMB; garden

zhāodàisuŏ – basic lodgings, a hotel or guesthouse

zhíwùyuán – botanical gardens

zhōng – middle

Zhou Enlai – an early comrade of Mao's, Zhou exercised the most influence in the day-to-day governing of China following the Cultural Revolution. His death triggered the Tiananmen Incident in 1976.

Behind the Scenes

THE LONELY PLANET STORY

The story begins with a classic travel adventure: Tony and Maureen Wheeler's 1972 journey across Europe and Asia to Australia. There was no useful information about the overland trail then, so Tony and Maureen published the first Lonely Planet guidebook to meet a growing need.

From a kitchen table, Lonely Planet has grown to become the largest independent travel publisher in the world, with offices in Melbourne (Australia), Oakland (USA), London (UK) and Paris (France).

Today Lonely Planet guidebooks cover the globe. There is an ever-growing list of books and information in a variety of media. Some things haven't changed. The main aim is still to make it possible for adventurous travellers to get out there – to explore and better understand the world.

At Lonely Planet we believe travellers can make a positive contribution to the countries they visit – if they respect their host communities and spend their money wisely.

THIS BOOK

This edition of *Shanghai* was written by Bradley Mayhew, who also wrote the 1st edition. James Farrer contributed the Identity section, and the 'Opening Up' and 'At Home with the Wu Family' boxed texts in the City Life chapter, as well as some of the book reviews in the Arts & Architecture chapter. Dr Victoria Buntine wrote the Health section in the Directory. The guide was commissioned in Lonely Planet's Melbourne office and produced by:

Commissioning Editor Michael Day
Coordinating Editor Andrea Baster
Coordinating Cartographer Daniel Fennessy
Layout Designer Tamsin Wilson
Editors & Proofreaders Melanie Dankel, Martine Lleonart, Lara Morcombe & Danielle North
Index Andrea Baster & Melissa Faulkner
Cover Designer Yukiyoshi Kamimura
Series Designer Nic Lehman
Series Design Concept Nic Lehman & Andrew Weatherill
Managing Cartographer Corinne Waddell
Mapping Development Paul Piaia
Project Manager Bridget Blair
Language Editor Quentin Frayne
Regional Publishing Manager Virginia Maxwell
Series Publishing Manager Gabrielle Green
Series Development Team Jenny Blake, Anna Bolger, Fiona Christie, Kate Cody, Erin Corrigan, Janine Eberle, Simone Egger, James Ellis, Nadine Fogale, Roz Hopkins, Dave McClymont, Leonie Mugavin, Rachel Peart, Ed Pickard, Michele Posner, Howard Ralley & Dani Valent
Special thanks to Martin Heng & Kyla Gillzan

Cover photographs Oriental Pearl Tower, Jorg Greuel/ Lonely Planet Images (top); Jade Buddha Temple, Dennie Cody/Getty Images (bottom)

Internal photographs by Phil Weymouth/Lonely Planet Images except for the following: p2 (#1) Glenn Beanland; p22 Bruce Yuan-Yue Bi; p125 Dallas Stribley; p135 Bradley Mayhew; p179, p181 Diana Mayfield; p187, p189 Keren Su/ China Span

THANKS

BRADLEY MAYHEW
My thanks as ever to Marie, Xiao Zhou and Lao Chen for a comfortable base and to Chris Torrens and Paul French of Access-Asia for their insights. Thanks to Andrea, Daniel and Michael (as ever), with whom it was great working on this edition.

Tina Kanagaratnam of Asia Media kindly helped keep the guide current with last-minute tips.

Finally, love to my wife Kelli, who was with me during our research trip in 2000 and who deserves much of the credit for the good stuff in the 1st edition.

OUR READERS

Many thanks to the travellers who used the last edition and wrote to us with helpful hints, useful advice and interesting anecdotes. Your names follow:

Alessandro Alocco, Jorge Alves, Bob Applebaum, Luke Arnold, Ruth Baetz, Steven Bailey, Jonathan & Penelope Bayl, Alex Bernikoff, Gary Booth, Harald Hjalmar Braakman, Bryan Brandsma, Derek Brennan, Marco Bresciani, Gerold Bruning, Helene Buckley, Elina Cabrera, Jim Calderwood, Chris Campbell, Guy Carrier, Clifford Chan, Caroline Child, Lawrence Chin, Alison Cribbs, Daniel Dahlmeier, Geoffrey Davis, Alaric De Arment, Rupert & Jemma de Smidt, Philip & Kerry Dean, Scott Delany, Hans Heinrich Doermann, Stephen Dolphin, WF Doran, Robert Doub, Daniel Dourneau, Alexandra Dubourg, Frank Dutton, Sean Dyde, John Easterbrook, Randal Eastman, Helen Egford,

Emily J Elliott, Paul Engels, J Evans, Angela Faerber, Craig Forman, Doug Fowler, Paul Fowler, Aymeric Fraise, Torsten Franke, Tom Frawley, Barry G, Anne Geursen, Anthony Ginn, Elizabeth Godfrey, Herb Goldstein, Lisa Grady, Stu Grant, Patricia Halter, Laurence Hamels, Nicky Harman, Manfred Hartmann, James Hawkins, Peter Heath, Robert & Tura Heckler, Moritz J Heidbuechel, Jan Henckens, Art Hilado, Jeanie Hore, Rhidian Hughes, Henrietta Irving, Laticia Jammes, Tess Johnston, Harold Jones, Jason Jones, Judith Karena, Pius Karena, Geoffrey Keating, Adeline Kee, David Kelly, Eldon Kendrew, Cameron Kennedy, Thom Kenrick, Matti Kinnunen, Peter Klein, John Koehler, Remko Koppius, Annett Kraske, George Kulstad, Aston Kwok, Alex Lauder, Davina Law, Jean Lennane, Mikelson Leong, Mike Lieven, Jo-Ann Lim, Ping Lim, Charles Locher, Adam Lotery, Cedric Maizieres, Don Mallory, Kai Markhof, Cindy Marleau & family, Jay Martin, Piet Meijer, Yves Mestric, Jo Mitchell, S Nadolni, Raquel Neto, Carmen & Robin Niethammer, Alex Nikolic, Bill Northby, Sebastian Nowozin, Rip Noyes, Holden Osborne, Joe Park, Renate Pelzl, David Perrin, Piergiorgio Pescali, Eric Phan-Kim, Hong Xiu Ping, Steven Plummer, John & Wendy Preston, Erik van Raaij, Jennifer Richmond, Matthew A Rifkin, Gernot Roth, Evelyn Saal, Fredrik Sand, Ed Schlenk, Esther Schouten, Birte Schulz, Ian Seccombe, Sven Serrano, Cynthia Simmons, Maxine Simmons, Lesley Singleton, Cameron Smith, Christopher Smith, Jacco Snoeijer, Kenneth So, Suzanne Soh, Walter Stanish, Nikola Stankovic, Kun Won Tang, Michel Mark Te, Suet Lan Tham, Michael Thomas, Judith Thrower, Sissel Topple, Steven P Tseng, Debora & Laura Tydecks, Darlene

Joy Uy, Ruud van Ammers, David van Driessche, Sophie Ruth Vaughan, Bernard Vixseboxse, John Vogel, Jessica Wahlberg, Qian Wang, Yau Wan-kong, Ann Warden, Georg Weber, Libby Whitmore, Anna Willmer, Kathy & Rick Wilson, Fran Wong, Anthony Wreford, Theodosia Zeleznik, Oliver Zoellner

SEND US YOUR FEEDBACK

We love to hear from travellers – your comments keep us on our toes and help make our books better. Our well-travelled team reads every word on what you loved or loathed about this book. Although we cannot reply individually to postal submissions, we always guarantee that your feedback goes straight to the appropriate authors, in time for the next edition. Each person who sends us information is thanked in the next edition – and the most useful submissions are rewarded with a free book.

To send us your updates – and find out about LP events, newsletters and travel news – visit our award-winning website: www.lonelyplanet.com.

Note: We may edit, reproduce and incorporate your comments in Lonely Planet products such as guidebooks, websites and digital products, so let us know if you don't want your comments reproduced or your name acknowledged. For a copy of our privacy policy visit www.lonelyplanet.com/privacy.

Notes

Notes

Index

See also separate indexes for Eating (p238), Drinking (p239), Shopping (p239) and Sleeping (p240).

Index

000 map pages
000 photographs

Index

000 map pages
000 photographs

Index

SLEEPING

000 map pages
00 photographs

MAP LEGEND

ROUTES

Freeway	One-Way Street
Primary Road	Mall/Steps
Secondary Road	Tunnel
Tertiary Road	Walking Tour
Lane	Walking Trail
Under Construction	Walking Path

TRANSPORT

Ferry	Rail
Metro	Rail (Fast Track)
Metro (Planned)	Cable Car, Funicular
Light Railway	

HYDROGRAPHY

River, Creek	Canal
Intermittent River	Water

BOUNDARIES

State, Provincial	Regional, Suburb

AREA FEATURES

Airport	Cemetery, Christian
Area of Interest	Cemetery, Other
Building, Featured	Land
Building, Information	Mall
Building, Other	Park
Building, Transport	Sports
Campus	Urban

POPULATION

✪ **CAPITAL (NATIONAL)**	◉ **Large City**
● **Medium City**	◉ **Small City**
● Town, Village	

SYMBOLS

Sights/Activities
- Buddhist
- Christian
- Confucian
- Hindu
- Islamic
- Jain
- Jewish
- Monument
- Museum, Gallery
- Point of Interest
- Ruin
- Shinto
- Sikh
- Taoist
- Zoo, Bird Sanctuary

Eating
- Eating

Drinking
- Drinking
- Café

Entertainment
- Entertainment

Shopping
- Shopping

Sleeping
- Sleeping

Transport
- Airport, Airfield
- Bus Station
- General Transport
- Taxi Rank

Information
- Bank, ATM
- Embassy/Consulate
- Hospital, Medical
- Information
- Internet Facilities
- Parking Area
- Petrol Station
- Police Station
- Post Office, GPO
- Telephone
- Toilets

Geographic
- Lookout
- Mountain, Volcano
- National Park

Map Section

SHANGHAI CITY

Planned Metro Lines

0 — 2 km
0 — 1 mile

To Jiangwan Zhen
(Terminal) (1km)

E — F — G — H

Fudan
University

Wenshui
Donglu
汶水东路站

Jiangwan Lu

Planned Metro
Line 8

Chifeng Lu
赤峰路站

Tongji
University
同济大学

15

19 同济大学
45

Yangpu

Luying Lu
Hongkou Stadium
虹口足球场站

Lu Xun
Park

Dalian Xilu

Kongjiang Lu

Jiangpu Lu

Hongkou

Dalian Lu

Siping Lu

Heping
Park

Linping Lu

Zhoujiazui Lu

Changyang Lu

37

25

Yangpu
Bridge

Luoshan Lu

To Ramada
Plaza Pudong
Hotel (10km)

Zhabei

East Baoxing Lu
东玉兴路站

See The Bund & Nanjing Donglu
Map (p244)

See Pudong Map (p253)

Planned Metro Line 4

Tianmu Donglu

Wusong Lu

Dongdaming Lu

Yangshupu Lu

River

Huangpu

Xizang Beilu

Zhongshan Dong Yilu

Nanjing Donglu

Huangpu

Yan'an Donglu

Lujiazui Lu

Century Ave

Pudong Dadao
浦东大道

36

49

Dongfang Lu
东方路

Zhangyang Lu

Yanggao Zhonglu

3

Huaihai
Donglu

Zhongshan Nanlu

Zhongshan Dong Erlu

Dongjiadu Lu

Luwan

Lujiabang Lu

Xujiahui Lu

Liban Lu

Nanshi

Pudong
New Area

18 31

26

39

28

29

Century Ave
(Shiji Dadao)

Century
Square

12

Shanghai Science and
Technology Museum
上海科技馆

13

Century
Park
世纪公园

38

Century Park
世纪公园

To Shanghai New
International Expo
Centre (500m); Tomson
Golf Club (1.5km)

Nanpu
Bridge

40

42

43

Zhongshan Nan Yilu

Zhongshan Nanlu

Naimatou Lu

Pudan Lu

Pudong Nanlu

Pujian Lu

Pudong Nanlu

Yanggao Nanlu

Longyang Lu

Longyang Lu
龙阳路

MagLev
Terminal
上海磁浮列车

To Pudong Airport (40km);
Shanghai Wild Animal
Park (45km)

See Old Town Map (p255)

Proposed Site
of Expo 2010

Planned Hua Qiao
(Flower Bridge)

Lupu
Bridge

Huangpu River

4

5

6

SHOPPING — (pp141–54)
Dongjiadu Cloth Market
董家渡轻纺面料市场 **21** F4
Guyi Antique 古意古典家具 **22** B5
Henry Antique Warehouse
亨利古典家具 **23** B5
Zhong Zhong Jia Yuan Antique
Furniture 中中古典家具商行 **24** B5

SLEEPING — (pp155–70)
Changyang Hotel 长阳饭店 **25** G2
Courtyard by Marriott
齐鲁万怡大酒店 **26** G3
Cypress Hotel 龙柏嘉店 **27** A5
Holiday Inn Pudong
上海浦东假日酒店 **28** G4

Hotel Nikko Pudong
上海中浦日航大酒店 **29** G4
Huamao Hotel 华贸宾馆 **30** A5
Intercontinental Hotel
新亚汤臣洲际大酒店 **31** G3
International Airport Hotel
国际机场宾馆 **32** A5
International Exchange Service Centre
华东师大国际交流服务中心 **33** B3
Longhua Hotel 龙华宾馆 **34** D6
Marriott Hongqiao
万怡虹桥大酒店 **35** A5
Novotel Atlantis
海神诺富特大酒店 **36** G3
Shizeyuan Hotel 师泽园宾馆 **37** G2
Sofitel Jinjiang Oriental Pudong
东锦江大酒店 **38** G4
St Regis Shanghai 瑞吉红塔大酒店 .. **39** G4

TRANSPORT
Bus Terminal 汽车站 **40** F4
Buses to the Bund **41** F4
Ferry 轮渡站 **42** F4
Ferry 轮渡站 **43** F4
Long Distance Bus Station
长途汽车站 **44** D2
Sightseeing Tour Buses .... (see 10)

INFORMATION
Bank of China 中国银行 .... (see 32)
German Centre **45** F1
Longhua Hospital 龙华中医 **46** D5
Mandarin Centre
复旦大学汉语中心 **47** C5
Shanghai Worldfield Convention
Centre & Hotel
上海光大会展中心国际大酒店 .. **48** A5
Tourist Information & Service Centre
旅游咨询官务中心 **49** G3

243

THE BUND & NANJING DONGLU

A   **B**   **C**   **D**

Children's Park

Zhongxing Lu

Huiwen Lu

Congqing Lu

Baoshan Lu
宝山路

Baoshan Lu 站
宝山路站

Jiangxi Beilu

Wujing Lu

Hailing Lu

Wusong Lu 吴淞路

91

Tianmu Donglu
天目东路

Shanxi Beilu

Hailing Lu

Sichuan Beilu 四川北路

Zhapu Lu

Kunshan
5

88
79

28

Wuchang Lu

Huaxing Lu

Zhejiang Beilu

Kange Lu

Anqing Lu

新疆路
Xinjiang Lu

Fujian Beilu

Tangqu Lu

Henan Beilu 河南北路

Tiantong Lu

58

Changzhi Lu

33

Xizang Beilu 西藏北路

Qufu Lu

Tiantong Lu

Suzhou Beilu
Suzhou Nanlu

86

50 65
90

Garden Bridge

Jinyuan Lu

Xizang Zhonglu 西藏中路

Xiamen Lu

Wusong River (Suzhou Creek)

Henan Zhonglu

Sichuan Nanlu

Jiangxi Nanlu

Yuanmingyuan Lu

Huangpu Park
黄浦公园

72
Pedestr
Tunnel

Xinzha Lu 新闸路

Beijing Donglu
北京东路

Huangpu

Shanxi Nanlu

Henan Zhonglu
河南中路

Ningbo Lu

Dianchi
Lu

76

37

80

Huangpu River

Beijing Xilu 北京西路

Huanghe Lu

Fengyang Lu

Fujian Zhonglu 福建中路

Tianjin Lu

Henan Zhonglu

38
17

47
18
84

1

63
64

60
61

Jiangxi Zhonglu

Guizhou Lu

Zhejiang Zhonglu

7

Shandong Zhonglu

M
42
16

35 57
83
8

2

Zhongshan

14

89

Huanghe Lu 19

78
43
44
22
54
53
48
92
95
93
52
69

41

Jiujiang Lu

Hankou Zhonglu

56

51
21
23

Dong Yilu

Yan'an
Dong Tunnel

62
34

60
Nanjing Donglu
南京东路

49
66
40
67
55

82

Fuzhou Lu
福州路

46

45

70

Guangdong Lu

Renmin Park
人民公园

6
71

36
81
25

11

15
85

Renmin Square
人民广场

24

26

Fujian Nanlu

Yan'an Donglu 延安东路

59

13

Renmin (People's) Square
人民广场

32

Yunnan Lu

29

Yan'an Donglu
延安东路

Yongjia Lu

Ninghai Donglu

Jinling Donglu

20

39

Henan Nanlu 河南南路

Renmin Lu 人民路

Huangpu Beilu

9
31
3
94

96

12

Xizang Zhonglu

10

Sanjiao
Park

87

30

77

Wusheng Lu

Huaihai Donglu
淮海东路

Fuyou Lu

Old Town

SIGHTS & ACTIVITIES (pp57–84)

Art 4 U Gallery 听雨轩画廊	1 D4
Church of the Holy Trinity 三一圣堂	2 C5
Grand Theatre Gallery 大剧院画廊	3 A6
Huangpu River Cruises	(see 75)
Jiangyin Lu Bird & Flower Market	
江阴路花鸟鱼精品市场	4 A6
Jingling Church 景灵堂	5 D2
Mu'en (Moore) Church 沐恩堂	6 B5
New Shanghai Metropolis Flower Market	
大都市鲜花店	7 A4
Room With a View Gallery 顶层画廊	8 C5
Shanghai Art Museum 上海美术博物馆	9 A6
Shanghai Museum 上海博物馆	10 A6
Shanghai Museum of Natural History	
上海自然博物馆	11 D5
Shanghai Urban Planning Exhibition Hall	
上海城市规划展示馆	12 A5
St Joseph's Church 天主教堂	13 D6

EATING (pp97–116)

Bonomi 波诺米咖啡店	14 D5
Croissant de France 可颂	15 D5
Croissant de France 可颂	16 C4
Donghai Café 东海咖啡馆	17 D4
Gino Café 季诺意大利休闲餐厅	18 D4
Huanghe Lu Food Street	
黄河声美食街	19 A5
Juelin Restaurant 觉林素菜馆	20 C6
M on the Bund 米氏西餐厅	21 D5
Manabe Café 真锅咖啡	(see 1)
Prego	(see 70)
Shanghai No1 Provisions Store	
上海第一食莫商店	22 B5
Three on the Bund	23 D5
Wang Baohe Restaurant 王宝和	24 B5
Wuyune Renjia	(see 89)
Xinghua Lou 杏花楼	25 C5
Xinjiang Restaurants 新疆饭店	26 B5
Xinya Restaurant	(see 66)
Yunnan Lu Food Street 云南路美食街	27 B6
Zhapu Lu Food Street 乍浦路美食街	28 D2

ENTERTAINMENT (pp123–40)

Glamour Bar	(see 21)
Great World Entertainment Centre	
大世界	29 B6
Noah's Bar	(see 51)
Shanghai Concert Hall 上海音乐厅	30 B6
Shanghai Grand Theatre 上海大剧院	31 A6
Yifu Theatre 逸矇舞台	32 B5

SHOPPING (pp141–54)

Centre of Tea From Home & Abroad	
中外名茶总汇	33 D3
D-Mall & Hong Kong Shopping Plaza	34 B6
Duoyunxuan Art Shop 朵云轩	35 C4
Foreign Languages Bookstore 外文书店	36 C5
Friendship Store 友谊商店	37 D4
Guan Long Camera Shop	
冠龙照相材料商店	38 C4
Guan Long Camera Shop	
冠龙照相材料商店	39 D6
Haishang Qinghuai Alley	(see 1)
Hualian Department Store	
华联商厦	40 B5
Jinguan Silk & Woollen Store	
金光绸缎呢绒商店	41 C5
Laokaofook Silk & Woollen Store	
老介福丝绸呢绒商店	42 C4
New World 新世界百货	43 A5
No 1 Department Store 上海第一百货商店	44 B5
Shanghai Antique & Curio Store	
上海古玩市场	45 C5
Shanghai Drama Costume & Accessories Shop	
上海戏剧会装用莎门	46 C5
Shanghai Musical Instrument Factory Store	
上海乐器厂	47 D4
Shanghai Zhejiang Tea Store	
上海浙江茶店	48 B5
Silk King 真丝商厦	(see 18)
Watson's 屈臣氏	49 B5
Zhongyang Market	(see 17)

SLEEPING (pp155–70)

Broadway Mansions 上海大厦	50 D3
Captain Hostel 船长青年酒店	51 D5
Central Hotel 王宝和饭店	52 B5
Chunshenjiang Hotel 春申江宾馆	53 B5
East Asia Hotel 东亚饭店	54 B5
Howard Johnson Plaza Hotel	55 B5
Metropole Hotel 新城饭店	56 D5
Nanjing Hotel 南京饭店	57 C4
New Asia Hotel 新亚宾馆	58 C3
New Asia Star Dafang Hotel	
大暖饭店	59 C6
New World Hotel (under construction)	
新世界大酒店（在建）	60 A5
Pacific Hotel 金门大酒店	61 A5
Park Hotel 国际饭店	62 B5
Peace Hotel 和平饭店	63 D4
Peace Palace Hotel (Peace Hotel South)	
和平汇中饭店	64 D5
Pujiang Hotel 浦江饭店	65 D3
Ramada Plaza	
南新雅华美达大酒店	66 B5
Seventh Heaven Hotel 七重天宾馆	67 B5
Shanghai Railway Hotel	
上海铁道宾馆	68 B4
Sofitel Hyland Hotel 海仑饭店	69 B5
Westin Hotel 威斯汀大饭店	70 C5
Yangtze Hotel 杨子饭店	71 B5

TRANSPORT

Bund Sightseeing Tunnel	
外滩观光隧道	72 D4
Ferry Booking Office	
上海港船票顶售处	73 D5
Ferry to Pudong 浦东轮渡站	74 D5
Huangpu River Cruise Dock	
黄浦江游船	75 D5
Railway Booking Office	
火车票预售处	76 C4
Train Ticket Office 火车票预售处	77 B6

INFORMATION

Air Canada 加拿大航空	(see 94)
Air France (Novel Plaza)	
法国航空（永新广场）	78 A5
Alliance Française 喃国文化协会	79 D2
Austrian Airlines 瑞士航空	(see 94)
Bank of China (main branch)	
中国银行	80 D4
Bank of China ATM 中国银行	81 C5
Bank of China ATM 中国银行	(see 63)
British Council 英国文化教育处	82 C5
Cai Tong De 蔡同德堂	83 C5
China Telecom 中国电信	84 D4
Citibank 花旗银行	(see 63)
CITS 中国国际旅行社	85 D5
CITS 中国旅行社	(see 18)
DHL	(see 94)
Goethe Institute	(see 82)
International Post Office 国际邮局	86 C3
Main Telecommunications Building 上海电信大楼	87 A6
Post Office 邮局	(see 70)
PSB 公安局	88 D2
Royal Thai Consulate-General	
泰王国领事馆	89 D5
Russian Consulate-General	
俄罗斯领事馆	90 D3
Shanghai First People's Hospital	
上海市第一人民医院	91 D1
Shanghai No1 Dispensary	
第一医药商店	92 B5
Shanghai Spring International Travel Service	
春秋国际旅行社	(see 6)
Tourist Information & Service Centre	
旅游咨询商务中心	93 B5
Virgin Atlantic 维珍航空	(see 14)

OTHER

Bund Centre	(see 70)
Central Plaza 奥地利航空	94 A6
Century Square 世纪广场	95 A6
Shanghai Government Building	
上海市人民政府	96 A6

FRENCH CONCESSION

A Wuding Xilu

B Wanghangdu Lu 万航渡路

C Beijing Xilu 北京西路 | Jiaozhou Lu | Changde Lu

D Tongren Lu

1 ⊞ 60

Yuyuan Lu 愚园路

M Jiangsu Lu 江苏路

2 Dong Zhu'anbang

Zhenging Lu

Nanjing Xilu 173 ●

M Jing'an Temple 静安寺
Jing'an Park 静安公园
⊞ 38 Yan'an Zhonglu

52 ⊞
76 ⊞ Fumin Lu
67 ⊞ 3

157 ⊞ 101
124 ⊞
156 ⊞ 160 ⊞

🏛 3
90
96

✚ 175

⊞ 117 169 ● Huashan Lu 华山路
176 ✚

Wulumuqi Beilu

⊞ 136 ⊞ 122

3 Lixi Lu

Jiangsu Lu

Yan'an Xilu 延安西路

Changle Lu
Changshu Lu
🏛 9

⊞ 69

Huaiing Lu

🏛 142

19 🏛
⊞ 119 Anfu Lu ⊞ 115
148 ⊞ Wuyuan Lu
180 ⊞
M Changshu L 常熟路

103

Ding Xiang Garden 丁香园
86 ⊞
31 ● 15 ● Fuxing Xilu 复兴西路
1 ⊞
49 ⊞
178 😊
188 ⊞
107 ⊞

Baoqing Lu 宝庆路

To 1221 (300m)

164 ⊞

4 Pingwu Lu

Xingfu Lu
Huashan Lu 华山路
Xinguo Lu
Wukang Lu
Yongfu Lu

100
54 ⊞ Taojiang
182 ⊞
Dongping Lu
75 143 77 ⊞ 92
88 ⊞

70 ⊞
22

Niujiao Bang
To Bodhi Bikes (250m)

42 ⊞
187 ⊞ 80 ⊞
81 ⊞
7 ⊞

184 ⊞

Yueyang Lu

Panyu Lu ● 2

5 ⊞ 149
⊞ 116

Fahuazhen Lu

10 ● Huaihai Zhonglu 淮海中路
25 ⊞
95 ⊞

Waiping Lu
Wuxing Lu
Gao'an Lu
Hengshan Lu 衡山路
91 ⊞

48 ⊞ 33 ⊞
57 ⊞
71 ⊞

Wulumuqi Nanlu
Yongjia Lu
133 ⊞

Xinhua Lu Huaihai Xilu 淮海西路

Jiaotong University

6

165 ⊞ 59 ⊞

154 ⊞ 37 ⊞ Guangyuan Lu
11 158 ⊞

177 ◎

Kangping Lu
Tianping Lu
Yuqing Lu
Hengshan Lu 衡山路
Gao'an Lu

62 ⊞

185 ✚

Ding'an Lu

98 ⊞

FRENCH CONCESSION (pp246–7)

FRENCH CONCESSION (pp246–7)

Old Manhattan Bar................................**101** C2
Shanghai Sally's 上海故乡餐厅.........**102** G3
Time Passage 昨天今天明天.................**103** B3
Woodstock...**104** F3
YY's...**105** F2

ENTERTAINMENT ☺ (pp123–40)
Ark House..(see 58)
California Club......................................(see 68)
CJW...(see 58)
Conservatory of Music.......................**106** E3
Cotton Club 棉花俱乐部......................**107** D4
Golden Cinema Haixing
  嘉华海兴影城......................................**108** G5
Guandii 官邸...**109** G2
House of Blues & Jazz
  布鲁斯与爵士之星.............................**110** F3
Kun Opera House
  上海昆剧团..**111** G4
Loft...**112** H3
Lyceum Theatre 兰馨大置院...............**113** F2
Planet Music Pub.................................**114** G4
Real Love Disco 真爱......................(see 48)
Rojam Disco.....................................(see 126)
Shanghai Dramatic Arts Centre
  上海话剧中心......................................**115** C3
Shanghai Film Art Centre
  上海影城..**116** A5
Shanghai Theatre Academy
  上海置剧学院......................................**117** B2
UME Cinema...**118** H2
Yonglegong (Paradise) Cinema
  永乐沟电影院......................................**119** B3

SHOPPING 🛍 (pp141–54)
1001 Nights 夜.................................(see 136)
Arts Craft Store of the Chinese Nationalities
  民族工艺品商店..................................**120** H2
Benetton..**121** G2
Chinese Printed Blue Nankeen Exhibition Hall
  中国蓝印花布馆..................................**122** D2
Dress Shops..**123** E2
Foreign Languages Bookstore
  外文书店..**124** C2
Fuxing West.......................................(see 31)
Golden Dragon 金龙...........................**125** F2
Hong Kong Plaza 香港广场................**126** H1
Isetan 伊势丹..**127** G2
Lu..**128** F3
Luo Ben...(see 31)
Lyceum Jewellery & Antique Store
  兰馨珠宝文物商行.............................**129** F2
Made in Heaven................................(see 136)
Maison Mode 美美百货公司..............**130** D3
Mandarava 曼陀罗................................**131** F1
New Hualian Commercial Building
  上海新华联大厦..................................**132** G2
New Ray Photo Making Ltd
  新之光摄影图浦谱幝.........................**133** D5
Pacific Department Store
  太平洋百货..**134** H1
Parkson Department Store
  百盛购物中心......................................**135** F2
Passepartout 七侶八士.......................**136** D2
Printemps 上海巴黎春天百货............**137** F2
Shanghai Central Plaza
  中环超市..**138** H1
Shanghai Harvest Studio 泰康路.......**139** G4
Shanghai Tang..**140** F2
Silk King 您庭保健会所.......................**141** G2
Silk King 丝丝商厦...............................**142** D3
Simply Life...(see 147)
Simply Life...**143** D4
Simply Life...(see 130)
Taikang Antique Market
  泰康古玩市场......................................**144** H4

TOTS 原创玩具......................................**145** G2
Watson's 屈臣氏..............................(see 159)
Weald Outfitter 旷野户外用品专门店...**146** H2
Xintiandi 心天地...................................**147** H2
Zhenjianzhai Antique Shop
  甄鉴斋古玩商店..................................**148** C3

SLEEPING 🛏 (pp155–70)
Conservatory of Music Guest House
  上海音乐学院外宾招待所............(see 106)
Crowne-Plaza Shanghai
  海银星皇冠酒店..................................**149** A5
Donghu Hotel (New block)
  东湖宾馆（新楼）...............................**150** E3
Donghu Hotel 东湖宾馆......................**151** E2
Education Hotel 教育宾馆...................**152** E3
Garden Hotel 花园饭店.......................**153** F2
Hengshan Hotel 衡山宾馆.................**154** C6
Hengshan Moller Villa
  衡山马勒别墅饭店..............................**155** E1
Hilton Hotel 上海静安希尔顿酒店....**156** C2
Hotel Equatorial...................................**157** C2
Jiangong Jinjiang Hotel
  建工锦江大酒店..................................**158** C6
Jinchen Hotel 金晨大酒店.................**159** F2
Jing'an Hotel 静安宾馆.......................**160** C2
Jinjiang Hotel 锦江饭店......................**161** F2
Jinjiang Tower 新锦江大酒店............**162** F2
Mason Hotel...**163** F2
Moller House......................................(see 155)
Radisson Plaza Xingguo Hotel 兴国宾馆...**164** A4
Regal International East Asia Hotel
  东亚富豪国际大酒店.........................**165** C5
Ruijin Guest House 瑞金宾馆.............**166** G3
Taiyuan Villa 太原别墅.......................**167** E5

TRANSPORT
Jinjiang Sightseeing Bus Stop
  锦江旅游车站......................................**168** F2

INFORMATION
Air China 中国国际航空.......................**169** B2
Air Macau 澳门航空........................(see 157)
Bank of China 中国银行......................**170** G2
Bank of China 中国银行......................**171** E3
Bank of China 中国银行......................**172** H1
China Eastern Airlines
  中国东方民航......................................**173** C2
CITS 中国国际旅行社.......................(see 174)
CYTS 中国青年旅行社........................**174** H1
DHL..(see 138)
FASCO...(see 161)
Huadong Hospital 华东医院外宾门诊...**175** B2
Huashan Hospital 华山医院................**176** B6
Internet Centre 音高点网络休闲中心...**177** B6
New Zealand Consulate-General....(see 188)
Pharmacy 药曜..................................(see 176)
Post Office 邮局....................................**178** D3
Post Office 邮局....................................**179** G2
Ruijin Hospital 瑞金医院....................**180** G4
Shanghai China Travel Service (SCTS)
  上海中国旅行社..................................**181** E1
Shanghai CYTS (STA Travel)
  中国青年旅行社..................................**182** D4
Shanghai Ko Sei Dental Clinic
  厚诚医院..**183** E2
Shanghai Library 上海图书馆.............**184** C4
Shanghai Medical University Children's Hospital
  上海医大儿童医院.............................**185** D6
Tourist Information & Service Centre
  旅游咨询咨务中心.............................**186** G2
UPS..(see 138)
US Consulate-General 美国领事馆.....**187** C4

OTHER
Qihua Tower 启华大楼........................**188** D3

A Shiquan Lu

B Guangxin Lu

C

D Panjiawan

1

Langao Lu

Zhongshan Beilu 中山北路

Zhenping Lu/ Zhenhuan Lu 镇坪路站

Moganshan Lu

2 Putuo Park 普陀公园

Yichang Lu

Shanxi Beilu

Xikang Lu

Aomen Lu

Aomen Lu

1

Putuo Lu

Changde Lu

Changshou Lu 常熟路

Jiangning Lu 江宁路

Changhua Lu

Shanxi Beilu

16

5 🏨

3 Dongxin Lu

Xinhui Lu

Xinhui Lu

Anyuan Lu

Shanxi Beilu

Guangfu Xilu

Changshou Lu 常德路

Haifang Lu

4 Wuning Lu 武宁路

Yuyao Lu

Changping Lu

Yanping Lu

Jiaozhou Lu

Changde Lu

Kangding Lu

Jing'an

Kangding Lu

Wanchun Jie

Wuding Lu

Wuding Lu

Xinzha Lu 新闸路

Jiaozhou Lu

5 Wanghangdu Lu 万航渡路

Wuding Xilu

Jiangsu Beilu

30 🚻

6 Changning Lu

🏧 35

63

28 🚻

18 🏨

Jing'an Temple 静安寺

6 🏨

Yuyuan Lu 愚园路

Jing'an Park 静安公园

69

PUDONG

A   **B**   **C**   **D**

1   **2**   **3**   **4**   **5**   **6**

0   500 m
0   0.3 miles

Zhoujiazui Lu

Dalian Lu

Tangshan Lu

Kunming Lu

Changyang Lu

Lintong Lu

22

Dantu Lu

Haimen Lu

Zhoushan Lu

Huoshan Lu

7

Gongping Lu

Gaoyang Lu

Tangshan Lu

Shangqiu Lu

15

20

19

Wuzhou Lu

Dongchangzhi Lu

1   26

东大名路

Yangshupu Lu

Dongdaming Lu

Daming Lu 大名路

32

Huangpu River

31

25

Pearl Park
浦东公园

9

Yincheng Beilu

Yincheng Zhonglu

35

Pudong Nanlu

Changyi Lu

3

34

27

10

Pedestrian Tunnel

23

8

Liujiazui Lu
陆家咀

Liujiazui
Park
陆家咀公园

Yincheng Donglu

Jimo Lu

Pudong Dadao 浦东大道

28

Fenghe Lu

2

Liujiazui Donglu

Qixia Lu

Liujiazui Lu

Zhongyang Dadao

中央大道

Liujiazui Xilu

17

M

13

4

21

11

Pudong Nanlu 浦东南路

Dongchang Lu
东昌路

29

Riverside Park

24

12

M

Yan'an Donglu
Tunnel

Huayuanshiqiao Lu

6

Rushan Lu

Yincheng Xilu

Haixin Lu

Yincheng Nanlu

Dongchang Lu

Pucheng Rd

Zhongshan Dong Erlu 中山东二路

30

Pudong
New Area

Shenjialong Lu

33

Yangzhou Lu

16

18

Zhangyang Lu

OLD TOWN

0 ————————— 500 m
0 ————————— 0.3 miles

OLD TOWN

Yunnan Lu

Huaihai Donglu 淮海东路

Jinling Zhonglu

32

34

28

13

Huaihai Park
淮海公园

9 • 14 23
20 ᴄʜᴏɴɢᴅᴇ Lu
Chongde Lu

24
26 Dongjiadu Lu

• 7

Shouning Lu

Dajing Lu 4
5

Qinglian Jie

Renmin Lu 人民路

Xizang Nanlu 西藏南路

Jinja Fang

Jingxiu Lu

Menghua Jie

Jin'an Lu

Ji'an Lu

Fuxing Zhonglu 复兴中路

Shunchang Lu

6

Zhizaoju Lu 制造局路

Fuyou Lu

Old Town
C 8

P
河南南路 Henan Nanlu

Fangbang

Dajing Lu 4
25
18

Zhoujin Lu

Xueyuan Lu

11

Fuxing Donglu 复兴东路

Wangjun Lu

Henan Nanlu 河南南路

15
3

Wenmiao Lu

Fangxie Lu

Xilin Lu

Zhonghua Lu 中华路

Daxing Jie

Pengfai Lu

Shangwen Lu

1

Daiji Lu

Dalin Lu

Sanmenxia Lu

Liyuan Lu

Lujiabang Lu 陆家浜路

Huining Lu

Jianguo Donglu

Yongnian Lu

Xiexu Lu

Jumen Lu

Huining Lu

Xietu Donglu

Mengzi Xilu

Liangbang Lu

Xietu Lu

Zhizaoju Lu 制造局路

Xilingjiazhai Lu

29

Xinzhaozhou Lu

Bachin Lu

Nanchechan Lu 南车站路

Quxi Lu

Quxi Lu

Zhongshan Nan Yilu 中山南一路

Tiedao Lu

Gaoxiong Lu

Old Town

2 17
31
Lujiachang Lu

Zhonglu

Anren Jie

16
12
27
10

19

Guangqi Nanlu

Ningjie Lu

Huangjia Lu

Xundao Jie

Dongjiadu Lu 董家渡路

*To Dongjiadu Church (400m);
Dongjiadu Fabric Market (500m);
Buses to the Bund (550m)*

Nanshi

Jianglin Jie

Huining Lu

Puyu Xilu

Puyu Donglu

Guohuo Lu

Haichao Lu

*To Bus
Terminal (400m);
Ferry (500m)*

Zhongshan Nanlu 中山南路

Bangsongyuan Lu

22

Yangshou Lu

Zhonghua Lu

Zhongshan Lu

A B C D

1

2

3

4

5

6

255

HONGQIAO & GUBEI

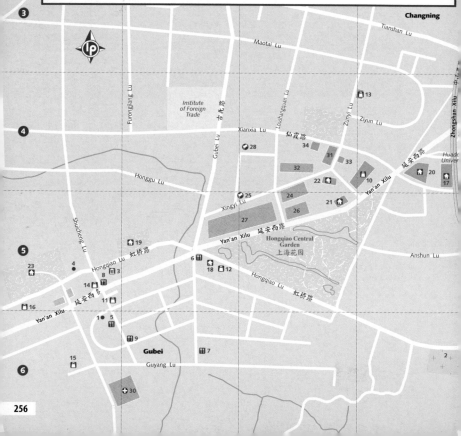

XUJIAHUI & SOUTH SHANGHAI

0 ———————— 500 m
0 ———————— 0.3 miles

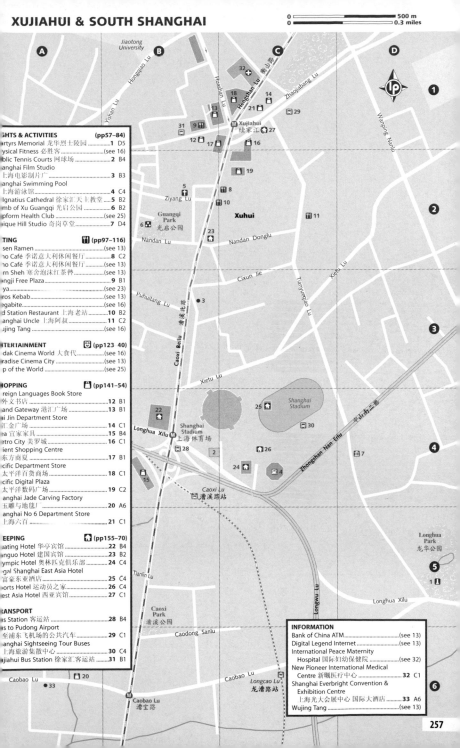

SHANGHAI TRANSPORT NETWORK

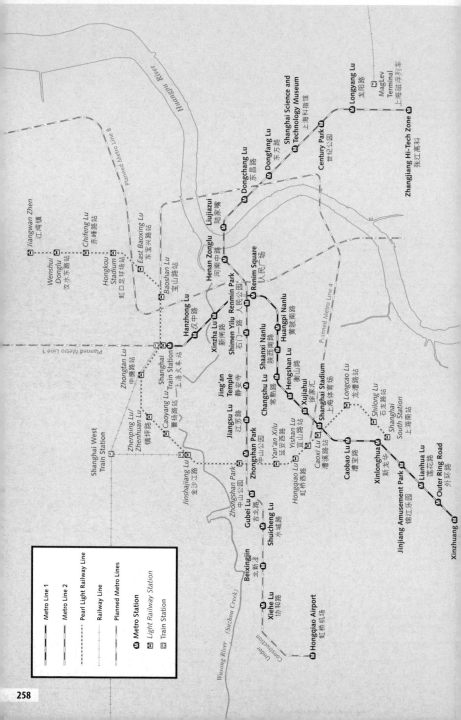

Key:
- Metro Line 1
- Metro Line 2
- Pearl Light Railway Line
- Railway Line
- Planned Metro Lines
- Ⓜ Metro Station
- Ⓔ Light Railway Station
- Ⓔ Train Station